CAMBRIDGE
Brighter Thinking

Challenge and Transformation: Britain, c1851–1964
A/AS Level History for AQA
Student Book

Thomas Dixon and Alan Gillingham
Series Editors: Michael Fordham and David Smith

CAMBRIDGE
UNIVERSITY PRESS

University Printing House, Cambridge CB2 8BS, United Kingdom

Cambridge University Press is part of the University of Cambridge.

It furthers the University's mission by disseminating knowledge in the pursuit of education, learning and research at the highest international levels of excellence.

www.cambridge.org
Information on this title: www.cambridge.org/9781107572966 (Paperback)
www.cambridge.org/9781107573000 (Cambridge Elevate enhanced edition)

© Cambridge University Press 2016

This publication is in copyright. Subject to statutory exception and to the provisions of relevant collective licensing agreements, no reproduction of any part may take place without the written permission of Cambridge University Press.

First published 2016
First edition 2016

A catalogue record for this publication is available from the British Library

ISBN 9781107572966 Paperback
ISBN 9781107573000 Cambridge Elevate enhanced edition

Additional resources for this publication at www.cambridge.org/education

Cambridge University Press has no responsibility for the persistence or accuracy of URLs for external or third-party internet websites referred to in this publication, and does not guarantee that any content on such websites is, or will remain, accurate or appropriate. Information regarding prices, travel timetables, and other factual information given in this work is correct at the time of first printing but Cambridge University Press does not guarentee the accuracy of such information thereafter.

NOTICE TO TEACHERS IN THE UK
It is illegal to reproduce any part of this work in material form (including photocopying and electronic storage) except under the following circumstances:
(i) where you are abiding by a licence granted to your school or institution by the Copyright Licensing Agency;
(ii) where no such licence exists, or where you wish to exceed the terms of a licence, and you have gained the written permission of Cambridge University Press;
(iii) where you are allowed to reproduce without permission under the provisions of Chapter 3 of the Copyright, Designs and Patents Act 1988, which covers, for example, the reproduction of short passages within certain types of educational anthology and reproduction for the purposes of setting examination questions.

This textbook has been approved by AQA for use with our qualification. This means that we have checked that it broadly covers the specification and we are satisfied with the overall quality. Full details of our approval process can be found on our website.

We approve textbooks because we know how important it is for teachers and students to have the right resources to support their teaching and learning. Please note, however, that the publisher is ultimately responsible for the editorial control and quality of this book.

Please note that when teaching the course, you must refer to AQA's specification as your definitive source of information. While this book has been written to match the specification, it cannot provide complete coverage of every aspect of the course.

A wide range of other useful resources can be found on the relevant subject pages of our website: www.aqa.org.uk

Contents

About this Series iv

Part 1 Victorian and Edwardian Britain, c1851–1914 — 1

1 Reform and challenge, c1851–1886 — 1
- The political system: Parliament and the workings of mid-19th-century democracy — 2
- Political developments under Gladstone and Disraeli — 12
- Economic developments — 20
- Society and social changes — 28
- Social movements and policies — 36
- Ireland and Anglo-Irish relations — 43

2 Challenges to the status quo, c1886–1914 — 52
- Political developments 1886–1905 — 53
- Politics and the constitution 1906–14 — 62
- Economic developments — 69
- Social change — 77
- Social policies — 87
- The condition of Ireland and Anglo-Irish relations — 94

Part 2 The World Wars and their Legacies: Britain, 1914–64 — 105

3 The Great War and its impact, 1914–39 — 105
- The impact of war on British politics — 106
- Political developments in the interwar years — 113
- Economic changes — 122
- Social developments — 131
- Social policies — 140
- Ireland and Anglo-Irish relations — 147

4 Transformation and change, 1939–64 — 158
- The impact of the Second World War on British politics — 159
- Developments in the political parties — 168
- Economic developments and policies — 176
- Social changes and divisions — 184
- Developments in social policy — 193
- The condition of Ireland and Anglo-Irish relations — 202

Glossary 212

Bibliography 215

Acknowledgements 218

Index 219

About this Series

Cambridge A/AS Level History for AQA is an exciting new series designed to support students in their journey from GCSE to A Level and then on to possible further historical study. The books provide the knowledge, concepts and skills needed for the two-year AQA History A-Level course, but it is our intention as series editors that students recognise that their A-Level exams are just one step on to a potential lifelong relationship with the discipline of history. The book is thus littered with further readings, extracts from historians' works and links to wider questions and ideas that go beyond the scope of an A-Level course. With this series, we have sought to ensure not only that the students are well prepared for their examinations, but also that they gain access to a wider debate that characterises historical study.

The series is designed to provide clear and effective support for students as they make the adjustment from GCSE to A Level, and also for teachers, especially those who are not familiar with teaching a two-year linear course. The student books cover the AQA specifications for both AS and A Level. They are intended to appeal to the broadest range of students, and they offer not only challenge to stretch the top end but also additional support for those who need it. Every author in this series is an experienced historian or history teacher, and all have great skill both in conveying narratives to readers and asking the kinds of questions that pull those narratives apart.

In addition to quality prose, this series also makes extensive use of textual primary sources, maps, diagrams and images, and offers a wide range of activities to encourage students to address historical questions of cause, consequence, change and continuity. Throughout the books there are opportunities to critique the interpretations of other historians, and to use those interpretations in the construction of students' own accounts of the past. The series aims to ease the transition for those students who move on from A Level to undergraduate study, and the books are written in an engaging style that will encourage those who want to explore the subject further.

Icons used within this book include:

- Key terms
- Speak like a historian
- Voices from the past/Hidden voices
- Practice essay questions
- Taking it further
- Thematic links
- Chapter summary

About Cambridge Elevate

Cambridge Elevate is the platform which hosts a digital version of this Student Book. If you have access to this digital version you can annotate different parts of the book, send and receive messages to and from your teacher and insert weblinks, among other things.

We hope that you enjoy your AS or A Level History course, as well as this book, and wish you well for the journey ahead.

Michael Fordham and David L. Smith
Series editors

PART 1: VICTORIAN AND EDWARDIAN BRITAIN, C1851–1914
1 Reform and challenge, c1851–1886

In this chapter we will examine political, economic and social conditions in Britain and Ireland in the third quarter of the 19th century. In particular, we will look into:

- the political system: Parliament and the workings of mid-19th-century democracy: the Queen and Parliament; ruling elites; prime ministers; parties and party realignment

- political developments under Gladstone and Disraeli: liberalism, conservatism and the bases of their support; the extension of the franchise

- economic developments: agriculture, trade and industry; economic ideologies; boom and 'the workshop of the world'; the onset of the Depression

- society and social changes: class and regional division; prosperity and poverty

- social movements and policies: self-help; trade unions; education and social reform legislation

- Ireland and Anglo-Irish relations: land agitation and the political response; the Home Rule movement.

A/AS Level History for AQA: Challenge and Transformation: Britain, c1851–1964

Key terms

First Great Reform Act: Passed in 1832, this gave the vote to middle-class men for the first time, reformed the political system and got rid of many of the smaller constituencies, replacing them with ones that better reflected the new centres of population, among other significant changes.

Chartist movement: A working-class political movement that was active from 1836 to 1848, which petitioned for further political reform following the 1832 Reform Act. Their charter comprised six demands, including universal male suffrage, secret ballots and annual parliaments.

Tory paternalism: An element of Conservative ideology focused on the idea that the elites should look after the lower classes as a parent would look after their children. It was seen as the motivation for social reform and a counter to growing demands for further reform and, later, socialism.

Democracy: 'The rule of the people', from the Greek *demos* (people) and *kratos* (rule). A democracy is a system whereby the people choose the government; this is normally done through the election of representatives. A 'full' or 'true' democracy will have universal suffrage for adults.

House of Commons: The lower house of Parliament in Britain where laws are debated and voted on. The House of Commons is composed of elected MPs from Britain's constituencies. During the 19th century the House of Commons became more powerful than the House of Lords.

The political system: Parliament and the workings of mid-19th-century democracy

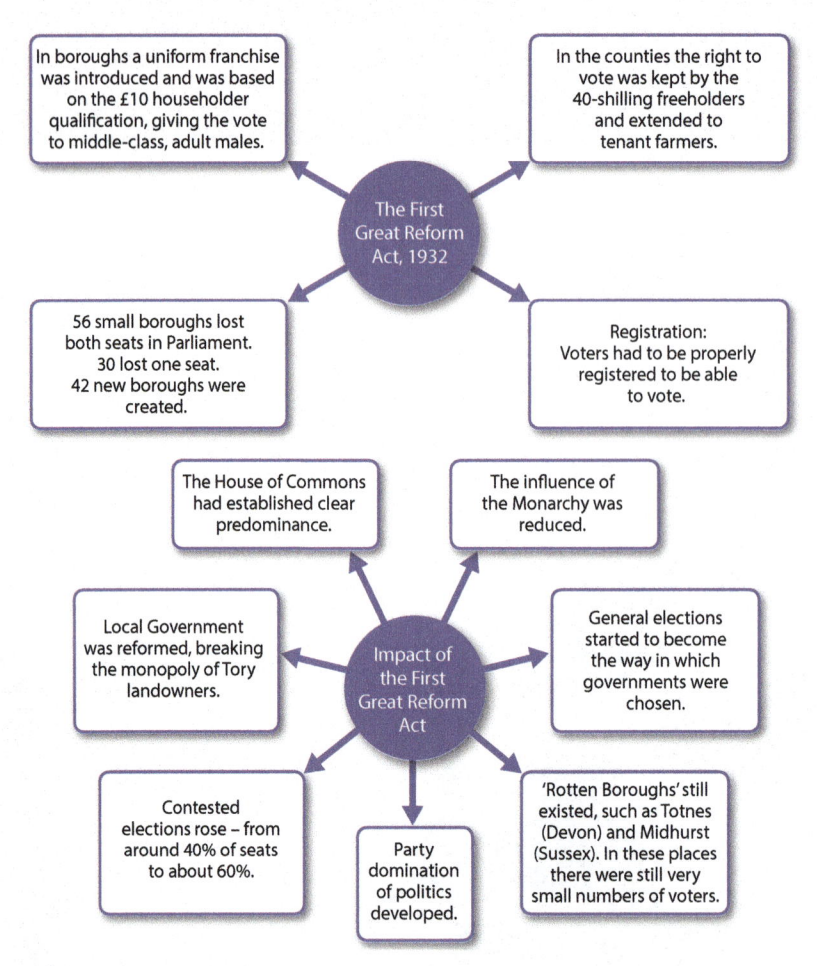

The First Great Reform Act, 1932
- In boroughs a uniform franchise was introduced and was based on the £10 householder qualification, giving the vote to middle-class, adult males.
- In the counties the right to vote was kept by the 40-shilling freeholders and extended to tenant farmers.
- 56 small boroughs lost both seats in Parliament. 30 lost one seat. 42 new boroughs were created.
- Registration: Voters had to be properly registered to be able to vote.

Impact of the First Great Reform Act
- The House of Commons had established clear predominance.
- The influence of the Monarchy was reduced.
- Local Government was reformed, breaking the monopoly of Tory landowners.
- General elections started to become the way in which governments were chosen.
- Contested elections rose – from around 40% of seats to about 60%.
- Party domination of politics developed.
- 'Rotten Boroughs' still existed, such as Totnes (Devon) and Midhurst (Sussex). In these places there were still very small numbers of voters.

Figure 1.1: The 1832 Reform Act

Britain's political system underwent massive changes in the period c1851–1886, in which further steps towards establishing full democracy were made. The first half of the 19th century had seen popular discontent and the enfranchising of many middle-class men in the **First Great Reform Act** in 1832, followed by further political agitation from the **Chartist movement**. As social and economic change continued apace, the political system came under close scrutiny. The political parties needed to adapt to an evolving political system and growing electorate, which essentially changed some of the old rules of the game. The parties competed for political advantage from the changes and sought to guide the newly enfranchised into the political sphere. After 1851, the ruling elites saw their power challenged by the growing electorate and the emerging power of the middle classes, so they needed to find new ways to assert their control, for example through Disraeli's **Tory paternalism**. In Benjamin Disraeli and William Gladstone, Britain had two of its greatest and most famous prime ministers. The Liberal and Conservative parties emerged during this period, following the party realignment over free trade.

Britain was not truly a **democracy** around 1851. Queen Victoria, although not directly involved, held considerable influence. The unelected House of Lords could veto legislation and provided many influential ministers, including prime ministers. Even following the 1832 Reform Act, the **House of Commons** was only elected by about one in six of the adult male population. The distribution of seats did not match the distribution of the population: many small constituencies kept their MPs while the northern towns and cities remained massively under-represented. MPs were not paid, so a political career remained the reserve of the wealthy. There was no secret ballot, and voters were vulnerable to bribes and threats, further increasing the political power of the ruling elites.

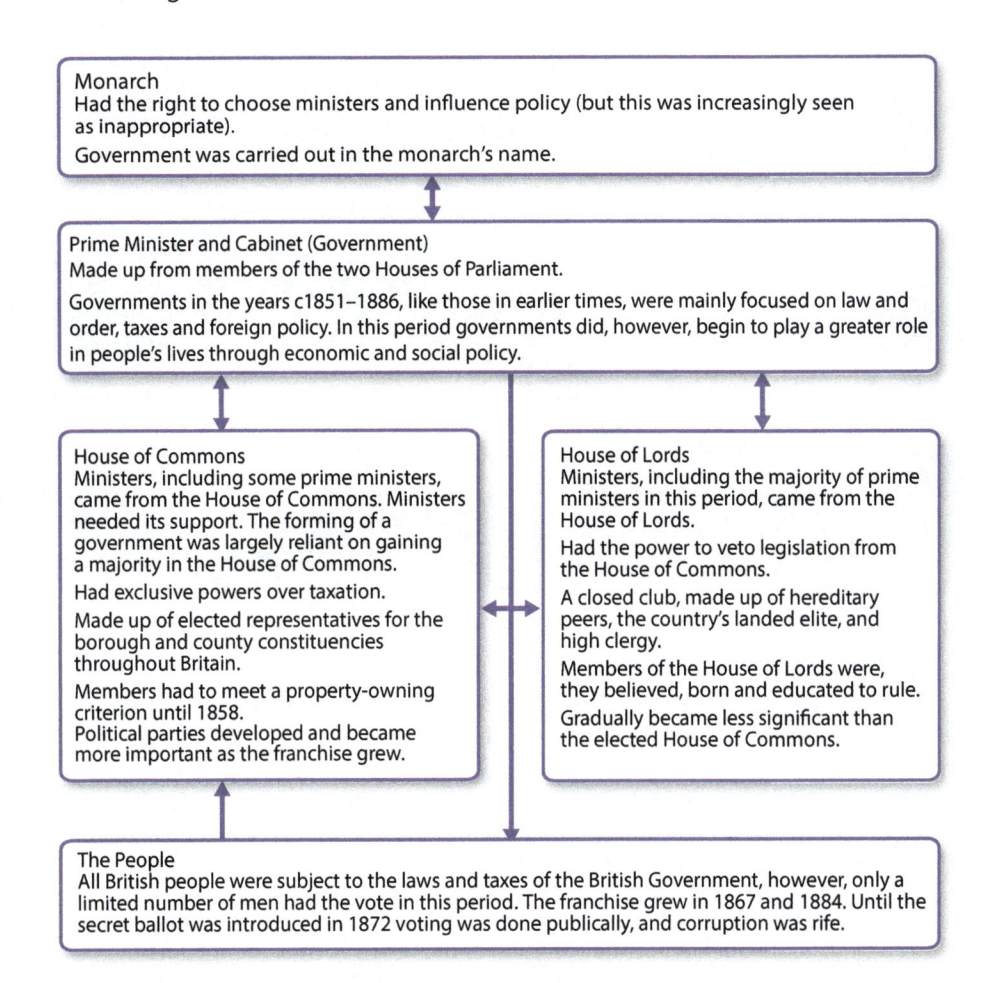

Monarch
Had the right to choose ministers and influence policy (but this was increasingly seen as inappropriate).
Government was carried out in the monarch's name.

Prime Minister and Cabinet (Government)
Made up from members of the two Houses of Parliament.
Governments in the years c1851–1886, like those in earlier times, were mainly focused on law and order, taxes and foreign policy. In this period governments did, however, begin to play a greater role in people's lives through economic and social policy.

House of Commons
Ministers, including some prime ministers, came from the House of Commons. Ministers needed its support. The forming of a government was largely reliant on gaining a majority in the House of Commons.
Had exclusive powers over taxation.
Made up of elected representatives for the borough and county constituencies throughout Britain.
Members had to meet a property-owning criterion until 1858.
Political parties developed and became more important as the franchise grew.

House of Lords
Ministers, including the majority of prime ministers in this period, came from the House of Lords.
Had the power to veto legislation from the House of Commons.
A closed club, made up of hereditary peers, the country's landed elite, and high clergy.
Members of the House of Lords were, they believed, born and educated to rule.
Gradually became less significant than the elected House of Commons.

The People
All British people were subject to the laws and taxes of the British Government, however, only a limited number of men had the vote in this period. The franchise grew in 1867 and 1884. Until the secret ballot was introduced in 1872 voting was done publically, and corruption was rife.

Figure 1.2: Parliament and the workings of mid-19th-century democracy

The Queen and Parliament

The monarch
Queen Victoria's government (1837–1901) ruled in her name, but not with her direct involvement. The 1689 Bill of Rights had curtailed royal authority and moved the British system towards parliamentary **government**. In addition, 'Economical Reform' from 1789 reduced royal control of **Parliament**. Queen Victoria did, however, have some important powers and influence – ministers lacking the monarch's confidence, for example, were generally dismissed. She could:

- appoint the prime minister
- summon Parliament
- 'influence' Commons elections through patronage of candidates.

Queen Victoria personally disliked not only political reform and the extension of the **franchise**, but also social reform – yet both of these happened during her reign. Although Victoria had both power and influence it can be argued that this was limited due to the increasing independence of the government from the monarch.

Key terms

Government: This group of politicians, called ministers, is led by the prime minister, and each has particular responsibilities. The two houses of Parliament and the civil service run the government of Britain under the leadership of the government. Senior members of the government, such as the Home Secretary and Foreign Minister, belong to the cabinet. Ministers are, in most cases, drawn from the two houses of Parliament.

Parliament: The legislature (law-making body) of Britain comprising the upper house (the House of Lords) and the lower house (the House of Commons).

Franchise: The right to vote in political elections, also referred to as suffrage.

Figure 1.3: Queen Victoria, Prince Albert and their young family

Two years into her reign, the 1839 Bedchamber Crisis had highlighted the risks of interference by the monarch in government: the Queen had attempted to keep the Earl of Melbourne in power despite Sir Robert Peel's electoral victory, and had been seen as having exceeded her constitutional role. Later in her reign she was criticised for withdrawing from political life following the death of Prince Albert. The public mood did, however, start to change after her son Albert Edward, Prince of Wales, became seriously ill before making a remarkable recovery.

She strongly disliked Gladstone, and she tried to prevent him becoming prime minister for the second time in 1880. She said he talked to her as he would to 'a public meeting' and is even said to have described him as 'half-crazy'. Her politics were much more in line with Conservative than with Liberal views but for the most part she avoided becoming involved in partisan politics, setting a precedent that is still observed. At times she effectively played the role of mediator, most notably over the disestablishment of the Church in Ireland in 1869 and during the arguments over the Third Reform Act in 1884.

In the later part of her reign Victoria's standing with the public grew. Her children married into Europe's royal households, increasing her importance in foreign relations. On a personal level she had a very happy marriage, but seemed not to like her children or grandchildren very much. Prince Albert was a great influence and helped guide her away from political controversy. He persuaded her that the right course was to work with the key politicians of the day, even if she did not like them or support their views.

1 Reform and challenge, c1851–1886

Speak like a historian

Professor Eric Evans

Professor Eric Evans is one of the foremost historians on British political and social history. The following is an extract from *The Complete A–Z: 19th and 20th Century British History Handbook*.

Victoria's early political life was dominated by two powerful men, the Earl of Melbourne, who acted as her first tutor in political matters and whom she adored and, after her marriage, her husband Prince Albert, to whom she was absolutely devoted and to whom she bore nine children. Reasonably intelligent and well-read, though often wilful, prejudiced and opinionated, she was usually happy to take her lead on political matters from Albert. Albert taught her to respect the talents of Sir Robert Peel, whom she had taken strongly against over the Bedchamber Crisis in 1839. There is no doubt that the death of Albert in 1861 was a blow from which she never truly recovered. She attracted considerable criticism both on the grounds of neglect of duty and, among those who knew about it, her ambiguous relationship with a Highland manservant, John Brown (who died in 1883). In the 1860s, a significant republican movement grew up. She was coaxed back into public life from the late 1860s, not least by the efforts of Benjamin Disraeli who flattered her shamelessly, manipulatively and with success.[1]

Discussion points:

1. Using your understanding of the historical context, how convincing are the arguments in this extract, regarding the political influence of Queen Victoria?
2. Why might Queen Victoria's political influence have declined during her reign?
3. What differences were there between the political power of Queen Victoria and the current Queen?

Queen Victoria and Prince Albert

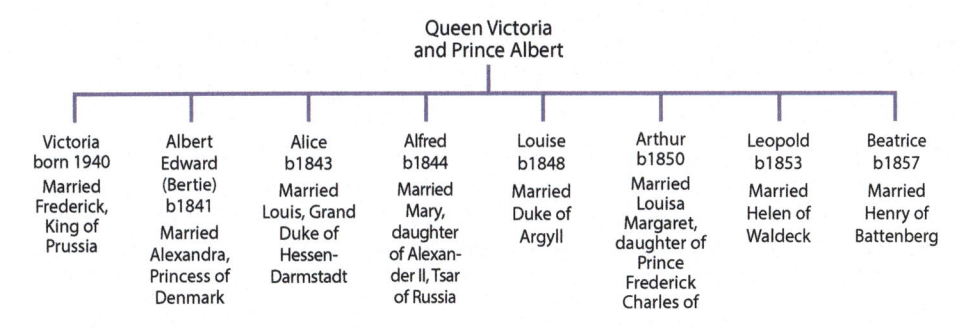

- Victoria born 1940, Married Frederick, King of Prussia
- Albert Edward (Bertie) b1841, Married Alexandra, Princess of Denmark
- Alice b1843, Married Louis, Grand Duke of Hessen-Darmstadt
- Alfred b1844, Married Mary, daughter of Alexander II, Tsar of Russia
- Louise b1848, Married Duke of Argyll
- Arthur b1850, Married Louisa Margaret, daughter of Prince Frederick Charles of
- Leopold b1853, Married Helen of Waldeck
- Beatrice b1857, Married Henry of Battenberg

Figure 1.4: Victoria and Albert's children and their links with European royalty

The House of Lords

The **House of Lords** held considerable power during this period. The prime ministers – the Earl of Aberdeen, the Earl of Derby, Earl Russell, the Marquis of Salisbury and Disraeli after 1876 (Earl of Beaconsfield) – sat in the House of Lords, as did a great number of cabinet ministers. The House of Lords could amend or veto any legislation. The aristocrats of the House of Lords often dominated government and in this time of social hierarchy and deference this hold was not significantly dented.

Key terms

House of Lords: The upper house of Parliament in Britain, where laws are debated and voted upon. The House of Lords in the 19th century comprised hereditary peers along with bishops and archbishops from the Church of England.

Key terms

Hereditary peer: Someone who becomes a peer (holder of high social rank such as Duke, Earl, Baron or Marquis) when it is passed to them following the death of a relative who had been the holder of the peerage.

Borough: A town that sends an MP or MPs to Parliament, traditionally a town with a corporation and privileges granted by a royal charter.

Paper duties: Taxes on paper and printing industries, notably on newspapers.

Constituency: An area in which a group of voters live. In the 19th century in Britain there were two types of constituency: boroughs (urban centres) and counties.

County: The main subdivision of the UK (such as Yorkshire and Lancashire). Traditionally counties sent MPs to Parliament to represent the rural community.

Figure 1.5: The six demands of the Chartists (1838)

The House of Lords was made up of **hereditary peers**, bishops and archbishops. Senior churchmen tended to come from the wealthy elites. Charles Longley, for example, who was Archbishop of Canterbury from 1862 to 1868, was from a wealthy family and married to the daughter of a baron. The aristocrats in the House of Lords had further influence on British politics, as in many cases they controlled **borough** seats. In a borough or 'nomination borough', the aristocrat would essentially choose the MP by controlling the voters through bribery and threats. Sir Robert Peel, for example, represented his father's borough of Tamworth.

The balance of power was gradually shifting from the House of Lords to the House of Commons. In 1832, for example, the Commons had forced the unwilling House of Lords to accept the Great Reform Act. Further examples of the Commons supremacy would come with their victory over the Lords in the conflict over **paper duties** in 1860/1861 and a further shift towards democracy with the 1867 Reform Act.

The House of Commons

The House of Commons was made up of members of parliament (MPs), each one elected to represent a **constituency**. The boroughs had been established centuries before and did not accurately reflect where the British people lived. The House of Commons in 1851 reflected the system established by the 1832 Reform Act, and subsequent demands for further reform by the Chartist movement had been rejected. The **county** seats represented the rural areas of Britain. General elections were scheduled to take place every seven years, but at times occurred much more frequently when governments fell because they lost the confidence of Parliament.

Chartist support and activity fluctuated in the 1830s and 1840s. As the economic situation became worse Chartist support grew and when the economic situation of the workers improved the level of support tended to fall. The Chartist movement largely collapsed in 1848.

> **Thematic link: Legacy of the 1832 Reform Act**

In modern Britain the House of Commons is central to our democracy, but in 1851 many aspects of the operation of the House of Commons were far from democratic. There were many in the House and outside who felt that any movement towards democracy would be unwelcome and potentially dangerous. The property qualification (£300 yearly income in boroughs, £600 in counties) required from MPs until 1858 also ensured that MPs came only from the wealthier upper echelons of British society.

A key role of the House of Commons was approving finance bills. An annual budget, presented by the Chancellor of the Exchequer and combining the passing of a number of finance bills through the House of Commons, was established in this period when Gladstone made up one large bill from a number of separate finance bills for the 1861 budget. This proved to be a more effective and much quicker way of passing financial legislation. Gladstone was determined to have the 'Paper Bill' pass and added it to the budget, calculating that the House of Lords would not reject the entire budget to overturn this single aspect. Gladstone won the day and the Commons still pass an annual budget.

Between 1806 and 1831, fewer than 40% of seats in the House of Commons were contested, but from the Great Reform Act until 1865 it was 59%. Voting was public, so corruption, violence and intimidation were still commonplace.

The evolution of the election system

Elections in the 1850s were characterised by:

- bribery
- treating, which gave the impression the borough was having a fete or celebration
- colourable employment
- quite possibly violence, or the threat of it, either between the supporters of rival candidates or towards voters – possibly fuelled by the provision of free ale.
- no secret ballot – everyone could see who voted for each candidate.

Ruling elites

British society was highly hierarchical and the country's elites, the landed aristocracy, were educated and groomed to rule. The aristocracy maintained a strong hold on British politics, most notably through their dominance of the House of Lords. The perception remained among the elites that they were born to rule and deference among the middle and working classes was much more marked than in the modern day. In the 19th century, a man who had inherited his title and wealth would be considered socially superior to, and would likely look down on, the man who had worked hard to earn his income. Politics was the largely the reserve of the landed gentleman as wealth was needed to win elections, connections and often patronage, in order to rise through the ranks. Someone seeking a political career needed the income to be able to dedicate themselves to politics without the distraction of having to earn it.

Key terms

Treating: Giving or offering food and, more often, drink in order to influence how people vote.

Colourable employment: Giving people fictitious or nominal jobs as a cover for paying them to vote for a particular candidate.

Voices from the past

Walter Bagehot (1826–77)

Walter Bagehot, a liberal political journalist, wrote *The English Constitution* just before the 1867 Reform Act. He did not believe in universal suffrage and argued that the working classes lacked the intellectual ability and education to be given the responsibility of the vote or make good decisions on their own behalf.

The masses are infinitely too ignorant to make much of governing themselves and they do not know their mind when they see it. Rank they comprehend, and money they comprehend, but, except in the vague phrase, 'He be a sharp hand', their conception of the abstract intellect is feeble and inexpressible.

The existing system … is a very curious one. The middle classes rule under the shadow of the higher classes. The immense majority of the borough constituencies … belong to the lower middle class and the majority of the county constituency is … by no means of the highest middle class. These people are the last to whom any people would yield any sort of homage if they saw them. They are but the 'dry trustees' of a fealty given to others. The mass of the English lower classes defer to the English higher class but the nominal electors are a sort of accidental intermediaries, who were not chosen for their own merits and do not choose out of their own number …

The result of our electoral system is the House of Commons, and that House is our sovereign. As that House is, so will our Cabinet be … We have vested, therefore, the trust of our supremest power in persons chosen upon no system, and who if they elected people like themselves would be unbearable. Yet a simple system would be fatal. Some eager persons indeed who are dissatisfied with what they call the imbecility of our present Parliament – meaning by that, not its want of sense or opinion, but its want of vigour in action – hope to get an increase of energy by a wholesale democratic reform … They think that as there are passions at the bottom of the social scale so there is energy. But ideas are wanted as well as impulse, and there are no ideas among our ignorant poor.[2]

Discussion points:

1. What are Walter Bagehot's views on the different classes in Britain?
2. Where does he say power lies in the British political system?
3. What is his attitude towards reform of the political system?

The writings of Charles Darwin were causing a big stir in mid-Victorian England and his cousin Francis Galton applied Darwin's ideas to people. He wrote a book called *Hereditary Genius* in 1869 in which he produced family trees of Britain's notable families (including his own), arguing that he could prove that ability was inherited. Galton's work was the start of the 'science' of eugenics. In a time of great social and political change it was used as evidence that the 'great' aristocratic families were the 'fittest' to run the country's government and key institutions.

The leaders of business and manufacturing, along with the middle classes started to take an increasing role in British politics. The wealthier middle classes looked to emulate the ruling elites, buying estates in the country and sending their sons to public schools, such as Eton and Westminster, then on to university. The possibility of social mobility was certainly evident in British politics with several leading political figures coming from outside the traditional ruling elites. Probably the best example of social mobility was the Peel family: Sir Robert Peel, 2nd baronet, was prime minister on two occasions. His father Sir Robert Peel, 1st baronet, was a leading industrialist who made his money as a mill owner and later politician. His father Robert Peel was a yeoman farmer who went on to make his fortune as a mill owner. The Peel family therefore moved from yeoman farmer to baronet to prime minister in three generations.

Speak like a historian

Norman Gash

Norman Gash's book *Aristocracy and People, Britain 1815–1865* is considered a seminal work on the changing position of the ruling elites. He argues that in 1865, despite the social and economic transformation of Britain, the elites still had real strength:

In the structure of the state, in government, in parliament and the electoral system, in the church, the armed forces, civil service in local government and in society. They had shown themselves on most occasions intelligent and flexible; they had made political concessions and yielded privileges when public opinion clearly demanded such surrenders … They had played a useful and sometimes prominent role in the social, religious, educational and other philanthropic movements of the period and had been rewarded by the moral approval of the public in addition to their existing social and political advantages. What was remarkable was not that British society was slowly slipping beyond the elites control, but that by a process of astute adaptation they had maintained that control so long and with so little resentment on the part of the rest of the community.[3]

Discussion points:

1. What is Gash arguing about the power of the ruling elites in 1865?
2. According to Gash how did the rest of society think about the ruling elites?
3. Gash is writing about 1865. Using details from the rest of Chapter 1, evaluate how accurate Gash's view would be if applied to 1886.

The repeal of the Corn Laws in 1846 appeared to signify a loosening on the grip of power by the ruling elites. The Corn Laws had protected the income of the landed classes at the expense of the labouring classes and urban population as a whole. The repeal of this law seemed to suggest that the interests of the ruling elites would no longer be allowed to override those of the wider population. Peel was in fact setting out to justify aristocratic rule and reduce class division by showing that aristocratic government would work in the national interest, not self-interest.

There were increasing worries among the ruling elites about whether their wealth and dominance would continue. The Earl of Derby stated on 23 August 1885 that his family's wealth was down to 'chance rather than our work' and questioned whether the family's prominent position and wealth would last.[4]

Prime ministers

There were significant issues within the political parties which led to frequent changes in government, for example:

- There were divisions over the Corn Laws among the Tories leading to Russell and the **Whigs** coming to power in 1846.
- A breakdown in relations between Lord John Russell and Lord Palmerston led to an effective vote of no confidence, which brought down Russell's government in 1852.
- Earl Derby's short-lived minority government in 1852 illustrated the continued divisions within the emerging **Conservative Party** between traditional Tories, **Peelites** and a group of around 100 MPs who favoured free trade being extended beyond wheat, known as 'free traders'.
- The Earl of Aberdeen formed a government in 1852 that was made up of Whigs, Peelites and 'free traders'. His government included the feuding Lord Russell (Foreign Minister) and Lord Palmerston (Home Secretary).
- Palmerston's government saw tension between the traditional Whigs and Radicals such as Cobden and Bright over issues of foreign policy.
- The Earl of Derby's second short-lived minority government proposed an extension of the franchise and fell when it was defeated. It was at this point that the Willis's Rooms meeting took place and it is said that the **Liberal Party** was formed.
- Palmerston died in 1865 and was replaced by Lord John Russell.
- Lord Russell in his short second term as prime minister again saw splits between the Whigs, Liberals and Radicals in his party as he sought to extend the franchise.
- Lord Derby became prime minister with Disraeli as his key man in the House of Commons. This government pushed through the Second Reform Act in part to strike a blow against Gladstone and the Liberals.

The frequent changes shown in the timeline illustrate the challenges faced by governments in the period.

Timeline of prime ministers, 1846–86

Years	Prime minister	Party
1846–52	Lord John Russell	Whig
1852	Earl of Derby (Edward Smith Stanley)	Conservative
1852–55	Earl of Aberdeen (George Hamilton Gordon)	Whig
1855–58	Viscount Palmerston (Henry John Temple)	Whig
1858–59	Earl of Derby (Edward Smith Stanley)	Conservative
1859–65	Viscount Palmerston (Henry John Temple)	Liberal

ACTIVITY 1.1

Research and write detailed profiles of:

- The Earl of Derby
- Viscount Palmerston
- William Gladstone
- Benjamin Disraeli.

Figure 1.6: Viscount (Lord) Palmerston

Key terms

Whigs: A political faction that became a political party. They supported the powers of Parliament and the rights of Nonconformists. In 1859 the Whigs combined with the Radicals and Peelites to form the Liberal Party.

Conservative Party: The political party that emerged from the Tory Party in the 1830s under the leadership of Robert Peel.

Peelites: Supporters of Robert Peel's repeal of the Corn Laws in 1846, which caused the Conservative Party to split.

Liberal Party: A political party many agree was formed in 1859 at the Willis's Rooms meeting. It was a coalition of Whigs, Radicals and Peelites who united together.

Figure 1.7: The Earl of Derby

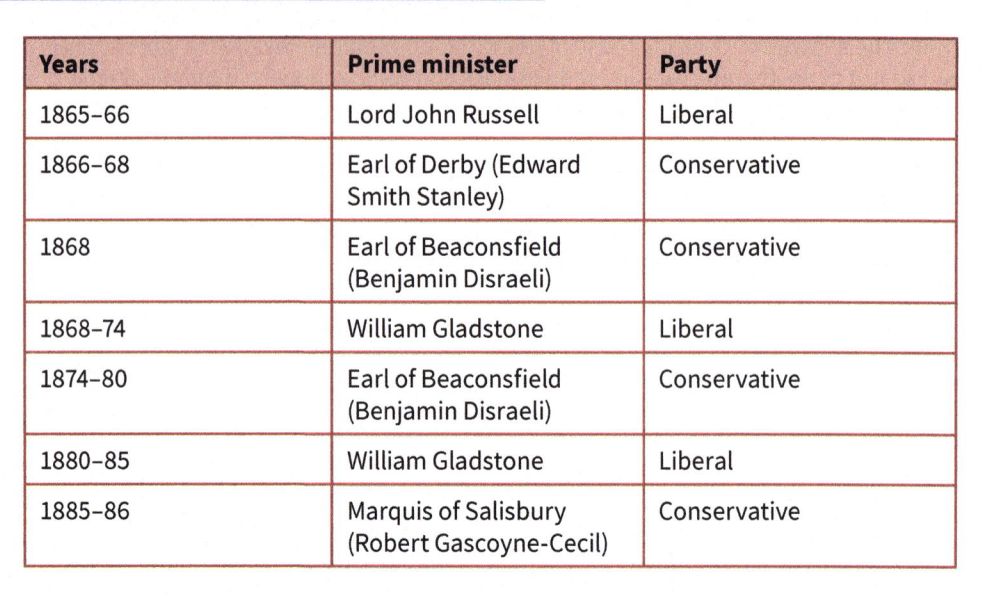

Years	Prime minister	Party
1865–66	Lord John Russell	Liberal
1866–68	Earl of Derby (Edward Smith Stanley)	Conservative
1868	Earl of Beaconsfield (Benjamin Disraeli)	Conservative
1868–74	William Gladstone	Liberal
1874–80	Earl of Beaconsfield (Benjamin Disraeli)	Conservative
1880–85	William Gladstone	Liberal
1885–86	Marquis of Salisbury (Robert Gascoyne-Cecil)	Conservative

Parties and party realignment

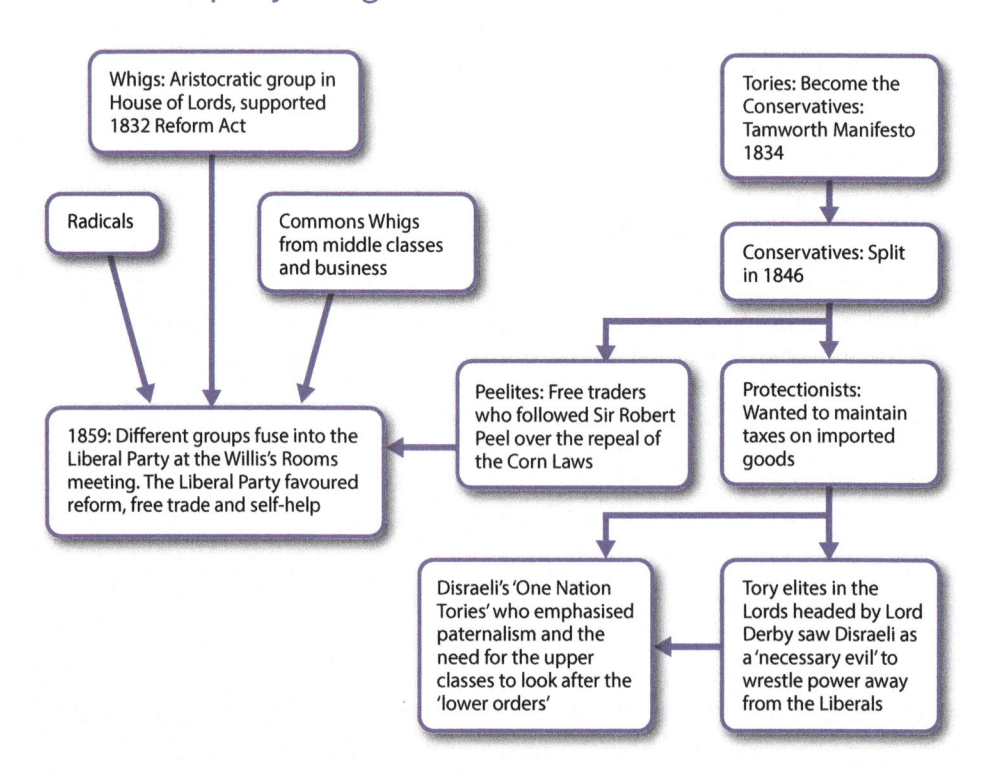

Figure 1.8: William Gladstone

Figure 1.9: The development of the main political parties

The period until 1867 and beyond was one of rapid and dramatic political change. As the franchise and key aspects of the political system changed the political parties had to adapt and evolve. The aristocrat-dominated political groupings from before 1832 started to develop into something approaching modern political parties. This process would not be complete until after later changes to the franchise and voting system but during this period the central ideologies and new party lines came to the fore. In 1867 two main political parties – the Liberals and the Conservatives – were emerging, which would go on to dominate British politics, though it was not the case that they had fully formed by 1867. The Liberals emerged from a coalition of groups including the Whigs, while the Conservatives had emerged out of the **Tory** party.

The Conservative Party is largely seen as emerging from the old Tory Party with Peel's Tamworth Manifesto in 1834. In this manifesto Peel and his supporters accepted the

Key terms

Tory: A parliamentary party that supported the established church and political order. The term has continued to be used in reference to the Conservative Party and its supporters.

1 Reform and challenge, c1851–1886

1832 Reform Act and moved forwards into the new era where the middle-class vote become key. Peel was significant in the formation of the Conservative Party and he was also responsible for a major split in the party in the 1840s. The Conservative Party split when Peel repealed the Corn Laws. The party split between the free traders headed by Peel (known as Peelites) and the protectionist rump of the Conservative Party. The years 1846 to 1865 were poor for the emerging Conservative Party, with only two short-lived minority governments, in 1852 and from 1858 to 1859.

> **Cross-reference: Economic ideologies**

The historical debate about Peel and his role in the collapse of the Conservative Party has raged for a long time. Within the Conservative Party at the time there was a debate about a new way forward to re-establish themselves as a political force. At this time a new star of Conservatism emerged in the form of Benjamin Disraeli. His leadership of the Conservatives in the House of Commons and rivalry with Gladstone, the leader of the Liberal Party, did much to shape British politics. Disraeli stealing a march over Gladstone over reform in 1867 and his ideology of 'one nation' Conservatism, based on the principle of paternalism, helped revive the Conservatives' fortune. He was, however, not universally liked in his own party, in part due to his Jewish background. His skill as a speaker and debater did, in fact, increase distrust of him among many of the old-school Tories in the House of Lords. Despite this distrust Disraeli proved to be vital to Conservative development in the 1850s and 1860s.

Figure 1.10: Benjamin Disraeli

The Liberal Party emerged largely out of the old aristocratic Whig Party, but also contained Radicals and Peelites. This diverse group fused together over time and the key moment that most historians pick out is the Willis's Rooms meeting in 1859. The Whigs in the House of Lords were from aristocratic families. They were, generally speaking, in favour of controlled political reform and extension of the franchise, which differentiated them from the Tories. After 1832 a distinctive Whig group emerged in the House of Commons, made up of both the landed classes and middle classes (both business and professional) who pushed for more progressive policies on freedom of religion (many were Nonconformists), press and trade. These would become important underpinning principles of the Liberal Party.

Radicals in the House of Commons pushed for much greater political reform and extension of the franchise. They sought policies that would shift the balance of the power away from the traditional elites and towards the ordinary people. The leading light of the Radical movement was John Bright.

The Peelites were a key component of the emerging Liberal Party, in particular William Gladstone who, first as Chancellor of the Exchequer and then as the Liberal leader, did more than anyone else to shape the new Liberal Party. The term 'Gladstonian liberalism' is often used to describe the party's ideology at this time. The Liberal Party was, however, far from united at this period with the ideas of free trade and self-help clashing with the doctrine of utilitarianism. This promoted the idea that the central aim should always bring the 'greatest pleasure to the greatest number of people', which often led to calls for more government intervention to help the poor.

ACTIVITY 1.2

Using the information in this section, and any other sources available, write a profile of Radical minister John Bright.

> **Thematic link: The extension of the franchise**

> **Key terms**
>
> **Nonconformist:** A member of a Protestant church that dissents (disagrees with and differs) from the established Church of England.
>
> **Free trade:** International commerce (trade) which is not subject to tariffs, quotas or other interference from government.
>
> **Laissez-faire:** An economic system that is free from government intervention.

The 1867 Reform Act was significant in the development of the party system for a number of reasons:

- The creation of the Bill by the Conservatives was in part due to Disraeli's desire to succeed where Gladstone had failed.
- The parties believed that passing a Reform Act would give them an electoral advantage, which was essential for these developing parties.
- There was some fear of popular revolt following the Hyde Park riots in 1866.
- The Conservatives saw the act as a way of deepening the divisions in the Liberal Party between those who favoured and those who opposed reform (Adullamites), taking advantage of Liberal weakness following the death of Lord Palmerston.

Political developments under Gladstone and Disraeli

Liberalism, conservatism and the bases of their support

Liberalism

The Liberal Party was made up of a loose coalition of old aristocratic Whigs, representatives of business and the professions, Peelite free traders and Radicals. Officially, the Liberal Party was formed on 6 June 1859, but really it was a process over time. The pact of 1859 served to bring down Derby's minority government. Gladstone committed himself to the Liberal Party, but there was not yet a nationally organised party with a membership or a party machine. With the formation of the National Liberal Federation in 1877, the party started to emerge as a modern mass party.

Liberalism developed under Gladstone and his beliefs and principles were key in the development of Gladstonian liberalism. He saw liberalism as 'an attitude of mind, a moral outlook, rather than a coherent set of principles',[5] which may partly explain how his own political position evolved over time from traditional Tory to an arguably radical Liberal. The Conservatives certainly hoped he would return to the Conservative fold in the 1850s. His 1866 Reform Bill was blocked by a group of Whigs who opposed reform. The cornerstone of 'Gladstonian' or 'Classical' liberalism was the idea of freedom. The Liberal Party beliefs and aims included:

- Removing all restraints on personal liberty: protect people from discrimination and ensure they can express their views: allow **Nonconformists** to work in the universities; remove Paper Duties allowing the growth of the popular press; create meritocracies in the military and civil service.
- Self-help: hard work, self-improvement and sound personal financial management should enable a good standard of living. The government should not interfere. Government help, it was believed, would encourage people to become reliant on the state or charity. Liberal governments were therefore very reluctant to interfere in the treatment of adult male workers. Gladstone once remarked that, 'The best thing the government can do for the people, is to help them to help themselves.'[6] Exactly what helping them to help themselves involved remained a key debate among the Liberal Party and party's stance on this issue changed over time.

> **Thematic link:** Liberal social reforms

- **Free trade** and **laissez-faire**: the government should not interfere in the workings of economic markets. When the repeal of the Corn Laws (tax on imported corn) split the Conservatives in 1846, the 'Peelites', including Gladstone, joined the Liberals. As part of his policy of reducing taxes and government intervention in all aspects of the economy to a minimum, Gladstone pursued a policy of abolishing duties on goods.

1 Reform and challenge, c1851–1886

- Inexpensive and accountable government: government should be as cheap as possible, so that taxes could be as low as possible. Gladstone believed that individuals were more effective in determining how their money should be spent than governments. As Chancellor of the Exchequer in the 1850s, he had wanted to get rid of income tax – he was unsuccessful because of the cost of the Crimean War, but he did reduce it.

Other key figures in the development of Liberalism and its ideology included John Bright and John Stuart Mill, who justifiably described the Liberal Party as a 'broad church'. The Liberal doctrine of small government and not interfering in people's lives or business could clash with a Radical desire to intervene to improve the lives of the poor and disadvantaged. Liberal bills that dealt with workers' conditions, and so on, could therefore be written more as guidelines than as compulsory measures. The ideology of the Liberal Party towards the economy, social policy and the role of government would later change, but at this point Gladstone's belief in free trade and self-help dominated.

Support for Liberalism

Reputedly, it was the Nonconformist northern industrialists who provided the main support for Liberalism, but this was far from being the full picture. Members of Parliament had to satisfy the property qualification. They were not paid, so they generally came from the wealthiest section of society with notable exceptions after 1874 when a small number of MPs were sponsored by trade unions. Wealth could be due to land, business, manufacturing or a profession, and many sat in several categories (Gladstone for one). What is clear is that there were still many Liberal MPs who were country gentlemen (figures vary between historians but numbers are normally around 40%). There were businessmen, such as John Bright and Richard Cobden, who were a close match to the popular perception. There were also bankers, stockbrokers, engineers, lawyers (about a quarter of Liberal MPs in 1874). It was easier for a barrister or a landed gentleman to be an MP than for someone running a business on a daily basis, which in part explains the prominence of lawyers and landed elites in the Liberal Party.

The majority of Liberal MPs after the 1868 election were Anglicans, not Nonconformists (282 Anglicans, 64 Nonconformists). Support came from the 'Radical Celtic Fringe', who gained real control in Ireland (36) and Scotland. Scottish Tory Sir Walter Scott had warned in 1826 that, following reform, Scotland could become 'completely liberalised', and he was largely right. Liberal strength was concentrated in the North, Midlands, Wales, Scotland and Ireland (until the 1870s), so they were a British, rather than an English, party. The Liberals were much stronger in the boroughs than the counties. Liberal voters prior to 1867 tended to be shopkeepers, independent producers, craftsmen and small farmers.

Outside Parliament there were a number of key Liberal organisations, which were driven by Nonconformists. These included the Liberation Society, led by the Nonconformist Minister Edward Miall, which had its own newspaper, *The Liberator*; the United Kingdom Alliance (a temperance organisation), which sold 25 000 copies weekly of its *Alliance News*; and the National Education League, which had a newsletter with over 20 000 subscriptions. Nonconformists may not have dominated in Parliament, but they were the backbone of Liberalism on the ground.

Thematic link: Trade unions

The Liberal Party also gained support from the new model unions, or **trade unions**, which emerged in the 1850s. The members were the elites of the working classes enfranchised in the 1867 Reform Acts. They hoped that their support for the party

ACTIVITY 1.3

Carry out some further research into Liberal organisations and pressure groups from the 1860s, 1870s and 1880s. What were their aims and how big an impact did they have on the Liberal Party?

Key terms

Trade union: A union of skilled workers from particular crafts or skills (such as the Amalgamated Society of Carpenters). These organisations sought to improve the conditions of their members and focused on self-help and self-education.

could lead to protection of their legal position, most notably protecting their funds (which Gladstone's government did in 1871).

The ideology of Conservatism

The Conservative Party had emerged from the old Tory Party in the 1830s, and had then split over the issue of tariff reform in the 1840s. The years between 1851 and 1886 were not an easy period for the Conservative Party. The Liberals enjoyed almost a monopoly on power until 1865: the only Conservative ministry of substantial length was that of Benjamin Disraeli from 1874 to 1880.

The Conservative Party abandoned its commitment to protective tariffs in the 1850s (as demonstrated in Disraeli's budget in 1852), since it was clearly electorally very damaging. The various attempts to reunite the Conservative Party with the Peelite group in the Liberal Party all failed, some argue because of Disraeli, since the return of Palmerston and, in particular, Gladstone would have stifled his own ambitions. In the 1850s and 1860s there was a great deal of infighting in the Conservative Party. Disraeli proved to be a highly divisive character: the Tory old guard never fully trusted him, and many actively disliked him, but very few other Conservatives had Disraeli's debating skills in the House of Commons. This is possibly best illustrated by the scornful nickname given to the 1852 Conservative Government which was referred to as the 'Who? Who? Ministry'.

Conservatives in the House of Lords, led by Lord Derby, stood for traditional values: defence of landed interest, protection of the position of the Anglican Church, opposition to electoral reform and strong foreign and imperial policy. In the 1860s, as the demands for further electoral reform grew stronger and the Liberal Government failed with its Reform Bill in 1866 Derby and Disraeli saw a chance to shift the party's position on electoral reform and gain advantage.

Disraeli did, however, bring about significant ideological change within the Conservative Party with his ideology of 'One Nation Conservatism' or 'Tory Democracy'. He was determined to broaden the appeal of the party after the Conservatives failed to achieve electoral victory following the 1867 Reform Act.

The beliefs of One Nation Conservatism

- Preservation of the power of the **establishment** – the long-established institutions of the Anglican Church, aristocracy and monarchy: these institutions should work in the interests of the whole country with the privileged taking a paternalistic interest in the rest of society. Disraeli spoke about the 'two nations' living in Britain, the rich and the poor. He saw it as essential that the rich ensured that the poor had 'pure air, pure water', placing the health and wellbeing of the people as the highest priority.
- The Conservatives are the party of both the aristocracy and working classes: rather than removing the class structure that existed, Disraeli sought to create an alliance between the upper classes and the working classes. He believed this would strengthen the aristocracy and monarchy as well as bringing benefits to the working classes. Disraeli saw the Liberals as the party of the middle classes that both attacked the wealth and position of the privileged and failed to support the working classes with their ideology of self-help.
- The Conservatives should defend and, if possible, extend the British Empire as well as competing with countries such as the USA, Russia and Germany. Disraeli thought the Liberals weak on foreign policy and empire.

One Nation Conservatism has remained a strand within the Conservative Party ever since Disraeli, and later leaders such as Baldwin and Macmillan were strong supporters of it. Historians, however, have debated how far Disraeli stuck to it. His rivalry with Gladstone is legendary, and his social reforms can be seen as attempts to compete with Gladstone, rather than deliberate policy. Reforms and policies were made up of a series of reactions to circumstances. Disraeli's second government (1874–80), however,

Key terms

Establishment: The elite group which dominated British politics, key institutions such as the church, armed forces and civil service and, to an extent, British society as a whole.

ACTIVITY 1.4

Find examples to illustrate the influence of Disraeli's 'One Nation Conservatism after his death in 1881.

How significant was Disraeli's ideology in the development of the Conservative Party?

did introduce social reform such as The Public Health and Artisans' Dwellings Act in 1875 and Factory Acts of 1874 and 1878.

> **Taking it further**
>
> A number of historians have written about Disraeli's ideology and motivation for changing the Conservative Party and introducing reform. Research the views of some or all of the following historians, or others: J.K. Walton, Robert Blake, T.A. Jenkins, Ian St John.

Support for conservatism

The Conservative Party was traditionally the party of the establishment and of the counties; it dominated the vote outside the towns. The Liberal 1884 Reform Act was largely intended to break the Conservative stranglehold on county seats. It had been the party of protectionism, championing the interests of landowners over the interests of manufacturing and industry. This changed in the 1850s as the Conservatives underwent a conversion to free trade, but the support from the landed classes remained strong and was strengthened as those who would previously have supported the Whigs moved away from the Liberals.

The Conservatives had a permanent majority in the House of Lords, where many key party members – most notably Lord Derby – sat, which reinforced the Conservatives as the party of the establishment and elites. Their influential upper-class power base was an advantage for party funds and offered an electoral advantage in an age when social class mattered and many still deferred to 'social superiors'. Before the Secret Ballot Act, local aristocrats could directly influence the way people voted.

A number of Conservatives, however, were also elected to borough seats, in places not now considered natural Conservative strongholds: Liverpool, for example, was solidly Conservative in the mid-Victorian period. The Conservatives were also seen as the party of the Anglican Church, as opposed to the Liberal movement with its strong Nonconformist influences (the strongly Anglican Gladstone had originally been a Conservative). When Gladstone's policies were seen as a threat to the established Church and, notably, when he disestablished the Church in Ireland, the Anglican Church became a bastion of Conservative support.

Following the Reform Act of 1867 the Conservative Party actively sought to expand the basis of its support. Local party associations grew in each constituency, including Conservative working men's associations and clubs (there may still be a Conservative club in your local town or city). Conservative clubs offered snooker and beer, and were often more attractive to working-class men than their Liberal equivalents, since Nonconformist influence often forbade alcohol. The National Union of Conservative and Constitutional Associations (NUCCA) was formed in 1867. The man who probably did most to develop the Conservative Party's relationship with new supporters was John Gorst, who was appointed party agent in 1870. He established the Conservative Central Office and became Secretary of the NUCCA, using these organisations to spread Conservative propaganda and policies to local party associations.

The Primrose League, named after Disraeli's favourite flower and aimed at promoting Conservative values, was set up in 1883 (Disraeli had died in 1881 and Queen Victoria sent primroses to his funeral). It was progressive in that it gave equal status to female members. It was only small during this period, but would grow in later years to have a very large membership (reportedly as high as one million in 1906). The League followed Disraeli's earlier principle of connecting the classes together, with many of the ambitious working classes (especially the women) taking great pleasure from brushing shoulders with those from high society. The Primrose League, though not of Disraeli's making, was a legacy of the transformation by him and Gorst of the Conservative Party, from a party of the landed elites and establishment to a party of mass appeal.

> Thematic link: Ruling elites

The extension of the franchise

The workings of mid-19th-century democracy were affected by the expansion of the franchise and its changing nature: there were significant shifts in the franchise in 1832, 1867 and 1884 (Figure 1.11). Key areas of change included:

- redistribution of seats so they better reflected the populations in the boroughs
- adjustments to the qualification for the franchise in the boroughs
- adjustment to the qualification for the franchise in the counties.

The franchise c1851

Country	Type	No of seats	Largest constituency	Electorate	Smallest constituency	Electorate
England	Borough	1	Salford	1497	Reigate	153
		2	Westminster	11 576	Thetford	146
		4	City of London	18 584	-	-
	County	1	Isle of Wight	1167	-	-
		2	West Riding of Yorkshire	18 056	Rutland	1296
		3	Cambridgeshire	6435	Oxfordshire	4721
	University	2	Oxford University	2496	Cambridge University	2319
Wales	Borough	1	Flint Boroughs	1359	Brecon	242
	County	1	Pembrokeshire	3700	Merionethshire	580
		2	Carmarthenshire	3887	Denbighshire	3401
Scotland	Burgh	1	Aberdeen	2024	Wigtown Burghs	316
		2	Glasgow	6989	Edinburgh	6048
	County	1	Perthshire	3180	Sutherland	84
Ireland	Borough	1	Carrickfergus	1024	Lisburn	91
		2	Dublin	7008	Waterford	1241
	County	2	County Cork	3835	County Kildare	1112
	University	2	Dublin University	2073	-	-

Table 1.1: Largest and smallest constituencies (by size of electorate) in the 1832 election

The 1832 Reform Act had failed to resolve several problems of the political system:

- There were still over 60 boroughs with fewer than 300 voters in 1832. Such seats were particularly vulnerable to corruption and being dominated by a local landowner.
- There was a uniform qualification of occupying a house with a £10 yearly rental value. (This criterion had been used since the 1820s for tax purposes and so was easy to administer.)
- Although the franchise was seemingly uniform and carefully worked out to enfranchise only the middle classes, there were variations from borough to borough due to differing rental values. In London, where rents were higher than elsewhere, some of the skilled working classes (artisans) were enfranchised while in parts of the North, middle-class men, who were the target of the Reform Act, found that they did not qualify to vote.
- It was not only the 'interests' of manufacturing and new industry that were awarded new representation. Older industrial towns, such as Stroud and Frome, gained representation, as did the spa towns such as Cheltenham and Brighton.
- Some substantial urban areas, however, such as Doncaster and Loughborough, had populations in five figures, but no MPs.
- In the counties the voting qualification was holding, or being a tenant farmer on, a 40-shilling freehold. This ensured the continued dominance of the county seats by the landed elites.
- The counties were still disproportionally under-represented, with almost 60% of the population and just over 30% of the seats.

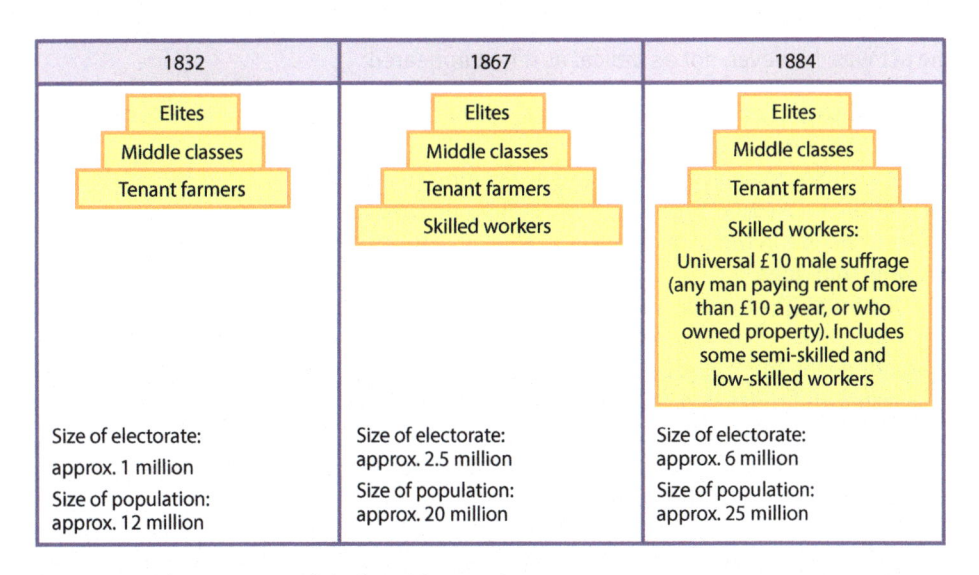

1832	1867	1884
Elites	Elites	Elites
Middle classes	Middle classes	Middle classes
Tenant farmers	Tenant farmers	Tenant farmers
	Skilled workers	Skilled workers: Universal £10 male suffrage (any man paying rent of more than £10 a year, or who owned property). Includes some semi-skilled and low-skilled workers
Size of electorate: approx. 1 million	Size of electorate: approx. 2.5 million	Size of electorate: approx. 6 million
Size of population: approx. 12 million	Size of population: approx. 20 million	Size of population: approx. 25 million

Figure 1.11: The extension of the franchise

The 1832 Reform Act was seen at the time as the final word in terms of extending the franchise. The majority of politicians and commentators believed that the middle classes had proven worthy of the vote, but to open the door to the working classes would be unwise and potentially disastrous. Over time these attitudes would change.

The Reform Act of 1867

Gladstone and his Liberal Government failed in an attempt to pass a reform bill in 1866. By reducing the rental value qualification from £10 per year to £7, the proposed bill would have given the franchise to 200 000 men, largely from the skilled artisans class (considered to be the 'respectable' elite of the working class). The bill split the Liberal Party: some thought the enfranchising of this number of the working class too radical.

The failure of the bill led to popular demands for reform and some public anger. The Reform League organised a series of rallies and demonstrations in protest against the defeating of Gladstone's bills. A demonstration in Hyde Park in July 1866, also known as 'Hyde Park Railings Affair', was the clearest expression of this. It involved 200 000 people who stormed the park. The overwhelmed police called for military support. The then Home Secretary Walpole intended to take a firm stance and perhaps even use force against the demonstrators, but he backed down. The Reform League continued to push for reform.

Disraeli seized the opportunity to score a point against his great rival Gladstone. He believed that the Conservatives, by widening the franchise, might gain electoral advantage. He also saw the opportunity to deepen the divide in the Liberal Party, giving further advantage to the Conservatives. The reform bill proposed by the Conservatives during the same Parliament aimed to enfranchise all male householders in the boroughs who had been resident in their property for two years and paid their own rates. It was estimated that these measures would enfranchise 400 000 men.

Amendments that made the bill more radical were proposed and accepted: the residency qualification dropped from two years to one, and compounders (men who paid their rates along with their rent) were to be given the vote. With these amendments, the Reform Act of 1867 enfranchised 700 000 men. In some boroughs, such as Leeds and Birmingham, the number of voters increased by over 25 000 men. A number of boroughs now had a working-class majority. The Reform Act was thus a big step towards democracy and it caused alarm in the Conservative Party. There were a number of resignations and Disraeli was accused by Lord Cranbourne of conceding the principle of a democratic political system 'which would sweep away the aristocracy'.

The act was, however, not as radical as it first appeared:

- The redistribution of seats was limited, leaving London, the Midlands and the North still under-represented.
- The rural South and West were still over-represented.
- A number of smaller boroughs were still dominated by the local landowner.
- The franchise in the counties was still based on highly restrictive property ownership rules.
- In the boroughs the one-year residency rule disenfranchised as many as 30% of working-class men. The group most strongly discriminated against – younger, single working-class men who still lived with their parents – were disenfranchised, as were servants and those in receipt of poor relief. Overall 40% of men in boroughs were excluded from the vote.
- The power of the elites and wealthy were also maintained through **plural voting** (7% of all votes in the boroughs).

The Secret Ballot Act (1872) and the Corrupt Practices Act (1883)

Earlier practices continued to a certain extent, however, including bribery and corruption, and candidates' expenses rose; for example, voters could now get away with taking bribes from both candidates. The Secret Ballot Act was an improvement and 11 years later the Corrupt Practices Act brought in further controls:

- strict penalties and limits on election spending
- banning of colourable employment and treating
- restrictions on transporting voters to polling stations
- candidates allowed one agent only
- strict election accounts required.

Thematic link: The evolution of the election system

Key terms

Plural voting: A situation where some people had more than one vote. For example, if they lived in one constituency and had business premises in another, they would have a vote in each constituency. This system favoured the wealthy and meant that there was no level playing field in British democracy.

The acts did lead to a reduction in corruption and in spending on elections. Corruption was not completely ended, but this legislation made it much more difficult to successfully influence elections through bribery or intimidation.

> **Taking it further**
>
> Research and write about an election in the 1880s following all the changes detailed in the section 'Political developments under Gladstone and Disraeli':
> - Identify similarities and differences between an election in the 1850s and one at the end of the 1880s
> - Find and evaluate contemporary accounts of elections and/or changes to the political system.
> - Find and evaluate historians' views of the development of democracy in Britain 1851–86 and how far things had changed.

The Reform Act of 1884 and the Redistribution Act of 1885

The 1884 Reform Act added an unprecedented 2.5 million voters. Henry Maine wrote in 1886 that the reforms had brought about 'unmoderated Democracy'. The bureaucratic and complex voter registration system, however, disenfranchised a number of men who were entitled to vote, and there remained a bias against young working-class men. No women yet had the vote; nor did a large proportion of men. The unelected and aristocratic House of Lords still had a veto on legislation. It would appear that Sir Henry Maine's claim was a little premature.

Arguably, Gladstone was less keen on widening the franchise generally than on attacking Conservative dominance of the counties by enfranchising rural labourers. The Conservatives seemed to have a permanent majority in the House of Lords and opposed the reforms on principle, but their leader Lord Salisbury worried that they would be seen as reactionary and acting out of self-interest. Gladstone and Salisbury met at Salisbury's London home and agreed what became known as the 'Arlington Street Compact'. This agreement set the basis for the 1884 Reform Act and the 1885 Redistribution Act to pass through Parliament. Together they revolutionised 19th-century British politics: not only were a large number of working-class men enfranchised, but new principles were established over constituencies. The first new principle was that constituencies were to be of equal size (approximately 50 000) and an independent Boundary Commissions was set up to ensure this.

These new boundaries defined in the Redistribution Act were drawn up according to the 'pursuits of the people', along socio-economic grounds. For example, a constituency made up of middle-class suburbs was defined next to a constituency made up of working-class areas. This created what was known as 'Villa Toryism' and led to a substantial increase in Conservative representation in the boroughs, as the middle classes abandoned the Liberals for the Conservatives.

The 1885 Redistribution Act also established the idea of single-member constituencies. The reforms severed historic links and broke party dominance over old borough and county seats, as many were now subdivided into multiple constituencies. British politics was substantially changed and the outcome was not the Liberal dominance Gladstone was hoping for. The new middle-class constituencies in the boroughs greatly benefited the Conservatives and their Villa Toryism, while the new working-class constituencies not only favoured the Liberals, but would have major long-term consequences as they made the emergence of a working-class party a possibility (though barriers to this still remained).

By 1886 the Liberal Party's position was slightly precarious. The Conservatives were benefiting from the Redistribution Act and enjoyed growing middle-class support. The

> **Hidden voices**
>
> ### Sheffield: a case study for Villa Toryism
>
> Until 1884 Liberal dominance of the boroughs had been increasing, especially those in the growing industrial towns and cities of the Midlands and the North. The Liberal Reform Act of 1884 was a clear attack on Conservative power in the counties, so the Conservatives needed to improve their chances of winning seats created by the 1885 Redistribution Act. Villa Toryism gave the Conservatives a foothold in the towns and cities and created a number of constituencies that went on to have unusual histories. One such was Sheffield Hallam: Sheffield is not a city renowned for Conservative support, but apart from a brief period between 1916 and 1918, Sheffield Hallam was a Conservative seat from 1885 to 1997.

ACTIVITY 1.5

Carry out research to discover other aspects that make Sheffield Hallam stand out from the other constituencies in Sheffield.

Find other examples of 'Villa Toryism' from around the country.

Key terms

Lib-Lab MPs: These were Liberal MPs financially supported by trade unions. Alexander McDonald and Thomas Burt, both supported by the Miners' Federation of Great Britain, were the first two such MPs to be elected in 1874.

1884 Act opened the door for the growth of a working-class party, and the first sign came in the form of the **Lib-Lab MPs**. In Ireland the Home Rule Party started to eat into Liberal support. The principle of reform was, however, strongly embedded and although Britain was still not fully democratic, the period 1867–85 had seen a dramatic transformation of the British political system: a substantial increase in the franchise, acceptance that the working classes were worthy of the vote, and a clampdown on the old corrupt practices, largely thanks to the introduction of the secret ballot.

Taking it further

Draw a table like this and use it to record how democracy and political organisations in Britain changed over time. Use the content of this chapter and add extra details from your own research. What evidence can you find of continuity and change?

	1831	1851	1867	1885
Monarch				
House of Lords				
House of Commons				
Liberals				
Conservatives				

Economic developments

Agriculture, trade and industry

Agriculture

The mid-Victorian period is most famous for the development of British trade and industry, but agriculture and land remained the cornerstones of wealth in Britain during this period. Britain was still, as E.J. Hobsbawm wrote, 'a place where plants grow and animals feed'.[7] The landowning class dominated the House of Commons (until 1885) and the social structure: 4000 landlords owned about 60% of the cultivated land between them and let it to 250 000 farmers who employed about 1 250 000 people. Agriculture was, in its own right, a key British 'industry' and, like all industries in this period, it modernised and faced foreign competition.

Figure 1.12: Sheffield steel works in the 1800s

Agriculture certainly faced challenges with the repeal of the Corn Laws in 1846. These had protected British farmers against cheap imported corn, keeping the price of cereal crops (and therefore bread) artificially high. British farmers now had to face foreign competition as Britain entered a period of free trade.

The ideas of James Caird, a farmer whose pamphlet *High Farming* appeared in 1849, were key to the development of British agriculture. He argued that land should be farmed more intensively in order to increase the **yield** and that the latest techniques and inventions would enable the producers to remain profitable even at lower prices. The years through to 1853 saw a difficult period of adjustment, but there followed a 20-year golden age for British agriculture. Farmers who followed Caird's advice and invested were rewarded with their incomes as much as doubling, and the countryside experienced a period of prosperity. The rapid population growth of the time also increased demand. British wheat faced stiff competition from the USA and Russia, but the prices of fresh produce (meat and dairy – not refrigerated, of course) increased significantly.

Key terms

Yield: In agriculture it is the amount of crops/produce that can be grown on a given piece of land, a higher yield means more produce. In investments the yield is the amount of profit made on an investment.

Between 1853 and 1873 **high farming** methods brought real benefits. There were several key developments and advances:

- A move to mixed farming: growing crops (root vegetables as well as wheat) and keeping animals such as sheep, cows and pigs, so that farmers spread their risk on crop prices. Manure from the livestock could be used help the crops grow and any excess crops could be used to feed animals.
- Artificial fertilisers: this included nitrate of soda, superphosphates, imports of Peruvian guano (bird droppings) and German potash.
- Machinery: the more spectacular and advanced machines, such as steam ploughs, were not widely used, but improved ploughs and hoes and the widespread use of the horse-drawn reaper, had a significant impact.
- Animal husbandry: saw improvements to pedigree breeds such as Hereford and Aberdeen Angus cattle, particularly noted for the quality of their beef.
- Scientific farming: was encouraged by the Royal Agricultural Society of England, which published a journal, carried out research and ran agricultural shows.
- Development of the railways: this was possibly most important for many farmers who were distant from towns and cities (see the section 'Railways').

The boom was also due to good weather – between 1850 and 1873 there were many summers leading to good harvests. However, the 'good times' would not last forever. A depression struck agriculture from 1873 and would last for a very long time. Some areas of British agriculture would never recover to the heights of this golden age as foreign competition became stronger.

Key terms

High farming: farming that was considered to be excellent, often involving new techniques, technology and ideas that improved production.

Trade and industry

In 1851 Britain's wealth and prestige was demonstrated at the Great Exhibition, housed in the Crystal Palace (a highly impressive building made of glass and cast iron, over half a kilometre long and 30 metres high) in Hyde Park. The Great Exhibition displayed all the triumphs of British manufacturing, including cutting-edge steam machines (railway locomotives, steam ploughs, steamships); Lancashire cotton; Nottingham lace; and various inventions and oddities, such as an unsinkable deckchair. There were also exhibits from other countries to display Britain's commitment to free trade. The exhibition was open for five months and received over six million visitors, many from abroad. The exhibition made a profit of £186 500. This was invested in buying land in Kensington, which was developed over the next 50 years for the Victoria and Albert Museum, the Albert Hall, the Science Museum, the Natural History Museum and Imperial College of Science and Technology. The exhibition gave British industry a lift. The international prestige that resulted helped usher in a 20-year boom.

International trade was being transformed by the development of the steamship and the railway. Britain, as the first industrial nation, led the way and dominated international trade. This was particularly true in the period between the repeal of the Corn Laws in 1846 and the onset of the depression in 1873. Britain had industrialised first, giving it an advantage. Germany was not completely united until 1871 and so did not fully become the power it would until after this point and the USA was consumed by the Civil War that raged from 1861 until 1865.

British trade with its own empire became particularly important: India became an essential market for British cotton and other exports. One of the biggest growth area in British trade was in invisible trade (services such as finance, banking, insurance and shipping). Britain's dominance of shipping meant that it also dominated world trade. Goods going out, as well as going into, Britain were carried on British ships, as was much else of the world's trade that never landed in Britain. Trading agreements with British colonies and dominions often meant that goods they produced had to be carried on British shipping and had to travel to Britain first, even if it was ultimately being exported elsewhere. Almost all shipping (British or otherwise) was insured in the City of London and British banks also financed most mercantile ventures.

1800	£300 million
1830	£400 million
1870	£2000 million

Table 1.2: The value of International trade[8]

1840	£160 million
1850	£250 million
1873	£1000 million

Table 1.3: The value of British investment abroad[9]

> **Key terms**
>
> **Balance of payments:** The difference between revenue from exports and spending on imports – this can be a surplus (revenue greater than spending) or a deficit (spending greater than revenue).

Aspects of trade that boosted British trade in the short term may well have damaged it in the long term. For example, large profits were made from developing industry in other countries, supplying experts, machinery, machine tools and raw materials. These countries would go on to become rivals for British industry or, in the long term, not require British imports.

During the period between c1851 and 1868 British trade made up around 25% of the total of world trade. British trade consistently ran at a surplus but there was a dramatic increase in imports, most notably of food. The fact that most of this was carried on British ships, insured by British firms, meant that the impact on the **balance of payments** was negative overall. It was, however, the case that during this period, in which Britain was considered the workshop of the world, that a higher value of physical goods were being imported into Britain than were being exported.

Railways

The growth of the railways played a significant part in British industrial strength. The increase in the amount of track in Britain – it rose from 9 500 km in 1850 to 22 000 km in 1875[10] – rivalled the 'Railway Mania' of the 1840s, and created jobs and growth in a variety of industries:

- iron and steel: production of track and rolling stock, also used in repair centres (notably in Crewe and Swindon)
- coal: the railways aided distribution and enabled new coalfields to develop
- agriculture: enabled rapid transport of produce over greater distances
- manufacturing: enabled rapid transportation of goods around the country and to ports for export.

Railway track and machinery were also important exports. The export of railway iron and steel rose from 2 846 000 tons in the years 1850 to 1854 to 4 040 000 in the years 1870 to 1875, and railroad machinery exports rose from 8600 tons in 1850 to 1854 to 44 100 tons in 1870 to 1875.[11] Britain was therefore not only benefiting from its own rapid railway expansion but also from the growth of railways in other countries. The development of transport that could move industrial and manufactured goods rapidly helped reinforce Britain's economic advantage.

Shipping

Britain dominated merchant shipping. By 1890 Britain had more registered shipping tonnage than the rest of the world put together. British ships transported goods entering and leaving Britain and a great deal of other trade that never came near British ports. The growth of the City of London as a financial centre also benefited because British firms (especially Lloyds of London) dominated shipping insurance, and merchants used the worldwide branches of British banks. British ships had laid the Atlantic cable between Britain and the USA in 1866, enabling almost instantaneous messages, which further boosted London's international financial markets.

Shipbuilding was a boom industry, creating large amounts of work in areas such as Glasgow, Belfast, Tyneside and Liverpool. It enjoyed high prestige: during the American Civil War the Confederacy sent agents to Britain to try to buy ships to break the Union's blockade of their ports. Shipbuilding was further stimulated by the movement from sail to steam and the development of ironclads – a highly advanced new type of battleship that effectively made earlier warships obsolete.

When the Suez Canal opened in 1869, only British steamships were narrow enough to pass through – large sailing ships were too wide. The canal further increased the flow of international trade from Europe and the USA through to Asia. New docks were built to accommodate the growth in trade. London alone saw the opening of five new docks, including the Royal Victoria and Royal Albert docks, between 1852 and 1886.

Britain led the way with the development of naval technology. Multiple expansion steam engines, developed in Britain, gave ships more power and the ability to travel much greater distances without re-coaling. In 1884 Sir Charles Parsons invented the steam turbine, which would further revolutionise shipping.

Cotton

The cotton industry, largely based in Lancashire, was one of the most important in Britain. Raw cotton was imported from the USA and turned into cloth. The average annual production of cotton textiles almost doubled between the 1850s and the 1870s.

However, the American Civil War led to a significant drop in the imports of US cotton. Cotton was grown on the slave plantations of the Confederacy, and the Union blockaded southern ports to cut off Confederate exports. The resulting 'cotton famine' in Lancashire meant reduced production and the loss of many jobs. Despite their hardship, the mill workers backed the Union cause, which aimed to end slavery, and this persuaded Gladstone and others that the workers were worthy of the vote.

> **Thematic link: The extension of the franchise**

Supplies of cotton were brought in from elsewhere in the world and new markets, most notably India, were found for British cotton textiles. The cotton industry continued to be an integral part of the British economy and a main export, increasingly to the developing world rather than to other major economic powers.

Coal

The industrial revolution was based on steam power, so coal was vital. It powered trains and steamships and iron and steel production, as well as the cotton industry. The growing population also increased the demand for coal for heating homes and cooking food. Coal production grew from 60 million tons in 1855 to 109 million tons in 1870.[12] New coalfields were opened up, for example in South Wales.

Germany and the USA were mechanising their mining industry, but in Britain most of the coal was still extracted by hand. Coal mines were run by private businesses which were reluctant to invest large amounts of money in mechanised equipment. About half a million men were employed in the mines, so it was a hugely significant industry, and the miners who undertook the difficult and dangerous work of hewing (cutting coal out of the rock face) were some of the best paid industrial workers.

Iron and steel

High quality British iron was not only the basis of many significant engineering projects in Britain, but was also in high demand throughout the world. Output of British iron continued to grow through this period (2.9 million tons in 1855 to 5.9 million tons in 1875)[13] and technological advances also put Britain at the forefront of steel production. In the mid-19th century Sheffield produced 90% of British steel, which accounted for nearly half of Europe's total production.

Successive engineers improved iron and steel production: In 1850 George Parry improved the hot blast furnaces by recycling some of the heat, making iron works more profitable; Henry Bessemer's converter system, patented in 1856, meant that steel could be produced in large amounts (3 tons per hour) far cheaper than the existing crucible system; and in 1867 a German engineer working in Britain (William Siemens) devised the open-hearth process.

Steel was a superior metal and it was now affordable. Railway companies switched to using it for rails, and shipping companies started to use it for metal-plating their ships. The Forth Bridge was built using steel between 1882 and 1889. Steel production required the use of non-phosphorous iron ore (most British-mined iron ore contained phosphorus). This requirement was overcome by the 'Basic Process', an advance for British steel that turned Middlesbrough into a boom town. The USA and Germany also had large deposits of phosphorous iron ore which they could now turn into steel, so Britain's key competitors benefited from a British innovation.

Economic ideologies

During the period following the repeal of the Corn Laws in 1846, Britain moved strongly away from protectionism and towards free trade. The ideology of free trade can be traced back to the writing of Adam Smith in the 18th century, in particular in his book *Wealth of Nations*. Smith argued that a system of a freely operating markets was the ideal economic model, as these markets would ensure competition that would drive down prices and benefit the consumer. The markets would prove a rigorous test for efficiency of production and also ensure the most effective allocation of resources to different parts of the economy. Smith argued that markets should be free from government intervention at both a national and international level: government interference was always to the detriment of the consumer and led to higher prices, since governments tended to intervene to protect producers (a small group) to the detriment of consumers (the whole population).

According to free trade theory, if manufacturers did not have to pay tariffs on goods, they could operate with lower costs, making exports more competitive on the world market. This was particularly true of goods where raw materials were imported and then the finished goods exported. Free trade would also benefit the working classes, as cheap imports would force down the price of food (the percentage of income spent by an average family on food was much higher then than it is today). A thriving manufacturing sector would help to keep unemployment down, also benefiting the working classes.

There were those who criticised Adam Smith's work, including Alfred Marshall who argued that people were as important as money, and services as important as goods. He demonstrated that Smith's theory of the 'invisible hand' of the market did not lead to fair market prices where a firm or small number of firms dominated a market.

Neither Adam Smith, nor indeed many other writers and economists, advocated markets completely free of government constraint. Smith, for example, backed state education, a state post office and government control of paper money. Gladstone, a free-trade convert, sought to keep government expenditure and taxes as low as possible. He even went as far as to describe 'excessive' public spending as a 'great moral evil'.

Free trade was supported by Radicals in the Liberal Party, such as Cobden (who believed it was key to international peace) and Bright, and increasingly by the Conservative Party as they moved away from their traditional support of protective tariffs. Free trade appeared to win the debate over protectionism, but there was still a debate about the economic role of Britain's colonies. Disraeli predicted that Britain's colonies would 'drop like ripe fruit' in the 1850s, but they (especially India) continued to be central to British economic policy and power.

ACTIVITY 1.6

To what extent did British governments pursue free trade policies between 1851 and 1873?

Gladstone and Peel
- Free trade
- Reduction of income tax
- Combining small finance bills into a single budget

Gladstone and Disraeli
- Public health acts
- Factory acts
- Labour relations and trade union legislation

Great Depression
- Agriculture and industrial slump
- Limited government action
- Splits in the Liberal Party over social reform

Figure 1.13: A summary of economic policy 1851–86

Cross-reference: Debates over protectionism, tariff reform and free trade (Chapter 2)

Boom and 'the workshop of the world'

	1856	1870
Coal	65 million tons	110 million tons
	1850	1875
Iron	2 million tons	6 million tons
Steel	60 000 tons	2 million tons

Table 1.4: The growth of coal, iron and steel production[14]

Britain, as the first industrial nation, had a great advantage over other nations in terms of economic development, by 1851. The next three decades were to be dominated by steam power, and by iron and steel, in which Britain led the way technologically. Britain was manufacturing more than other nations in the key products of the day (coal, iron, steel, cotton textiles) and dominated in key areas of engineering, such as the production of machine tools and screw-making machines.

- Production in all significant areas grew (coal, iron, steel, railways, shipping, cotton) and industrial growth ran at about 3.5% per year.
- Britain had good deposits of the vital raw materials for its industries and could meet the growing demand.
- Trade grew dramatically, both imports and exports. In 1850, Britain's share of world trade was 20%. In 1875 it was 25%.[15]
- Overall standards of living increased, unemployment fell and wages increased more quickly than prices.
- The British were increasingly better off, so they consumed more and further fuelled the boom.
- The number of agricultural labourers fell by almost half a million between 1851 and 1871, while employment in all the key industries increased significantly.

- The British population grew by almost 6 million in 20 years, aiding the growth in demand.
- Unlike France, Germany and the USA, Britain had so far been relatively untouched by war.
- British governments pursued free trade and laissez-faire economics, which helped feed the boom. Firms and individuals were encouraged to show initiative and enterprise. The Limited Liabilities Acts of 1855 and 1862 encouraged the buying of shares in firms as the level of risk was limited to the value of the investment.

Britain was seen as the 'workshop of the world', yet there is strong evidence to counter this. Britain was actually importing goods of a higher total value than it was exporting during this period.

Year (average of 5 years)	Net imports (£ million)	Exports of UK products (£ million)	Balance of commodity trade (£ million)[16]
1846–50	87.7	60.9	−26.8
1851–55	116.4	88.9	−27.5
1856–60	158	124.2	−33.8
1861–65	201.2	144.4	−56.8
1866–70	246	187.8	−58.2
1871–75	302	239.5	−62.5

Table 1.5: The balance of commodity trade, 1846–75

Britain's overall balance of trade during this period was positive, but this was due to income from services (such as shipping, insurance and banking) and income from interest and dividends from investment abroad. So, although Britain was certainly economically very strong and dominant in trade, it is not clear that the term 'workshop of the world' was fully appropriate. By the end of this period, Britain was struggling to compete, in terms of production of key industrial goods and materials, with the USA and Germany where the economies were growing more rapidly.

- They had larger populations than Britain and greater resources of raw materials.
- They outperformed Britain in areas such as education (male illiteracy was 17% in Britain in 1875, compared with 2% in Germany) and the training of engineers and scientists (British universities produced far fewer scientists and engineers than those in the USA, and, from 1850, German *Realschule* pioneered technically focused secondary education, as opposed to the classical British syllabus).
- Investment in new technologies, as evidenced by US mass production, was being pioneered through the birth of the modern assembly line and mass production of guns, clocks and sewing machines.
- Britain had industrialised first, but by the 1880s this was arguably a disadvantage. In Germany and the USA industries were being started up with the latest technology and were quick to adopt new techniques (for example in mining and in the early use of electricity as a power source). The older British industries now had outdated machinery and techniques.
- British industry was more typically made up of smaller firms than in Germany and the USA. At individual firm level, they were less likely to have the capital available to invest in new machinery. This was particularly true after 1873 when production continued to increase, but prices and profits fell.

In this period the percentage of British exports going to the developed world fell markedly and the majority of British exports were now being sold in the developing world, most notably in her colonies.

ACTIVITY 1.7

To what extent did Britain warrant the claim to being the 'workshop of the world' in the period 1851–86?

1 Reform and challenge, c1851–1886

The onset of the Depression

Historians debate whether the period from 1873 to the end of the century can be called the 'Great Depression'. The historian S.B. Saul, in his 1985 book *The Myth of the Great Depression*, argued that there was no depression in the British economy, but rather an overall average fall in business profits, which caused many at the time to see economy in a pessimistic light.

Arguments against a depression	Arguments in favour of a depression
Falling prices can be seen as part of a long-term trend due to advances in industry reduction in the cost of production and the failure of governments to alter the money supply in line with increasing trade.	Profits were falling, largely due to falling prices.
Although there were years of high unemployment, there were also some years in the period 1875–95 when unemployment of trade union members was 2%, compared with the 4.6% average in the boom years.	To cut costs, companies would lay off workers. The average unemployment rate among trade union members fluctuated, but gradually increased, during this period (see Figure 1.14).
British production of coal, iron, steel and cotton all increased during this period.	The percentage share Britain held in world production of key industrial goods, such as steel, iron and coal, fell during this period.
The economy continued to grow, albeit at little more than 1% a year.	
As the European and US markets became more competitive, Britain expanded new markets in the developing world.	The economies of Germany (three times) and the USA (almost four times) were growing significantly faster than Britain's.
Failure to invest in new machinery and premises was due to complacency and mismanagement by British businessmen, not a depression (the historians Hobsbawm and Wiener have blamed the class structure in Britain, saying that businessmen were trying to emulate the aristocracy rather than develop their businesses).	Britain failed to adopt new industries, such as electrical engineering, chemicals and dyestuffs and production of new machines, such as typewriters and sewing machines.
There was much to be positive about in this period, including the bicycle and telephone industries, as well as in retail (argued, in particular, by the historian Martin Pugh).	European countries and the USA protected their industries against British goods using protective tariffs, while Britain maintained free trade.
In general, the cost of living fell as prices fell, so that in real terms wages increased.	Falls in profits meant that British firms did not have the money to invest in new premises and machinery.

Table 1.6: Was there a depression in the last quarter of the 19th century?

Those who accept that Britain did suffer a depression identify a number of causes:

- Increased foreign competition especially from Germany and the USA, both of which had vast natural resources at their disposal.
- Britain failing to match the educational advances, in particular in science and engineering, of other countries. Science was only really taught to medical students at university.
- Introduction of protective **tariffs** across Europe and the USA.
- Failure of British industry to keep up with advances in technology and continue with old machinery.

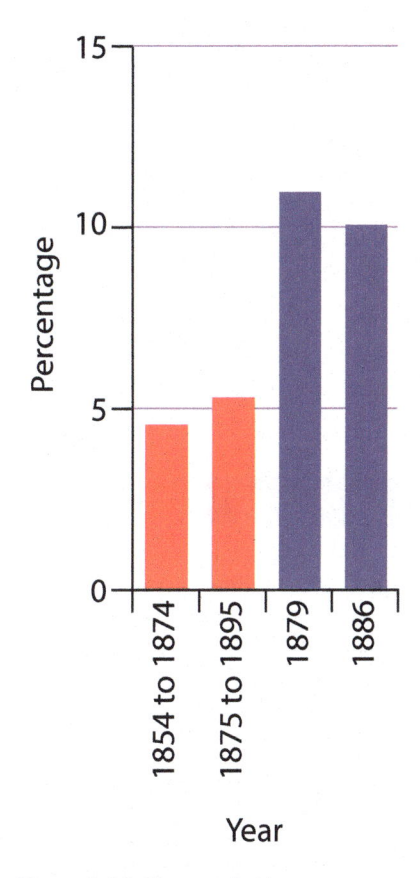

Figure 1.14: Changes in the average unemployment rate among trade union members (%)

ACTIVITY 1.8

Choose a reason from Table 1.6 and argue that it was the key reason that there was or was not a depression.

Then rank all the reasons in order of importance.

- British firms tended to be fairly small family firms compared with very large US and German companies. British firms were headed by the families of the man who started the firms, while in the USA and Germany men were recruited on merit.
- British industrial base was less diverse than other countries with less development of new industries.

The Great Depression and agriculture

Arguably, there was a much clearer Depression in agriculture in Britain following 1873. Following a series of good summers and high yields there was a change in weather and, therefore, harvests, in 1873 and 1875 and subsequently. Wet weather ruined crops and led to the spread of diseases among livestock, such as foot and mouth, liver rot and swine fever.

Farming production and profits both tumbled as cheap foreign imports benefited from free trade and the technological advances in shipping (steamships increased in size and speed from the late 1860s, and refrigerated ships were introduced in the 1880s). Britain was flooded with wheat from the USA, Canada, India and Australia, and then frozen meat from New Zealand, Australia and Argentina. The modern 'traditional English breakfast' started in this period with the importing of Danish bacon.

Agricultural wages fell, increasing the gap between the living standards of industrial and agricultural workers. Low food prices were very good news for industrial workers, but not for agricultural workers, whose average earnings were about half of those working in industry.

Some farmers shifted from crop production to dairy farming (the demand for milk grew and this was not affected by foreign competition) and poultry farming or growing fruit and vegetables. British meat struggled to compete on price, but did compete effectively on quality with foreign imports. Some farmers even switched to growing flowers, giving up on food produce as they could no longer make it profitable.

A significant political consequence of the agricultural depression was that many among the landowning class dropped out of politics, since they could no longer afford to take part, and were replaced by men from business and the professions.

Society and social changes

Class and regional division

In Britain's highly hierarchical Victorian society, position was of great importance. There were hierarchies and divisions within the classes as well as between them. There were gradations of working class, and there was arguably a greater division between the higher and lower tiers of the working classes than between the higher tiers of the working classes and the lower tiers of the middle classes. A skilled artisan from the higher tiers of the working classes may well have earned more than a clerk who would consider themselves middle class. There was also a narrowing gap and, increasingly, some degree of intermarriage between the affluent people at the top of the middle classes and the upper classes, as trade and industry started to overtake land as the best source of wealth. The relationship between the classes changed as the British economy and politics changed when first the middle classes, then some of the working classes acquired the franchise and greater affluence.

The upper classes

In mid-Victorian Britain the upper classes could largely be divided into two groups; the landed aristocracy and the landed gentry (see Table 1.7).

The powerful aristocracy dominated the House of Lords. They also dominated and exerted great influence over society in terms of lifestyle (leisure activities, education, food and drink), manners and fashion. The gentry and many of the middle classes

> **Key terms**
>
> **Tariff:** Taxes imposed on imported goods by a government to protect the country's own industries against foreign competition.

> **ACTIVITY 1.9**
>
> Using the information in this section and further reading carry out a debate on the motion that 'There was no depression in Britain in the 1870s and 1880s.'

aspired to emulate them and showed a considerable degree of deference to the highest ranks in British society. An important ambition for many a member of the gentry was to see their son or daughter married into the aristocracy (Mrs Bennett in Jane Austen's *Pride and Prejudice* is a prime example of this).

Aristocracy	Gentry
Included about 800 people	Included about 3000 people
Annual income generally over £10 000 (Duke of Northumberland £130 000)	Annual income £1000–£10 000
Land over 10 000 acres	Land 1000–10 000 acres
House and estate in the countryside	House and estate in the countryside
Own or rent a house in London	—
Up to 50 staff/servants	At least six servants
Title such as Duke, Earl, Marquis, many sat in the House of Lords	Possible minor title, many sat in the House of Commons

Table 1.7: Characteristics of the upper classes

There were also tensions, with some of the gentry being resentful of the aristocracy's dominance of key positions in the localities and on the national stage. The 'occupation' of the ruling classes had always been land ownership – money earned from any actual work or trade was considered rather vulgar – but during the period 1851–86 it became increasingly common for the landed elites to marry their children to the children of leading families from the worlds of banking and commerce. (Winston Churchill's mother, for example, was the daughter of a wealthy US financier; she married Lord Randolph Churchill in 1874.)

The middle classes

The middle classes were, in general terms, people who derived a steady income from non-manual labour in business or the professions. To be considered truly middle class it was generally accepted that you would need a minimum annual income of £100. Some earned much more than this and were, financially at least, as well off as the upper classes. The middle classes played a major role in the development of Britain as an industrial and commercial power. Their influence in politics grew, as did their wealth and numbers. The middle classes in many ways looked up to the upper classes in terms of trying to mimic their fashions, manners and lifestyle. For some of the most successful of the middle class their ultimate ambition was to set themselves up like the landed aristocracy, with a country estate and a house in London and adopt the lifestyle of an aristocrat. In the elitist class culture of 19th-century Britain 'new money' (earned money) was always looked down on by 'old money' (inherited wealth from land). Though some of the middle classes did achieve great wealth the majority did not, but their standard of living did, however, generally improve.

The middle classes comprised different levels:

- rich industrialists, bankers, financiers and merchants
- richer clergy, doctors, university professors, public school headmasters
- yeoman farmers, lawyers, mill managers
- teachers and clerks.

The real incomes of the middle classes increased between 1851 and 1871 as the economy grew strongly and prices were pushed down by cheap imports and falling prices of industrial and manufactured goods. The numbers of the middle class also increased rapidly, faster than the population in general, despite many middle-class families starting to limit the sizes of their families, which suggests a degree of social mobility at the time.

The middle classes separated themselves from the poor by moving south and west out of the city centres (the best directions to move to get away from the smoke) and into the suburbs. It was during this period that suburbs started to emerge on the leafier outskirts of towns and cities. These suburbs were often clustered around the stations of railway branch lines. The railway season ticket started to become a mainstay of many a middle-class family's budget.

A feature that distinguished the middle classes from the working classes was their ability to employ servants. The number of servants varied, from a single maid employed on an occasional basis, to up to three full-time servants performing various duties. The employment of servants – in emulation of the lifestyle of the upper classes – helped create greater leisure time for the middle classes, especially middle-class women. Books and magazines about fashion, lifestyle and household management were aimed at them. One of the most successful, Mrs Beeton's *The Book of Household Management*, helped middle-class women cope with the new challenges of managing and paying servants, entertaining, purchasing of the latest fashions and cooking the latest foods for every day and for dinner parties. The middle classes also sought to emulate the upper classes in the education of their children. The more affluent of the middle classes sent their boys to rub shoulders with the landed elites at public schools, such as Eton and Westminster.

The middle classes considered themselves, rather than the upper classes, to be the driving force behind Britain's economic and industrial power. This confidence, and their growing affluence and numbers, meant that the middle classes were now well placed to claim dominance in British politics and society. They promoted the idea that positions should be based on merit and not on birth, and the Liberals introduced reforms to the army and civil service that reflected this. The self-made men of the middle classes believed that through hard work and ability the best men would rise up through society.

While they had an eye on taking over from those above them in the social structure, many in the middle classes also cast a less-than-kind eye on the poor who, they believed, were in that position due to lack of hard work and thrift (good money management), and because of a poor moral character (often displayed through drinking or gambling).

The working classes
Among the working classes, the biggest divide was between the unskilled working classes and the skilled, or artisan, class, who took care to defend their position and income. The lower the skill level of a worker, the more volatile their working life tended to be. Skilled working classes formed friendly societies and trade unions.

ACTIVITY 1.10

In 1997 the future British deputy prime minister claimed, 'We are all middle class now.' Using the information in this section evaluate how accurate this statement is regarding mid-19th century standards, consider:
- standards of living
- attitudes towards wealth
- attitudes towards poverty.

Cross-reference: Trade unions

The less-skilled workers in particular were liable to be laid off when there was an economic downturn or drop in demand. Many, such as dressmakers during the London 'season', had work that was largely dependent on the time of year. Many with no regular job simply took what work they could in local industry or local agriculture. Living arrangements were often similarly unstable, with working classes moving regularly from one lodging to another. The development of technology and processes of mass production threatened the position of the artisan class also, causing them to organise to defend their position.

1 Reform and challenge, c1851–1886

> **Taking it further**
>
> Parallels have been draw between the lives of mid-Victorian working classes and modern day workers on zero-hours contracts. Produce a table to show similarities and differences.

The rural poor, whose work was already seasonal, were particularly affected by the Great Depression after 1873, which hit agriculture harder than industry. Agricultural mechanisation and the advent of high farming also reduced the demand for agricultural workers. Changes to the Poor Law in 1834 required someone to be resident in a parish for five years to be eligible for poor relief. This led landowners to restrict labourers to four years of employment and then evict them. Landowners restricted the amount of land available for housing, creating 'closed villages'. The poor would be forced into the 'open villages' that formed nearby – but not too near, to avoid paying poor relief – and these became places of real poverty and poor housing. There followed angry disturbances by rural labourers, including a spate of arson attacks.

Working-class consciousness grew during this period and the artisans (the elite of the working class) gained greater prosperity and the vote. The lower working classes benefited from falling prices, especially for food, but life remained a struggle with the instability of work and housing being two major issues. The conditions for many among the working classes were terrible, with very high infant mortality, low life expectancy, dangerous conditions in work and squalid overcrowded conditions at home. Governments during this period started to address issues of poverty and public health. As more working-class men gained the vote in 1884 and working-class constituencies were created in 1885, the scene was set for more powerful working-class movements to emerge.

> **ACTIVITY 1.11**
>
> What barriers still remained to the creation of a working-class party in 1886?

Regional differences

Britain was not a uniform place. In terms of religion, politics and economics, Ireland was a vastly different place from the rest of Britain. Scotland stood out in terms of its more developed education system and higher literacy rate; Northern England, the Midlands and South Wales had developed industrially with the production of cotton, coal, iron and steel, as well as in the transport industries of railways and ship building. London stood out from the rest of the country in terms of the size of its population and as a major international centre of commerce, as well as being the centre of government. Much of the South-East and South-West remained largely agricultural, and the South-East in particular was over-represented in Parliament.

In modern Britain, we talk about the North/South divide, but the picture was different in the period 1851–86. Northern areas that are now economically depressed were booming in the mid-Victorian period. In the industrial areas there was competition for workers, which pushed up wages and meant that pay in the North was higher than in the South. In very general terms, housing in the North was better for workers than in the South and rents were lower, as were the costs of other key commodities, such as coal. Some areas in the North, however, had very poor conditions, notably the back-to-back housing in Yorkshire.

All major towns and cities had slums where casual workers lived near to local industry. The worst conditions were found in London which had the highest rents and highest coal prices. There was a huge influx of people but very little industry. Many relied on casual seasonal work, leading to terrible poverty in the winter. Health conditions were terrible in the capital too, especially during cholera outbreaks.

In some places life was notably better – for example, Nottingham was noted for having much better housing for the working classes than other major cities, as did the new towns, often with much more space per person and some amenities, such as gas lights and low rents, unheard of elsewhere – but there was little worker mobility. These towns needed to make themselves more attractive to workers so that they would be willing to uproot themselves and their families and move.

This period was notable for migration, both within the country and emigration out of Britain. Growth in industry was one factor; for example, when new coal fields opened in Nottinghamshire, miners came from other mining areas. This started to break down some traditional differences, but regional accents and dialects remained strong. Many people left to seek a new life and opportunity in the USA or the dominions of the British Empire (Canada, Australia and New Zealand).

Prosperity

The gap between rich and poor in Britain during the period 1851–86 was vast. During a period of prosperity for the British economy as a whole between 1851 and 1873, food prices fell and real wages for the majority of British people increased; people were arguably more prosperous during this period than during the earlier stages of industrialisation. It is certainly true that the middle class grew and that, therefore, a greater number of people shared in some aspects of the prosperous lifestyle of the upper classes. There was also, however, terrible poverty among many in British society, in the slums in cities and towns, and acute poverty for many in rural areas.

At the top of society, and to a degree among the middle classes, this was a period of great prosperity. Around the British Isles splendid stately homes have been restored to display the lavish lifestyle of the ruling elites at this time, also captured in books, films and TV dramas.

The very rich lived a life of luxury, waited on by servants. Living on wealth that was both inherited and generated by their extensive lands, they were free to develop hobbies, travel extensively and attend a great range of social events. The life of the wealthy was one of leisure, fine food and drink and a series of social occasions. The year for some was structured as follows:

- Easter into the summer months (generally fitting in with the sitting of Parliament): the 'season' in London (balls, theatres, dinner parties, riding and driving in Hyde Park, exhibitions and picnics)
- summer: holidays by the sea or abroad
- August: shooting
- winter: hunting.

Aristocrats would have several homes and would move around during the year: out of London for hunting and fishing, and into London for the 'season' – the highlight of the year and especially important with regard to the marriage market. Wealthy families wanting to make a good match for their son or daughter ensured they met the 'right' people at the 'right' events and occasions. On coming of age and completing her education an aristocratic girl would 'come out' and be presented to the monarch and to society as a marriageable debutante. A wealthy girl might bring with her a dowry worth up to £15 000 a year and a good match could open up a whole new social circle to a family. Amounts unthinkable to their servants, or to the working classes in general, were spent on dresses and dinner parties during the season. Charlotte Brontë was paid £20 a year (over twice the average wage of a labourer in London) as governess to the girls of a wealthy family, while an aristocratic lady would have a good number of dresses that would have cost at least £50 each and jewellery that might cost ten times as much.

ACTIVITY 1.12

Use a variety of sources to produce a magazine-style report on the lifestyle of the aristocracy in the mid-Victorian era. You may want to include details from literature or examples from local stately homes.

1 Reform and challenge, c1851–1886

The growing prosperity of the upper and middle classes is demonstrated by the following points:

- The number of people in service increased from around 750 000 in 1851 to 1 200 000 in 1871.
- The number of people keeping horses and carriages grew during the period, as did the use of the railways.
- Taking an annual holiday became a key sign of prosperity, and spa towns and seaside resorts grew. To middle-class people such 'excursions' were good for their health and they could now afford them.
- Expenditure by the middle and upper classes grew much more quickly than the increase in the costs of goods, suggesting that the standard of living for this group was increasing, even if this was not always their perception.

For the ruling elites and growing middle classes this was a period of prosperity – arguably at the expense of the working classes who worked long hours, six days a week, for low pay to produce the goods the wealthy consumed, or who waited on them as servants.

Some among the working classes experienced improvements in living standards: developments in technology and manufacturing gave them access to some goods that had previously been the reserve of the wealthy The invention of the sewing machine, for example, with paper patterns and department stores, made fashionable clothes more accessible. Falling food prices and cheap food imports were also benefits.

Poverty

The widely held ideas of laissez-faire and self-help suggested that it was not the government's job to intervene in the economy to support the poor, sick or elderly, or to interfere with workers' conditions or hours of work. So, terrible poverty existed in close proximity to great wealth. Canon Girdlestone, vicar of Halberton in Devon, thought 'the labourers did not live in the proper sense of the word, they merely didn't die',[17] and this applied to many in the working classes, who faced a number of challenges.

Low wages

Wages were very low for unskilled or semi-skilled workers. Rates can be a misleading guide to income, since a person might not work a regular number of hours or might have additional sources of income, and a family might have a number of wage earners, including the children. A sole wage earner would not earn enough to provide all the necessities of life for a family. Even with both adults and children bringing in a wage, many working-class families could not afford enough to eat. They lived on a very basic diet made up largely of potatoes and bread. Meat would be a rare luxury and families would often go without food, especially when work was harder to come by or if they could not sell what they produced.

The low wages for adults meant that the working classes did not all support restrictions on working hours for children or themselves, as they needed the wages. Low wages inevitably led to other health problems. Poor diet and living conditions, combined with a lack of money to pay for medical treatment, led to high infant mortality and low life expectancy. With no money to fund education, many were trapped in a life of poverty with little chance of escape.

Some of the poor found ways to supplement their income: street selling, taking in washing, home-based crafts or running an allotment. Others were forced to find means outside the law, such as poaching, petty crime or prostitution (rife in Victorian England – it is estimated that successful prostitutes could earn £2 a week, which was more than twice the average earnings of a coalminer).

ACTIVITY 1.13

What does 'poverty' mean? Create a diagram to display the key characteristics of poverty. What is the difference between 'relative' and 'real' poverty?

The low wages were, to a degree, mitigated by charity both from within the working-class communities and from charities created by the middle classes.

Dangerous working conditions

Employees also faced danger at work. Mining was notorious, as mine owners were unwilling to invest in modern machinery. At Hartley Colliery in Northumberland 204 men were entombed when the beam of the pumping engine snapped and fell down the single shaft. Between 1860 and 1897 nearly 24 000 men died in mining accidents.

Working conditions in other industries, such as match factories and brickyards, were highly damaging to workers' health. In matchmaking the phosphorous fumes ate away at the workers' (often young girls) teeth and jawbone, leading to 'phossy jaw'. Agricultural workers also suffered with poor health, with rheumatism and bronchitis brought on by working long hours in the cold and wet.

The dangerous and health-damaging working conditions contributed to the continuing poverty of the working classes. Medical treatment was expensive and days missed from work meant no pay. People were forced by poverty to continue working in terrible conditions when unfit, further damaging their health and lowering their productivity.

High rents and poor living conditions

In this period workers would spend between a quarter and half of their wages on rents, which were pushed up by various factors. In the countryside there was a very limited supply of housing and in the rapidly growing urban areas the demand for housing was high. Government attempts to improve housing and clear slums meant that newly built housing (much better quality, with sinks and outdoor toilets) was too expensive for the poorest, but slums were scarcer. Areas where accommodation was available at more reasonable rates and in better condition were the exception rather than the rule.

Living conditions for many of the working classes were terrible: massive overcrowding; poor sanitation; poorly built accommodation, including back-to-back housing, constructed by unscrupulous developers looking to make profit; outbreaks of devastating disease, such as cholera; and buildings in very poor states of repair. Legislation was brought in to improve conditions, but slums were not cleared with any haste (with perhaps the exception of Birmingham) and the terrible conditions continued.

Some of the working classes preferred the 'freedom' of the slums – despite the low-quality, damp, draughty and dilapidated housing, communal privies, cramped courtyards and unclean water supplies – to the imposed standards of middle-class morals of the new model housing developments. Few workers' houses had solid roofs, walls and floors that kept out the weather. Families were often crammed into a single room (5% of the Glasgow population also had a lodger). Gas lights were becoming more common and furniture was becoming cheaper, but the poor lived a life without luxury. Food was often of a low standard and frequently adulterated, for example graphite and black lead in tea.

> **Cross-reference: Social reform legislation**

Child labour

Child labour was common in both industry and in agriculture. There was increasing legislation to try to limit the long hours of work. Much of the work was dangerous, for example: extreme heat working in the potteries; moving huge weights in the brick yards; inhaling soot while cleaning chimneys; spending hours in the cold and wet in the field scaring birds; or working as part of an agricultural 'gang'. Child labour kept adult wages down, denied thousands of children the chance of an education and caused serious long-term damage to their health.

The Poor Law and the workhouse

There was no state support for the old, the ill or the unemployed. Some workers organised friendly societies and trade unions to support themselves, others were reliant on charity. When there was no other option the poor would be forced to seek poor relief and face being put into the workhouse.

The Poor Law raised money locally through **rates** to support the poor who could not support themselves. The Poor Law was amended in 1834 to shift responsibility from individual parishes to 600 poor law unions. Poor relief was mainly offered through a workhouse. In applying for poor relief a man had to accept that he and his family would be placed in a workhouse, buildings designed to hold those who could not support themselves. A person entering the workhouse was, in effect, giving up the power to support their own family. Husbands, wives and children were separated into different wards, all had to wear the workhouse uniform and give up any personal belongings (returned on leaving the workhouse). They would be expected to work for their keep and conditions were deliberately harsh so people would seek to avoid the workhouse.

The New Poor Law had been introduced in 1834, setting up a new framework under poor law unions for organising poor relief and workhouses. It was largely designed for the agricultural South and faced resistance in the industrial North. At times of economic depression there were insufficient places and outdoor relief (support from the rates to a person in their own home) was issued. Some education was provided for children in the workhouses and the conditions were largely down to the personality of the master of the workhouse.

> **Key terms**
>
> **Rates:** local taxes, usually calculated on the basis of the value of a person's property or dwelling.

Figure 1.15: Charles Dickens' *Oliver Twist*: Oliver asks for more.

ACTIVITY 1.14

Carry out research into a workhouse of your choice (possibly the one nearest to where you live). What were conditions like? What individual accounts can you find? What does the workhouse tell us about Victorian attitudes to poverty and the poor?

The standard of living of the British people in this period is much debated. Contemporary reports may have exaggerated or simply picked out the very worst cases. Details of the true scale of working-class suffering may have been watered down by those who profited from the workers' low pay. Historians are equally divided. Left-wing writers are likely to stress the suffering and exploitation of the workers, while right-wing writers may stress the function of the market in ensuring that standards of living improved for all.

The working classes arguably enjoyed a better standard of living and higher real wages during the period 1851–86 than during the first half of the 19th century or earlier. Conditions were, nevertheless, terrible and poverty was at a level hard to conceive of in modern Britain. Industrialisation had spread wealth more widely, but the lower working classes saw little improvement. It was in this period that Karl Marx was writing *Das Kapital* in London, theorising on the exploitation of the workers, ultimately leading to revolution and the collapse of capitalism.

Social movements and policies

Self-help

Many Victorian Britons believed that the working classes should support themselves and not be reliant on ratepayers, charity or the government. Thomas Malthus (1766–1834), among others, had predicted dire consequences if the population were allowed to grow unchecked. Support from poor relief, and cheap food, thanks to the repealing of the Corn Laws, would encourage population growth and cause greater misery for the poor. The idea of self-help is most closely associated with Samuel Smiles whose best-selling books *Self-Help* (1859) and *Thrift* (1875) set out the key principles of individualism – how people should support themselves and strive for self-improvement. Smiles promoted the idea of self-discipline, perseverance and learning from experience.

Self-help in practice was largely carried out through friendly societies. Friendly societies were organisations made up of workers who paid a subscription (normally weekly). Members of the friendly society would then receive benefit payments from the society if they were unemployed or sick. Friendly societies would also pay the

Voices from the past

Samuel Smiles (1812–1904)

Extract from *Self-Help* (1859)[18]

The spirit of self-help, as exhibited in the energetic action of individuals, has in all times been a marked feature in the English character, and furnishes the true measure of our power as a nation. Rising above the heads of the mass, there were always to be found a series of individuals distinguished beyond others, who commanded the public homage. But our progress has also been owing to multitudes of smaller and less known men … Even the humblest person, who sets before his fellows an example of industry, sobriety, and upright honesty of purpose in life, has a present as well as a future influence upon the well-being of his country; for his life and character pass unconsciously into the lives of others, and propagate good example for all time to come. Daily experience shows that it is energetic individualism which produces the most powerful effects upon the life and action of others, and really constitutes the best practical education. Schools, academies, and colleges, give but the merest beginnings of culture in comparison with it. Far more influential is the life-education daily given in our homes, in the streets, behind counters, in workshops, at the loom and the plough, in counting-houses and manufactories, and in the busy haunts of men … For all experience serves to illustrate and enforce the lesson, that a man perfects himself by work more than by reading, – that it is life rather than literature, action rather than study, and character rather than biography, which tend perpetually to renovate mankind.

Discussion points:

Summarise Smiles' ideology in your own words. How influential were his ideas on:

1. friendly societies and trade unions?
2. government policy?
3. social change?

funeral costs of members. Unlike trade unions, friendly societies did not play any role in terms of negotiating pay and conditions or any other issues in the workplace. The friendly societies were regulated to ensure that the members received the benefits they required and their financial interests were looked after. Several Acts of Parliament were passed to ensure that the friendly societies were tightly regulated by law and their members' interests protected.

The 1855 Friendly Societies Act recognised that friendly societies held large amounts of money, and this money was given greater protection. The societies had to be registered with the government and make regular reports; they also had the right to sue any official who stole from the society's funds. This act and other legislation was consolidated in the 1875 Friendly Societies Act, which meant all friendly societies had to publish annual accounts, reports and rulebooks. Societies were not required to pay stamp duties. The supporting legislation suggests that the friendly societies had government backing, as they largely fitted into the political thinking of the time and helped promote the fact that members of the working class were worthy of the vote. It is, however, notable that membership was made up of the wealthier upper echelons of the working classes and that many of the working classes did not qualify to join a friendly society, as they lacked the skills and training and could not afford weekly contributions. Self-help, therefore, did not reach all in the working classes.

Another form of self-help seen at this stage was through consumer cooperatives. In 1851 there were about 140 of these, increasing to over 1200 by 1875. The principle of these cooperatives was that they were owned by the members, who would pay a weekly subscription and then receive a 'dividend' from the profits made by the cooperative. They would also have the right to buy food from the cooperative. Goods were sold with a small profit margin and were generally cheaper than elsewhere; the food was also guaranteed to be 'pure'. Government again supported these self-help ventures and gave them the same protection as friendly societies. Cooperatives grew to buy property, develop their own manufacturing plants and produce a range of goods. They became nationally coordinated in 1863 in England and Scotland in 1868, giving them greater bulk-buying power and further reducing prices.

Trade unions

A trade union is an organisation of workers that aims to maintain or improve pay and conditions of employment of the workers. Trade unions give workers greater strength in interaction with their employers through collective bargaining. Trade unions also offer a range of other benefits to their workers, in exchange for a subscription fee.

Trade unions had faced severe challenges from both employers and government over the years and in the 1850s a new type of union started to emerge: the new model unions. The first of these was the Amalgamated Society of Engineers, Machinists, Smiths, Millwrights and Pattern-Makers (ASE). The ASE and new model unions were less radical than their predecessors and did not want to bring about socialist ideals or bring down the system of ownership or government. The new model unions had a full-time secretary and headquarters, were highly selective in who they admitted (health, age, years of experience, work skills and reputation) and charged a high subscription of 5d. a week that would insure against sickness, pay pensions and funeral expenses and give emigration grants. They sought respectability and had moderate policies on striking.

The strongest evidence of this moderate position came through the trade councils in the 1860s, most notably the London Trades Council (the Junta): the secretaries of the major new model unions would coordinate policy across the country, not to cause maximum disruption, but to minimise strikes and settle disputes through negotiation or arbitration. The ASE had 33 000 members and 308 branches by 1867. Other new model unions were also large, but there were problems:

- For many in trade unionism they were too moderate.
- They only covered the elites of the working classes, causing a greater gulf between the elite artisans and the unskilled workers.
- The new model unions put a great deal of effort into trying to protect their members' jobs and pay from encroachment by less skilled, lower-paid workers; effectively they were defending the wealthiest workers from the poorer workers, rather than taking on the employers.

Trade unionism faced some major problem in the 1860s. One major scandal concerned the Sheffield Outrages. Non-unionists in the cutlery trade were being intimidated and threatened by members of the cutlery makers' trade union. This intimidation included 'rattening', which was stealing the tools of a 'blackleg' (someone who crossed a picket line and did the work of striking trade union members). Matters came to a head when the home of a 'blackleg' was blown up, allegedly by trade union members. The Sheffield Outrages seriously damaged the image of respectability that the trade unions were trying to build.

The *Hornby v Close* case in 1867 posed further problems for trade unions. The Bradford Boilermakers had £24 stolen out of their fund box. They believed their funds were protected by the Friendly Societies Act of 1855, but it was judged that trade unions were not covered by this legislation. This meant that trade union funds were not secure – a potential threat to the funds and thus the unions themselves. Trade unions now needed support in Parliament to change laws in their favour. A Royal Commission, set up to inquire into the trade union movement, the legal position of its funds and the legality of its actions, published a largely positive report in 1867 suggesting that this was possible (but also questioning the legality of picketing, in the light of the Sheffield Outrages). In 1868 the Trades Union Congress (TUC) met for the first time with 34 delegates representing 100 000 members; by 1875 there were 153 delegates representing 1 million members. In 1871 the TUC Parliamentary Committee was set up to further union interests; its secretary Henry Broadhurst was a moderate Liberal.

Year	Legislation	Consequences
1871	The Trade Union Act	Gave trade unions the right to register under 1855 Friendly Society Act and legal acceptance.
1871	Criminal Law Amendment Act	Aimed at preventing repeats of the Sheffield Outrages. A three-month prison sentence for anyone who committed 'any form of molesting or intimidation' during a strike. The rather vague phrasing of this act meant that it threatened the act of picketing. In 1873, for example, seven wives of striking workers were convicted for having shouted insults at blacklegs. This act and its consequences led to many workers withdrawing support from the Liberals.
1875	Conspiracy and Protection of Property Act	The Conservatives, having benefited from the workers' greater support, responded with this act that allowed non-violent picketing and meant striking was a potent weapon. Though trade union influence could have been expected to grow at this point, the economic depression meant that trade unions, particularly in the agricultural sector, were not in a strong position.

Table 1.8: Legislation affecting trade unions in the 1870s

In the 1880s a new phenomenon appeared in trade unionism, the New Unions. These were unions for the unskilled workers. They were far more inclusive than the other unions, often covering whole industries rather than individual crafts, and charged a very small weekly subscription. They were far more militant than traditional unions and can be seen as a symbol of social change and political change. The working classes became more class-conscious and determined to fight for a higher standard of living. Agricultural workers too, being newly enfranchised, increasingly believed they could bring about change.

> **Cross-reference:** Trade unions and new unionism (Chapter 2)

Education

It is difficult to argue that, before 1870, Britain had what could be convincingly described as an education system. The government played very little role in education in the 1850s and 1860s, and schools were run by private individuals, companies and religious groups. There were, therefore, many different sorts of school (as shown in Table 1.9).

None of these schools was free to all. Attendance in school was not compulsory. The Newcastle Commission reported in 1861 that about 15% of the population received some sort of education, but the majority could not read a newspaper or write a letter.

	Public schools (Eton, Harrow, Westminster, St Paul's, for example)	Grammar schools	Private schools
Secondary	<ul><li>High fees, boys boarded at the school.</li><li>For the sons of aristocrats, landowners and wealthy industrialists.</li><li>Education based on the classics (Greek and Latin).</li></ul>	<ul><li>Fee paying, though some free places for poor children.</li><li>Boys needed to be local as there was no boarding.</li><li>Not as illustrious as the public schools, but similar focus on the classics.</li></ul>	<ul><li>Newer than public or grammar schools.</li><li>Fee paying.</li><li>More modern curriculum, including maths, science and modern languages</li></ul>
Elementary	**Voluntary schools** Offered elementary education (primary) including basic reading, writing and arithmetic. Charged fees though often gave support to the poorest students.		
Basic	**Dame schools**<ul><li>Types of voluntary school, run by elderly ladies, often seen as little more than childminding.</li></ul>	**Charity schools, Factory schools and Ragged schools**<ul><li>Types of voluntary school.</li><li>Basic education for poor students.</li></ul>	**Church of England schools and Nonconformist schools**<ul><li>Religious voluntary schools run by either the Church of England or the Nonconformist, British and Foreign Schools Society.</li><li>Basic reading, writing and arithmetic. Main focus on religious instruction.</li></ul>

Table 1.9: Varieties of school

The first major action taken on education by the government came in 1862 when Robert Lowe (Head of the Education Department in the Liberal Government) introduced payment by results. Schools were inspected and the pupils tested in reading, writing and arithmetic. The results would determine the grant a school received and the teachers' wages. This led to an education based on cramming and reciting of lists of facts learned by heart so they could be reproduced in the tests. There was considerable opposition to the strain this placed on teachers but the system survived until 1897. Supporters of the policy claimed that it made the education

Key terms

Denomination: A sub-group of a major religion, for example, Anglican, Baptist and Roman Catholic are all different Christian denominations.

ACTIVITY 1.15

How far did education policy in the years 1862 to 1883 fit with the ideas of self-help and laissez-faire?

What impact do you think educational policy would have had on:

- social mobility
- Britain's economic development?

system more efficient, but ultimately it would be seen as failing to help Britain to catch up with other major powers.

Forster's Education Act (1870) brought major changes in the way government intervened in education. The act was something of a compromise and was the focus of a great deal of religious argument. It allowed both Anglican and Nonconformist voluntary schools to continue. New boards were set up to organise 'board schools' for children aged 5 to 12 where no school existed. These schools received a government grant and collected a special local rate. Religious education, if the board decided to include it, should take the form of Bible studies and not follow a particular **denomination**. Despite this, different religious groups fought for control of the school boards. Religious schools received no money from the boards. Many Nonconformists were upset at having to pay rates towards 'godless' board schools or having to send their children to an Anglican school if it was the only school in the area.

School was neither compulsory nor free in 1870. In 1876 a further Education Act by Disraeli's government set up local committees to encourage school attendance and remind parents of their responsibility in ensuring the instruction of their children. In 1880, A.T. Mundella's Education Act finally made education compulsory for five to ten-year-olds. Board and voluntary schools had a fee of about 3d. per child per week (though the local school board might pay this for the poorest children). The government believed that the voluntary system would fill any gaps, keeping cost down. Voluntary schools were still the majority (there were 11 000 Anglican schools, compared with 3700 board schools, in 1883). The number of children receiving an elementary education doubled from about 1.5 million in 1870 to about 3 million in 1880. The wealthy continued to use public, grammar and private schools, and girls' education was generally given less priority: even the daughters of the wealthy received education from a governess rather than attending secondary education.

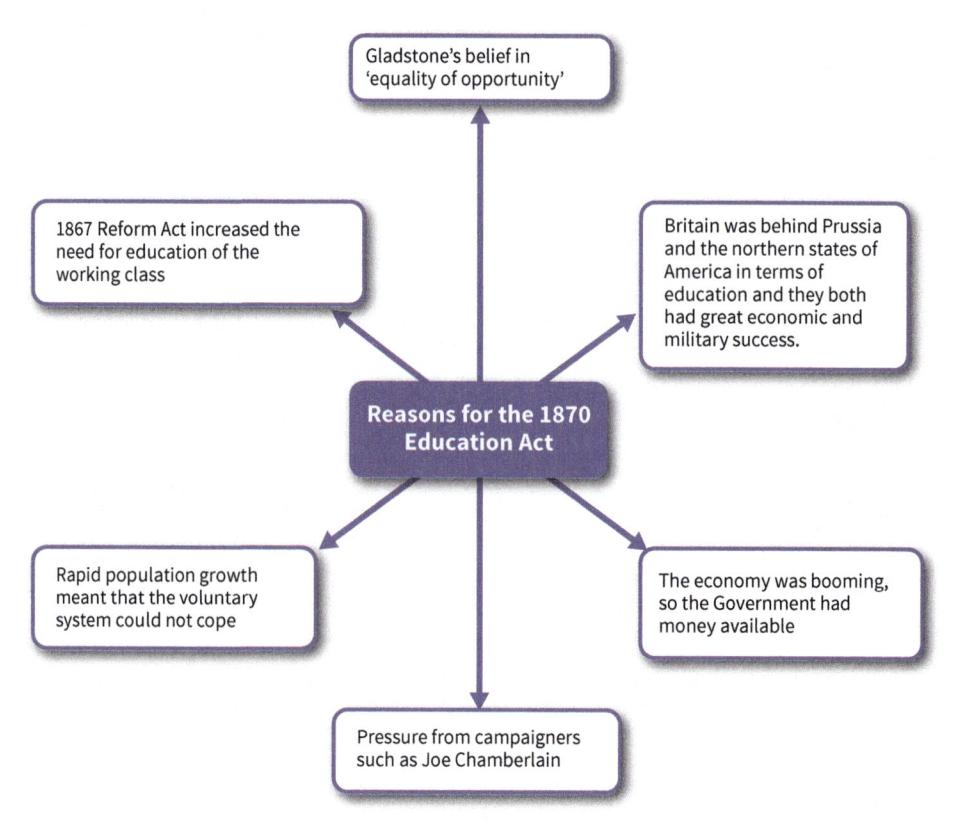

Reasons for the 1870 Education Act:
- Gladstone's belief in 'equality of opportunity'
- 1867 Reform Act increased the need for education of the working class
- Britain was behind Prussia and the northern states of America in terms of education and they both had great economic and military success.
- Rapid population growth meant that the voluntary system could not cope
- The economy was booming, so the Government had money available
- Pressure from campaigners such as Joe Chamberlain

Figure 1.16: Reasons for Forster's Education Act

Social reform legislation

A range of social reform legislation in this period aimed to protect or support different members of society, enabling organisations, such as friendly societies, cooperatives and trades unions. These were underpinned by political reforms: the extension of the franchise gave a voice to the working classes who could, therefore, expect legislation that would improve their lives. This catalyst for change was, to some degree, countered by the prevailing ideologies of laissez-faire, self-help and free trade.

Motivation for introduction of social reform legislation

The motivation for introducing reform for both the Conservatives and the Liberals is an issue of historical debate. For Disraeli's government it can be seen as fitting with his ideology of 'One Nation' Conservatism and, therefore, long-term ideological belief. On the other hand, it can be seen more as short-term pragmatism – a response to outside pressure (for example public health) and as attempts to gain electoral advantage by widening their support among the working classes. The acts can be seen as the work of individual ministers and therefore not part of a major plan or overall strategy. Notably Disraeli and the Conservatives made no mention of social reform in the 1880 election campaign, despite their seeming success in this area, suggesting they did not see it as being of central importance.

With regard to Gladstone and his Liberal government it can be viewed as being motivated by political ambition in terms of gaining electoral advantage or as acting based on moral and religious grounds. Much of the Liberal social reform, while undoubtedly having a significant impact, was still based on the idea of 'self-help'. In education, for example, a completely new system was not created, but rather a relatively cheap system was added to plug any holes that existed. Liberal social reform was, to a degree, an attack on privilege, but certainly held back from having the state take over from voluntary organisations. Liberal policies can also be seen as being driven by their Radical elements and traditions, which sought to improve the lives of the working classes.

Public health

A key area of social reform was public health. Edwin Chadwick, for example, wrote about the terrible conditions in the 1840s in the poor areas of towns and cities.[19] Increasingly, there were calls for action as research showed the connection between insanitary conditions and outbreaks of disease, such as cholera (over 50 000 people died of cholera in 1849–50). In 1854 Dr John Snow showed that the Broad Street pump was the cause of a local cholera epidemic and that cholera was carried in water.[20] Appropriate powers were urgently needed. In 1867, the extension of the franchise increased pressure on the parties to take legislative action.

The Public Health Act (1872), passed by Gladstone's Liberal Government, was an attempt to improve public health, but was largely considered a disappointment. The government did not invest enough money and failed to intervene sufficiently and Gladstone was not fully committed to the policy. Local boards of health were created to improve public health but, in keeping with Liberal economic principles, they focused on keeping spending as low as possible.

The weaknesses of the Liberal Act of 1872 were largely removed by the Conservative Public Health Act (1875). It gave clear guidance on the responsibilities of local authorities and made these duties compulsory. Local authorities had to ensure there was adequate water supply, drainage and sewage systems. Contaminated food was to be sought out and destroyed and cases of infectious disease were to be reported to the Medical Officer. They also were given responsibility for street markets, street lights and burials, as well as removal of waste. The compulsory nature of these responsibilities was a major step forward in terms of government intervention to bring about social change and improve the lives of large numbers of people.

ACTIVITY 1.16

Explain the conflict in Liberal ideology about government intervention on issues such as public health.

The Artisans' Dwelling Act (1875), also passed under Disraeli, fell short of the Public Health Act in that it made no compulsory stipulations. The act allowed local authorities to clear slum housing where there were insanitary properties and replace them with better-built modern accommodation that would improve the inhabitants' health. There was strong opposition to the act from inside and outside the Conservative party, claiming that the act was an attack on landlords' rights, so the provisions of the act were advisory, not compulsory.

The health of the working classes had been undermined over a long period by the adulteration of food. Foodstuff was often bulked out with products such as sand and sawdust and even very harmful material, such as lead. This was widespread and well known, and people had turned to the new cooperatives to ensure they were buying unadulterated food. The Sale of Food and Drugs Act (1875) set out very tight regulations on the preparation and adulteration of food.

Changes to structural privilege

Entry into the civil service had been based on being recommended by an MP or a peer, demonstrating that it was 'not what you know but who you know'. Posts were awarded on the basis of friendships, family or even ability to pay, but it was not an effective way of recruiting able people to run the increasingly complex administration of the country. Gladstone favoured efficiency and equality of opportunity and introduced the principle of recruitment based on examination. There was resistance from the aristocrats who dominated the civil service, notably in the Foreign Office, which was initially left out of reform. Although less eye-catching than other reforms, the Civil Service Reform Act (1871) did aid social mobility and can be seen as undermining aristocratic dominance.

Similarly, the army reforms under Gladstone, steered through by Edward Cardwell, widened access to senior ranks. Officer ranks in the army had been bought and sold, so that promotion was based on the ability to pay rather than merit. The House of Lords initially defeated the proposal to abolish the buying of commissions, but then passed it when Gladstone threatened to bypass them. Promotion was to be based on merit. The treatment of ordinary soldiers also improved, with an end to flogging in peacetime and a halving of the time spent in service abroad. The army became much more professional, following the example of the highly successful Prussian army. These reforms were largely successful, though the Duke of Cambridge used his position as Commander-in Chief to slow down and block further reforms.

Intervention in industries and trade

Drunkenness and the social problems associated with alcohol were widespread in mid-19th century Britain. For Gladstone, the need for greater control of public houses and of the profits made by brewers was a moral issue, though this conflicted with Liberal laissez-faire economics, and the brewing industry, of course, objected. The Licensing Act (1872), seen overwhelmingly by the working classes as too harsh, was thought too mild by those in the Liberal Party who supported temperance movements:

- Magistrates were given the power to issue or refuse licences for the opening of public houses depending on the number of pubs in the area.
- Pubs in towns had to close at midnight; in country at 11 p.m.
- Adulteration of beer was outlawed. One of the most dangerous actions had been adding salt to beer to make the drinker thirsty so they drank more.

The impact of the act was more political than social. The liquor trade moved solidly behind the Conservative Party and the Conservatives could present themselves to the working classes as the defenders of their right to drink and relax in their local pub. There were a number of disturbances when police tried to impose closing hours. Above all, the act illustrated the fact that at this time government social reform was seen by many as an attack on personal liberty.

In 1862 the Children's Employment Commission was set up to investigate the conditions children were working in. Progress had been made with the conditions in textile mills, but campaigners such as Lord Shaftesbury wanted these improvements to be brought into other industries. In 1867 the Conservative government extended the regulations restricting children's working hours in mills and other industries to all other workshops employing more than 50 people and to workshops and ordinary houses where fewer than 50 people were employed. In 1871 a moving speech by Lord Shaftsbury led to the regulations being further extended to brickfields. The Factory Act (1874), passed under Disraeli, built on the regulations of 1850. The working day was reduced from 10.5 hours to ten hours. The age at which a child could be employed increased from eight to ten. To start full-time work, you now needed to be 14 (previously 13). The Factory and Workshops Act (1878) made the 1867 regulations of houses and workshops employing fewer than 50 people more rigorous. The act brought these businesses under a government inspectorate, which proved more effective than inspection by local authorities.

A campaigner called Samuel Plimsoll pushed for regulation on the repair and loading of merchant ships. Shipping was unregulated and ships were often in poor repair and massively overloaded, as owners aimed to make as much profit as possible. This search for profit had been at the cost of seamen's lives. After a protracted battle (at one point he literally shook with rage in the Commons having become frustrated with Disraeli's failure to act) Plimsoll's demands were formalised in the Merchant Shipping Act 1876. These regulations included the drawing of a 'Plimsoll Line' on merchant ships to show their maximum load. This was not, however, truly effective until 1890 – until then the height of the line was determined by the ship-owner.

Ireland and Anglo-Irish relations

The Act of Union in 1800 united Ireland with the rest of Britain, creating the United Kingdom of Great Britain and Ireland. The Act of Union was not universally popular and there was early opposition as well as demands for **Catholic emancipation** (which came about in 1829). The fact that the Church of Ireland was established as the state church alongside the **Church of England** caused dissatisfaction among the largely Catholic Irish population. In the 1840s there was a campaign for the repeal of the Act of Union and also some support in Ireland for the creation of a federal system.

Between 1845 and 1848, the Great Famine (also known as the Irish Potato Famine) led to around one million deaths. As a result, a further million Irish people chose to emigrate to the USA, so in total the Irish population decreased by over 20%. The famine was in essence caused by 'potato blight', a disease that devastated potato crops. It spread throughout Europe, but had by far the biggest impact in Ireland, because of their greater reliance on the potato and issues surrounding land ownership and the Corn Laws. The Great Famine caused resentment against British rule in Ireland and demands for reform and **Home Rule**. Following an abortive uprising by the group 'Young Ireland' in 1848, unrest continued for a range of political, economic, cultural and religious reasons.

Land agitation and the political response

Ireland was a largely agrarian society. The majority of land was owned by Anglo-Irish landlords who were frequently absent from the country. The situation was often made more complicated by the subletting of land by tenants and the fact that the land agents and bailiffs who looked after the landlords' estates would often evict tenants without good notice or good reason. Irish agriculture was not able to advance like the rest of Britain, in part because most farmers were employed on small farms. They rarely had the money to invest in improvement, but if any improvements were made by a tenant, their rent was increased.

> **Key terms**
>
> **Catholic emancipation:** The process by which historic restrictions on Irish Catholics were lifted, giving them equal civil rights to non-Catholics. Emancipation was granted by the Roman Catholic Relief Act (1829).
>
> **Church of England:** The founding church of the now-worldwide Anglican Church; the established church in England following the reformation in the 16th century. It is headed by the British monarch and combines Protestantism with some Catholic traditions.
>
> **Home Rule:** A system by which Ireland would have its own Parliament, responsible for Irish domestic affairs, but would also remain under the ultimate control of the Westminster Parliament. Westminster would be responsible for foreign and defence policy, and Ireland would remain part of the British Empire.

Figure 1.17: Searching for potatoes in a stubble field

In these circumstances Irish farmers remained poor and the yields achieved in Ireland were much lower than those in the rest of Britain. Those farmers who were evicted would find themselves in the workhouse and in a cycle of poverty they could not escape from, which was another reason to seek a new life in the USA. It also created resentment against the landowners, who were British and Protestant, and the British government, which was doing little to relieve their suffering. The immediate focus of anger, however, were the bailiffs and land agents who were subject to violent attacks, arson and even murder in extreme cases.

Year	Number of families evicted
1849	16 686
1850	19 949
1851	13 197
1852	8591
1853	4833
1878	980
1879	1238
1880	2110
1881	3415
1891	1098

Table 1.10: Evictions in Ireland

ACTIVITY 1.17

Draw a graph to represent the information in Table 1.10.

Then explain the following trends using the information in the rest of this section:

a. the high number of evictions in the late 1840s
b. the fall in evictions during the 1850s
c. the rise in evictions from 1878 to 1881
d. the drop in evictions by 1891.

Key terms

Established church: In Britain, the Church of England is the established church. It hosts official ceremonies such as coronations, royal weddings and funerals, and so on.

Disestablishment: The process of removing a church from its status as the official, 'established' state church. In Irish terms, this meant ending the established status of the Anglican Church.

Gladstone was determined to solve the various problems in Ireland and to reduce the level of agitation. It is said that on finding he had won the 1868 election he announced, 'My mission is to pacify Ireland.' Gladstone believed that a key cause of unrest was religion. The 1869 Disestablishment of the Church of Ireland was designed to quell this unrest and fitted well with the Liberals' attitude towards the **established church**. Almost 90% of the Irish population was Catholic. This led to a situation in which most of the population (5.3 million out of 5.8 million) were paying a tithe (10% of income) to the Anglican Church – a church which they did not attend. **Disestablishment** of the church was a popular idea among Irish Catholics, especially as only a quarter of the assets of the Church was used to improve schools, hospitals and workhouses. The poor in Ireland therefore benefitted from disestablishment. The bill faced fierce opposition in Parliament, most notably from the bishops in the House of Lords. Queen Victoria strongly disapproved of it, but Disraeli knew there was no realistic chance of defeating it, given the Liberal majority in the House of Commons. Gladstone believed that the Irish Church Act would bring about an end to violence in Ireland and to Irish violence in Britain by groups such as the Fenians.

The Fenians

The Fenians were a society formed by James Stephens in the USA in the 1850s, which started operating in Britain in 1867. The Fenians were a militant nationalist group who wanted to end the Union with Britain. They were willing to use violence to try and achieve their aim of an independent Ireland. This was demonstrated in their failed uprising in Manchester in 1867. The US wing (which had developed from Irish emigrants, angry at the British reaction to the Irish Famine) was known as the Fenian Brotherhood. The Irish wing was called the Irish Republican Brotherhood (IRB).

Much to Gladstone's surprise, the violence did not subside. The two main issues causing the unrest had not been addressed: first, the desire for an independent Ireland, or at least Home Rule; and second, land ownership, rents and evictions.

Disestablishment not having succeeded, Gladstone turned his attention to the issue of land reform.

1870 Land Act

Ireland lacked the industry that existed in the rest of Britain. The linen industry had not been able to compete with more-advanced English industry following the introduction of free trade with the Act of Union in 1800. The disappearance of herring, which had provided the backbone of the fishing industry, from Irish shores was a further blow to the country's industry. This meant that the Irish people were more reliant on working the land than their mainland compatriots. The population increase before the Great Famine put increased pressure on the amount of land available and brought about the practice of sub-letting small parcels of land.

In the 1850s the Irish Tenant League fought for the protection of tenant farmers. They demanded the **three Fs**: **fixed tenure**, fair rents and **free sale** – the ability to sell their 'interest' in a piece of land to someone else (subletting). In Ulster there was a custom by which tenants were secure in keeping their tenure as long as they paid their rent on time. This made them more likely to carry out improvements to their land. Ulster tenants were also helped by the right to 'sell' their interest in the land to an incoming tenant. The Ulster Custom was responsible in part for greater prosperity in that region, compared with the rest of Ireland. As the name suggests though, this was merely a tradition and was not legally enforceable. This meant that, if circumstances demanded, landlords could simply ignore the custom.

The Land Act of 1870 started to address the tenant farmers' demands and gave legal weight to some aspects of the Ulster Custom:

- Tenants were not to be evicted while up to date with their rent. They were given the right to 'free sale' of their holding, if giving up their tenancy to a new tenant deemed acceptable by the landlord. These two aspects of the Ulster Custom were given the force of law where the custom existed.
- The principle of rent control was introduced.
- Evicted tenants had to be paid compensation by the landlords for any improvements they had made. A scale of payments was set out by the act. The aim of this element of the act was to prevent unjustified eviction in pursuit of profit. The amount a landlord would have to pay was deliberately set at a high rate to try to protect the tenants.
- An element of the act (added by the Radical minister John Bright) allowed tenants willing to buy their holding from their landlord to borrow two-thirds of the purchase price from the state.

Gladstone hoped that the act would calm the situation in Ireland and encourage Irish landowners to develop a more positive relationship with their tenants. He was disturbed at the number of absentee landowners, not rooted in the communities to whom they let property. He saw the act as a moderate one, translating customs into law and encouraging reasonable behaviour by landlords. It was seen by his opponents as anti-property and anti-landlord. However, the bill passed through the Houses of Parliament with little opposition.

MPs hoped that an improvement in Irish living conditions would end opposition to British rule. In reality, the act did not achieve its aims. It encountered numerous problems and did not fully address some of the major concerns of the Irish people. First, it was very hard to identify where the Ulster Custom had been in place. Also, tenants could not afford to buy land: they did not have one-third of the purchase price. Meanwhile, landlords had no real reason to sell. The eviction clauses were largely ineffective, as the rent control was not effectively imposed. (The concept of 'excessive rent' was never properly defined.) Finally, tenants on long leases were not covered by the provisions of the act.

> ### Voices from the past
>
> The following extract is taken from the Fenian Oath, 1859
>
> I … in the presence of Almighty God, do solemnly swear allegiance to the Irish Republic, now virtually established, and that I will do my utmost, at every risk, while life lasts, to defend its independence and integrity.[21]
>
> #### Discussion point:
>
> What conclusions can you draw from the oath about:
>
> 1. the aims, and
> 2. the tactics of the Fenians?

> ### Key terms
>
> **Three Fs:** This was the stated aim of the Land League: fair rents, fixity of tenure, and free sale.
>
> **Fixed tenure:** The principle which ensured that tenants had a guaranteed right to remain on their land for a fixed period of time, without threat of eviction.
>
> **Free sale:** The principle which allowed a tenant to sell their 'interest' in a piece of land to the next tenant.

> **Cross-reference:** The Second Home Rule Bill (Chapter 2)

As a result, violence and unrest continued. Gladstone returned to repression, introducing the Coercion Act of 1871, which gave police extra power over arrests and imprisonment. The need for this act can be directly traced to the failures of the 1870 Land Act. A more effective Land Act may well have halted unrest, and the demands for ending British rule may have died down.

Taking it further

Types of nationalism

In general terms, Irish nationalism refers to a desire on behalf of the Irish people to be free from British (and especially) English influence. Nationalist feeling became increasingly prominent after the Act of Union of 1800. However, nationalism took a variety of forms. Militant nationalism refers to the use of violent, usually illegal, methods with the aim of achieving an independent Ireland, free from British government control. This was the approach of the Fenians, of Young Ireland and later of the Irish Republican Army (IRA). Constitutional nationalism was the method favoured by Daniel O'Connell, who campaigned successfully for Catholic civil rights during the 1820s. This involved the use of democratic, peaceful, political action in order to achieve the aim of an independent Ireland. Isaac Butt, Charles Stewart Parnell and, later, John Redmond followed a similar path to O'Connell. Finally, cultural nationalism refers to the promotion of Irish art, literature, music and sport, as well as the Catholic faith and the Gaelic language. Cultural nationalists also reject attempts to impose 'British' culture, the English language and the Anglican faith on Ireland.

Two interesting issues arise when we begin to analyse nationalism in these terms:

- How do we define a group like Young Ireland, who promoted Irish poetry and the Gaelic language, but also attempted a violent rebellion in 1848?
- Is it too simplistic to talk of Parnell as a constitutional nationalist? He was a leading figure in the political system and rejected violence personally, but was not afraid to use the tactic of brinkmanship (implying the threat of violence in order to force concessions) in his work both with the Irish Parliamentary Party (IPP) and the Land League. This was also true of Daniel O'Connell in an earlier generation. There were similar blurred lines in the relationship between the political party Sinn Fein and the militant nationalist group, the IRA.

1. Research Daniel O'Connell's role in Irish nationalism, particularly the campaigns for emancipation and repeal. How would you define his brand of nationalism?
2. Draw a table listing advantages and disadvantages of each form of nationalism.

The Land War

The recovery of Irish agriculture that had taken place since the end of the Great Famine ended abruptly in the early 1870s. There was a series of poor harvests between 1877 and 1879, making the situation worse. Famine returned, with a further failure of the potato crop. As in England, Irish agriculture suffered in the face of imported US grain, which was far cheaper than home-produced grain. Farmers' income fell dramatically, leading to them calling for reductions in rents. Some reduction did take place, but ultimately the outcome was mass evictions; it is estimated that around 6000 people lost their homes. Demands for change were widespread and numerous local organisations were established. The next stage was to be a national organisation that would lead rural Ireland into the so-called 'Land War'.

The Irish National Land League was formed by Michael Davitt in 1879. Davitt was a socialist who believed in the radical redistribution of land. He was joined by Parnell, who became President of the League, and John Devoy, a leading Fenian. The combination of Davitt's radical socialism, Parnell's constitutional nationalism and Devoy's militant approach made the League a powerful organisation, supported by a broad range of the population. The Land League provided practical help for evicted tenants, as well as carrying out a campaign of violence against selected landlords. Supported by wealthy US donors, the League encouraged tenants to refuse to work for landlords who continued to charge excessive rents. Its ultimate aim was to ensure that ordinary Irish farmers became owners of their land. It also set out to end the widespread custom of 'rack renting', whereby landlords would increase rents every year, as well as opposing evictions and oppression by landowners. Campaigning for the three Fs was a central part of the League's mission.

The Home Rule movement

While the Land League was using direct action to challenge the power of Irish landlords, significant developments were also taking place among constitutional nationalists. In 1870, Isaac Butt founded the Home Rule Association, which by 1873 had become a political party (known as the Home Rule League, which aimed to win home rule for the Irish as opposed to complete independence). The League received support from a variety of sources, including the Catholic Church and the Fenians, and in the 1874 general election, around 60 Irish MPs claimed to be in favour of Home Rule.

However, Butt was unable to convince Disraeli's government that the issue should be a priority. The Conservatives had a large majority in the House of Commons, so those Liberals who did support Home Rule struggled to make an impact. Frustrated by Butt's moderate approach, a group of Irish MPs regularly employed **obstructionist tactics** in parliamentary debates. This did little to persuade British politicians of the merits of the nationalist cause. When the Fenians withdrew support from the Home Rule League in 1876, it was clear that the movement needed new leadership. This was provided by Parnell, who had been elected in 1875 as MP for County Meath. His approach was more direct and confrontational than Butt's, enabling the Home Rule movement to make a greater impact from 1877 onwards.

The 1881 Land Act
The 1880 general election was an encouraging one for Parnell. The Home Rule League, now renamed the Irish Parliamentary Party (IPP), won 61 seats. In addition, Gladstone (who was more supportive of Home Rule than Disraeli) returned as prime minister. However, Gladstone's initial actions were repressive. He introduced the 1880 Coercion Act in response to the violence of the Land League, which had recently assassinated the leading landowner Lord Mountmorres. The act gave the authorities greater power of arrest in Ireland. Despite Parnell's efforts, the act was passed by the Commons. As a result, Davitt was imprisoned, and 36 IPP MPs were expelled from Parliament. However, this only served to increase support both for the Land League and the IPP.

Gladstone, a clever politician, soon understood the situation and began to construct a new bill that would improve living conditions for the Irish population. While he undoubtedly believed in the morality of this cause, he was also determined to create a situation in which the Land League had no further need to exist. Consequently, the Second Land Act was passed in 1881. This gave legal status to the three Fs and included the creation of land courts to ensure fair rents. This resulted in a 20% reduction in rent over the next few years.

Voices from the past

Charles Stewart Parnell (1846–91)

Parnell was one of the most important figures in the long history of Irish nationalism. Born in 1846 to a family of landowning Protestants, Parnell was educated at Cambridge University. He played a leading role in the Irish Land League's Land War of 1879–81; his vision was to create a relatively conservative society where the vast majority of people owned their land. His most important role was in the Irish Nationalist Party, for whom he was elected as an MP in 1875 and which he led from 1877. In this role, Parnell worked closely with successive British prime ministers, particularly Gladstone, and ensured that the Home Rule question was at the centre of British politics. His final years were a sad end to a monumental career – the failure of the 1886 Home Rule Bill was followed by personal scandal and political downfall when his affair with Kitty O'Shea was revealed.

Key terms

Obstructionist tactics: Blocking the passage of a bill through the Commons by talking for so long in a debate that the bill runs out of parliamentary time.

The Land Act put Parnell in a difficult position. He knew that vocal support for it would anger more radical nationalists at home, who believed that the act did not go far enough. On the other hand, he was also aware that excessive criticism of the new law would reduce his bargaining power with the British government, including Liberal MPs who supported Home Rule. Parnell chose to support parts of the act, but to criticise others, notably the land courts, with which he refused to cooperate. This led to his arrest and imprisonment in Kilmainham Jail; the British believed that he was attempting to incite trouble by wrecking the act. Once again, it soon became clear that repressive British tactics were having unintended consequences. Parnell's popularity in Ireland soared, and Gladstone recognised the need to release him.

Parnell's release (after six months) marked the beginning of a more cooperative era between the IPP and the government. The Land Act had reduced the power of the Land League, and as a result, Gladstone felt able to offer concessions. Enshrined in the Kilmainham Treaty of 1882, these concessions included amendments to the Land Act, such as providing greater support for tenants already in arrears, and the relaxation of the Coercion Act. In return, Parnell began to cooperate with the land courts, as well as reiterating his commitment to peaceful methods.

Parnell's growing influence

Parnell's hand was strengthened by an outbreak of violence in May 1882. The assassination of Lord Cavendish, the Chief Secretary for Ireland, and his under-secretary, T.H. Burke, by a militant group named the Invincibles, shocked both the British and the Irish public. While these killings, known as the Phoenix Park murders, led to further tough measures, including the Prevention of Crimes Act 1882, suspending trial by jury, they also provided Parnell with an opportunity. He distanced himself from such a militant approach, breaking with Davitt and setting up a new party, the Irish National League (INL), committed primarily to the cause of Home Rule. Parnell imposed strict discipline on the party, earning the nickname 'The Dictator'. (He relished this nickname, even naming his horse 'Dictator'!) He introduced 'the pledge', which forced INL MPs to vote with the party line on any issue where a majority of members had given their backing.

The INL had several early advantages. First, Parnell successfully gained the support of the Catholic Church, promising to protect its control of education at both school and university level. Second, the 1884 Representation of the People Act had increased the Irish electorate from 224 000 to 738 000. This meant that many landless labourers and tenant farmers, natural supporters of the INL, were able to vote for the first time. Finally, as another election loomed in 1885, both the Liberal and Conservative parties actively sought Parnell's support, knowing that the INL could soon hold the balance of power in the Commons and reassured by a couple of relatively peaceful years in Ireland.

Joseph Chamberlain attempted to make an agreement with Parnell whereby the INL would support the Liberals in return for reform of Irish local government. Meanwhile, Parnell also met Conservative peer Lord Carnarvon and, as a result, Parnell encouraged Irish people living in England to vote for the Conservative Party. The fact that the Conservatives dominated the House of Lords made it important for Parnell to woo them, to provide even a vague hope of a future Home Rule bill becoming law.

> **Cross-references:** The extension of the franchise; The First Home Rule Bill (Chapter 2)

To Parnell's delight, the 1885 general election results offered the best possible opportunity for Home Rule. Not only was a Liberal Government elected, but, with 86 seats, the INL held the balance of power. The remaining years of the decade would see Home Rule at the forefront of British political debate.

1 Reform and challenge, c1851–1886

Speak like a historian

D.G. Boyce, *The Irish Question and British Politics 1868–1986*

Gladstone's conversion to the policy of Irish self-government has occasioned much debate … the more sceptical have attributed it to Gladstone's bid to reassert his leadership over the Liberal Party … his conviction that he and he alone could settle Ireland suggests a strong personal motive … but he found it imperative to equate his own political future with the principle of great and good acts of government.[22]

Discussion points:

1. Use your work from other parts of this chapter to suggest why Gladstone needed to 'reassert his leadership'.
2. In your own words, summarise Boyce's arguments about why Gladstone supported Home Rule.
3. Using the information in the rest of this section, can you think of other reasons, not mentioned by Boyce, why Gladstone supported Home Rule?

Further reading

Richard Aldous, *The Lion and the Unicorn, Gladstone vs Disraeli* (New York, W.W. Norton, 2007) gives a really insightful and detailed examination of the two dominant statesmen of this period. E.P. Thompson's *The Making of the English Working Class* (London, Penguin, 2013) and John Benson's *The Working Class in Britain 1850–1939* (London, I.B. Tauris, 2003) give really useful examinations of the working classes during this period, offering a chance to examine history of the ordinary people rather than the more-traditional history of great men and key events.

Early Victorian Society: The Two Nations by Betty R. Easson and J.E. McIntyre (Edinburgh, Blackie, 1979), is good piece of social history, examining the changes in British society for both the wealthy and the poor. It offers an alternative way of examining history in Britain and the opportunity to understand both the differences and the similarities between Victorian society and today's society. Christine Kinealy's *A New History of Ireland* (Stroud, The History Press, 2008) offers an excellent overview of this period; its perspective is fairly sympathetic to the Irish and somewhat critical of the British, but not disproportionately so.

Practice essay questions

1. 'Electoral reform benefited the Liberals more than the Conservatives, in the years 1867 to 1885.' Explain why you agree or disagree with this view.
2. 'Britain suffered a depression in the years 1873 to 1886.' Explain why you agree or disagree with this view.
3. With reference to these extracts and your understanding of the historical context, which of these two extracts provides the more convincing interpretation of the position of the aristocracy in the 1880s?

Extract A

N. Gash, *Aristocracy and People: Britain 1815–1865*. Hodder and Stoughton, 1991 [1979]

[The aristocracy] had shown themselves on most occasions intelligent and flexible; they had made political concessions and yielded privileges when public opinion clearly demanded such surrenders … They had played a useful and sometimes prominent role in the social, religious, educational and other philanthropic movements of the period and had been rewarded by the moral approval of the public in addition to their existing social and political advantages. What was remarkable was not that British society was slowly slipping beyond the elites' control, but that by a process of astute adaptation they had maintained that control so long and with so little resentment on the part of the rest of the community.[23]

Extract B

D. Cannadine, *The Decline and Fall of the British Aristocracy*. Yale University Press, London, 1990

The British Aristocracy were the prisoners of time. Whether they liked it or not, whether they knew it or not, and whether they fully understood it or not, it is clear that from 1880 onwards, their circumstances and consciousness changed and weakened. The rate of change varied: the very rich survived better and longer than the less well off aristocrats, the erosion of status and power was different in every case. By investigating the decline and fall of the British aristocracy it is possible to see the process almost at full stretch. The story of the unmaking of the British upper classes most appropriately begins in the 1880s.[24]

> **Chapter summary**
>
> By the end of this chapter you should have an overview of how British politics, economy and society developed from 1851 to 1886. You should understand:
>
> - the reasons for, and extent of, the changes to the workings of democracy in Britain in the years 1851 to 1886
> - the extent, and significance, of developments in Liberalism and Conservatism under Disraeli and Gladstone, and the basis of their support
> - the reasons for, and consequences of, the economic boom and the onset of the depression that followed
> - the nature of British society with its class divisions, the changes that took place and the debates over prosperity and poverty
> - the impact of social movements and policies; changes and continuities in educational and social legislation as well as the development of trade unions
> - the importance of the land question in the relationship between Britain and Ireland, and the vital role played by Parnell in the campaign for Home Rule.

Endnotes

[1] E. Evans, *The Complete A–Z 19th and 20th Century British History Handbook*. London, Hodder & Stoughton, 1998.
[2] W. Bagehot, *The English Constitution*. London, Chapman and Hall, 1867, pp. 327–29.
[3] N. Gash, *Aristocracy and People: Britain 1815–1865*. London, Hodder & Stoughton, 1991 [1979], pp. 349–50.
[4] D. Cannadine, *The Decline and Fall of the British Democracy*. Yale University Press, London, 1990.
[5] M. Winstanley, *Gladstone and the Liberal Party*. London, Routledge, 1990, p. 28.
[6] Quoted in N. Lowe, *Mastering Modern British History*. London, Palgrave Macmillan, 2009, p. 228.
[7] E.J. Hobsbawm and C. Wrigley, *Industry and Empire: From 1750 to the Present Day. Volume 3*, The Penguin History of Britain. London, Penguin, 1968, p. 173.
[8] Ibid, p. 139.
[9] Ibid.
[10] D. Taylor, *Mastering Economic and Social History*. London, Palgrave Macmillan, 1988.
[11] E. Hobsbawm, *The Age of Capital, 1848–1875*. London, Weidenfeld & Nicolson, 1975.
[12] Taylor, *Mastering Economic and Social History*.
[13] Ibid.
[14] N. Tonge, *Industrialisation and Society 1700–1914*. London, Thomas Nelson and Sons, 1993, pp. 337–40.
[15] Ibid.
[16] P. Mathias, *The First Industrial Nation: An Economic History of Britain, 2nd edition*. London, Methuen and Co. 1969, p. 279.
[17] 'Peasant Life in the West of England' (1872), available at https://archive.org/stream/peasantlifeinwes00heatuoft/peasantlifeinwes00heatuoft_djvu.txt.
[18] S. Smiles, *Self-Help*. London, John Murray, 1866, Chapter 1.
[19] E. Chadwick, *The Sanitary Condition of the Labouring Population (1842)*, Edinburgh, Edinburgh University Press, 1965 and *The Present and General Condition of Sanitary Science, 1889*. London, Meldrum 1889. Available at https://en.wikisource.org/wiki/The_present_and_general_condition_of_sanitary_science.
[20] Dr J. Snow, *On the Mode of Communication of Cholera, 2nd edition*. London, John Churchill, 1855.
[21] From the Fenian Oath, 1859, quoted in A. O'Day and J. Stevenson (eds), *Irish Historical Documents since 1800*. Dublin, Gill & Macmillan, 1992, p. 74.
[22] D.G. Boyce, *The Irish Question and British Politics, 1868–1986*. London, Palgrave Macmillan, 1988.
[23] Gash, *Aristocracy and People: Britain 1815–1865*, pp. 349–50.
[24] Cannadine, *The Decline and Fall of the British Aristocracy*, p. 25.

2 Challenges to the status quo, c1886–1914

In this chapter we will examine significant ideological shifts in politics; problems in industry and trade; social change, including the campaign for female suffrage and Liberal attempts at reform; and debates over Irish Home Rule. We will look into:

- political developments 1886–1905: reasons for Conservative dominance to 1905; problems in the Liberal Party; socialism and Fabianism; the emergence of the Labour Party

- politics and the constitution 1906–14: the ideology of New Liberalism; political crises and constitutional change; the development of the Labour Party

- economic developments: the Great Depression and its aftermath; problems of British industry and agriculture; staples, new industries and foreign competition; invisible exports; debates over protectionism, tariff reform and free trade

- social change: trade unions and new unionism; syndicalism; the issue of female emancipation; the growth of the urban population; the expansion of service industries; standards of living

- social policies: government legislation and local initiatives 1886–1905; taxation and welfare reform by 1914

- the condition of Ireland and Anglo-Irish relations: the Home Rule Bills; developments and opposition.

Political developments 1886–1905

Between 1886 and 1905 political changes began that would lead to a different political landscape once democracy became established in Britain. This section traces strongly interconnected themes: Conservative dominance was in part due to the problems of the Liberal Party; the Liberal Party faced strong competition in urban seats from the newly emerging Labour Party; the Labour Party emerged in part because the Liberal Party failed to offer the working classes an attractive alternative to the Conservative Party; the Labour Party and Liberals split the anti-Conservative vote in constituencies, contributing to Conservative dominance.

Election	Conservatives/Unionists	Liberals	Irish Parliamentary (Nationalists)	Labour or Lib-Lab
1885	247	319	86	1
1886	394 (317 Conservatives, 77 Liberal Unionists)	191	85	0
1892	314 (268 Conservatives, 46 Liberal Unionists)	273 (1 independent)	81	3
1895	411 (340 Conservative, 71 Liberal Unionists)	177	82	0
1900	402 (335 Conservative, 67 Liberal Unionists)	183	83	2
1906	156	398	82	29

Table 2.1: British election results 1886–1906

Reasons for Conservative dominance to 1905

Disraeli died in 1881, but his influence continued into the period 1886–1905. Arguably, he was responsible, alongside John Gorst, for making the party a modern organisation. He was important in establishing 'One Nation' Conservatism and the Primrose League, formed in his memory, had over a million members by 1905. The foundations laid by Disraeli did, therefore, arguably aid future Conservative dominance, though it must be remembered that he lost the 1880 election.

The leadership of the Conservative Party after Disraeli's death was split between Lord Salisbury in the Lords and Sir Stafford Northcote in the Commons. Northcote's leadership came under strong criticism (especially from a backbench group called the Fourth Party) and by 1885 Salisbury was in undisputed control.

> **Cross-reference:** The extension of the franchise (Chapter 1)

Villa Toryism saw the Conservatives gain the seats of middle-class suburbs in the big cities. The business and commercial classes started to turn away from the Liberals, who were focusing on radical causes. Salisbury's skill in negotiating the 1885 Redistribution Act therefore reaped great rewards as these middle-class constituencies were created.

Captain Middleton was appointed as the party's principal party agent in 1884 and he effectively coordinated the Conservative Party organisation, creating a highly successful electioneering machine. With the growth of the Primrose League and strength of Conservative working men's clubs which, unlike the Nonconformist-

ACTIVITY 2.1

Use the details in this chapter to create diagrams to show:

1. how the different themes of the chapter are connected, giving precise examples
2. continuity and change in British politics, comparing the years 1886–1905 with the years 1867–85.

dominated Liberal clubs, served beer, the Conservatives were able to build significant amount of working-class support. The Conservative support for imperialism also helped secure some working-class support.

Working-class Toryism was often fed by support among parts of the working classes for Conservative pro-empire policy. Conservative support was particularly strong in military towns such as Colchester, and naval ports such as Portsmouth. The same was true in areas where jobs were dependent on work in the armaments industry, such as Woolwich. There was also working-class support for the Conservatives based on anti-Catholic feeling in Northern Ireland, Lancashire and Central Scotland. The Conservatives were seen as the bastions of the Church of England, gaining them support from working classes in areas where there were significant and unpopular Catholic minorities.

The contrasting policies on licensing laws and attitudes to drink also increased working-class support – the 'drinking masses' disliked the Liberal moves to restrict drinking and Conservative Working Men's Clubs proved popular. In the countryside, deference continued to play a role, where those in service, in particular, tended to vote Conservative in line with their employers.

Act	Impact
Labourers' Allotment Act (1887)	Gave local authorities the power to buy land for allotments to enable the working classes to 'elevate' themselves. Not compulsory and ignored by most local authorities.
The Mines Regulation Act (1887)	Extended the level of legal protection for miners at work.
Local Government Act (1888)	Set up 62 county councils, borough councils set up in large towns and cities, London County Council established, unmarried women could vote in county council elections.
The Tithe Act (1890)	Tithes (a 10% tax on income or produce paid to the Anglican Church) to be paid by landowners, not tenants.
The Housing of the Working Class Act (1890)	Local authorities could identify uninhabitable dwellings and replace them with council-built houses.
Fee Grant Act (1891)	Abolished fees for elementary education.
The Factory Act (1891)	Minimum age for children employed in factories raised to 11, women's working day limited to 12 hours (with one and a half hours for meals)
Education Acts 1897 and 1902	School funding was increased and then LEAs created, with significant growth of secondary education through grammar schools.
Workmen's Compensation Act (1897)	Employers were required to pay compensation to workers who suffered illness or injury due to their work.

Table 2.2: Conservative policies of the late 1880s

ACTIVITY 2.2

For each of the acts in Table 2.2 evaluate how far it would have contributed to Conservative dominance.

Working-class support for the Tories was also, in part, due to the popularity of their foreign and imperial policy. This was partly due to patriotic feeling and because the working classes associated strong imperial policy with improvements in their economic position. The Conservative emphasis on empire and patriotism consolidated middle-class support as well as attracting working-class votes.

The skill and personality of Lord Salisbury was also important in the success of the Conservative party. He overcame competition from Sir Stafford Northcote and Lord Randolph Churchill (who resigned in 1886) and proved to be a shrewd party manager. A key success of the Conservatives during this period was attracting the support of the Liberal Unionists, who separated from the Liberal Party over Home Rule. Adding this group significantly affected parliamentary arithmetic (though only truly tipping the balance in 1886; see Table 2.1) but also brought highly able men, such as Joseph Chamberlain, into the Unionist Party. It can be argued that the combining of the Liberal Unionists with the Conservatives broadened the appeal of the Conservatives to the electorate more significantly than the simple addition of Liberal Unionist MPs on the government benches.

Salisbury was a strong believer in government not intervening too much in social or economic fields, but also tried to create circumstances in which the working classes could improve their own position.

Thematic link: Ideologies of laissez-faire and self-help

Cross-reference: Government legislation and local initiatives 1886–1905

Problems in the Liberal Party

There were numerous issues and differences in the Liberal Party in 1885:

- divisions over Home Rule in Ireland
- split between imperialists and anti-imperialists
- Radicals challenging the Liberal laissez-faire attitude to social reform
- competition between 'Grand Old Man' Gladstone and the forceful radical Chamberlain.

Cross-reference: The condition of Ireland and Anglo-Irish relations

The most destructive of these divisions was over Home Rule. On this issue Gladstone had become so convinced that it was the only possible answer to the Irish question that he had become blind to the damage it was doing to his party. Table 2.1 shows the significant impact which the resultant split had on the number of Liberal MPs. The Liberal Party was not only hit by the loss of Liberal Unionist MPs to the Conservative ranks (particularly significant in 1892), but also by the impression given to the electorate of a weak and divided party that was focused on an issue which was not of the utmost significance to many voters.

In 1885 the Liberal Government was brought down by a vote on increasing duty on beer and spirits, as Parnell and the 60 Irish Nationalists voted with the Conservative Party. This occurred following Conservative promises that they would drop the Coercion Acts and give support to tenant farmers. After the 1886 election that followed, the balance of power was on a knife edge. It was at this point that divisions over Home Rule fully emerged. Gladstone had, by now, privately converted to the idea of Home Rule for Ireland. This news emerged when his son, Herbert, leaked a private conversation they had had on the subject. The leak happened before Gladstone had the opportunity to talk to his party colleagues about this change of heart.

The leading lights of the Liberal Party, including Lord Hartington and Joseph Chamberlain, were outraged at having not been consulted on this major change in policy. Although the Liberals, along with the Irish Nationalists, managed to swiftly bring down the Conservative administration, the First Home Rule Bill that followed exposed big divisions in the Liberal Party. Hartington and other Whigs opposed the bill, as did Chamberlain and some of the Radicals. The split was disastrous as Chamberlain resigned to lead a breakaway group known as the Liberal Unionists. The Liberals, with Irish Nationalist support, managed to make it into power again, narrowly, in 1892. Gladstone again introduced a Home Rule Bill; again it was defeated, and in 1894 Gladstone resigned.

The Liberal Party had been stripped of many of its most-able men by the arguments over Home Rule and in 1895 suffered a terrible election defeat. The Liberal Unionists won 70 seats and the appointment of Chamberlain into the Conservative cabinet secured the merging of the two parties, ensuring that the Liberal split over Ireland was permanent. The loss of significant numbers of MPs and of front-benchers, such as Chamberlain, together with a loss of focus on other issues that were significant to the British people meant that the split over Ireland had dire significance for the Liberal Party at this time.

The issue of empire also became a divisive one for the Liberals, with Gladstone largely disapproving of the principal of empire, while others such as Chamberlain were enthusiastic supporters. Gladstone's policies met with varying degrees of success. Gladstone's ordering of withdrawal from Afghanistan and acceptance of independence for Transvaal, for many, showed weakness. The latter was particularly unpopular as it seemed that the Liberal Government was giving in to force. Imperialists like Chamberlain felt more in line with the Conservatives on the issue of empire.

This issue had not always been divisive. However, although Gladstone's action was seen as weak by other Liberals, sometimes the opposite was true and his actions were viewed as being too aggressive. The occupation of Egypt in 1882 on Gladstone's orders, for example, led to the resignation of renowned Radical John Bright who disagreed with the policy. This demonstrates that, while the Conservatives always found the issue of empire to be a unifying matter in the later part of the 19th century, with their championing of the 'Age of Imperialism', for the Liberals, imperialism was a difficult and divisive issue. The concept of imposing Britain's will on the people of foreign nations to suit Britain's interests above those of the local population did not fit well with Liberal ideology.

Taking it further

Investigate the development of radical and liberal ideology in the years 1885–1905. In particular, look at elements of continuity and change from earlier periods and areas of disagreement.

The Liberal Party had long been a broad coalition of differing views. Gladstone through, at times, sheer force of personality, held the party together, but the divisions within the party became increasingly significant. The party contained many traditional Liberals who believed in laissez-faire economics and minimal government intervention in social issues. They feared that too much government help would strip the working classes of the motivation and requirement for self-help and improvement. Increasingly, however, an alternative ideology was emerging from the Radical elements of the Liberal party who wanted to go beyond Liberal social policy. This group was headed by 'Radical Joe' Chamberlain who advocated a wide range of social reform that was proposed in the 1886 Unauthorised Programme, including:

- extension of power of local government to buy land at a fair price and let them as allotments, smallholdings (3 acres and a cow for agricultural workers) and high quality working-class homes
- creation of elected authorities in the counties
- free elementary education funded by higher taxes or Church disestablishment
- a graduated taxation system which would place a greater burden on the wealthy and less of a burden on the poor.

There was serious division between Radicals such as Chamberlain and the traditional Whigs such as Lord Hartington who were horrified at the ideas of disestablishment of the Church and abandoning traditional economic policy.

The Liberal Party split over the issue of Home Rule, with the new Liberal Unionist group being created. This group was itself far from united, containing right-wing Whigs, including Hartington, and Radicals, including Chamberlain, who strongly disagreed on social policy. The Liberal defeat in 1886 was a clear one, but in 1892 Gladstone and the Liberals returned to power with the backing of the Irish Nationalists.

Voices from the past

Joseph Chamberlain (1836–1914)

Joseph Chamberlain, a unique figure in British political history, can claim to have split two major parties (the Liberals over Ireland and empire, then the Conservatives over tariff reform). Having been a radical mayor in Birmingham, he was a brilliant but controversial MP in the Liberal Party until the mid-1880s. He resigned over Home Rule for Ireland and led a splinter group out of the Liberal Party. This independent group, the Liberal Unionists, supported the Conservatives over Ireland and some other issues. In 1895 Chamberlain entered the combined Conservative/Liberal Unionist cabinet (the alliance of these two parties was now referred to as the 'Unionists') as Colonial Secretary. He played a key role in the Unionist election victory in 1900 in what was known as the 'khaki' election, during which his clashes with Liberals over the Boer War became increasingly bitter. After the victory in the Boer War, Chamberlain turned his energy to the issue of tariff reform that would ultimately split the Conservative Party and cost them the 1906 election.

Chamberlain strove for a new politics based on mass support and greater government intervention.

At last the majority of the nation will be represented by a majority of the House of Commons, and ideas and wants and claims which have been hitherto ignored in legislation will find a voice in Parliament, and will compel the attention of statesmen. Radicalism, which has been the creed of the most numerous section of the Liberal party outside the House of Commons, will henceforth be a powerful factor inside the walls of the popular Chamber.

The stage of agitation has passed, and the time for action has come.

There is need, therefore, for the attempt which is made in the following pages to compile a definite and practical Programme for the Radical Party. The new necessities of the time can only be fully met by constructive legislation. New conceptions of public duty, new developments of social enterprise, new estimates of the natural obligations of the members of the community to one another, have come into view, and demand consideration.[1]

Discussion points:

1. How did the ideology of Joseph Chamberlain differ from traditional Liberalism?
2. What do you think he means by 'new estimates of the natural obligations of the members of the community to one another'?

A/AS Level History for AQA: Challenge and Transformation: Britain, c1851–1964

> **Taking it further**
>
> Using the 'Voices from the past' text and your own research into the career of Joseph Chamberlain (see the Further reading section at the end of this chapter), assess his contribution to the decline of the Liberal Party between 1885 and 1905.

Socialism and Fabianism

ACTIVITY 2.3

1. Draw your own version of the diagram in Figure 2.1.
2. Write an explanation for each connecting arrow.
3. Write an explanation for the different colours.

Figure 2.1: The development of the labour movement

Short timeline of key events in the labour movement

1881	Formation of the SDF
1884	Formation of the Fabian Society
1884	Extension of the franchise to include working classes in counties
1885	Redistribution Act creates some constituencies with working-class majorities.
1892	Keir Hardie becomes the first independent working-class MP
1893	Formation of the Independent Labour Party
1900	Formation of Labour Representative Committee
1901	Taff Vale decision
1903	Lib-Lab Pact

Figure 2.2: Karl Marx, the father of Marxism, who saw Britain as the most likely place for a socialist revolution

> **Thematic link:** The importance of political ideas and ideologies

Socialist ideas, such as those promoted by Karl Marx and Friedrich Engels, were slow to take hold in Britain. Following the 1870 Education Act, which ensured that more of the working class could read, ideas started to spread. Some key works included Marx's *Communist Manifesto* (with Engels, translated in 1850) and *Das Kapital* (translated in 1887); *Progress and Poverty* (1881) by Henry George, a US economist, and Robert Blatchford's journal *The Clarion*. The spreading of Marxist ideas led to the creation of socialist groups in Britain in the 1880s, though the number of socialists in Britain is estimated to have been as low as 2000 at this time. The socialists in Britain did not all share Marxist teaching about the need for violent revolution, but did all desire a more equitable society.

The Social Democratic Federation

This started life in March 1881 as the Democratic Foundation, before changing its name in 1884 to the Social Democratic Federation (SDF), largely due to the influence of Henry Mayers Hyndman who was a somewhat unlikely Marxist (he was a Victorian gentleman educated at Eton and Cambridge University). The SDF became a truly Marxist organisation, despite its roots in Radicalism, and favoured revolution over a democratic route to socialism. Hyndman was critical of trade unions which he saw as elitist, favouring a small number of skilled workers ahead of the rest of the working classes. He also believed that strikes were a waste of time and energy that could be better spent on activities such as producing propaganda. The SDF did contain trade unionists who were highly critical of Hyndman's views.

The SDF splintered in 1884 with the Socialist League being formed by a group from the SDF executive committee that included Eleanor Marx and William Morris. Morris dominated the Socialist League and was arguably important in the advancing of socialist ideas. The Socialist League itself, however, had little impact on British politics and never had more than about 700 members.

The most significant impact of the SDF came in 1886–87. Its campaigns in support of the unemployed and in favour of popular control of the Metropolitan Police culminated in a mass meeting in Trafalgar Square on 13 November 1887. This date was remembered as 'Bloody Sunday' as, in the violence that broke out, two demonstrators were killed by the police. A week later 40 000 people attended a meeting at Hyde Park, violence again broke out as mounted police charged the crowd. In the charge a demonstrator was fatally wounded. His funeral was attended by 120 000 people.

This seemed to suggest that the SDF was on the verge of becoming a significant mass movement. This did not, however, come to pass and the impact of the SDF is still debated. Hobsbawm suggests that Hyndman's leadership meant the SDF failed to collaborate with others and did not make the most of its opportunities. Crick, however, argues that the SDF played an important role in developing socialists who spread these ideas and went on to work in other organisations.

The Fabian Society

The Fabian Society was set up in 1884 and had very different beliefs from the SDF. Instead of revolutionary socialism the Fabians believed in evolutionary socialism – socialism which could be achieved by reform through national and local government. They took their name from a Roman general called Fabius, who defeated Hannibal by refusing to engage him and his troops in a set-piece battle. Fabius won through being patient, taking a gradualist approach and avoiding direct confrontation. The Fabians aimed to defeat their enemy 'capitalism' through gradual steps and by avoiding confrontation.

The members of the Fabian Society were almost totally middle class. Famous members included the writers George Bernard Shaw and H.G. Wells – in fact, 10% of the members were writers and journalists. The Fabians promoted their ideas through essays and pamphlets on a wide variety of topics. The driving forces behind the society were Beatrice and Sidney Webb, leading the writing on issues such as political reform and poverty. Fabian essays published in 1889 were widely read, for example, and 27 000 copies were sold in two years.

Key terms

Marxism: A political ideology devised by Karl Marx that sees human history as a struggle between the classes. It criticised free market capitalism and argued that workers were being exploited by those who owned businesses and that, in time, the workers would rise up in revolution.

Socialism: A political ideology which calls for the creation of a society in which property, wealth and work is shared out equitably and members of society work cooperatively. Socialists often disagree over how this society will be brought about.

ACTIVITY 2.4

Research the careers and influence of:
- Henry Mayers Hyndman
- William Morris
- Eleanor Marx.

> **Voices from the past**
>
> ### Kier Hardie (1856-1915)
>
> As a child, he worked in the coal-pits near Hamilton and learned to read from scraps of newspaper found in the street. Later, as a skilled worker in the coal industry, Hardie joined the trade union movement. He was a teetotal Nonconformist and initially a supporter of the Liberal Party. Disenchanted with the Liberals in the 1880s, in the 1890s he helped build an Independent Labour party (ILP) and then the Labour Representative Committee (LRC). He was a distinctive figure in Parliament in a tweed suit and deerstalker hat, deliberately standing out as a pioneer of working-class representation. This extract is from Hardie's address on 11 April 1914 at the 21st anniversary of the formation of the ILP:
>
> The Independent Labour Party has pioneered progress in this country, is breaking down sex barriers and class barriers, is giving a lead to the great women's movement as well as to the great working-class movement. We are here beginning the twenty-second year of our existence. The past twenty-one years have been years of continuous progress, but we are only at the beginning. The emancipation of the worker has still to be achieved and just as the ILP in the past has given a good, straight lead, so shall the ILP in the future, through good report and through ill, pursue the even tenor of its way, until the sunshine of Socialism and human freedom break forth upon our land.[2]

The Fabian Society still exists to this day and can be seen to have played a key role in the development of socialism and the Labour movement in Britain. It can, however, also be criticised in the period 1884 to 1906 in terms of their limited interactions with the working class and trade unions. Their seemingly divided loyalty among the Independent Labour Party, Labour Party and the Liberals can also be seen to affect their significance, especially as this reduced their role in establishing a unified left-wing in British politics.

The emergence of the Labour Party

The Independent Labour Party

Another key group in the development of the Labour Party was the Independent Labour Party (ILP) under the leadership of Keir Hardie. Hardie was hugely important in bringing together different left-wing groups and trade unions, leading to the formation of the Labour Representative Committee which then became the Labour Party.

Timeline: Kier Hardie

1877	Joined a Nonconformist church
1878	Became involved in trade union activity
1879	Sacked and 'blacklisted' because of his union activity
1881–86	Worked as a journalist
1886	Appointed Secretary of the Ayrshire Miners' Union; became Secretary of the new Scottish Miners' Federation
1887	Involved in a strike that troops used violence to break up; saw Lib-Lab MPs speaking and was disillusioned with their lack of support for his campaign for an eight-hour working day
1888	Passed over as Liberal candidate in Mid-Lanarkshire, he stood as an independent and received 8% of the vote; helped set up the Scottish Labour Party
1890	Put his name forward for seat of West Ham
1892	Won West Ham seat, becoming first independent working class MP; two other 'independent' Labour MPs were also elected – John Burns and Joseph Havelock Wilson; Scottish Labour Party put up five candidates in the general election
1893	Independent Labour Party founded; Hardie became president
1893–95	ILP grew rapidly from 200 branches to over 400
1895	ILP put up 28 candidates in the general election, but none was elected
1899	Support for ILP grew following a difficult time for trade unions; Amalgamated Society of Railway Servants (ASRS) pushed the TUC to secure representation of Labour interest in Parliament
1900	Formation of the LRC; Hardie was one of its two successful candidates in the General Election
1901	Taff Vale decision
1902–03	LRC won three by-elections.

| 1877 | Joined a Nonconformist church |
| 1903 | Lib-Lab Pact |

Figure 2.3: Keir Hardie addressing a crowd in Trafalgar Square in 1908

The Labour Party

The emergence of the Labour Party was linked to changes in the trade union movement. The party required financial support from the trade unions and, increasingly, the trade unions needed someone to offer strong representation of their interests in Parliament.

Between 1895 and 1899 the trade unions evolved and became more radical. There were some major setbacks, such as employers creating associations and federations which then took on the unions – in 1897–98, for example, the Federation of Engineering Employers organised a successful lockout of the Amalgamated Society of Engineers. The unions were also facing an increased number of legal challenges regarding the liability of their funds, owing to damage caused by their industrial action. There were also legal challenges to the right of peaceful picketing. The Conservative government encouraged firms to legally challenge the unions and could be seen to be overstating the threat of militant socialism.

The trade unions were also increasingly frustrated by the lack of support in Parliament from the Liberal Party (the Lib-Labs only numbered 11 to 13). The split of the Liberals over Home Rule also affected the unions' links with the trade unions as it meant that the key radical figures, notably Chamberlain, left the party.

The TUC voted by a narrow margin to hold a conference about raising parliamentary representation and as a result the LRC was created in 1900. The proposal of the Amalgamated Society of Railway Servants (ASRS) calling for all 'cooperative, socialistic, trade union and other working organisations' to 'secure a better representation of the interests of labour in the House of Commons' was passed. The unions, ILP, SDF and Fabians would pay for their own candidates. These candidates would be independent of all other parties. The LRC had an executive of 12 including: seven trade union delegates, two ILP delegates, two SDF delegates and one Fabian

ACTIVITY 2.5

1. Consider the obstacles in the way of the formation of an independent labour party 1880–1900. Explain how the following held the movement back:
   - the Liberal Party Libs-Labs
   - the restricted nature of the franchise
   - variation of views among the working classes
   - problems in financing the party
   - suspicion of state intervention
   - theory of removable inequalities (belief in ever-increasing prosperity and social mobility).
2. Rank the above reasons in order of importance.
3. Which of these obstacles had been overcome by 1905?

delegate. The original proposal was a committee of 18 but this was reduced (trade unions lost five and Fabians one) to help balance trade union representation and Socialist representation (some representatives were both). The franchise had increased, but the existing parties were not offering real social reform out of which a working-class party might emerge.

The LRC did not prosper in the 1900 election, which was due in part to the dire state of its finances and in part to the patriotic atmosphere of the election. The election is generally considered to have been a disaster – only two candidates were elected – but not all the evidence backs this up; for example, on average, the 15 candidates received over 4000 votes, higher than ILP averages in 1895 (1400 votes).

> **Cross-reference: Trade unions and new unionism**

The Taff Vale judgement of 1901 made a massive difference to the relationship between Labour and the unions. The number of affiliated union members rose from 350 000 in 1901 to 861 000 in 1902, the largest group of new members coming from the textile workers. Although the Liberals expressed some sympathy towards the trade unions, they were not in power. The Lib-Lab MPs were achieving very little in the House of Commons and this meant that trade unionists started to believe that an independent Labour group in Parliament might prove more effective. The Liberals and Labour Party would later work together to overthrow the Taff Vale decision when the Liberal Party supported the Trade Disputes Act proposed by the Labour Party.

In 1902 and 1903 three more LRC MPs were elected in by-elections and others came close. The LRC also made constitutional changes in 1903: these included raising the annual subscription rate for unions from ten shillings per 1000 members to one penny for each member; a parliamentary fund was also created to pay MPs during their term in office. These changes took financial control from the unions and placed it in the hands of the LRC.

The Lib-Lab Pact of 1903 was a major breakthrough for the Labour Representative Committee. Liberals and Labour agreed to not run rival candidates in numerous constituencies in order to avoid splitting the anti-Conservative vote in key seats and also to save party spending on elections. The Liberals were also impressed with how strong the LRC had become, believing they had a common cause against protection and that the LRC could attract working-class Conservative voters that the Liberals could not. Herbert Gladstone, the Liberal Chief Whip, was also key, as he was willing to deal with the LRC's Ramsay MacDonald.

Politics and the constitution 1906–14

The ideology of New Liberalism

What was New Liberalism?
New Liberalism was a substantive change to Liberal ideology. It inspired changes in social and economic policy; led to Liberal social reforms between 1906 and 1914 that were an important step towards establishing a welfare state; and changed the relationship between the state and the people. While Classical Liberalism focused on minimising the role of the state and promoting self-help, New Liberalism promoted state intervention in order to correct economic inequalities that limited the lives and opportunities of the less well off. Underlying these differences were fundamentally different beliefs about society. Classical Liberalism saw society as a collection of individuals, but saw those individuals as not being strongly connected; while New Liberalism saw society being made up of distinct elements that worked together. Classical Liberalism championed free-market economics and low taxation; New

Liberalism saw the economic system as containing flaws and elements that were unfair.

New Liberalism was distinct from Classical Liberalism, but also from socialism. Socialism emphasised exploitation and conflict between the classes and called for the destruction of the existing structure of society. New Liberalism called for greater cohesion between the different classes. It saw society as organic, with its different parts working together. However, there were some similarities with socialism, particularly in terms of movement towards greater state intervention to help the poor in society and redistributing wealth to a degree. Both New Liberals and socialists looked at unearned income as being different from earned income and talked of targeting it with higher taxation.

Speak like a historian

Alan Sykes

Alan Sykes, former lecturer in Modern History at the University of St Andrews, has also written on tariff reform and the radical right in British political history. This was written as an introduction for university students to the historical debates about the Liberal Party and Liberalism.

Nominally, New Liberalism built upon the Liberal tradition of liberation, but it ran too easily to expert committees that bore more relation to the ideas of Viscount Milner than those of Gladstone. It compounded social with intellectual condescension. The working classes were to be administered, inspected, policed and reformed, their incomes were to be compulsorily reduced for their own good, their choices restricted, but they were not to share power. The elevation of the state, as a positive force, the embodiment of the 'common good' through which the individual achieved his own liberty, provided a rationale for top-down government by bureaucracy. New Liberal ideology did not just build upon traditional Liberalism; it turned it inside out, providing the ideological basis that few understood for reforms that few wanted. Moreover, it was, like the economic policies that succeeded it in the 1920s, not only unintelligible in terms of traditional Liberalism, but often just unintelligible. Nothing had changed by 1929.[3]

Discussion points:

1. Explain Sykes' view in your own words.
2. How valid is this view? Find evidence to support it.
3. Write a counter-argument to Sykes' view.

ACTIVITY 2.6

1. Create a table, using information from this section and from your own research, to plot the similarities and differences between Classical Liberalism, New Liberalism and Socialism.
2. Make notes on the importance of ideas and ideology in the positioning of New Liberalism on the UK political landscape.

New Liberalism used the ideas of biology, viewing society as an organism and the people as the cells that make up that organism. According to New Liberalism individual liberty can only be achieved through society and what is good for the individual is inseparable from greater consideration for the good for society. Following from these beliefs the need for state intervention in given circumstances was measured against the need for social good. If there was strong evidence that problems in society could not be solved unless the state intervened, then New Liberals would support that intervention – for example, through Liberal reforms aimed at protecting children, the old, the ill and the poorest workers.

A/AS Level History for AQA: Challenge and Transformation: Britain, c1851–1964

> ### Key terms
>
> **Underconsumption:** J.A. Hobson argued that for the economy to perform well, the well-off needed to buy goods to feed the circulation of money through the economic cycle of shopkeeper–manufacturer–wages for the worker. If the well-off saved money instead, the economy would underperform.
>
> **Tariff reform:** A strengthening of the tariff system to boost protection.
>
> **National efficiency:** There was concern that Britain was declining compared with other world powers and that the reason for this was the poor health and education of the work force in Britain, making them increasingly inefficient compared with their German and US contemporaries.

According to New Liberalism tax could be graduated (higher rates of tax applying to higher earners) and targeted at one class to benefit the others, based on the idea of 'unearned' income from land and property. This was presented as society reclaiming income for its own use. The New Liberal thinker Herbert Samuel argued that improving one part of society (helping the poor) had benefits for the whole of society, so all members of society could be required to contribute. Society was seen as a single organism: what brought about the greatest benefit to the most people benefited society as a whole and, according to the economist J.A. Hobson, could be threatened by **underconsumption**.

> **Cross-reference:** The Beveridge Report (Chapter 4)

For the New Liberals the right to work was crucial (as it later was in the Beveridge report), since, without the means to support themselves, people would be unable to access the other key rights. Some New Liberal ideas were not accepted widely at the time, but have been considered and even adopted in Parliament since: a minimum 'living wage', nationalisation of railways and mines (and other industries and services suggested by Hobson) and a minimum standard of housing. Some would even be considered radical in the 21st century: in 1912 the Liberal MP Russell Rea suggested that the state should provide free heating, lighting and food for poor children to improve their life chances and society as a whole.

The growth of New Liberalism

In the early 1890s New Liberalism developed outside the official Liberal Party (which was not listening) in debating societies, lecture tours and the press, books and journals and specialised newspapers: *The Progressive Review*, *The Speaker* and its successor *The Nation*. Much was theoretical and no programme was agreed on, but there was a new language of reform. During all this the Liberal leadership focused on Home Rule and arguments over imperialism. The Liberal Party, united by horrors of the Boer War and 'Chinese slavery', the 1902 Education Act and the 1904 Licensing Act, came together and the New Liberal ideas started to permeate through the party. Before

> ### Voices from the past
>
> #### Key figures in the emergence of New Liberalism
>
> #### J.A. Hobson, economist (1858–1940)
>
> Hobson argued that Classical Liberalism concentrated too much on individual freedom. He argued that this idea was not valuable to the poorest in society as their circumstances took away their freedom of action. The businessmen who made vast profits, however, could not have done so without their workers. The economic system was, therefore, flawed and created inequality in terms of liberty.
>
> #### T.H. Green, Oxford don (1836–82)
>
> Green rejected Classical Liberal ideas of society as a collection of unconnected individuals and instead described society as being like a living creature made up of different parts and therefore more than the sum of its parts and dependent on all being healthy. Green promoted the idea of that what was best for society might not necessarily be so for individuals. Green also wrote about the need for the state to monitor, and even regulate, the behaviour of individuals where their behaviour damaged society as a whole.
>
> #### Herbert Samuel, Liberal MP and later Liberal leader (1870–1963)
>
> Samuel argued that improving one part of society, such as by helping the poor, would benefit the whole of society. Samuel argued that this meant that all members of society could be required to contribute to help a part of society that required it.

the election of 1906 Chamberlain split the Conservative Party over **tariff reform**, significantly weakening them. Liberals viewed the proposal of tariff reform as an attack on their fundamental beliefs, causing the party and its supporters to unify and rally. The Liberals then swept to power in 1906 and the ideology of New Liberalism had a significant impact on the Liberal Social Reform that followed.

The emergence of Liberalism was strongly linked to the debate over **National efficiency**. Around one in three volunteers for the **Boer War** at the start of the 20th century had been found to be unfit for military service and in poorer areas it was markedly higher; for example, around three-quarters of recruits from a working-class area in Manchester were deemed to be unfit.

The conversion of Lloyd George to New Liberalism was key to the advancement of the ideology within the Liberal Government from 1906 to 1914. It can be argued that Lloyd George was more focused on traditional Liberal ideas, such as Church disestablishment, land reform and temperance than New Liberal focus on Social reform. From 1908, however, he started to show greater commitment to the need for state intervention to address Britain's social problems. He visited Germany in 1908 and was deeply impressed by their labour exchanges and policy of social insurance. Lloyd George may well have been a late convert, but he made a crucial contribution to turning New Liberal ideology into policy and government action.

Political crises and constitutional change

The People's Budget

In 1909 'The People's Budget' and the House of Lords' reaction to it led to a constitutional crisis. The budget was a fundamental departure from traditional economic policy, with a clear aim to raise substantial amounts of money by taxing the wealthy (in particular the landed elites) to spend on policies to support the less well off through welfare schemes and the building of dreadnoughts which was urged by the popular press ('we want eight and we won't wait'). Its key features were:

- sixpence per pound on incomes of £5000 and over
- twopence increase in tax on unearned incomes over £3000 per annum
- a 20% tax on land sold at a higher value than it was bought, among other new taxes on land
- increase in death duties
- threepence tax on a gallon of petrol
- tax on motor vehicles based on horsepower
- duties increased by 33% on spirits and 25% on tobacco, along with increased duties on liquor licences

The budget appeared to be deliberately targeting the landed interests that were the backbone of the Conservative Party, which opposed the bill in the strongest possible terms. With the balance of power lying in the Liberals' favour in the House of Commons, the confrontation would come to the fore in the House of Lords. It has been argued that Lloyd George, the Liberal Chancellor of the Exchequer, deliberately provoked the House of Lords, aiming to bring about the constitutional crisis – the government had combined into the budget two important bills that the Lords had previously rejected (the Land Bill in 1907 and the Licensing Bill in 1908). The overriding consensus, however, is that the Liberals wanted to push through their reform programme and revitalise their rank-and-file supporters in the run-up to the next election and did not want to provoke a crisis that would slow down their programme.

The constitutional crisis

Because Britain's **constitution** is not codified, the relationship between different political institutions has changed over time. By convention in 1909, the House of Lords could veto any other bills (proposed laws) but it could not veto finance bills, which are

Key terms

Boer War: The Second Boer War took place from 1899 to 1902. It was fought in South Africa between the British and a group of settlers of Dutch extraction known as the Boers. Britain won the war, but at terrible cost and with great difficulty. The war raised many questions about empire and Britain's position as a great power.

Constitution: The set of rules that sets out how a country is governed, and defines the relationship between different political institutions and between government and the people. Some countries have a codified constitution (written in a single document) and others, such as Britain, have an uncodified constitution: an accumulation of laws, convention and precedent.

ACTIVITY 2.7

Using the table of Liberal social reforms in the 'Social policies' section of this chapter, address the following questions:

For each reform, identify which group in society was being targeted.

1. How strongly is New Liberalism evident in the reforms?
2. What other motivations could have led the Liberals to introduce these reforms?
3. Which of the reforms do you think would have been rejected by Classical Liberals? Explain your answer.

concerned with tax and government income. For over 200 years no finance bill had been rejected by the House of Lords.

> **Cross-reference:** The political system: Parliament and the workings of mid-19th-century democracy (Chapter 1)

This changed in 1909 when the unelected House of Lords stood in the way of the taxation and spending plans of a government with a secure majority in the House of Commons. The power of the landed elites had been eroded by the extension of the franchise and other political reforms such as the introduction of the secret ballot. This, combined with the economic depression of the latter stages of the 19th century and the continuing problems faced by British agriculture, made the landed elites feel that their traditional position was under threat. The party leaders, the King and the British people would all have a role in deciding whether the aristocracy would maintain its power or whether Britain would take a step closer to democracy and the House of Commons would gain political **hegemony**.

ACTIVITY 2.8

As you read through this section on crises and change, add to your notes on the development of democracy and political organisations in Britain.

Key terms

Hegemony: Dominance or power over others.

Timeline of the constitutional crisis

1906	Liberals win large majority in General Election.
1907	House of Lords rejects Liberal Land Bill.
1908	House of Lords rejects Liberal Licensing Bill.
1909	(April) People's Budget introduced. (Nov) House of Lords rejects the Budget. (Dec) Asquith dissolves Parliament.
1910	(Jan) Liberals and Unionists win about the same number of seats; Irish Nationalists and Labour keep Liberals in power. (April) People's Budget becomes Law. (May) The King (Edward VII) dies. (June) Constitutional conference held, but fails to find compromise. (Nov) Asquith asks for Parliament to be dissolved and for King George V to promise to make new Liberal peers to outvote existing Conservative peers, if the need arose, to push reform through. King insists there must be another election before Asquith could move against the Lords. (Dec) Liberals hold power following the second general election of 1910.
1911	The Parliament Bill becomes law (the Parliament Act) following disputes in the Conservative Party. The Lords could now only delay, not veto, any bill and the life of Parliament was reduced from seven to five years.

The confrontation had been building up between the Liberals and the Lords: numerous Liberal bills had been challenged and rejected by the Lords. The Lords was within its constitutional rights when it rejected these earlier bills, but not to reject a finance bill. Whether the budget was deliberately set to provoke or sidestep the House of Lords is debatable, but the Liberal Government had good reason to tackle the Lords over its rejection – the democratically elected House of Commons should have power over taxation; they had a huge majority giving them a clear mandate to carry out their policies; the Lords appeared to be acting to protect their interests and those of the Conservative Party rather than the national interests.

Parliament was dissolved and, following a general election, the budget was passed. The crisis was not, however, over. The final stage was for the Liberals to pass a

Parliament Act that would weaken the Lords and ensure the dominance of the Commons. The Liberals ultimately triumphed over the Lords through a combination of support from the people at the ballot box (and notably the Labour Party and Irish Nationalists) and an agreement with the new King George V that he would, if required, create enough new Liberal peers to ensure the Parliament Act would pass.

The consequences of the constitutional crisis were numerous. The crisis can be seen as being decisive in ending Balfour's leadership of the Unionist Party, which in the short term was bitterly split on how to respond to the crisis, giving further advantage to the Liberals. For the Conservatives, the crisis can in some ways be seen as positive, however, as Balfour, who had lost three elections, was replaced by Bonar Law who would prove to be key in ensuring the Conservatives would be in a strong position to deal with the new political landscape after the First World War.

The Liberal Party could clearly see itself as the victor of the power struggle with the House of Lords. The People's Budget and the Parliament Act can both be seen as impressive achievements for the Liberal Party. The elections of 1910 had, however, stripped the Liberals of their majority and left them exposed to the demands of the Irish Nationalists and Labour Party, on whom they were now reliant. The Lords used its newly designated powers to delay Liberal reforms and the reforming ministry rather lost its earlier momentum. The years 1909 to 1911 will ultimately, however, be seen as the standout period in the career of the Liberal leader Asquith and in the history of the Liberal Party as a whole. The reforming Liberal Government had taken a major step in creating a new relationship between government and the British people.

Taking it further

Research the arguments put forward by E.H.H. Green in his article 'Neutering Mr Balfour's Poodle' on how the constitutional crisis led to divisions among the unionist peers.[4]

Carry out further reading to find evidence to support this view.

Evaluate his argument that the British aristocracy had finally withdrawn from their role of the governing class in Britain by 1914.

The development of the Labour Party

The parliamentary party
The Lib-Lab Pact helped the Labour party make its first major breakthrough in terms of number of MPs when 29 Labour MPs were elected in 1906. This was a major step forward for the Labour Party with a now small but definite presence in the House of Commons. However, the Liberals had 397 MPs, a massive majority, and therefore had little reason to listen to their electoral-pact partners. Ideally, the Labour party would have hoped for a close-run election between the major parties, which would have given them leverage to push through some legislation. Although the parliamentary arithmetic was not in their favour the Labour Party managed a significant achievement in Parliament in 1906 in the form of the Trade Disputes Act. While the Labour Party MPs' support was not required by the Liberal Party to pass legislation, the adoption of New Liberalism meant the two parties had similar ideas about some key issues.

Cross-references: Government legislation and local initiatives 1886–1905; Taxation and welfare reform by 1914

The Trade Disputes Act was based on the Labour Party's bill. It reversed the Taff Vale decision, meaning that trade unions could now strike and peacefully picket without fear of legal actions draining their finances. This had a significant impact on trade unions and on their perception of the Labour Party, which could rightfully claim credit for this change in the law, as being a viable parliamentary representative of the trade union movement. The most significant evidence of this was the Miners' Federation of Great Britain (MFGB) affiliating to the Labour Party, switching its 12 sponsored MPs into the Parliamentary Labour Party. The MFGB were an amalgamation of the regional miners' union formed in 1888 and were highly involved in industrial action, including violent clashes in Featherstone in 1893 and Tonypandy in 1910. They were significant as they had a membership of over half a million and wielded great power within the trade union movement.

The ideological closeness of Labour to the Liberals (see the section 'The ideology of New Liberalism') also meant that the Labour Party managed to influence, to a degree, the Workmen's Compensation Act and acts regarding school meals and medical inspections. Their input was limited to a few minor amendments but, nonetheless, showed that the Labour Party could make a difference in Parliament and therefore were viable representatives for the working classes.

Because they were so ideologically close to the Liberals and their New Liberalism, it was hard for the Labour Party to present a clear differential between them and the Liberal Party. The Liberals allowed the Labour Party to contribute to Liberal bills and acts, which suggests that they did not see the Labour Party as a threat. The Liberals in a way seemed to have 'stolen the Labour Party's clothes' by promoting some redistribution of wealth, attacking the landed elites and offering support for the most vulnerable in society. If the Labour Party simply agreed with the Liberal reforms, then why would people vote for them? On the other hand, if they demanded more radical reforms, then the electorate might see them as too radical and be concerned about extreme socialist policies.

However, Labour won three by-elections between 1906 and 1909, and gained the 12 MFGB members, and this suggests that they walked the tightrope between these two fairly effectively. By 1914, however, Labour had lost eight seats in a combination of by-elections and the two general elections in 1910. Moreover, there were only around 90 constituencies with working-class majorities and they were competing with two long-established parties with developed party machines and politicians with great popular appeal.

Funding and organisation

The Labour Party faced great financial challenges, notably following the Osborne Judgement in 1909, which required union members to opt in to the political levy rather than opt out. This massively reduced the Labour Party's funding from the trade union movement, on which it relied to support its MPs, run election campaigns and manage the national party. From 1911, however, MPs were paid, and then in 1913 the Trade Disputes Act reversed the Osborne Judgement. These acts showed the increased influence of the Labour Party following the much closer elections of 1910, which meant that they had greater leverage in Parliament (see Figure 2.4). The changes they gained can be seen as too little too late and little reward for the Labour Party's help in keeping the Liberals in power. However, they would help lay the foundation for the further growth of the Labour Party in the years following the First World War.

Outside Parliament the Labour Party made some significant gains. The biggest success was in the growth of trade union support. The support of the Miners' Federation in 1909 brought 550 000 new members to the Labour Party. The party's membership rose from 1.4 million in 1910 to 2.1 million in 1915. Following the Trade Union Act of 1913 trade unions voted overwhelmingly to establish political funds for the Labour Party and trade union support was solidly behind the party by the outbreak of the First World War.

ACTIVITY 2.9

1. Create a diagram to show the positives and negatives of Labour's progress in the years 1906–14. This could for example be in the form of a set of weighing scales.
2. To what extent did the position of the Labour Party improve from 1906 to 1914?

The Labour Party also made progress in local elections. They had 91 council seats in 1906 and this rose to 171 seats in 1913. The Labour Party at a local level could offer programmes of social reform that meant they were distinct from the Liberals. Their support, however, was patchy and they did not have overall control of any councils. In 1914 over half of the party's councillors were in Yorkshire and Lancashire, suggesting that the party was not as yet a truly national one. The party under the leadership of Ramsay MacDonald was becoming increasingly well organised and had full-time agents and officers as well as seven senior staff in 1914. Before war broke out they were preparing to fight 150 seats at the next election (twice as many as in 1910) suggesting an increasingly confident party and one on a secure financial footing.

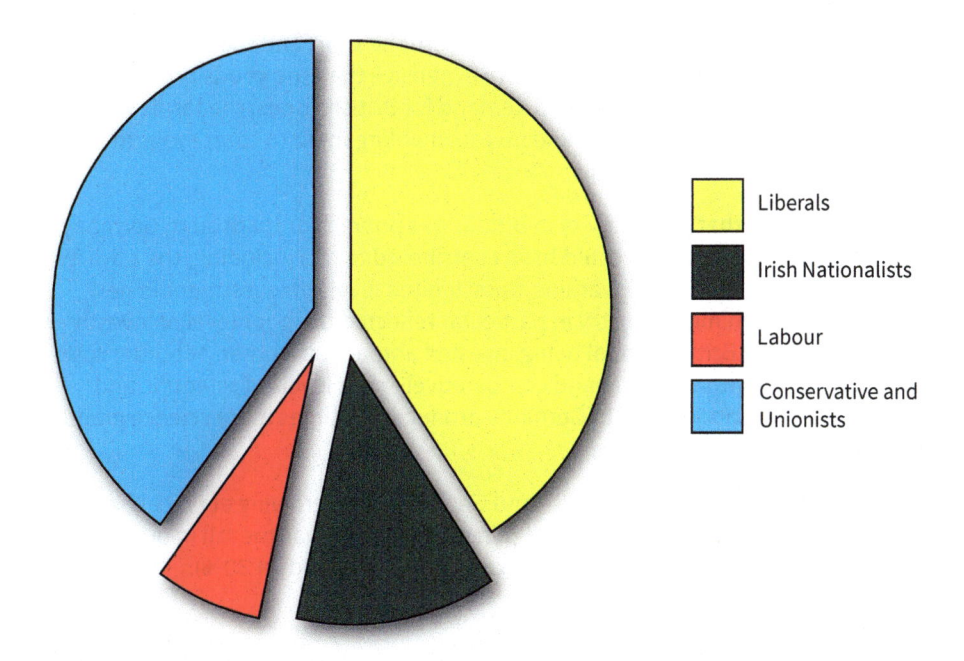

Figure 2.4: The balance of power in the House of Commons after the 1910 elections

Economic developments

The Great Depression and its aftermath

> **Cross-reference:** The onset of the Depression (Chapter 1)

The start of the Great Depression is normally placed in 1873 and it was still in effect in 1886, and a Royal Commission was set up to investigate the depression in industry and trade. The commission did not come up with radical proposals and stood firmly behind the free trade that many Conservatives were starting to question, but its existence demonstrates the degree of concern about Britain's economy at the time, among the governing classes: the landed classes and middle classes were seeing a fall in profits.

Historians still debate whether there truly was a 'Great Depression', and how far the British economy had recovered by 1914. The people at the time certainly considered there to be a Great Depression and, undoubtedly, Britain lost its world-leading economic position. The debate centres around whether the decline in British industry and agriculture was genuine or simply relative.

Clearly there were significant difficulties in the British economy. Many British firms experienced declining profits and they therefore invested less. British industry was made up mainly of smaller family firms, rather than the much larger firms in the USA or Germany, so their capacity to invest was hit harder by the drop in profits. Smaller firms had fewer resources to fall back on and investment in new technology and factories would require a higher percentage of their turnover. This lack of investment led to a degree of stagnation in British industry.

The export values of the early 1870s were not exceeded until the late 1890s, which strongly supports the idea of a Great Depression between 1873 and 1896. For example, cotton goods' export values of 1872 were not equalled until 1904, the worst year for the export of cotton goods being 1895.

Tariffs imposed by other countries on British goods from the 1860s onwards began to have a major impact on British exports, in both the short and the long term. In the short term they made British exports more expensive than the goods produced within the importing country, which reduced demand for British goods; the tariffs would also allow native industry to grow and invest, enabling them to compete with British produced goods in the long term.

Evidence suggests that productivity in Britain was poor in comparison to Germany and the USA. Various reasons could have contributed to this including: the poverty and poor health of the British working class; limited levels of investment in new technologies (the mining industry in particular reflected the poor level of investment in mechanisation); British capital being invested abroad rather than at home; costs of transportation within Britain; and comparatively poor levels of scientific and technological education. In 1913 Germany produced six times more science graduates than Britain.

The competing economies in the USA and Germany were growing at twice the rate of the British economy. A clear sign of the perceived decline was the fall in price of some industrial goods during this period (for example, textiles by over 30%).

> **Cross-reference:** Staples, new industries and foreign competition

Imports were not increasing at the same rate during the Great Depression as they had done previously, which suggests that the British economy was depressed. Britain did not impose import tariffs, so the imported goods were often cheap, most notably food products. Demand was not strong, however, due to unemployment and stagnant wage levels.

Overall there was a growing deficit emerging during the Great Depression in the visible **balance of trade**. Britain, traditionally the 'workshop of the world', was no longer a net exporter. British industry was struggling in foreign markets – manufacturers against mass-produced US and German goods, and agriculture against foreign imports. There was clearly a serious decline in agriculture.

In other parts of the economy, however, there was no real evidence of sharp decline – merely of slower growth. Overall levels of production and the volume of exports continued to rise in most industries through the period of the Great Depression. In 1896 Britain was still one of the world's leading economies. The City of London became a world leader in financial services. British entrepreneurial efforts shifted from traditional industry, which was beset with falling prices and competition, switching their focus to the service sector and commerce, areas in which Britain excelled. The level of invisible exports more than offset the deficit in the visible balance of trade and Britain's overall balance of trade remained positive.

Landed interests and middle-class businessmen were affected by the Great Depression – and possibly formed the traditional historical view of this period – but for the

Key terms

Balance of trade: The value of exports minus the value of imports. The visible balance of trade is based on the value of physical goods being exported and imported. The overall balance of trade is also affected by 'invisible' imports and exports: services and non-physical goods, such as city financial services for foreign firms.

working classes the impact of the economic changes was very different. Falling food prices increased 'real wages' and improved the standard of living of many in the working class. Historians such as S.B. Saul have even dismissed the whole idea of the Great Depression.[5]

The aftermath of the Great Depression would also suggest that the British economy was still functioning effectively. Between 1900 and 1913 GDP increased on average by 1.7% a year. Staple industries continued to increase output, for example, coal production increased from 223 million tons in 1900 to 287 million tons in 1913. British dominance of shipbuilding continued with about 60% of the world's merchant ships being built in British shipyards. Britain continued to increase foreign investment – from £50 million in 1901 to £200 million in 1913, suggesting the country was in rude economic health.

However, there was no longer the optimism about British economic progress that had been apparent in the mid-19th century. It was unclear whether Britain would be able to maintain its strong position in world markets in the staple industries. Books with titles such as *Made in Germany* and *American Invaders* were attaining a wide readership, emphasising the point that Britain was no longer the 'workshop of the world'. People started to look for reasons and there was a wider debate about 'National efficiency' (see 'The ideology of New Liberalism').

Some even turned to the writings of social-Darwinists such as Galton and spoke of 'physical deterioration' (the idea that there was a genetic decline in the British race) and saw solutions in terms of **eugenics**. The recruitment drive for the Boer War and reports by Seebohm Rowntree and William Booth exposed the terrible poverty that existed in Britain and begged the question as to whether the British worker could, in the long term, compete with the seemingly healthier and better educated German and American workers.

Britain's share of the world's manufacturing continued to fall even after the Great Depression ended. Britain had certainly been overtaken by the USA and Germany, but the decline was comparative not real: the British economy continued to grow and so did British production.

Problems of British industry and agriculture

Industry

In 1870 Britain produced 33% of the world's manufactured goods and 14% in 1913, when the USA produced 35% and Germany 16%. Although the latter appeared to be doing better, Britain had started from a higher base and was therefore likely to have a slower growth rate than the newly emerging economies. British industrialists were less dynamic and less flexible. They had more skilled craftsmen than the USA, so cost-reducing technical innovations – such as the Ford conveyor belt – were not adopted and Germany was well ahead in terms of technical and managerial education.

There are various theories about what was at the heart of British industry's problems:

- The 'early start' thesis states that the country that industrialises first faces a long-term disadvantage, as techniques and processes become outdated and the initial advantage is lost. Later starters can adopt recent techniques and equipment and learn from the experience of the initiator. Introducing electricity to the British cotton industry, for example, would have required redesigning the weaving sheds, while in the USA the whole production process could be put into place in one go. In the steel industry in the 1860s, Britain, the USA and Germany were all using the same British equipment. The other two updated their technology, but Britain stuck with the older, less-efficient methods. In shipbuilding, Britain had also had an early start, and here they continued to dominate. New industries – such as dyes, chemicals, electricity and motor cars – became better established in the USA and Germany

Key terms

Eugenics: The idea that society could be improved through promoting selective breeding and even sterilisation of some members of society.

than in Britain. Britain did develop chocolate or soap production, but these did not contribute significant manufacturing innovations to benefit the economy.
- Declining demand abroad is an alternative explanation for the problems of Britain's economic problems. Other countries developed their own raw materials and manufacturing, so Britain was no longer *the* 'workshop of the world'. Germany, the USA and other countries were now exploiting their own natural resources, which reduced British exports. The British policy of free trade put it at a disadvantage after 1880 as other countries imposed tariffs on British goods. British exports increased by 3% between 1899 and 1913, albeit significantly less than before the depression (see Table 2.3). Employment did not fall significantly, as falling exports might suggest, but there may be two reasons for this: emigration from Britain was high during this period; and the lack of modernisation meant that industry was still reliant on large numbers of workers.

Years	£ million
1840–49	124.5
1860–69	159.7
1870–79	218.1

Table 2.3: Total value of British exports[6]

- Low wages could also explain Britain's relative economic decline as this suppressed British demand for manufactured goods; in the USA workers received higher pay and so generated demand. British manufacturers, moreover, concentrated on high-quality goods aimed at the aristocracy rather than targeting the mass market with cheaper goods produced on production lines. So Britain was on the one hand reliant on shrinking export markets and on the other facing competition from cheaper imported German and US goods. The construction industry was also growing in the USA and Germany as infrastructure developed and new factories were built, but here too Britain fell behind.
- Supply-side factors meant the British economy was at a disadvantage compared with other economies. In the USA, the shortage in skilled labour forced industry to develop labour-saving machinery; in 1910, US textiles and tinplate industries produced the same amount as Britain with about 25% of the workforce. Britain had no need to develop efficiency in terms of labour or fuel, which were both abundant.
- British entrepreneurs dominated, but small family-run firms often focused on profits, not long-term reinvestment. The complacent sons and grandsons of the founders of family firms were more interested in being country gentlemen than leaders of commerce. During the Depression they preserved profits by cutting wages rather than investing in technology, moving to mass production, developing better management techniques and integration, for example by introducing economies of scale through having spinning and weaving on the same site.

However, entrepreneurship in retail was alive and kicking. Thomas Lipton and J.J. Sainsbury took mass retailing to a new scale. Lipton founded his first shop in 1872 and by 1898 had 242 branches, factories and overseas agencies. Jesse Boot, meanwhile, was transforming the economics of chemists, with stores for the middle classes.

Agriculture

British agriculture declined more sharply than industry. Because of cheap imported cereals, thousands of agricultural workers were laid off, farmers went bankrupt, and the amount of land used for growing cereal crops fell from 9.6 million acres in 1872 to 6.5 million acres in 1913. Much of the land was turned over to pasture and so improved the supply of British meat and dairy products, where farmers were better protected from cheap foreign imports because milk, in particular, could not be imported efficiently. Although refrigerated meat was now reaching Britain, British farm meat was

ACTIVITY 2.10

Research the history of the company founded by Scottish chemist Charles Tennant. To what extent does it exemplify the description given here of British family-run firms?

of better quality and many preferred to eat fresh, rather than frozen, meat. Livestock farmers were also boosted by the low price of animal feed. The number of livestock in Britain increased during this period and areas such as Lancashire and the West Country saw significant increases in the numbers of cattle and pigs.

There were significant issues within agriculture with loss of income leading to: a lack of maintenance of farm land; stagnant wages for labourers; a shrinking workforce; fields being left to become rough pasture. New technology was developed in response to the pressure to save labour costs, such as a self-binding reaper and a new plough that could work two farrows at the same time. There was also development in scientific approaches and courses on farming and breeding livestock.

While British farmers suffered as bread prices fell, there were benefits from the rising disposable income of the urban workers with the demand for dairy products, most notably milk. As a result, dairy farmers were in a much better position through this period than farmers in other sectors of agriculture.

After 1900 there was some limited recovery in British agriculture. Overall, agricultural output increased by 5% between 1900 and 1914 and, for the first time in almost half a century, prices also rose slightly. Government supported farmers moving to dairy and market garden farming (intensive farming near cities, producing fresh fruit, vegetables and flowers) and banned live cattle imports in 1892, which helped protect British farmers as well as providing support for smallholders. British farming would never truly recover to its previous highs and this had significant impact on British politics and society as well as the economy.

Staples, new industries and foreign competition

Britain was still a major force in the world economy in the staple industries, if perhaps over-reliant on its particular strengths in textiles and shipbuilding. These were strong in the mid-19th century, and had shaped the British economy by exploiting large export markets. However, this distortion meant that Britain was particularly vulnerable to changes in the world economy. By 1886 other countries were no longer reliant on British exports of coal, iron and steel, but were able to exploit their own resources. The USA and Germany not only had natural resources well in excess of Britain's, but their new industries and manufacturing techniques surpassed any developments in Britain, where many sectors faced challenges.

In the USA, the textile industry used electricity, modern machines, the latest spindles, all of which lowered costs. Lancashire, on the other hand, preserved older methods, even when 95 new cotton mills were opened between 1905 and 1907. In 1913, only 8% of British coal was cut mechanically in 1913 (over 25% in the USA) and the industry made limited use of electricity, concrete and steel and mechanical transport. More men than ever were employed, but productivity was very low compared with other countries and safety records were poor.

Britain was slow to adopt larger, cheaper and more efficient steel processes, sticking with the production of pig iron instead of steel. Any success in the steel industry can be linked to British dominance of shipbuilding and the naval race in the build-up to the First World War. There were major advances in shipbuilding, including the development of oil-fired turbines that were more efficient than the steam turbines. Although British inventions to improve shipbuilding were later adopted and developed abroad, for the time being Britain remained dominant in the shipbuilding industry.

By 1907, however, the staples of coal, textiles, iron, steel and engineering were still responsible for 50% of all British output and employed 25% of the workforce, which suggests that they maintained a key role in the British economy and continued to function even in the new, more competitive, world.

Staple industries

Annual average per decade	Imports of raw cotton (kg)	Exports of cotton cloth (metres)
1870–79	564 269	3269
1890–99	705 790	5057
1910–19	845 497	5460

Table 2.4: The textile industry[7]

Year	Output (million tons)	% exported
1870	108.6	13.4
1900	221.6	25.9
1913	282	—

Table 2.5: The coal industry[8]

Country	Tons of steel (millions)
USA	13
Germany	7
Britain	5

Table 2.6: Steel production in 1913

Year	Value in £ millions
1880–89	35.3
1890–99	32.5
1900–09	45.7
1910–19	62.9

Table 2.7: The value of British exports in iron and steel[9]

Year	Steamships (thousand tons)
1880–89	377.2
1890–99	500.9
1900–09	674.2

Table 2.8: Tonnage of ships built and first registered in Britain[10]

New industries

Britain's motor car industry was hampered by the 1865 Red Flag Act, which limited motorised transport to 4 mph and required a car to be preceded by a person carrying a red flag to warn other road users. This act was not repealed until 1896. By 1914 there were 132 000 cars in Britain. The majority were individually hand-built, such as the Silver Ghost manufactured by Rolls Royce in 1907. The quality of British craftsmanship was second to none, but US mass production – as demonstrated by the introduction of the Model T Ford in 1908 – made the car affordable to a much larger proportion of the US population.

Figure 2.5: A Model T Ford

The bicycle industry was also an important new industry, with firms such as Humber and Raleigh producing bicycles in large numbers that fed not only the domestic market, but also became a highly valuable export.

In the chemical industry, a key new industry, Britain failed to compete effectively – sticking to the old and less efficient Le Blanc method to produce soda, for example, while Germany and the USA quickly adopted the new more efficient Solway ammonia process.

This period also saw developments in the electrical industry. The first power station had been built in 1881 at Godalming and further power stations were built in large cities. The development of the steam turbine meant that electricity could be produced on a large scale and a grid of cables were developed to transport electricity to domestic and industrial customers. With advances that meant electricity could be used to power wireless telegraphy and modes of transport such as trams, the electrical industry was becoming increasingly important.

After the First World War, however, Britain did develop new and efficient industries in vehicles, aircraft, chemicals, electrical equipment, artificial fibres and oil. This suggests that decline was not terminal or permanent and that the issues that the British economy faced from 1886 to 1914 were surmountable.

Invisible exports

British industry and agriculture were struggling, but huge profits were being made in the invisible exports of shipping, trading and financial services, and these more than compensated for any deficit in the balance of visible trade.

The City of London was the economic hub of the world and the pound sterling the cornerstone of international trade. British investment abroad was buoyant throughout the period and reached £4000 million in 1913, while the combined foreign investment of France, Germany, Belgium, Holland and the USA was £5500 million. It was clear that in foreign investment Britain led the world and the dividends and profits of this investment flowed back into Britain. British investors found greater opportunities and profit margins in the new and emerging economies of the world and so this is where they invested their capital.

The British merchant navy contributed greatly to the level of invisible exports. In 1900 45% of all cargoes entering French ports and 55% of all cargoes entering US ports were carried by British ships. This gave Britain a key role in world trade and also ensured that profits would flow back into Britain. British shipping generated £100 million per year from 1911 to 1913 – two-thirds of invisible exports – and carried almost all trade between Britain and both Europe and the rest of the world. The only notable exception was the USA, whose ships were more technologically advanced, required fewer sailors and were quicker (they even received lower insurance premiums from Lloyds).

Britain dominated many financial markets in banking and insurance. One notable example was the insurance of shipping, in which Lloyds of London almost had a monopoly. Foreign traders, particularly from emerging economies in Asia, South America, the USA and Africa, who were exporting to Britain would engage a British merchant, use British merchant ships, insure their cargo with a British insurer and finance their venture from a British bank. British banks had branches across the world, from South America to India, Egypt and Hong Kong.

Twice as much capital was being invested abroad as was being invested at home in the years 1911 to 1913. While this helped the invisible balance of trade it can be argued that it was not helping technical innovation on a long-term basis in Britain.

ACTIVITY 2.11

Using the information in this chapter and your own research, address the question below. It is worth noting that you may find differing figures in different sources and you need to use your judgement to decide what is most useful and reliable.

1. To what extent was there a decline in the British economy between:
   - 1873 and 1886
   - 1886 and 1914.
2. What do you think was the key reason why Britain struggled to maintain its previous economic dominance?

Key terms

Protectionism: The policy of a government that 'protects' its country's industry from foreign competition through tariffs, quotas and so on (the opposite of free trade).

Debates over protectionism, tariff reform and free trade

From 1860 other countries defended themselves against British exports with tariffs. As the Great Depression of the 19th century took hold in Britain, questions were raised about whether Britain should take similar actions to defend its own industry. Ever since the repeal of the Corn Laws in the 1840s there had been consensus between the Liberal and Conservative Parties on the idea of following a policy of free trade. This cross-party consensus was ended in 1902 with the Conservatives introducing a one-shilling tariff on imported wheat to help pay for the Boer War. The consensus was then totally destroyed in 1903 by the proposals of the Secretary for the Colonies, Joseph Chamberlain, to introduce **protectionism**.

The argument for free trade

Free trade was popular, as the adoption of the policy had helped drive down food prices. Cheap food was essential to the working classes (notably for the agricultural workers who tended to vote Conservative): they had had no notable increase in wages, while prices fell by about 25% between 1880 and 1900, so their standard of living was directly benefiting from free trade. The middle classes also benefited from the influx of cheap manufactured goods from abroad, notably Germany and the USA.

Free trade, it is argued, encourages a nation's producers, industry and manufactures to become more efficient through competition. Competition from abroad drives down prices, leading to the requirement for innovation to produce goods that are better than the others in the market, and greater efficiency to drive down costs to be able to compete on price. Consumers are the biggest winners in this process, but it also helps improve the nation's businesses and industry.

The argument for protectionism

British agriculture and industry was struggling to compete with the USA, Germany and other countries in terms of price. This meant that Britain was facing an influx of foreign goods. At the same time these same countries had introduced tariffs to protect their industries against British imports. The supposed efficiencies and innovation that free trade was claimed to bring were arguably not evident in British industry. The supporters of protectionism pointed to the impact of free trade being unemployed British workers. Tariffs, it was argued, could raise money to be spent on reforms to help the poor.

Figure 2.6: The popular perception of the need for tariff reform

The events and outcomes of the debate

Joseph Chamberlain proposed a system of imperial preference: this would impose tariffs on goods from outside the British Empire while removing the wheat tariff from imports from the colonies, provided they in turn did not impose tariffs on British goods. Chamberlain saw this as a way to consolidate Britain's political, economic and military ties with its empire, while defending its economic position against Germany and the USA. He argued that the money raised would pay for educational reform and naval defence without the need to raise taxes. He proposed his scheme in May 1903 in a speech in Birmingham, on the same day Balfour (Conservative PM) spoke of scrapping the wheat tariff. The Cabinet split, while Balfour failed to act decisively one way or the other.

Chamberlain resigned in September 1903 and set up the Tariff Reform League. He moved away from his idea of imperial preference and embraced the idea of full protectionism. He continued to criticise Balfour and the split in the Conservative Party worked strongly in the Liberal Party's favour.

Social change

Trade unions and new unionism

In 1888 trade unions had about 750 000 members, representing about 10% of all adult male workers in the economy. The unions had been the reserve of the artisan class, but with the emergence of the 'new' unions, the movement began to include the semi-skilled and unskilled workers. Traditional unions and new model unions had focused on defending the interests of their members (often defending them against the encroachment into their trades from unskilled workers); the 'new' unions were more political and influenced by socialist ideas. New unionism emerged in part because of improving trade conditions, and was most prominent in industries that were starting to grow rapidly.

The unions' growth was also due to the terrible social conditions in which the new union members lived. These social conditions started to diminish people's belief in a system based on laissez-faire economics being able to produce a society for all. This led to the increase in socialism and the call for greater government intervention – these ideas were found within the new unions. They wanted fundamental changes to wealth and income distribution in favour of the low-paid workers. Annie Besant, the leader of matchgirls' strike of 1888, was a member of a socialist party (SDF) and the Fabian Society.

> **Cross-references:** Socialism and Fabianism; The emergence of the Labour Party

New unions were also known as 'general unions' as they admitted anyone within industry, regardless of their job, and charged very low subscriptions. The highly selective traditional trade unions focused on protecting the position of their skilled members from other workers in the industry and charged high subscriptions, beyond the reach of most artisans.

ACTIVITY 2.12

Using details from this whole section prepare for a class debate on whether to introduce tariffs to protect the British economy in the period 1886–1913.

Timeline: Trade unions

Summer 1888	Strike at Bryant and May match factory, women earning on average five shillings (25p) for a 70-hour week. The strike was successful and a matchgirls' union was formed the following year with 800 members.
March 1889	Gas Workers' and General Labourers' Union was created and had 20 000 members by the end of the year.
14 August 1889	Great London Dock Strike, lasted five weeks; by the second week over 100 000 workers were on strike. They demanded 6d. per hour, received support from within Britain and abroad (£30 000 raised by dockers in Australia). The employers gave in to dockers' demands. In the same year, a seamen's union and General Railwayworkers' Union were also formed.
1890s	Employers fought back: the Shipping Federation was created to break the hold of the Dockers' Union. In 1893, the National Free Labour Association provided blackleg labour to the federation and other employers. The Dockers' Union membership fell from 56 000 in 1890 to 23 000 by 1892.

The late 1880s and early 1890s saw a burst of activity from the new unions (see the timeline), and rapid growth in the years 1888–91. The new unions certainly had a significant impact, with the matchgirls and London Dockers succeeding in improving their pay and conditions. The massive numbers that were attracted into new unionism was also significant, as it showed growing political consciousness among the working classes and a greater sense of working-class solidarity, compared with the earlier trade unions that divided the upper sections of the working classes from the rest. In the 1890s, however, the continuing depression weakened the position of the workers and this was a period of retreat for the trade unions.

The timeline highlights that the new unions started to face problems in the 1890s as employers fought back. The continuing economic hardships meant that employers were able to find workers willing to break strikes. This suggests that the unions' aims of uniting the working classes had not fully succeeded. Once the new unions' strikes started to fail and they were unable to offer their members the success of the 1880s, their membership and popularity started to fall. The courts and government actions were also significant in the relative decline of new unionism as the unions failed to find support and key judgements, such as the Taff Vale and Osborne decisions, damaged their power. The trade union movement started to move away from supporting the Liberals in Parliament and towards seeking independent labour representation (see 'The emergence of the Labour Party').

The Taff Vale judgement of 1901 was a major blow to the trade union movement. The Amalgamated Society of Railway Servants (ASRS) had asked for a wage increase for its members, as the Taff Vale Railway Company was making higher profits from the increased demand created by the Boer War. The company refused to accept the unions' right to negotiate and brought in 'blackleg' labour from the National Free Labour Association (set up in 1893 to offer non-union workers to employers to break strikes). An injunction was put in place to stop the union picketing and they also sued the union for damages to compensate for lost revenue during the strike. The case went to the House of Lords and the union suffered a complete defeat and was ordered to pay £23 000 in compensation and costs. This sent shockwaves across the union movement, as it brought into focus the risk of being bankrupted through strike action and seemed to remove the movement's most important weapons of collective bargaining, striking and picketing. Increasingly, the unions sought representation in Parliament, as only here could the decision be overruled.

The Trade Disputes Act brought in by the Liberal Government (based on a Labour Party bill) in 1906 overruled the Taff Vale decision, strengthening the union movement and leading to an increasing number supporting the Labour party, which now had a growing number of MPs.

The Osborne Judgement dealt a blow to the relationship between trade unions and political parties. Walter Osborne, a member of ASRS, objected to paying the political levy that went to the Labour Party. The case went to the House of Lords which ruled in Osborne's favour. This hit the Labour Party hard, but elicited a great deal of sympathy for the Labour Party among trade unionists. The judgement was overturned by the Trade Union Act in 1913 and the majority of trade unionists voted in support of the political levy.

The trade union movement remained divided between moderates (Lib-Labbers) and radicals (socialists); however, almost all were able to find some common ground within the Labour Party.

Syndicalism

The period of 1908 to 1914 saw a wave of strikes and industrial unrest, with numerous large-scale strikes and associated outbreaks of violence between 1910 and 1914. This included the killing of a miner in Tonypandy in 1910 and troops shooting dead two strikers who attacked a train in Llanelli in 1911. There were a number of national strikes, notably the first ever national railway strike in 1911 and then the first ever national transport strike in 1912. In 1914 three of the biggest unions formed an agreement to take sympathetic action if ever one of them went on strike, though this didn't take force due to the outbreak of war. The strike wave of 1910–14 can be seen as having been more 'political' than earlier strikes: arguably, the idea of **syndicalism** was gaining ground.

> **Key terms**
>
> **Syndicalism:** A form of revolutionary socialism that aims to overthrow the capitalist system and replace it with a socialist system based on the trade union movement. Syndicalists looked to the trade unions as the workers' movement that had the power to bring down the employers and, through a general strike, the power to gain control over the economy and society.

Year	Total trade union membership (millions)	Number of stoppages (hundreds)	Number of working days lost in year through strikes (millions)
1908	2.48	3.89	10.79
1909	2.47	4.22	2.69
1910	2.56	5.21	9.87
1911	3.14	8.72	10.16
1912	3.41	8.34	40.89
1913	4.13	14.59	9.8
1914	4.14	9.72	9.88

Table 2.9: Union membership and strikes 1908–14[11]

In 1909 E.J.B. Allen, a former member of the SDF, wrote *Revolutionary Unionism*, which influenced the trade unionist Tom Mann (Mann was one of the leaders of the London Dock Strike of 1889, after which he had gone to Australia. He returned to England in 1910). He became the champion of British syndicalists and aimed to work within existing union structures to unite the workers and bring about a general strike. He and Guy Bowman launched a newspaper, the *Industrial Syndicalist*. Mann also helped set up the Industrial Syndicalist Education League.

Various events highlight the impact and influence of Syndicalism:

- the aggressive tactics of the ASRS and South Wales Miners' Federation in 1911 and 1912
- Mann's role in the creation of the National Transport Workers' Federation in November 1910 (it combined dockers', sailors' and firemen's unions)
- Mann's involvement in the miners' strike in South Wales and the dock strike in Liverpool in 1911
- The arrest and imprisonment of Mann and Bowman following the publication of an article entitled 'Open Letter to British Soldiers', often referred to as the 'Don't Shoot' leaflet: they were sentenced to up to nine months in prison for incitement to mutiny; following support from the trade union movement they were released early
- the triple alliance of the Miners' Federation, the National Union of Railwaymen and the National Transport Workers' Federation, in which they agreed to carry out sympathetic action if one of them went on strike – this was a possible step towards a general strike.

Although there was clear evidence of syndicalist action and involvement in the industrial unrest during 1910–14 their impact is largely dismissed. Syndicalism, it is argued, was only really involved in a minority of the key strikes of this period. It is also dismissed because the majority of union leaders were moderates and only in the strikes in South Wales and Liverpool was there strong evidence of syndicalist involvement. It appears that the syndicalists were trying to harness the anger of grass-roots trade unionists, but were not the root cause stirring it up and this again leads to the conclusion that syndicalism's importance should not be overstated.

The issue of female emancipation

There were two key groups pushing for female emancipation in the years from approximately 1886 to 1914:

- the suffragist movement (The National Society for Women's Suffrage, NSWS) dated back to the 1860s and pushed for reform, working within the law and society's conventions
- the suffragettes (Women's Social and Political Union, WSPU), formed in 1903, took a militant approach.

The impact of these two groups has been hotly disputed by those involved and by historians. Their shared goal gave them some common ground, but their differing approach meant they rarely saw eye to eye. They had a common enemy, the Anti-Suffrage League.

The constitutional approach

The 1884 Reform Bill proved to be a failure, as an amendment proposed by William Woodall for equal franchise for men and women was defeated. It became clear that the prime minister, Gladstone, did not support the amendment; in 1892 he overtly stated that he did not and would not support female franchise on ideological grounds. The suffragists had failed to convert the Liberals at the time of the Reform Bill and in the following years the tactic of getting MPs to pass a **private member's bill** also failed.

Some Liberal Party MPs did support female **suffrage** and the majority of Liberals had voted for female suffrage on various occasions between 1867 and 1886. However, this did not transform into action when the Liberals came into power. The Liberals did, however, give single women the vote in local government elections and allowed women to join school boards – key steps for women into the public domain and towards the franchise.

ACTIVITY 2.13

Research different interpretations of syndicalism and the impact they had. You may want to look at the views of Pelling in *A History of British Trade Unionism* (Pelican, 1987), Laybourn, *A History of British Trade Unionism c.1770–1990* (Alan Sutton, 1992) and Behagg, *Labour and Reform: Working-Class Movements 1815–1914* (Hodder & Stoughton, 1991).

ACTIVITY 2.14

Industrial unrest in the years 1910 to 1914 can be put down to a number of reasons. Carry out research into the importance of the following:

- economic context
- growing working class consciousness
- local issues
- government intervention
- disillusion with the political parties.

Key terms

Private member's bill: A bill put forward by a member of the House of Commons who is not a member of the government.

Suffrage: The right to vote in political elections, also referred to as franchise.

Conservatives seemed to warm to the idea of female enfranchisement after the Reform Act of 1884 (this was possibly motivated by the fact that they hoped middle-class women would vote for them). However, like the Liberals, when the Conservatives came into power they took no action to enfranchise women. The highly important Conservative organisation the Primrose League did, however, cater for women who played a very active role within it. Working- and middle-class women in particular were attracted by the opportunity to brush shoulders with the upper classes. The Primrose League did not support female suffrage, but it did not prevent its members from doing so.

The Liberal suffragists, like the parliamentary party, split over Home Rule. The suffragist movement split in the 1880s over whether to stick to a non-party approach. The NSWS restructured in 1888 and allowed groups affiliated to political parties to join. Suffragists such as Millicent Fawcett and Lydia Becker feared that the non-political organisations would be swamped by the much more numerous political organisations. The situation was made more divisive as the groups linked to the Conservative Primrose League were not allowed to affiliate to other organisations, meaning that almost all political groups joining the NSWS would be Liberal.

With the non-party approach clearly over, Becker and Fawcett created a breakaway group that did not follow the new rules. The bigger group was the one following the new rules (Parliament Street Society) rather than the splinter group, the Great College Street society. The Parliament Street Society then split again over whether to campaign for votes for married women or not. A third group (Women's Franchise League) split off, as it staunchly supported the idea of married women being included in any legislation emancipating women, while the other groups were willing to support measures that did not uphold votes for married women. The movement, originally made up of middle- and upper-class women, grew to include a growing number of working-class women by the end of the 1890s.

The militant approach

In October 1903 Emmeline Pankhurst set up the WSPU because she was dissatisfied with earlier campaigns. The trigger for the creation of the WSPU can be seen as being linked to the death of her husband, Richard Pankhurst. A socialist meeting hall was built in his memory and when the ILP branch that used the hall refused to allow women, Emmeline decided that something different was needed. The WSPU stood out from other groups as it was willing to use confrontation and violence. Frustrated by the lack of progress since the 1860s and the way the Liberal Government had ignored women's demands, the suffragettes became increasingly militant. Force was used against them, for example on 'Black Friday' in 1910 when Ada Wright was assaulted by the police, and they felt empowered by the precedent of militant action leading to extension of the franchise in 1832 and 1867.

The movement attracted a great deal of publicity and a strong reaction. Tactics such as window breaking and arson (including Lloyd George's country house) were often the WSPU's way of responding to political events and proved more shock value than a way of attracting support. The hunger strikes provoked sympathy and the forced feeding created such outrage that it was dropped as a policy by the government, providing a propaganda coup. In June 1913 one of the most significant events in the history of the WSPU took place when, at the Derby horse race, Emily Davison attempted to pin a suffragette rosette on the King's horse and grabbed its reins. The horse fell and Davison received fatal head injuries. The cause now had a martyr and her funeral was attended by huge crowds.

ACTIVITY 2.15

How important was the role of key individuals and groups and how were they affected by developments? Research the following figures:

- Emmeline Pankhurst
- Millicent Garrett Fawcett
- Syvia Pankhurst
- Emily Davison.

There were three phases of action of the WSPU:

	Dates	Actions
Phase 1	May 1906–June 1908	Confronting Parliament and ministers Campaigning at by-elections
Phase 2	June 1908–Jan 1910	Window breaking Technical offences (deliberately committing offences so they would be arrested) Hunger strikes
Phase 3	Nov 1911–Aug 1914	Window breaking on a larger scale Mass hunger strikes Arson attacks Attacks on property

Table 2.10: Militant suffragette action, 1906–14

ACTIVITY 2.16

Complete your own version of Table 2.10. Carry out some research so that you can add:

- examples of each technique
- an evaluation of whether each tactic was or was not effective.

Research different historians' views and representations of the impact of the WSPU and make judgements about their validity.

Campaigns against women's suffrage

While some organised groups campaigned for female suffrage, others campaigned against it: the Anti-Suffrage League had both men's and women's sections (by April 1912 it had over 10 000 members and 235 branches). The League lobbied MPs, used constitutional methods and remained clear of party affiliation. It received support from *The Times* and other national and regional papers. The League offered the following arguments:

- that many women (the league claimed the majority) did not really want the vote
- 'biological' arguments about women being less rational and more emotional and so unfit to vote, as well as being weaker and therefore incapable of fighting to defend the country like men
- the 'separate spheres' argument, that women should remain in the domestic sphere (house, family), which suited them, and men in the public sphere (politics and work), which suited them.

By 1914 only the Labour Party out of the major parties clearly supported female suffrage. There did seem to be growing public support across the social spectrum and within the Liberal and Conservative parties. The militant tactics of the WSPU created anger among some, while actions by the authorities such as the 'Cat and Mouse Act' evoked sympathy for the movement. Above all, the suffragette movement raised the profile of the issue of female suffrage.

ACTIVITY 2.17

Hold a class debate: Did the participation of women in campaigning by the Anti-Suffrage League undermine the League's argument about separate spheres?

The growth of the urban population

The expansion of towns

Rapid urbanisation continued in the period 1886–1914. The ratio of urban to rural population increased to around 3:1 (it had been 1:1 in the 1850s). There were both push and pull factors at work. Employment opportunities in agriculture continued to fall even as the Great Depression came to an end. In the towns and cities, especially in industrial heartlands and key shipping ports, work was available, urban wages were higher than rural ones, and towns and cities offered access to the developing working-class leisure activities. Attitudes towards public health had taken a leap forward when the Public Health Act was passed in 1875, helped by the work of Koch and Pasteur on germ theory.

Town	1881	1901	1921
Bath	52 000	50 000	69 000
Birmingham	546 000	760 000	919 000
Bolton	105 000	168 000	179 000
Bristol	207 000	329 000	377 000
Glasgow	673 000	904 000	1 034 000
Kings Lynn	19 000	20 000	20 000
Liverpool	627 000	685 000	803 000
Manchester	502 000	645 000	730 000
Middlesbrough	55 000	91 000	131 000
Norwich	88 000	112 000	121 000
Oxford	35 000	49 000	57 000
Sheffield	285 000	381 000	491 000
York	50 000	78 000	84 000
UK	34 940 000	41 540 000	47 170 000

Table 2.11: The growth of urban populations[12]

By 1900 towns were becoming more efficient in supplying water services and municipal gas. However, there were often still chronic shortages of accommodation, in particular near the factories. The lack of clear town planning and adequate transport meant that working classes lived in the smoke around the factories in overcrowded conditions. Things were, however, starting to improve.

The Housing of the Working Classes Acts (1890 and 1900) compelled local authorities to demolish unhealthy housing (owners of slum housing could be compelled to sell it to the council) and provide other accommodation for those made homeless. The 1890 act made loans to build new houses easier to obtain, but both acts failed to deal with strategic planning of the expanding towns.

In 1898 Ebenezer Howard published *To-morrow: A Peaceful Path to Real Reform* (later reprinted as *Garden Cities of Tomorrow*). He campaigned for overall town planning and his book offered a vision of towns with no slums and fresh air, but still all the opportunities of other towns. In 1903 Letchworth Garden City was founded following his ideas and his 'three magnets' diagram that kept industry and residential areas separate. It was the first city built with a designated green belt. In 1905 and 1907 competitions for the building of cheap cottages attracted national interest and sponsorship from the *Daily Mail*, which ultimately led to the newspaper launching the Ideal Home Exhibition.

ACTIVITY 2.18

1. Locate all the places in Table 2.11 on a map of Britain and find their current populations.
2. Work out the percentage increase in population for each town or city.
3. Research the key industry or business in each of the these towns and cities in the period 1886–1914.
4. What trends can you see and what conclusions can you draw from the data and from your answers to questions 1 to 3?

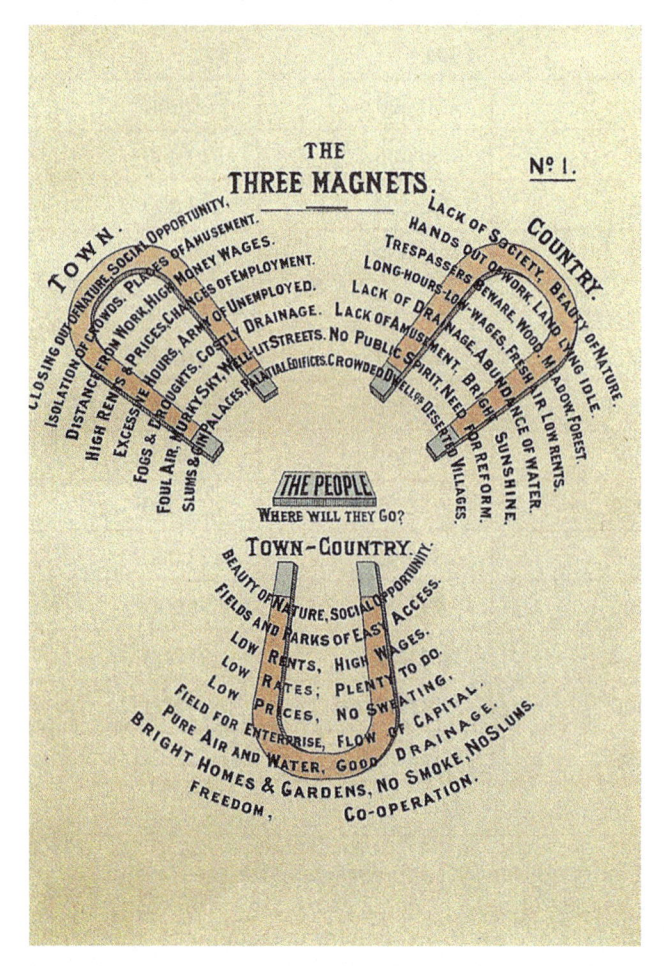

Figure 2.7: Ebenezer Howard's 'Three magnets' diagram

> ### Taking it further
>
> Study Ebenezer Howard's 'Three magnets' diagram in Figure 2.7. Conduct a class debate on the advantages and disadvantages of the ideas put forward by Howard.

The Housing and Town Planning Act (1909) was a Liberal Government measure which allowed local authorities to carry out town planning schemes to avoid piecemeal building. The impact of the act was minimal, as it was not compulsory and was overly complicated, so only one major scheme started before 1914.

The expansion of service industries

The position of British heavy industry and manufacturing was becoming less secure in the years 1886–1914, but in the **service industries** there was clear growth and new developments with the growth of retail, leisure and financial services.

The face of retail was radically altered in this period through the growth of retail chains such as Lipton, Boots and Sainsbury's, which were starting to become a fixture in British high streets. These new retailers were the next step on from the earlier cooperatives.

Key terms

Service industry: A business that does work for a customer, or provides goods, but is not involved in manufacturing.

> **Cross-references:** Self-help (Chapter 1); Problems of British industry and agriculture

The Lipton and Sainsbury shops offered a wider range of goods, including more imported goods, than had previously been available. They catered largely to the middle classes, but with food prices dropping in the last part of the 19th century some of the working classes gained access to this greater range of quality food products. Another new type of shop that developed during this period were the 'penny bazaars' that had a penny price limit on their goods – one such shop was Marks and Spencer.

There was a new focus on consumers, and companies such as Lever Brothers (a soap manufacturer) appealed to them through advertising campaigns. So, despite the industrial and agricultural depression in this period, new retail and related industries (such as advertising) were developing.

> **Taking it further**
>
> Research the following businesses that were growing during this period:
> - Lipton
> - Sainsbury's
> - Marks and Spencer.

Financial services were a vital cornerstone to the British economy. The City of London dominated banking, financial services and insurance markets. The London Stock Exchange offered the opportunity for businessmen to float their companies and raise income through selling shares.

> **Cross-reference:** Invisible exports

There was a marked growth in the leisure industry during this period. Blackpool and other seaside resorts flourished as people went on days out (the introduction of bank holidays in 1871 was significant here) and took short breaks (4 million people visited Blackpool in 1913). The working-class love of watching football thrived: the Football League was founded in 1888 and 100 000 people attended the FA Cup final in 1901. Other major leisure activities for the masses included watching and betting on horse and dog racing.

ACTIVITY 2.19

Carry out further research into the growth of the leisure industry, using the following headings:
- Holidays and resorts
- Sport and betting
- Newspapers (*Daily Mail* and *Daily Mirror*).

Standards of living

The rise of the Labour Party and growth of trade unions (and heightened unrest 1910–14), the new political ideology of 'New Liberalism' (which led to major social reform) and the debate over national efficiency all suggest that there were real issues of inequality and poverty during this period, and there was economic hardship in the Great Depression as British industry struggled to compete. On the other hand, there is strong evidence that falling prices led to improvement in 'real wages' and standards of living. The growth of retail and leisure industries, in particular those aimed at the working classes, would also suggest that standards of living were increasing. Reforms in public health and social reforms will have also have helped improve the standards of living for many.

Evidence of poverty

There were two key surveys into living conditions at the turn of the century, Charles Booth in London and Seebohm Rowntree in York.

Charles Booth's survey of 'Life and Labour in London' (1889) found that:

- 30% of London population lived below the poverty line
- 8.5% lived in 'primary poverty', unable to afford basics of food, clothes and housing
- 22% lived in 'secondary' poverty, making ends meet but at a minimal level (with no chance of saving for a rainy day).

Seebohm Rowntree's survey of York (1899) found that:

- 28% of the population were living in poverty
- poverty was caused by low wages, lack of regular work, ill health, old age and large families.

These two reports significantly undermined traditional attitudes towards poverty, as they demonstrated that 'thrift' and other Victorian remedies for poverty were not possible for almost a third of Britain's population. The message was clear: this group within British society was unable escape the poverty cycle by themselves, and would need government help. If these surveys had been done earlier in century their findings would probably have been even worse.

Evidence of rising standards of living

Various statistics point to rising standards of living in this period. Table 2.12 shows a comparative measure of overall prices in different years, and Table 2.13 shows one economist's estimate of incomes in 1904.

Year	Index
1880–84	100
1885–89	84
1890–94	82
1895–99	76
1900–04	86
1905–09	91
1910–13	102

Table 2.12: The Rousseau price indices for 1880–1913 (a measure used to compare prices from year to year, a lower index number indicates lower prices on average being paid for goods)[13]

Group	Number of people	Estimated total income
Rich	1 250 000	£585 000 000
Comfortable	3 750 000	£245 000 000
Poor	38 000 000	£880 000 000

Table 2.13: Sir Leo Chiozza Money's estimate of incomes in 1904[14]

During this period, even agriculture – the hardest hit and lowest paying of all industries – saw a growth in incomes year on year, which suggests that standards of living were increasing. The standard of living of the middle classes was certainly increasing and their lifestyle was growing closer to that of the upper classes. The upper classes remained very wealthy, though income from landed interests suffered considerably from falling prices.

Overall, Britain was more prosperous than ever, but wealth was very unevenly spread. The middle and upper classes continued to have a high standard of living and for some of the working classes there was a marked increase in their standard of living, but around 30% of the British population remained very poor.

Poverty in itself is hard to measure. It can be seen in absolute (as in Booth's and Rowntree's reports) or comparative terms (the measure most commonly used today). Any analysis of poverty – or of what constitutes an acceptable standard of living – over time must take account of these differences.

Social policies

Government legislation and local initiatives 1886–1905

The Conservative Government (1886–92)
In his Dartford speech in October 1886, Lord Randolph Churchill announced a programme of Tory democracy:

- smallholdings for agricultural labourers
- improvement of housing and public health
- compulsory national insurance
- provision of public amenities, such as public swimming pools, art galleries, museums and parks.

It appeared that the Conservatives were about to embark on a programme of social reform that would consolidate their support among the working classes who supported them in the election. Churchill, however, did not stay long in the Conservative Government and the actual reforms did not match the dynamic nature of his speech. The reforms included:

- The Labourers' Allotment Act (1887) gave local authorities the power acquire land for allotments. However, it was not compulsory for them to do so and no money was provided by central government to fund it, so many local authorities ignored it.
- The Local Government Act (1888) created 62 elected county councils, over 60 borough councils and London County Council, made up of 28 Metropolitan Boroughs. These new councils were responsible for roads and bridges and policing. The act demonstrably improved the quality of local government, but it did not address the key issue of poverty.
- The Fee Grant Act (1891) was a significant step towards improving education for the working classes. It abolished fees for elementary education, making education more accessible for the poorest families and also removing the burden of school fees for any of the working classes who were still having to pay them.
- The Factory Act (1891) raised the minimum age that children could work in factories to 11. This complemented the Fee Grant Act in aiming to ensure that working-class children received an elementary education. The act also introduced a 12-hour maximum working day for women, with 1 hr 30 mins for meals. This was an example of Conservative paternalism: the government stepped in to help women and children who could not help themselves.

The Liberal Government (1892–95)
The Liberal Government in the 1890s was not able to focus on social reform because its majority depended on the support of the Irish Nationalists, so other issues, notably Home Rule, dominated Liberal thinking.

ACTIVITY 2.20

Class discussion: Is what was considered poverty in Britain in 1900 different from what was considered poverty in 1851 and what is considered poverty today?

ACTIVITY 2.21

Using the information in this section and the rest of the chapter, produce a series of diagrams or tables that show two sides to the following debates:

1. Poverty was a significant issue in Britain in 1900.
2. The problem of poverty in Britain was diminishing by 1914.
3. The standard of living of the British people improved between 1886 and 1914.

ACTIVITY 2.22

Compare the achievements of the Conservatives by 1892 with the ideas set out by Churchill in 1886. Were his objectives met? Was anything additional done that was not part of his speech?

There were, however, a couple of significant pieces of legislation:

- The Local Government Act (1894) subdivided the county councils set up in 1888, which were becoming overwhelmed with work, into urban district and rural district councils. These newly created district councils became effective units in managing public health, roads and education. Women, both married and single, could vote and stand for election, which had an impact on the attitudes and policies of local government.
- The Liberal Budget in 1894 introduced death duties on all forms of estate. This could have provided money for social reform, but in the uncertain international situation of the time it was used to fund naval building instead (the Naval Race). This may well have been because any social reform proposals that the Liberals did bring forward were blocked by the House of Lords.

Local initiatives

Much of the social reforms during this period moved responsibility from central government to the recently established local councils, who now administered and often funded initiatives. However, acts passed by governments in Westminster would suddenly affect local action, and local voluntary bodies were often involved, so the outcome of these changes across Britain was variable, to say the least. Local government was often hamstrung by a lack of finances even when there was the will to follow social reforms.

Some councils showed remarkable things could be achieved. Birmingham was held up as the trailblazer in local initiatives in social policy. The driving force behind this was Joseph Chamberlain, both when he was mayor and then later when he was in Parliament. In Birmingham the following took place:

- The council bought the town's two gas companies and its waterworks, and these were expanded and modernised.
- A drainage board was set up to deal with proper disposal of waste water and refuse.
- Pavements and street lighting were extended.
- Six public parks were opened.
- In an improvement scheme, 90 acres of slum were cleared and replaced with quality housing for workers and a retail area.
- New libraries, museums and art galleries were opened.
- Birmingham was recognised as a city in 1889 and was seen as the best example of progressive local government.
- Chamberlain founded Birmingham University in 1900.

There were numerous other examples of local pride and displays of growing significance of local government around the country, such as in the building of town halls. Sheffield Town Hall, for example, was opened in 1897 by Queen Victoria and this is just one of many impressive town halls built in northern England during this period. Another key example of local initiative was the founding of civic universities. In Liverpool in 1892 the Victoria Building was completed, built in distinctive red brick (a term still used today to refer to the universities built around this time). Red-brick universities were also opened in Sheffield (1897, Royal Charter awarded 1905), Leeds (Royal Charter awarded 1904) and Bristol (Royal Charter awarded 1909) among others.

The Conservative and Unionist Government (1895–1905)

The Conservative leaders Salisbury and Balfour had very little conception of the problems of the working classes and believed in self-help. Much was made of Germany's economic strength and productive workforce, but they did not follow the example of Bismarck in Germany, who introduced sickness insurance in 1883 and old-age pensions in 1889. They did, however, take some steps in social policy.

ACTIVITY 2.23

1. Produce a table with all the social reforms in this section that have an element that is voluntary for local authorities.
2. For your local area, or another of your choice, research the degree to which these policies were pursued. The council website and archives at local libraries will be a good place to start.

ACTIVITY 2.24

1. What does the example of Birmingham demonstrate about what could be achieved by local government?
2. How can you explain the fact that not all local authorities followed Birmingham's example?

The controversial Education Act of 1902 made councils responsible for education and gave state funding from the rates to voluntary and church schools. The act also led to the first state grammar schools being set up, offering opportunity for some of the working classes to access secondary education. The new grammar schools modelled themselves on existing private schools, so technical education was still inadequate.

The Unemployed Workmen Act (1905) enabled local committees to provide work for the unemployed, supported entirely by voluntary fundraising. No financial support was given by government, and local authorities were not compelled to fund the scheme, which therefore failed.

The Royal Commission on the Poor Laws was set up in 1905 but took four years to report. The Commission included a small group who wanted to see radical changes to social policy and the Poor Law removed. Most notable were Charles Booth, the future Labour MP George Lansbury and Beatrice Webb, a key member of the Fabian Society. The Commission became bogged down in debates between those who believed in collectivism (that society should collectively fund support for the poor through government intervention, since the poor could not help their poverty, which was due to economic and social structure) and those who believed in individualism (that individuals had responsibility to look after themselves, and the cause of a person's poverty was their own lack of work ethic and morality).

The chair of the Commission, Lord George Hamilton, and 14 other committee members, were all individualists. They compiled the Majority Report, while Webb and her supporters compiled the Minority Report. The Minority Report called for the abolition of the Poor Law and the creation of a Ministry of Labour to help the poor. The Ministry of Labour would organise public work schemes to generate work during economic downturns and run labour exchanges. There would also be a designated government department to look after people who could not work owing to ill health. This report was not enacted, but elements of it can be seen in the Liberal social reforms and in the later creation of the welfare state by the 1945 Labour government.

The Majority Report maintained that the Poor Law was still fit for purpose and that the causes of poverty were largely 'moral', that is, poverty was generally the fault of the poor, although the report did accept there was some contribution from the economic cycle. By the time the report was produced in 1909 the Liberal Government was already tackling elements of poverty, so its impact was not great. The Poor Law, however, stayed in place.

Taxation and welfare reform by 1914

Taxation
Government policy through the 19th century had been based on the idea of minimal state intervention in the economy, in tandem with free trade and the promotion of self-help. Taxation was at a much lower rate than we are used to today, which meant that the poor paid very little tax. However, the low tax rates across all income brackets meant that the government received comparatively little income and therefore did not have the resources to tackle poverty directly (nor did it believe it was its job to do so).

There were, however, major changes taking place at the turn of the century. The cost of the Boer War and the naval race put pressure on government spending. The Boer War led to Balfour's government introducing a small tariff on wheat to raise revenue; the need for money to build dreadnought battleships (a new type, far superior to those already in service) was one of the reasons for Lloyd George's People's Budget (1909). Furthermore, the decision to embark on welfare reform, such as old-age pensions, meant that the government needed much more money than before.

Lloyd George's People's Budget deliberately targeted the rich to pay for these areas of expenditure. Taxes were placed on high incomes (6d. per pound over £5000), mining

ACTIVITY 2.25

1. Look at the Minority Report, which can be found by searching online for 'The Minority Report of the Poor Law Commission'.
2. Compare the recommendations of the report with Liberal social reforms between 1906 and 1914. How similar are the recommendations to the reforms enacted by the Liberal Government?

royalties and, in a very controversial move, a 20% tax on the increased value of land when it was sold. Tax was also raised on cars and petrol; at this point only the rich could afford to drive. The landed interests in particular felt they were being unfairly targeted, especially by the land tax.

> **Cross-reference:** Political crises and constitutional change

Tax was also increased on tobacco and on spirits. This was not on health grounds, as it would be today, but because these items were seen as things that the poor should not be spending money on.

Timeline: Liberal social reform

Year	Reform	Detail
1906	Trade Disputes Act	Reversed the Taff Vale judgement and therefore protected the unions' right to peacefully picket and strike.
1906	Workmen's Compensation Act	Extended compensation for injury at work and disease caused by work to 6 million workers.
1906	Provision of Free School Meals	Local authorities could provide free school meals for poor children (voluntary).
1906	Merchant Shipping Act	Improved conditions for seamen on British ships and imposed these standards on vessels using British ports.
1907	Education Act	Two key components: medical inspections and medical treatment of children. The former was compulsory, but the latter was voluntary, meaning many local authorities did not offer treatment.
1908	Coal Mines Act	Maximum eight-hour day for miners – the first time hours of work for adult males had been regulated.
1908	Children Act	Designed to improve the lives of children. It prevented imprisonment of children under 14 (juvenile courts and remand homes were set up) and banned children from entering pubs or buying cigarettes. The act also aimed to reduce child neglect and abuse.
1909	People's Budget	See the section 'Constitutional Crisis'.
1909	Old Age Pension	Five shillings a week was paid to people over 70, whose incomes were less than £21 per year (there were exclusions for those who had been in prison or had frequently not worked – those who met these criteria were, however, unlikely to live to 70).

Year	Reform	Detail
1909	Labour Exchanges Act	Set up labour exchanges (job centres) across the country making it much easier for the unemployed to find out about local vacancies. Previously, the unemployed would have to go from business to business enquiring about work. By 1913, 430 were established across the country, but the system remained voluntary.
1909	Trade Boards Act	Set up boards to oversee pay and conditions, including setting minimum wages in industries such as tailoring, box-making, lace-making and chain-making. These were 'sweated industries' which traditionally employed large numbers of women and children. This was a step towards a state-set minimum wage.
1910	Housing and Town Planning Act	Introduced compulsory slum clearance and gave powers to councils to build new houses with regulations on banning back-to-back housing and the number of houses per acre (12). There was no government money to fund the house building.
1911	National Insurance Act	National Health Insurance: The principle was that a worker paid into the insurance fund along with their employers and the state (worker 4d., employer 3d. and the state 2d.). If the worker was off ill they would receive 10 shillings a week for up to 13 weeks and entitlement to free medicines and treatment. There were further grants if the illness was TB and there was also a maternity grant. The scheme did not cover spouses or children. It did not cover those earning more than £160 a year. Unemployment Insurance (only applied to certain industries): Workers and employers paid 2½d. each a week, the state 2d. The benefit paid was 7 shillings a week for up to 15 weeks per year.
1911	Shop Act	Gave shop assistants a half day off a week (did not set limit on working hours).
1912	Miners' Minimum Wage Act	Boards created set minimum wages in different districts.
1913	Trade Union Act	Reversed the Osborne Judgement, meaning that trade union members had to opt out of paying into the unions' political fund.

Reasons for social reform

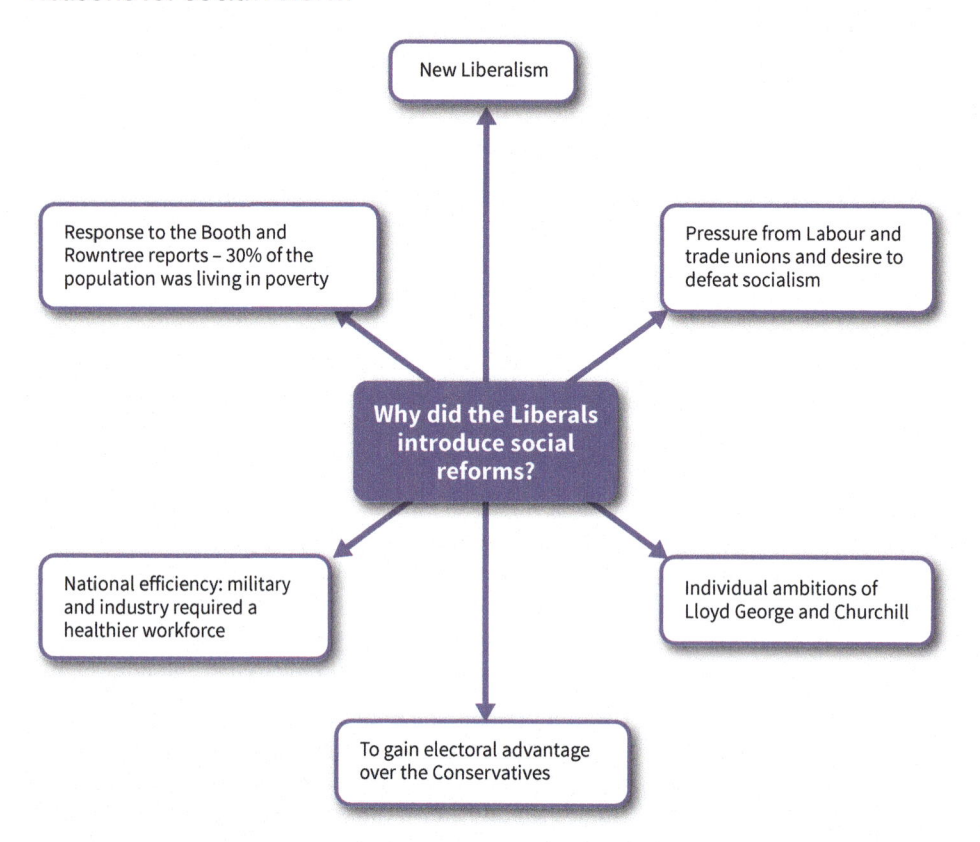

```
                        New Liberalism
                              ↑
Response to the Booth and                    Pressure from Labour and
Rowntree reports – 30% of the                trade unions and desire to
population was living in poverty             defeat socialism
         ↖                                          ↗
              Why did the Liberals
              introduce social
              reforms?
         ↙        ↓          ↘
National efficiency: military              Individual ambitions of
and industry required a                    Lloyd George and Churchill
healthier workforce
                    ↓
              To gain electoral advantage
              over the Conservatives
```

Figure 2.8: Reasons for Liberal social reforms

ACTIVITY 2.26

Split into groups and allocate each group one reason from the diagram in Figure 2.8. Research the significance of your reason and then argue the case for it being the most significant in a whole class debate.

Liberal reforms: positive aspects

One positive aspect of the reforms was help for children. Free school meals, and medical inspections and treatment, were founding principles still present in the British welfare state. The Liberals also built on free elementary education introduced by Balfour in 1902, but also stipulated that 25% of secondary school places had to be free of charge where the school received government funding (this gave rise to the 11+ exam). There were laws to protect children from abuse and neglect, a designated court system and rules preventing the sale of tobacco or alcohol to children – so it can be argued that the Liberal social reforms did much to improve the life chances of poor children in Britain. For the first time, the government was accepting responsibility for looking after the most vulnerable in society.

Liberal social reforms also established important new principles regarding help for workers. Not least of these was that, if required, the government would step in to legislate in support of adult male workers. For example, miners' working days were restricted to eight hours, and shop workers were protected. Important steps were taken to protect people against low pay; for example, 400 000 of the poorest-paid and most vulnerable in society were ensured a reasonable wage by the Trade Boards Act.

The acts in support of the trade unions were significant in ensuring that workers could continue to stand up for themselves in negotiations over pay and conditions, and in preventing the legal system being weighted against the unions.

The National Insurance Act came out of genuine concern over the numbers of deaths from tuberculosis, as well as a desire to improve national efficiency. Lloyd George would have gone further if it had been affordable to, but he had underestimated the costs of pensions. The principle had nevertheless been created that the government's remit included supporting people in times of illness and unemployment, and this would re-emerge as a key foundation of the welfare state in the 20th century.

Figure 2.9: Schoolchildren in the East End of London being served free school meals, c1910

Another important principle was established by the clearing of slums and their replacement with good quality council houses. Although this was not fully realised, Lloyd George would continue his work after the war with homes 'fit for heroes'.

As with the measures to help children, pension provision was a key step towards our modern welfare state and another example of the state taking responsibility to support the most vulnerable in society. The act helped not only the old, but also their families who, before this, would have been supporting their elderly relatives out of their own meagre wages. The fact that the pension was a right paid at the Post Office, not a charity handout was highly significant, not only in the take-up of the pension but also in the dignity it offered. Pensioners were heard to shout 'God bless Lloyd George!' as they went to collect their first payments.

Liberal reforms: criticisms

Many aspects of the bills, however, were not compulsory. Fewer than half the education authorities were providing free school meals in 1914 and the government had to make grants available in 1912 before local authorities would offer children medical treatment, rather than just inspection. The **Children's Charter** was too vague and still did not offer enough protection; for example, children could still be sold alcohol in sealed containers.

With regard to workers, the Trade Disputes and Trade Union Acts were, arguably, simply to please the Labour Party rather than offering genuine support for the trade union movement. Various other acts on specific trades or industries did nothing for people not in those industries. Even for those covered there were glaring loopholes; for example, the Shop Act gave a half-day off a week, but did not set working hours, so employees could be forced to make up the hours elsewhere in the week. The Miners' Minimum Wage Act was mainly designed to reduce industrial unrest and fell short of a national minimum wage. The Trade Boards Act could have gone much further and been a step to a national minimum wage. The labour exchanges could have been compulsory, to ensure all potential jobs were known to the unemployed.

The state's contribution to the National Insurance Act was low. To be truly effective, the figure needed to at least match the amount paid by the employee and employer. The government, it seemed, was making the worker save for sickness and unemployment rather than offering help in times of need. In any case, Booth's and Rowntree's research had shown that 30% of the population were unable to save. Time limits

ACTIVITY 2.27

Create your own summary of Liberal social reform, think about how you will present the information to cover all the different aspects, and both positives and criticisms.

1. What evidence can you find of the continuation of the policies in Liberal social reform in modern Britain? How have the arguments about social policy changed from then to now?
2. Create a diagram that shows links and contrasts to ideas and ideologies from the first two chapters of this book.
3. A key debate about Liberal social reform is whether it was the start of the welfare state. Look at Chapter 4 and look for the connections between Liberal social reform and the creation of the welfare state by the Labour government 1945–51.

Key terms

Children's Charter: A collection of measures of 1906–09 introduced as part of Liberal social reform to help children. It included free school meals, compulsory medical inspections in schools, separate courts for child offenders and a 'free place' system in secondary schools for bright working-class children.

were placed on benefits, there was no cover for children and spouses, and not all trades were covered by unemployment insurance. The act was also criticised by Conservatives as an attack on the right of employees to use their own wages as they chose.

Although the Liberal government took action on slum housing, no money was offered to local authorities to build good quality council houses in their place. So in most cases local authorities did not, and a key aspect of the life of the poor was not improved.

The Labour Party attacked the pension provision as not being enough to live on. It was 5 shillings a week, below the 9 shillings a week paid through health insurance and 7½ shillings a week paid under unemployment insurance. It was known that 30% of the population were unable to save, but the pension provision assumed that people would have savings to help support them. The pension provision can also be criticised as it was not available until people were 70. Given the low life expectancy and poor health of the working classes in Britain, it was argued that this age was much too high.

The condition of Ireland and Anglo-Irish relations

The First Home Rule Bill

The results of the 1885 general election played a major role in Gladstone's decision to introduce the First Home Rule Bill. His Liberal Party lost all 13 of their seats in Ireland; meanwhile, the Irish Party won 86 out of the 103 available seats, many with large majorities. Gladstone suspected that, unless he offered Home Rule, the increasingly confident nationalists would set up their own Irish Parliament. The Liberal majority over the Conservatives was just 86, so Gladstone also needed the support of the Irish MPs to guarantee that legislation was passed by the House of Commons. Added to this, as the election results were being counted, Herbert Gladstone (the prime minister's private secretary, and his son) leaked the news to the press that 'Mr Gladstone has definitely adopted the policy of Home Rule for Ireland'. This revelation, known as the Hawarden Kite, left Gladstone with little choice but to press ahead with his plans.

The key proposals of the Home Rule Bill were:

- Ireland would have an Assembly (a Parliament) with two orders (houses). One order would contain 204 directly elected MPs, and the other order 28 peers and 75 members elected by leading Irish property owners.
- The Irish Parliament would raise its own taxes, and would control services such as education and transport. Ireland would also provide the British Treasury with £3 242 000 towards the empire and the national debt.
- The British Parliament would maintain supreme power – this meant it could choose to abolish the Irish Parliament if it wished. Britain would continue to control defence, foreign policy and issues relating to empire.
- There would no longer be any Irish MPs at Westminster.
- The Lord Lieutenant would be the British representative in Ireland; he was not accountable to either order of Parliament.

The Home Rule plans also included a land purchase scheme, whereby the government would lend tenants money to buy their holdings. This was meant to reassure landowners, who could sell their land and take the money, free from worries about what the Irish Parliament might do to their estates.

Reaction to the bill

Gladstone's decision to introduce the bill had a huge impact on the Liberal Party. Politicians such as Lord Hartington, who were identified as Whigs, believed that Home Rule would lead to the collapse of the British Empire.

Voices from the past

William E. Gladstone (1809–98)

I ask you to show to Europe and to America that we too can face political problems which America twenty years ago faced, and which many countries in Europe have been called upon to face, and have not feared to deal with. I ask that in our own case we should practise, with firm and fearless hand, what we have so often preached – that the concession of local self-government is not the way to sap or impair, but the way to strengthen and consolidate unity. I ask that we should apply to Ireland that happy experience which we gained in England and in Scotland ... that the best and surest foundation we can find to build upon is the foundation afforded by the affections, the convictions, and the will of the nation; and it is thus, by the decree of the Almighty, that we may be enabled to secure at once the social peace, the fame, the power and the permanence of the Empire.[15]

Discussion points:

1. What arguments is Gladstone using to persuade the House of Commons to support Home Rule?
2. Why do you think the Commons was not convinced by these arguments?

> **Cross-reference:** The problems of the Liberal Party

Joseph Chamberlain, who had previously proposed administrative reform as a way of dealing with the Irish Question, feared that Home Rule would lead to the collapse of the Union, especially as it was not linked to a wider review of the status of England, Scotland and Wales. John Bright shared this fear and joined Chamberlain in his opposition to the bill. On 13 March, Chamberlain resigned from the Cabinet.

Meanwhile, the Conservative Party, led by Lord Salisbury, was united in its opposition to Home Rule. While Salisbury's reasons were similar to those of Chamberlain and Hartington, he also knew that the failure of the bill would exacerbate Liberal divisions, potentially leading to a long period of Conservative rule. The most vocal opposition to the bill came from the Irish Protestant minority, who feared a Parliament dominated by Catholic politicians. In Belfast, unionists and nationalists clashed, with 32 deaths. When the House of Commons debated the bill, 93 Liberal MPs joined the Conservatives in voting against. As a result, Gladstone's proposals were defeated by 30 votes. The prime minister resigned and, in the subsequent general election, the Gladstonian Liberals won only 192 seats. Chamberlain's new Liberal Unionist Party had 77 MPs; they supported Salisbury's Conservatives, who, with 316 MPs, formed a new government. The performance of the Irish Party was similar to 1885, but the new prime minister was less reliant on its support than Gladstone had been.

Parnell's decline

The 1886 election was the beginning of Parnell's decline as a significant figure in Irish politics. The growth of radical nationalism in the same year was a threat to his more respectable constitutional approach. A notable example was the 'Plan of Campaign', which involved tenants meeting together to agree an acceptable level of rent. If landlords disagreed, then the tenants would refuse to pay; those who were evicted were then given support from the Land League. Meanwhile, Parnell was the victim of a forger, Richard Pigott, who wrote a series of letters in Parnell's name, expressing support for violent nationalism.

Although the truth emerged, and Parnell received sympathy both from Liberals and Conservatives, his reputation was soon ruined for very different reasons. When Parnell was named in a high-profile divorce case between Captain O'Shea and his wife Kitty, many of his Nonconformist supporters in the Liberal Party were outraged, as was the Irish Catholic Church. 44 of his more conservative MPs, led by Justin McCarthy, left the Party in 1890. Parnell's death in 1891 failed to quell the growing conflict within the Irish Party; for the rest of the decade, it was split between John Redmond's Irish National League, and John Dillon's Irish National Federation.

Speak like a historian

F.S.L. Lyons

F.S.L. Lyons lectured in history at Hull University and Trinity College, Dublin. His works on Parnell and on the Great Famine are among his most acclaimed. Lyons was viewed as a 'revisionist' historian since he refused to blame the British government for the suffering of the Irish people during the famine.

Parnell was neither a creative thinker nor a radical innovator. All the ideas to which at different times he lent the force of his personality – the 'new departure', 'the land for the people', the concept of independent opposition, the vulnerability of an Irish parliamentary party at Westminster, Home Rule itself, had been originated by other men. Furthermore, his notions about the ultimate form an Irish settlement might take tended to be less evolutionary than circular. Indeed, his speeches in 1889 even suggest that, if the divorce suit had not released the avalanche, it was well within the bounds of possibility that he might have ended by accepting from Gladstone a federal solution not very far from that propounded by the ageing Butt and excoriated by the youthful Parnell. To say this is not to minimize his achievement – it is rather to define it more precisely by emphasizing, in a way the Parnell myth conspicuously fails to do, that the greatness of the achievement lay in Parnell's ability to realize his potential despite the limitations inherent in his own character and in the Irish context within which he had to work. The essence of what he did can be summed up in a single sentence. He gave his people back their self-respect.[16]

Discussion points:

1. Summarise Lyons' interpretation in no more than 50 words.
2. Explain two pieces of evidence which support Lyons' view that Parnell 'gave his people back their self-respect'.
3. What was Parnell's greatest achievement? Write one paragraph, explaining your view.

The Second Home Rule Bill

Politics after 1886 was dominated by the Conservative Party, which governed for 16 of the next 19 years. When Gladstone was briefly returned to power in 1892, he used the opportunity to introduce a second Home Rule Bill. Like its predecessor, the bill proposed an Irish Assembly with two houses. Again, the Lord Lieutenant would continue to hold significant executive power; however, the Irish government would be responsible for appointing judges. One-third of Irish revenue would go to the imperial government in Westminster. A major difference from the first bill was that 80 Irish MPs would be elected to the British Parliament. This was an important concession, as Gladstone's Liberals had formed a minority government, and needed the support of the Irish Party to pass legislation. Unlike the 1886 proposals, the Second Home Rule Bill was passed by the House of Commons by a majority of 34. To Gladstone's disappointment, the Conservative-dominated House of Lords rejected the bill by 419 votes to 41. Although Gladstone failed, Home Rule was to remain a Liberal commitment until the outbreak of the First World War.

Conservative policies towards Ireland

Conservative governments between 1886 and 1905 had a dual strategy for governing Ireland. On the one hand, Salisbury claimed that Ireland needed 'twenty years of resolute government'. This was put into practice by Arthur Balfour, Irish Chief Secretary from 1887 to 1891, who supported the shooting of rioters at Mitchelstown in 1887 – three were killed. Balfour's Crimes Act also gave magistrates new powers to deal with rioters. However, his brother and eventual successor as Chief Secretary, Gerald, exemplified the other Conservative approach, which he referred to as 'killing Home Rule with kindness'. This aimed to improve the standard of living for the Irish, in order to eliminate their desire to leave the Union. Also known as 'constructive unionism', it led to a number of reforms:

- Land Purchase Acts were passed in 1887, 1891 and 1896. The 1887 act went further than Gladstone's 1881 legislation, ensuring that leaseholders benefited from fair rent.
- The 1891 act gave £33 million to tenants to buy their land; 55 000 did so. The act established congested district boards to tackle the issue of over-population. The boards helped to move people from over- to under-populated areas. This involved building around 3000 new houses, and giving out over 2 million acres of land.
- The Recess Committee was established in 1895, followed by an Irish Department of Agriculture and Technical Instruction in 1899. Both of these bodies, led by Horace Plunkett, aimed to improve Irish agriculture through the encouragement of new farming methods.
- In 1898, the Local Government (Ireland) Act introduced a system of county councils and district councils, elected by male householders. This shifted control away from Protestant landowners and towards middle-class nationalists.
- The 'Wyndham' Land Purchase Act of 1903 was the creation of the 1902 Irish Land Conference, made up of tenants and landowners. The act gave landlords £12 million to encourage them to sell their land. Tenants would be given all the money they needed to buy land; they would then repay the loans over 68 years, at 3.25% interest. This was lower than their normal rent.

Assessing the 1903 Land Act

By providing large subsidies to encourage landowners to sell, the act undoubtedly had an impact. By 1919, 72% of tenants had bought their land. However, the sale of land remained voluntary, and landless labourers continued to be vulnerable. In terms of its impact on nationalism, the act worked in the Conservatives' favour. William O'Brien, a close friend of Parnell and a participant in the Land Conference, left the Irish Party, as part of a more conciliatory attitude towards the British.

Other nationalists, such as John Dillon, were left with a dilemma. They welcomed the opportunities offered by the act, but realised that improved economic conditions would start to undermine Irish support for Home Rule. Ultimately, their worst fears were unfounded, as constructive unionism ended in 1905. This was partly the result of the Liberal landslide in the 1905 election, but was also caused by growing unionist fears about a proposed scheme to devolve power to the Irish. The creation of the Ulster Unionist Council in 1905, combined with a growing nationalist backlash against constructive unionism, meant that the early years of the new century would continue to be fraught with tension.

The attempts to introduce an Irish Parliament led to an increasingly polarised Ireland by 1900. Unionists were determined to fight against Home Rule, while some nationalists wanted not just Home Rule, but full independence. Despite this division, the British government's third attempt at Home Rule very nearly succeeded. Had it not been for events thousands of miles away in Eastern Europe, the course of Irish history could have been very different.

> ### Hidden voices
>
> #### Arthur Balfour
>
> Born in 1848, Balfour was elected as Conservative MP for Hertford in 1874. Within four years, he had become private secretary to his uncle, Lord Salisbury, who was Disraeli's Foreign Secretary. Along with a group of MPs known as the 'Fourth Party', Balfour played a leading role in the defeat of the 1886 Home Rule Bill. When Salisbury became prime minister in 1886, Balfour became Secretary of State for Scotland, and then for Ireland. He gained a reputation for combining a hard-line approach to rebellion with a genuine desire to improve the economic conditions of the Irish people, calming nationalist feeling in the process.

Developments and opposition

The growth of unionism and nationalism

The introduction of the Home Rule Bill in 1886 was the catalyst for the growth of unionist feeling. There were growing fears that Home Rule would equal 'Rome Rule' – unionists noted that 80 of the 86 Nationalist MPs elected in 1885 were Roman Catholics and that Catholic clergy were heavily involved in the Home Rule campaign. The O'Shea scandal gave the Church an opportunity to reiterate its moral authority, while the writings of nationalist leader Patrick Pearse (who edited the Gaelic League's newspaper) emphasised the close links between Catholicism and nationalism.

During the 19th century, unionist politics had been dominated by landowners, who had significant pockets of support in the south of Ireland. They were supported by the academics of Trinity College Dublin, as well as a thriving working-class unionist movement in the city. However, by 1910, unionism had become a predominantly northern movement, focused on Ulster. As early as 1886 an 'Ulster party' had emerged at Westminster, led by Colonel Edward Saunderson, primarily in response to the fact that Parnell had won 17 of the 33 Ulster seats. The growth of Ulster unionism was partly the result of the decline of southern unionism, a process which began after the widening of the franchise in 1884. New, working-class, southern voters tended to support nationalist politicians.

At the same time, the creation of a wider franchise strengthened the position of unionism in Belfast. Unionist feeling was strong among the factory workers of the city, many of whom had the vote for the first time. Northern workers believed that it was the Union, and particularly free trade within the British Empire, which had brought prosperity to Ulster. Some 50% of Irish industrial jobs were in Ulster; of these, up to 40% were based in Belfast. Between 1850 and 1900, Belfast had the fastest economic growth of any city within the UK – it was widely feared that Home Rule would bring an end to this prosperity.

The rise of Ulster unionism, dominated by the middle and working classes, was also the result of the Land Acts of 1870 and 1881. These acts reduced the influence of southern unionist landowners. The disestablishment of the Anglican Church in Ireland also reduced the influence of southern unionists. Northern Presbyterian unionists and Anglican landowners were now equal in the eyes of the law: 'old hatchets, if not buried, were put aside, in the face of the mutual enemy, Catholic Nationalism'.[17] The new face of unionism was represented by populist MPs such as Tom Sloan, who served as Independent Unionist MP for South Belfast between 1902 and 1910.

As unionist feeling developed in the north, Irish nationalism increased in the south. The late 19th and early 20th centuries were marked by the growth of cultural nationalism, involving the promotion of Irish traditions. The Gaelic Athletic Association (GAA), founded in 1884 by Michael Cusack, encouraged traditional Irish sports such as hurling and Irish football. Its close links to the Catholic Church, the Irish Party, and the Irish National Brotherhood made it much more than simply a sporting organisation. The founding of the Gaelic League in 1893 was an attempt by Eoin MacNeill and Douglas Hyde to publicise Irish literature and preserve the Gaelic language, especially in education. Like the GAA, many of its leading members had militant political views. A notable example is Patrick Pearse, who went on to lead the Easter Rising of 1916. Despite the growth of more militant, cultural nationalism, the moderate Irish Party remained popular. Sinn Fein, the political party established by Arthur Griffith in 1905, received limited support in its campaign for independence. Griffith, who edited the *United Irishman* newspaper, was a relatively isolated figure among those who wished to separate from Britain, mainly because of his support for the monarchy and his rejection of violence.

The Liberal Government (1906)

Henry Campbell-Bannerman became prime minister in 1906, with a majority of 270. Encouraged by the scale of their victory, the new Liberal Government's priority was an ambitious programme of social reform. This made Ireland less prominent an issue than it had been for Gladstone. Nevertheless, improvements were made to Irish higher education – a National University was created in order to educate Catholics, while the Presbyterian Queen's College Belfast became a full university. Another Land Act (in 1909) introduced compulsory purchase by tenants in certain over-populated areas. However, it was not until 1909–10 that Ireland moved up the Liberals' agenda. This followed the constitutional crisis caused by Lloyd George's 'People's Budget' and resulting in the Parliament Act.

> **Cross-reference:** Political crises and constitutional change

The Third Home Rule Bill

The passing of the Parliament Act in 1911 was soon followed by the introduction of another Home Rule Bill. This was no surprise: the removal of the Lords' veto meant Home Rule now had a good chance of success. In addition, the Liberals' tiny majority made them dependent on the parliamentary support of the Irish Party. The Liberals also wished to honour their commitment to Home Rule, which had begun with Gladstone, and which Asquith had reiterated during both election campaigns of 1910. The Third Home Rule Bill was very similar to the second. An Irish Assembly would be established, with 40 members in its upper house and 164 in the lower house; this Parliament would be able to raise taxes; 42 Irish MPs would sit at Westminster and the Lord Lieutenant would play an important administrative role.

Reaction to the bill

The Irish Party, under John Redmond, strongly supported the Bill. However, the bill's lack of provision for Ulster, which would remain part of a self-governing Ireland, led to fierce opposition from both the Conservative Party and unionists. Conservative leader Andrew Bonar Law claimed he could imagine 'no length of resistance to which Ulster can go in which I should not be prepared to support them'.[18] As in 1886 and 1893, Ulster Protestants feared that Ireland under Home Rule would be dominated by the Catholic Church. In addition, Ulster businessmen believed that an Irish Parliament would be influenced by farmers who knew little of northern industry.

In 1912, Ulster Unionists produced a Solemn League and Covenant, outlining their opposition to Home Rule. It was signed by 450 000 people, including Edward Carson, leader of the Irish unionists at Westminster. The formation of the Ulster Volunteer Force (UVF) in 1913 also demonstrated the strength of unionist opposition to Home Rule. This was a paramilitary group, which had recruited and trained up to 100 000 members by the summer of 1914. In an audacious act, it imported 35 000 rifles and 5 million rounds of ammunition from Germany in April 1914. Known as the Larne gun-running incident (after the seaside town where it occurred), it made clear that the government could no longer ignore the claims of Ulster to be exempt from Home Rule.

Figure 2.10: Edward Carson becomes the first person to sign the Solemn League and Covenant

In response to the creation of the UVF, the Irish Volunteers were formed as a nationalist paramilitary force in November 1913. The Volunteers claimed they were established neither to harass the British government nor to combat the UVF, but they were susceptible to pressure from radical elements. The Irish Party was initially critical of the Volunteers, opening the way for the militant IRB to influence the group. By the outbreak of the First World War, the Volunteers had 160 000 members. Their importing of 25 000 rounds of ammunition and 1500 Mauser guns led to intervention by the army; this angered nationalists, who had not forgotten the limited British reaction to the Larne incident.

Voices from the past

The Solemn League and Covenant

Being convinced in our consciences that Home Rule would be disastrous to the material well-being of Ulster as well as the whole of Ireland, subversive of our civil and religious freedom, destructive of our citizenship and perilous to the unity of the Empire, we, whose names are underwritten, men of Ulster, loyal subjects of his Gracious Majesty King George V, humbly relying on the God whom our fathers in days of stress and trial confidently trusted, do hereby pledge ourselves in solemn Covenant throughout this our time of threatened calamity to stand by one another in defending for ourselves and our children our cherished position of equal citizenship in the United Kingdom and in using all means which may be found necessary to defeat the present conspiracy to set up a Home Rule Parliament in Ireland. And in the event of such a Parliament being forced upon us we further solemnly and mutually pledge ourselves to refuse to recognize its authority. In sure confidence that God will defend the right we hereto subscribe our names.

September 1912[19]

Discussion points:

1. What did those who signed the Covenant pledge to do?
2. How do the pledges within the Covenant link to the formation of the UVF?
3. What does the wording of the Covenant suggest about the type of people who wrote and signed it?

Negotiations over Home Rule

Meanwhile, the British government struggled to decide how best to proceed with the bill. Although the Commons supported Asquith's proposals in January 1913, the Lords still had the power to delay a bill. They voted against Home Rule, leaving the Liberals in a difficult situation. It was clear that partition – the splitting of Ireland, allowing parts of Ulster to remain fully within the UK – could increase Conservative and unionist support for the bill. However, Redmond was hostile to the idea, claiming that it would be tantamount to the 'mutilation of the Irish nation'.

The urgency of finding a compromise was heightened by the Curragh mutiny of March 1914. Concerned at the possibility of having to ask Ulster-born British soldiers to fight the UVF, the government issued orders that any soldier who wished to be 'absent from duty' in Ulster would have permission to leave the country. If soldiers chose to stay but then disobeyed instructions, they would be dismissed. However, these orders were conveyed in a confused fashion, and 58 cavalry officers mutinied, claiming they would rather be sacked than take up arms against unionist soldiers. Soon after, the government assured army generals that they would never be asked to use force against Ulster Unionists. This made a political compromise the only alternative.

Speak like a historian

Christine Kinealy

Christine Kinealy is Professor of History at Drew University in the United States, where her specialist subject is 19th-century Ireland. Praised by some academics for shedding new light on the Great Famine, she has also received criticism from others for placing too much blame on the British government.

Between them, Gladstone and Parnell had not only brought significant benefits to Ireland but had laid the foundations for a new phase of nationalism that was organized, confident and determined. Their common failure, however, was in ignoring the views and aspirations of Irish Protestants, despite the fact that they themselves were Protestant. Both men had underestimated the strength of feeling and consequent opposition of Irish and British Protestants. Because they failed to woo or convince them, a schism had emerged in Ireland that proved more difficult to heal than earlier political divisions. The voice of liberal Protestantism shrank and was drowned out by conservative elements.[20]

Discussion points:

1. In your own words, summarise Kinealy's interpretation of Gladstone's and Parnell's policies towards Ireland.
2. Find evidence in this section to support and oppose the interpretation.
3. Do you agree with Kinealy's interpretation? Write a paragraph to explain.

Asquith drafted proposals to allow Irish counties an opt-out system, where they could choose to be exempt from Home Rule for six years. Both the Irish Party and Carson were critical of the idea in public, Carson claiming it was merely a 'stay of execution' for Ulster, and Redmond continuing to oppose any form of partition. However, both men privately accepted that compromise was necessary, and when the issue was discussed at a special conference at Buckingham Palace, it was generally agreed that the four most 'Protestant' counties of Ulster should be excluded from Home Rule. The

ACTIVITY 2.28

Produce two parallel timelines, one summarising political developments in Ireland between 1886 and 1914, and the other summarising Ireland's economic developments during the same period. Annotate your timelines to show the links between the two sets of developments.

status of Tyrone and Fermanagh, also in Ulster but with a more significant Catholic population, was more difficult. The conference broke up without agreement.

Two months later, Archduke Franz Ferdinand was assassinated in Sarajevo, and the First World War began. Home Rule was put to one side and British military decisions made during the war would change the course of Irish history for ever.

Further reading

Bernard Harris' *The Origins of the British Welfare State: Society, State and Social Welfare in England and Wales, 1800–1945* (Basingstoke, Palgrave Macmillan, 2004) is particularly useful for the sections of this chapter examining social policy and social change. Martin Pugh's *The Making of Modern British Politics: 1867–1945* (Oxford, Wiley, 2002) offers a detailed examination of British politics for both this chapter and Chapter 3. Donald Read's *Edwardian England* (London, Harrap, 1972) and Roy Hattersley's *The Edwardians* (London, Abacus, 2006) both offer interesting insights into Britain during this period.

Alan Sykes' *The Rise and Fall of British Liberalism 1776–1988* (Harlow, Longman, 1997) offers a really good, detailed examination of developments of the Liberal Party. Jonathan Parry's *The Rise and Fall of Liberal Government in Victorian Britain* (Yale University Press, 1993) is also useful on this topic. *Irish Home Rule 1867 to 1921* by Alan O'Day (Manchester University Press, 1998) is an accessible summary of the key issues involved in the failure of the three Home Rule bills and the impact of that failure.

Some good biographies include: *Gladstone and the Liberal Party* by Michael Winstanley (London, Routledge, 1990); *The Chamberlains* by Roger Ward (Stroud, Fonthill, 2015); *Radical Joe: A Life of Joseph Chamberlain* by Denis Judd (London, Faber, 1993); and *Charles Stewart Parnell* by F.S. Lyons (Dublin, Gill & Macmillan, 2005)

Practice essay questions

1. 'Standards of living improved in Britain in the years 1902 to 1914.' Explain why you agree or disagree with this view.
2. 'The policies of British governments successfully stabilised the situation in Ireland between 1886 and 1905.' Explain why you agree or disagree with this view.
3. With reference to these extracts and your understanding of the historical context, which of these two extracts provides the more convincing interpretation of New Liberalism.

Extract A

Sykes, *The Rise and Fall of British Liberalism*, p. 271.

New Liberalism built upon the Liberal tradition of liberation, but it … bore more relation to the ideas of Viscount Milner than those of Gladstone. It compounded social with intellectual condescension. The working classes were to be administered, inspected, policed and reformed, their incomes were to be compulsorily reduced for their own good, their choices restricted, but they were not to share power. The elevation of the state, as a positive force, the embodiment of the 'common good' through which the individual achieved his own liberty, provided a rationale for top-down government by bureaucracy. New Liberal ideology did not just build upon traditional Liberalism; it turned it inside out, providing the ideological basis that few understood for reforms that few wanted.[21]

Extract B

Roy Hattersley, *The Edwardians*. London, Abacus, p. 140.

Winston Churchill had become not only a Liberal but a 'new Liberal'. In his two years at the Board of Trade and at least part of his time at the Home Office, he was the main exponent of the 'constructive radicalism' which Gladstone – ten years after his death, still a major influence on Liberal thinking – so deplored. Churchill's enthusiasm for active intervention in the economy was confirmed by his determination to improve wage levels in what was called 'sweated industries' – an initiative that ran at the same time as his proposals to encourage the creation of labour exchanges and one which was more important in terms of the government's acceptance of social responsibilities.[22]

Chapter summary

By the end of this chapter you should have a broad overview of how British politics, economy and society developed in 1886–1914. You should understand:

- the reasons for Conservative dominance to 1905: the problems of the Liberal Party; the importance of the ideologies of socialism, Fabianism and the reasons for the emergence of the Labour Party
- the significance of the ideology of New Liberalism; the causes and consequences of political crises and constitutional change; causes and significance of developments in the Labour Party
- economic developments and their effects: the Great Depression and its aftermath; problems of British industry and agriculture; staples and new industries, foreign competition; invisible exports; significance of debates over protectionism, tariff reform and free trade
- social changes and their effect: significance of trade unions and development and impact of new unionism and syndicalism; significance of the issue of female emancipation; the reasons for, and significance of, the growth of the urban population; causes and consequences of the expansion of service industries; debates over the standards of living
- the impact of social policy legislation and local initiatives; reasons for, and consequences of, changes in taxation and welfare reform by 1914
- effects of the failure of the first two Home Rule bills and the fall of Parnell, and of successive Conservative governments on nationalism and unionism.

Endnotes

[1] Adapted from the Preface to *Joseph Chamberlain, The Radical Programme* (1885), at https://archive.org/details/radicalprogramme00chamiala.

[2] http://labourlist.org/2014/04/keir-hardies-sunshine-of-socialism-speech-full-text.

[3] A. Sykes, *The Rise and Fall of British Liberalism, 1776–1988*. Harlow, Longman, 1997, p. 271.

[4] E.H.H. Green, 'Neutering Mr Balfour's poodle', *Modern History Review*, 7.4, April 1996, p. 26.

[5] S.B. Saul, *The Myth of the Great Depression*. Basingstoke, Macmillan, 1969.

[6] C. Cook and J. Stevenson, *Handbook of Modern British History, 1714–1987*. Harlow, Longman, 1988, p. 194.

[7] D. Taylor, *Mastering Economic and Social History*. Palgrave Macmillan, 1988, p. 424.

[8] Ibid.

[9] P. Mathias, *The First Industrial Nation: An Economic History of Britain, 2nd edition*. London, Methuen and Co. Ltd, 1969, p. 434.

[10] Ibid, p. 457.

[11] D. Peaple and T. Lancaster, *British History for AS Level, 1867–1918*. Ormskirk, Causeway Press, 2000, p. 142.

[12] Mathias, *The First Industrial Nation*, p. 417.

[13] Ibid, p. 421.

[14] H. Perkin, *The Rise of Professional Society: England Since 1880*. London, Routledge, 1989, p. 29.

[15] Gladstone's speech in the House of Commons, introducing the Home Rule Bill, April 1886, quoted in Joseph L. Altholz, *Selected Documents in Irish History*. London, Routledge, 2000.

[16] F.S.L. Lyons, *Charles Stewart Parnell*. Dublin, Gill & Macmillan, 2005, p. 644.

[17] D.G. Boyce and A. O'Day, *The Ulster Crisis*, Basingstoke, Palgrave Macmillan, 2006, p.3.

[18] Bonar Law, quoted in T.P. Coogan, *De Valera: Long Fellow, Long Shadow*. London, Arrow Books, 1993, p. 46.

[19] A. O'Day, and J. Stevenson (eds), *Irish Historical Documents since 1800*, Dublin, Gill & Macmillan, 1992, p. 149.

[20] C. Kinealy, *A New History of Ireland*. Stroud, The History Press, 2008, p. 183.

[21] Sykes, *The Rise and Fall of British Liberalism*, p. 271.

[22] R. Hattersley, *The Edwardians*. London, Abacus, p. 140.

PART 2: THE WORLD WARS AND THEIR LEGACIES: BRITAIN, 1914–64

3 The Great War and its impact, 1914–39

In this chapter we will examine the many different ways in which the First World War affected the years that followed. In particular, we will look into:

- the impact of war on British politics: coalition government; the decline of the Liberals; the position of the Conservatives and the influence of Labour
- political developments in the interwar years: electoral reform; Conservative and Labour governments; the National Government; the abdication crisis and the emergence of radical political movements
- economic changes: increased state involvement during wartime; problems of the staple industries and mines; the General Strike, government finances and the gold standard; the Depression; economic realignment
- social developments: changes in the role of women during and after war; the working classes; regional divisions; changing attitudes in the 1920s and the 'hungry thirties'; the growth of the media
- social policies: legislation and reforms in housing; education and welfare
- Ireland and Anglo-Irish relations: the Easter Rising; the Anglo-Irish War; the Government of Ireland Act and the Anglo-Irish Treaty; divided Ireland before the Second World War.

The impact of war on British politics

Coalition government

Timeline: First World War

June 1914	Assassination of Franz Ferdinand
Aug 1914	Germany invades Belgium; Britain enters the war; First British involvement in the fighting as the BEF fight Germans at Mons
Sept 1914	Battle of Marne ends German hopes of a quick victory over France
Oct–Nov 1914	Battle of Ypres, casualties are very high, but the BEF prevents the Germans reaching Channel ports
March–Sept 1915	Stalemate on the Western Front, large numbers of British and Dominion volunteer troops sent to fight in Europe
March–Dec 1915	Disastrous Gallipoli campaign sees 250 000 injured and 43 000 killed. –No relief for Russia via the Black Sea; Bulgaria joins the Central Powers
May 1915	A German torpedo attack sinks the liner *Lusitania* killing 1000 passengers
July–Nov 1916	The Battle of the Somme: 21 000 British killed on the first day of fighting; total killed and wounded – France 194 000, Britain 418 000, Germany 650 000
Jan 1917	Unrestricted submarine warfare leads to the convoy system
April 1917	USA enters the war
June–Nov 1917	Battle of Passchendaele: Britain suffers 324 000 casualties for a 4-mile advance
Dec 1917	Russia leaves the war following the Bolshevik Revolution
March–May 1918	German spring offensive
Aug–Nov 1918	Allied counter-offensive
11 Nov 1918	Armistice signed

ACTIVITY 3.1

On an A3 sheet of paper draw a timeline across the middle. Below the line plot the military events of the war, above the line plot the political events in Britain. Use the rest of this section to help you.

Figure 3.1: Recruitment poster featuring Lord Kitchener

The reasons the coalition was formed

At the start of war, the Liberal prime minister attempted to run the war effort using the existing structures of party government. The only addition to the existing government was Lord Kitchener as minister of war. He was given the job based on his reputation as a commander in the Sudan and in the Boer War. He was, however, not prepared for the logistical challenges and demands of the adoption of trench warfare and he struggled with the political demands of his job – in part because he was unfamiliar with civilian methods and having others question him and his ideas. The Liberals were perhaps not the natural party of government in wartime and they would stay in sole power for less than a year.

On 14 May 1915 the 'Shell Scandal' broke, when an article in *The Times* stated that the War Office had failed to supply the front lines with enough shells to bombard enemy positions. The next day news broke of the resignation of Admiral Sir John Fisher, who had clashed with Winston Churchill (First Lord of the Admiralty) over the disastrous Gallipoli campaign. The combination of these two events called into question the competency of the Liberals to run the war effort. The response was the setting up of a **coalition** government. At the time Asquith was completely unaware that he was bringing to an end the last solely Liberal government for at least a century.

Member	Post	Party
H.H. Asquith	Prime minister	Liberal
R. McKenna	Chancellor of the Exchequer	Liberal
Sir E. Grey	Foreign Secretary	Liberal
Lord Kitchener	Secretary of State for War	—
A. Bonar Law	Secretary of State for the Colonies	Conservative
D. Lloyd George	Minister of munitions	Liberal
A Henderson	President of the Board of Education	Labour
A. Balfour	First Lord of the Admiralty	Conservative
A. Chamberlain	Secretary of State for India	Conservative
J. O'Connor	Solicitor general for Ireland	Irish Nationalists

Table 3.1: Selected list of members of the Coalition Government in 1915

The coalition was mainly made up of Liberals and Conservatives, but also included a representative each from the Labour Party and Irish Nationalist so it encompassed all of the parties in the House of Commons. The benefit of this was that the government could claim to stand for the whole country and political efforts would be concentrated

> ### Key terms
>
> **Coalition**: An alliance between different political parties which is temporary. Parties form a coalition when no party has a clear majority, or at a time of national emergency when party differences are put to one side. A Coalition government was created in May 1915.

ACTIVITY 3.2

Read the profiles of Asquith and Lloyd George in Voices from the past. Then research and write profiles of the other cabinet members in Table 3.1.

Voices from the past

Herbert H. Asquith (1852–1928)

Herbert H. Asquith was prime minister from 1908 to 1916. In this period he oversaw a constitutional crisis, key social reforms and took Britain to war. He is often overshadowed by other ministers from his government, notably Lloyd George and Churchill, who did more to drive social reform. He was a highly intelligent man from a middle-class family in Yorkshire. He won a scholarship to Oxford University and became a barrister before entering politics. He was a notable imperialist, against female emancipation, a free trade advocate and pro-Home Rule.

He was removed from power in 1916 by a combination of Lloyd George and the Conservative Party, following the conflict over conscription. He was perceived as a weak war leader and this has affected his legacy. He has also been criticised for his actions in dealing with the challenges to the Liberal Government 1910–14. Historian Adelman, while criticising Asquith over industrial relations and female franchise, is positive about his handling of the constitutional crisis (see Further reading). Roy Jenkins, one of Asquith's biographers, argues his cautious approach was well suited to the political problems of the time.

David Lloyd George (1863–1945)

David Lloyd George, who became prime minister in 1916 – and was certainly one of the most brilliant and controversial that Britain has ever seen – was renowned for his intellect and quick (and at times cruel) wit. He was not short of confidence, declaring himself a genius when he was 13. His controversial People's Budget led to the constitutional crisis of 1909–11 and he manoeuvred to replace Asquith in 1916.

In 1911, John Burns, a cabinet colleague, famously said, 'Lloyd George's conscience is as good as new for he has never used it.' He was renowned for his unconventional methods and energy. The historical controversy over Lloyd George is about whether he was doing all he could to ensure the future of the Liberal Party, or whether he was responsible for its destruction as he sought personal power.

on the national good and not on political point-scoring. The idea was now the parties would have collective responsibility for Britain's war effort and, therefore, share in any successes and failures. This should have led to positive working relationships as they worked towards a common goal, leaving to one side the political difference and bickering of peace time.

The cabinet was made up of 23 men – too many, as a large cabinet meant that decision-making was slow and cumbersome. The inter-party unity that the coalition was supposed to create was also lacking: the Conservatives were bitter about the Liberals maintaining the key cabinet posts, and their overriding view was that Asquith was not up to the job of being a wartime leader. This view spread to some members of the Liberal Party as the war continued and some of the most difficult decisions had not been made. It was from within the Liberal Party that the biggest challenge to Asquith's leadership would come. Lloyd George had been a major success as minister of munitions and became more powerful in July 1916 when he took over as minister for war (Lord Kitchener drowned when the cruiser *HMS Hampshire*, on which he was a passenger, hit a mine en route to Russia).

The decline of the Liberals

Wartime splits

Figure 3.2: Herbert H. Asquith

Figure 3.3: David Lloyd George

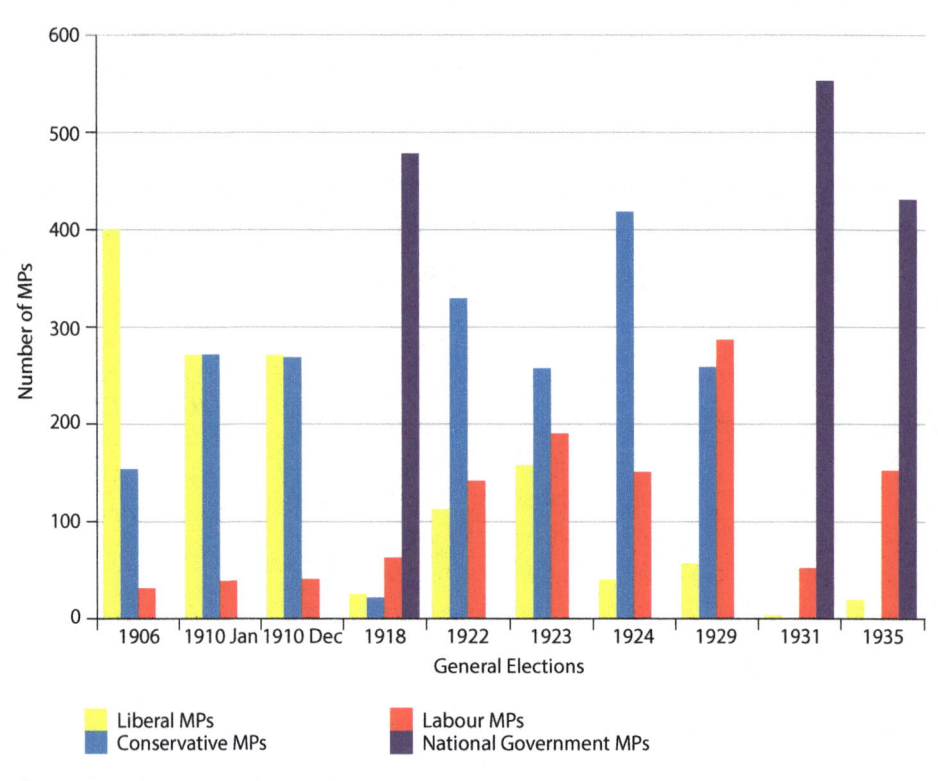

Thematic link: The importance of political ideas and ideologies

Figure 3.4: Election results 1906–1935.
(Breakdown during periods of National Government: *Coalition Government 1918*: Coalition Conservatives 335, Coalition Liberals 133, Coalition Labour 10. *National Government 1931*: Conservatives 473, National Liberals 68, National Labour 13. *National Government 1935*: Conservatives 388, National Liberals 33, National Labour 13)

Following the Shell Crisis in May 1915 Lloyd George became minister for munitions, a role in which he excelled, and he achieved almost instant results. He used his position to push for greater control over Britain's war effort. He believed that **conscription** was essential to ensure that the British war effort matched the demands of the war of attrition on the Western Front. Conscription, however, did not fit with the Liberal ideology of individual freedom and Asquith and other Liberals were very uncomfortable with the idea.

In October 1915 the 'Derby Scheme' was introduced as a compromise: it categorised the adult male population by age, occupation and marital status – a clear precursor to conscription. The scheme, however, did nothing to counter the declining number of recruits (55 000 per month, down from a height of 450 000 in September 1914). Asquith was backed into a corner and, with great reluctance, introduced conscription in January 1916. John Simon, the Liberal Home Secretary, resigned over this divisive issue.

On becoming minister for war in July 1916, Lloyd George focused on the issue of the creation of a smaller war cabinet. John Simon's resignation had started a split, which became clearer over this issue, exacerbated by the battle of the Somme and its mounting casualty list. Lloyd George had already had discussions behind closed doors with the Conservative leadership by the time his call for a small war cabinet reached its climax in December 1916 (see the timeline).

> **Key terms**
>
> **Conscription:** The calling up of people for compulsory military service.

Timeline: Small war cabinet, 1916

1 December	Lloyd George calls for a small war cabinet, with himself as chair and with the other members being Conservative leader Bonar Law and Edward Carson (Ulster Unionist). Asquith was not to sit in the war cabinet, but would remain as prime minister. Asquith rejects the idea and is furious with Lloyd George
3 December	Asquith accepts the plan after the Conservatives threaten to resign from the government
4 December	*The Times* publishes an article on the formation of the small war cabinet. The article is highly critical of Asquith, portraying him as a weak leader who needs to be sidelined. The article causes Asquith to change his mind and reject the idea of the small war cabinet. Lloyd George and Conservative cabinet members resign.
5 December	Asquith resigns.
6 December	A conference of party Leaders (Asquith, Lloyd George, Bonar Law, Balfour and Henderson) takes place at Buckingham Palace. The position of prime minister is offered to Conservative leader Bonar Law, he refuses unless Asquith will serve under him (which he will not).
7 December	The Conservatives are willing to serve under Lloyd George who is offered the position and accepts. Asquith and other Liberal ministers resign, but Lloyd George has the support of 100 Liberal MPs, the Conservatives and the Labour Party. Asquith and the other Liberals move into opposition. The Liberals are now split.

Was Lloyd George responsible for the split? Should Asquith have taken the blame? Asquith could have seen off the split by accepting the war cabinet or serving under Bonar Law. What is certain is that this was a key turning point in British political history. Lloyd George proved to be a very able war leader and showed that effective leadership was not necessarily built on a strong party base. The Liberal Party never recovered from the split and, arguably, the very heart of Liberal ideology suffered greatly under the test of war.

George Dangerfield's *Strange Death of Liberal England* (1935)

There is an argument that the Liberal Party was already in terminal decline, even before the war. This may at first seem counter-intuitive, given that the Liberal Party was in government, had survived and triumphed in a constitutional crisis and brought about a radical set of social reforms. The idea of the 'strange death of Liberal England' was presented by the historian George Dangerfield. In this he argued that there had been a four-fronted attack on the Liberals and liberalism in the years 1910–1914 and that the Liberal Party would have been torn apart if war had not broken out. He therefore argues that the Liberal Party collapse was already assured before the First World War and not caused by the Lloyd George/Asquith split during it. The four attacks he identified were:

1. the attack of 'die-hard' Tories on Liberal social and tax policies, which reached their height with the rejection of the People's Budget
2. the attack by unionists (in both England and Ireland itself) on the Liberal Government over Irish Home Rule
3. the attack of the trade unions, driven by syndicalist ideas, on the government in the form of the strike wave of 1910–13.
4. the attack on the Liberal government by militant suffragettes.

> **Cross-references:** Chapter 2: Politics and the constitution 1906–14; Social change; The condition of Ireland and Anglo-Irish relations

According to Dangerfield, if the war had not intervened there would have been:

- a general strike and a bitter struggle over a national living wage
- civil war in Ireland with Ulster Unionists who were willing to fight Home Rule, apparently with the support of key Conservatives
- further unrest and chaos from increasing suffragette militancy; the Liberal Party would have been stuck between effective response and their liberal principles, having already had their ministers attacked and Lloyd George's home burned to the ground.
- a sustained effort to delay all Liberal acts in the House of Lords.

Dangerfield's book is a compelling read and full of interesting argument but his thesis has been widely attacked and dismissed by historians. Criticisms of Dangerfield's theories include the following:

- He underestimates the impact of New Liberalism and how it reinvigorated support for Liberalism and Liberal ideology.
- He fails to acknowledge the many achievements of the Liberal government during 1910–14. They dealt effectively with the House of Lords, the suffragette challenge and the Irish problem. The threat of syndicalism is seen by many as having been exaggerated by Dangerfield.
- He does not examine the problems of the other political parties. Conservatism was arguably having a crisis of its own, being seen as out of touch with much of the electorate, and the Labour Party was failing to make progress.
- He gives the date of the 'death' of the Liberal Party incorrectly, ignoring the events both during and after the war that contributed to the Liberal split and failure to reunite.
- The rise of organised Labour (trade unions) and their affiliation to the Labour Party, along with the changing franchise, were responsible for Liberal decline.

ACTIVITY 3.3

Using Chapter 2 and other sources examine the significance of each of Dangerfield's 'attacks' on the Liberal Party and liberalism. You could record your findings in a table like this:

Attack on Liberalism	Evidence of significant threat	Evidence there was no significant threat	Conclusion on how damaging the challenge was to the Liberal Party
House of Lords			
Unionist attack on Home Rule			
Revolutionary syndicalism			
Militant suffragettes			

Speak like a historian

Michael Bentley

Dr Michael Bentley is a lecturer at Sheffield University who has written on aspects of 19th- and 20th-century British political history, including works on the Liberal Party. He has also published on historiography. His most famous work is *Politics Without Democracy, 1815–1914*.

Liberal language after 1913 developed an optimistic future-tense about the 1915 election. Of course, the mood required qualification. The Labour party refused to renew an electoral pact; and since the Osborne judgement had been reversed by the Liberals in 1913 the possibility of Labour fielding 100, even 150 candidates at the next election called for consideration. Some Conservative resurgence in by-elections also brought its daunting moments, but, seen overall, the performance of the government in by-elections since 1910 seemed no worse than one might expect. Besides, unless it wanted to jump back into the hole it had dug itself over food taxes, the Tory party could talk only about Ireland … The Conservative party would find itself with an awkward manifesto to write. To foresee in the 1915 election a Liberal victory, followed by a renewed understanding with part or all of the Labour party, seemed neither stupid nor unrealistic. Nor does anything in the historical record make nonsense of the contention.[1]

Discussion points:

1. What is Bentley's view of the state of the Liberal Party in 1913–14?
2. How could this view be used to counter George Dangerfield?
3. How valid is the view?

The position of the Conservatives and the influence of Labour

The Conservative Party

In the short term it can it can be argued that the outbreak of war in 1914 denied the Conservatives an electoral victory (in 1915) and a return to government for the first time in a decade. There is, however, no certainty about this and historians are divided over the issue.

In the middle of the war the emergence of Lloyd George as the dominant figure in British politics can also be seen to have pushed the Conservative Party into the role of supporting cast until 1922. The period 1906–22 is the longest without a Conservative government in modern British history.

The war can also be seen as the springboard for the Conservative dominance of the interwar period. The Liberals split during the war and ultimately became a spent force in British politics. In the period 1915–45 there were only two periods – nine months during the first Labour Government of 1924 and two years during the second Labour Government of 1929–31 – when the Conservatives were not part of the government.

The formation of the wartime coalition government gave ministerial experience to men such as Bonar Law, Balfour and Austen Chamberlain. It helped restore Conservative confidence and unity following the bitter divisions over tariff reform and the constitutional crisis. The demands of war can also be seen to have better fitted with Conservative ideology than with that of the other political parties. They were better suited to dealing with issues such as conscription (as they did not have the same reservations as the Liberals over individual freedom when it came to defending Britain) and had been advocating anti-German policy and more armaments before the war broke out.

The Conservatives remained united during the war, while the Liberals remained splintered with no general election to pull them back together. Bonar Law, who had not had the full support of the Conservative backbenches before Asquith's downfall, gained their support through his part in bringing down Asquith, who was deeply unpopular with the Conservative backbenchers.

The fact that the Conservatives had the majority in the government at the end of the war meant that, although Lloyd George was 'the man who won the war', the Conservatives could justifiably claim to be the party that won the war. This association with Britain's success certainly helped them going into the postwar era.

The Labour Party

There is a historical debate here. Some claim that the Labour Party was already on the rise before the war and in a position to overtake the Liberals as the main alternative to the Conservatives. Others see the war as key in transforming the position of the Labour Party, along with the extension of the franchise in 1918, which led to Labour emerging as a potential party of government.

> **Thematic link:** The emergence and development of the Labour Party

Arguably, the Labour Party came of age during the war, gained experience in government, assured the country that it placed national interest over sectional concerns, and emerged as one of the two major parties following the Liberal Party split. The Labour Party itself had been split by the war: Ramsay MacDonald resigned his position in the party and, with some other members of the Labour Party, went into opposition; while the bulk of the party joined the coalition government in 1915. Unlike the Liberals, the split in the Labour Party was not a disaster and the party reunited

---

ACTIVITY 3.4

Look back at the graph in Figure 3.4 and examine the performance of the Conservative and Labour parties in the elections from 1910 to 1924.

Research details about the shifting share of the vote they received. What impact did the war have on the electoral support for:

a. the Conservative Party?
b. the Labour Party?

in 1917. None of the Labour members who had refused to join the government were disciplined or dismissed from the party. Those outside the government did not campaign against the war, but rather for the prevention of future wars and protection of soldiers' families from poverty. Even the Labour MPs in the government were never fully supportive of all aspects of government policy.

The 'Doormat Incident' of 1917 took the Labour Party out of the government and led to it establishing its own distinct identity. Arthur Henderson was left 'on the doormat' while the war cabinet (of which he was part) discussed his behaviour towards Russia. Henderson, who was already frustrated by Lloyd George's attitude towards him, decided that this was the final straw.

Following years in the Liberals' shadow, Henderson wanted to establish the Labour Party as a fully independent and distinct party. The job of drawing up a new constitution was given to Sidney Webb. The constitution contained:

- a commitment to full employment and a national minimum wage for men and women
- development of unemployment insurance and abolition of the Poor Law
- development of health services
- commitment to common ownership through nationalisation of key industries, including the major staple industries – this was the famous Clause IV of the Labour constitution seen as the 'socialist' commitment at the heart of Labour ideology; this commitment remained in place until the leadership of Tony Blair in the 1990s; it was vague enough to not alienate middle-class or non-socialist union support
- special taxes on capital and high incomes
- abolition of conscription
- freedom for Ireland and India.

Thematic link: The increased role of the state in wartime

The Labour Party was now ideologically clearly distinct from the Liberals. State intervention in the economy was now increasingly accepted, thanks to Liberal social reform and to the unprecedented level of government intervention in the economy during the war. This helped the Labour Party, as it showed that state intervention could bring benefits and should not necessarily be feared.

Thematic link: Electoral reform

The biggest factor affecting the future of the Labour Party's future, however, was undoubtedly the Representation of the People Act of 1918. Only once all the working classes were enfranchised could the Labour Party hope to become a major party.

Political developments in the interwar years

Electoral reform

Two important acts extended the franchise during this period: the Representation of the People Act (1918) introduced votes for all men over 21 and all women over 30. Elections were to be held on a single day. The '**first past the post**' system was to be maintained, and **proportional representation (PR)** was not introduced. The Representation of the People Act (1928) introduced votes for all men and women over 21. However, peers, lunatics and felons (criminals) were excluded from voting.

ACTIVITY 3.5

Research the 'Doormat Incident'. Was Arthur Henderson badly treated?

ACTIVITY 3.6

Which party gained more from the war, Labour or the Conservatives?

Were the gains of the two parties due to their own actions, to the failures of the Liberals, or to circumstance?

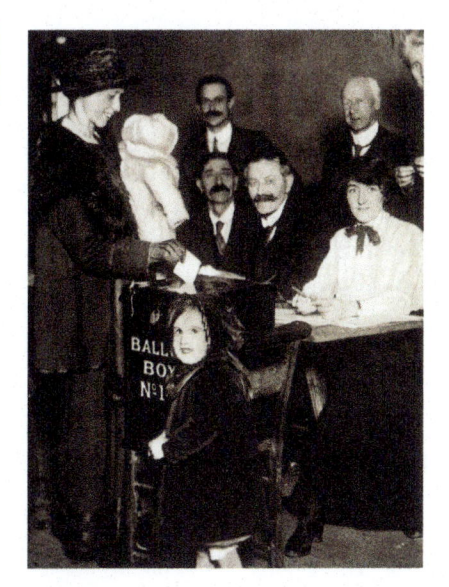

Figure 3.5: Women voting in 1918

A/AS Level History for AQA: Challenge and Transformation: Britain, c1851–1964

Key terms

First past the post: A voting system whereby the country is divided into constituencies (areas) of roughly equal population. The votes at an election are counted for the constituency and the candidate with the most votes wins the seat. This system can lead to the number of seats a party wins not reflecting their share of the overall vote across the country.

Proportional representation (PR): A voting system whereby the number of seats a party receives is based on the share of the vote the party received. For example, if a party wins 25% of the vote then they gain 25% of the seats in Parliament.

Thematic link: How did democracy and political organisations develop in Britain?

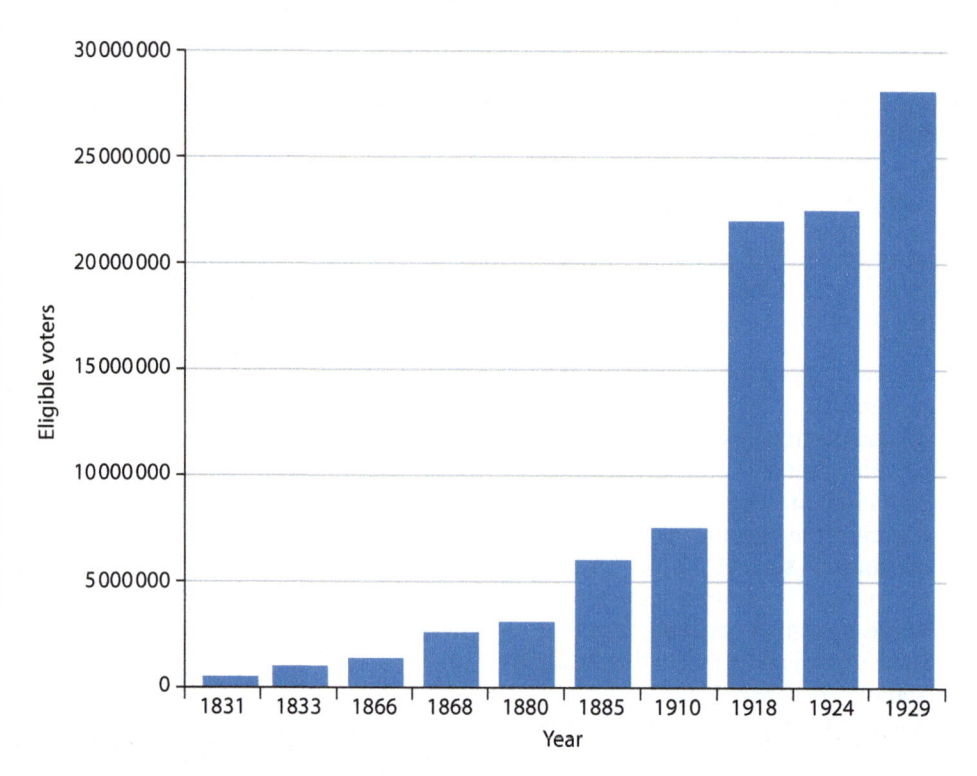

Figure 3.6: The growth of the electorate, 1831–1929

Taking it further

Examine the details of the 1918 Representation of the People Act. Using the views of academic historians, consider its electoral impact.

Reasons for electoral reform

Historians still debate whether full democracy was established in Britain by the Representation of the People Acts of 1918 or 1928. The 1918 act enfranchised far more people than any previous reform acts and can be said to have established genuine democracy. Women had been granted the vote in general elections for the first time, albeit not on exactly the same terms as men. Two explanations are offered for this:

- At the time it was argued that women took longer to mature than men and would not be able to make rational decisions until they were 30.
- The age difference prevented women becoming the majority of the electorate.

The unequal treatment of women, however it is explained, is one of the reasons why Britain can be considered not to have been a full democracy in 1918. Further reasons include the continuation of plural voting, and the fact that the deposit a candidate had to pay to stand in a general election was the considerable sum of £150. This would disadvantage individuals and parties that were less affluent.

There were also problems with the 'first past the post' system:

- In 1918, Lloyd George and his supporters gained 47% of the vote and almost 70% of seats.
- In 1922, the Conservatives gained 37% of the vote and 330 seats; Labour gained 29.4% of vote and 142 seats; the Liberals (combining the 3 groups) gained 29.1% of vote and 116 seats.
- In 1929 Labour won fewer votes than the Conservatives, but more seats.

This issue could perhaps have been addressed, as the Reform Act in 1918 made it possible for PR to be trialled in 100 constituencies, but this was never done.

There were further issues inhibiting full democracy. The unelected monarchy and members of the House of Lords still held office on grounds of heredity, and Members of Parliament, once elected, could:

- switch party
- break a promise they had made in the election
- support policies that their constituents opposed.

Unless an MP was convicted of a crime, he could not be removed until the next election.

However, for democracy to function it is not necessary for representatives to directly reflect the views of their electorate, or their manifesto. The MP is chosen to represent the people of the constituency and in doing this the electorate are demonstrating their trust in the MP to make the right decisions. At the next election they can vote for or against the MP, depending on whether this has been fulfilled.

Conservative and Labour governments

The Coalition government (1918–1922)

The first election following the First World War is often referred to as the '**coupon election**'. The Progressive Centre Alliance of Lloyd George's Liberals and the Conservatives swept to power with an overwhelming majority. The alliance was in part a marriage of convenience (working with Lloyd George would give the Conservatives a greater chance of winning power and vice versa), in part based on fear of the potential spread of socialism and in part to keep the Labour Party out of power.

> **Thematic link:** The roles of key individuals and groups and how they were affected by developments

After the 1918 election, the Coalition government had, in effect, a majority of 322 and the opposition parties' leaderships were stripped of key figures: Asquith (Liberal), Henderson, MacDonald and Snowden (all Labour) all lost their seats. The alliance between the Lloyd George Liberals and the Conservatives was never properly formalised after the election (despite a petition from 95 Conservatives to do so in early 1920). Lloyd George was seen in 1918 as 'the man who won the war' but would go on to become 'the prime minister without a party'.

The fall of Lloyd George is a complex issue with many causes, including economic depression, the failure of reconstruction, problems in Ireland, foreign policy failings, and the honours scandal, which was rooted in the fact that he lacked a political base following the Liberal split. The Conservatives increasingly saw Lloyd George as a liability as numerous problems mounted. Interestingly, though, he outlasted any other Allied leader from the First World War.

ACTIVITY 3.7

Research the positive and negative impacts of the electoral reforms of 1918 and 1928 on:

- the Labour Party
- the Liberal Party
- the Conservative Party.

Key terms

Coupon election: In the general election of 1918 there was a coalition between the Conservatives and the Liberals who chose, after the **Maurice debate**, to follow Lloyd George. The term 'coupon' was a reference to a letter every official coalition candidate had received, signed by Bonar Law and Lloyd George, endorsing them and ensuring they were not opposed by another Conservative or Lloyd George Liberal. Of those with a 'coupon', 88% were elected.

Maurice debate: In May 1918 General Sir Frederick Maurice, the retired Director of Military Operations, accused Lloyd George of misleading the House of Commons about the numbers of British troops in France and his promises to hold troops back in Britain. Asquith called for a select committee to look into the allegations and was supported by 98 Liberal MPs. This incident led to the Liberals splitting into two completely separate parliamentary parties.

ACTIVITY 3.8

David Lloyd George was a brilliant, dynamic and highly controversial political figure. A.J.P. Taylor called him 'the most inspired and creative statesman of the twentieth century'. Kenneth Morgan described him as having both 'pioneered a new role for the interventionist state' and 'aroused distrust and hostility to an astonishing degree'.

Research the impact Lloyd George had on British politics from 1906 to 1922. Look at historians' views and draw your own conclusions.

Issue	Events/actions
Demobilisation of troops	Policy of demobilisation based on profession (key workers being demobbed first) caused controversy and led to strong protests from rank-and-file troops. The policy was abandoned and replaced by 'first in, first out'. This was more popular and over 4 million men were demobbed by the end of the summer 1919. The majority went straight into work.
Strikes and industrial unrest	As government price controls were removed there was an increase in the cost of living, which sparked a series of strikes (more than 2000 in 1919 and 1920). Cross-reference: Economic changes
Government income and expenditure.	The level of government expenditure rose dramatically in 1921 as the economy slumped and 2 million people were out of work.
Tensions between Lloyd George and the Conservatives	Bonar Law, who had always been key in ensuring that Lloyd George had a clear idea of Conservative backbench opinion and that the coalition functioned effectively, resigned due to ill health in 1921. His replacement Austen Chamberlain was ill-suited to the role, which required excellent communication. Splits developed over the partition of Ireland Cross-reference: Ireland and Anglo-Irish relations The 'honours scandal' seriously damaged Lloyd George: he was accused of selling honours to raise money (the Liberals under his control were very short of funds).

Table 3.2: The record of the Conservative-Liberal coalition 1918–22

Baldwin's Conservative Government (1923)

Following the resignation of Lloyd George there was a difficult decision for the King. Who should follow the interim Bonar Law to become prime minister; Lord Curzon or Stanley Baldwin? The King chose the unknown Baldwin, possibly because it was no longer acceptable to have a prime minister in the House of Lords.

The first solely Conservative government since 1906 had a fairly strong majority but was divided with some 'Lloyd George Conservatives', led by Austen Chamberlain, being outside the fold. The government faced a difficult time in foreign policy, but had some success at home, for example Neville Chamberlain's housing legislation.

ACTIVITY 3.9

Using the information in this section and your own further reading:

1. Create your own version of Table 3.2 and add an extra column evaluating the level of success of the coalition Government
2. Evaluate the extent to which Lloyd George was 'a prisoner' of the Conservatives
3. Explain why the coalition ended.

Thematic link: Social policies

Stanley Baldwin called a general election. He wished to bring in protectionist tariffs as a way of addressing unemployment and, given his change of policy, he needed a **mandate** from the electorate. The calling of the election was typical of 'honest' Stanley Baldwin, who was a stark contrast, in many ways, to Lloyd George. Baldwin may well have been hoping to outmanoeuvre Lloyd George in order to prevent him from uniting with some of the Tories in a Centre Party.

The Liberals united under Asquith in defence of free trade, but the 159 seats they won made it clear that they were no longer the main opposition, since Labour won 191.

Key terms

Mandate: The political authority to carry out a policy, or set of policies, based on legitimate political power. For example, a political party that wins a clear majority in the House of Commons is said to have a mandate from the electorate to carry out its manifesto.

Baldwin had won the most seats (258), but not a majority and, therefore, had lost the debate over tariffs, which were strongly opposed by the Liberals and Labour.

MacDonald's Labour government (1924)

The first Labour government was a **minority government**, so it was not well placed to bring in major reforms. The Labour leader Ramsay MacDonald was determined to show that Labour could be trusted. However, wild fears spread that Labour might:

- disband Britain's armed forces
- end the empire
- take drastic action against the rich and opponents in the civil service
- outlaw religion
- confiscate post office savings
- emancipate women, bringing in an era of free love and destroying the family unit.

MacDonald chose a cabinet that would help show that Labour was fit to govern and need not be feared by the middle classes. Key figures in the government were:

- MacDonald, who served as both prime minister and Foreign Secretary (he certainly had successes in foreign policy, most notably the instigation of Dawes plan)
- Arthur Henderson as Home Secretary (who had cabinet experience from the War Coalition Government)
- Philip Snowden as Chancellor of the Exchequer (who was teetotal and essentially believed borrowing was evil).

The cabinet also included former Liberals and former Conservatives. The fact that eight ministers in this first Labour Government had been to the top English public schools suggests that this was not going to be a radical government. Some have argued that its ministers were dominated by civil servants as they learnt the ropes. Perhaps MacDonald had a deliberate policy of giving positions to people who would struggle with their particular department, to ensure that things continued pretty much as they had before Labour came to power – or perhaps he was simply not good at appointing his cabinet ministers.

The fall of the Labour Government was largely due to what became known as the Campbell case. J.R. Campbell, a man with a good war record, was serving as acting editor for a communist newspaper, *Workers' Weekly*. The paper published an article calling for troops not to fire on 'fellow workers'.[2] Campbell was charged with inciting mutiny, but under pressure from its backbenchers the Labour government overturned the charges. Asquith called for a committee of inquiry, while the Conservatives accused Labour of interfering in the course of justice. MacDonald could have allowed the committee to be set up, but instead he resigned (having apologised to the House for misleading them, though he had not).

During the election the *Daily Mail* printed a forged letter claiming to be from the Bolshevik, Grigory Zinoviev, calling on the Communists in Britain to follow instructions from Russia and set up a revolution. This suggestion that Communists had strong influence over the Labour Party certainly had an impact: the *Daily Mail* believed it had won 100 seats for the Conservatives with the article.

Baldwin's second Conservative Government (1924–29)

Baldwin's decisive victory in the election gave him a strong position at the head of a unified Conservative Party. He did, however, appear determined to offer stability rather than a strong legislative programme. His only controversial action was appointing Winston Churchill as Chancellor of the Exchequer.

> **Key terms**
>
> **Minority government:** A party that does not have over 50% of the seats in the House of Commons so has to rely on the support of other parties to pass legislation and is vulnerable to a vote of 'no confidence'.

Thematic link: Social policies

The government was not responsible for wide-ranging reform, but did introduce some changes to pensions and unemployment insurance. The Local Government Act (1929) was probably its biggest reform. Other major innovations were:

- The Central Electricity Board was appointed by the minister of transport and made responsible for the distribution of electricity. It was responsible for the setting up the National Grid and connecting the power stations. This was completed in 1933.
- The British Broadcasting Company (BBC) became a public corporation. The BBC offered a wide range of programmes with news, educational programmes, cultural programmes (the BBC had its own symphony orchestra) and light entertainment programmes. Some politicians adapted well to the new medium (Baldwin and Snowden) while some did not (Lloyd George and MacDonald).

Thematic link: Economic developments

Baldwin's government was possibly most defined by the General Strike. Overall, it failed to solve (or do anything about) unemployment, which was the biggest issue of the day. There were also other economic problems, such as the decline of coal and a balance of payments crisis. Of the whole government only Neville Chamberlain seemed to offer any energy and inspiration. Baldwin set out to be the opposite of the dynamic Lloyd George and he seemed to succeed.

During the 1929 Election, the Conservatives promised more of the same with their 'Safety first' slogan. The Labour Party's campaign focused on the controversial 1927 Trade Disputes Act and the need to reverse it. By far the most radical manifesto came from the Liberals under the title 'We Can Conquer Unemployment'. It was based on the new economic ideas of John Maynard Keynes and William Beveridge. The Labour Party won the most seats, but failed to get a majority.

Cross-references: The National Government; The Beveridge Report (Chapter 4)

MacDonald's Labour government (from 1929)

The second Labour government, weakened by being a minority administration, faced an enormous challenge when the Wall Street Crash plunged the world into an economic crisis. The government was unable to cope with the rising unemployment rate and took little action to solve the problem. They could have done more, since the Liberals suggested – and would have supported – a massive spending programme, as did the then junior member of the Labour cabinet, Sir Oswald Mosley. He consulted Keynes, who suggested bringing in subsidies for farmers (to reduce food imports), government control of banks, lending money to industry, paying old age pensions from 60, and raising the school leaving age from 14 to 16. Mosley had some support in the Labour Party, but the leadership rejected his ideas and he left to found the British Union of Fascists.

Thematic link: Radical movements: the British Union of Fascists

The government suffered a financial crisis, so they proposed severe pay cuts for public sector workers (including a 20% pay cut for teachers) and, following a large withdrawal of gold from the country by foreign investors, a vote in the cabinet over a 10% cut in unemployment benefit. The motion was highly divisive and passed by 11 votes to nine. MacDonald saw this as too narrow a margin and offered to resign. To the amazement of the party, he allowed himself to be persuaded to stay on as prime minister of what became known as the National Government. This led to accusations that he had betrayed the Labour Party, and even to caricatures of him as 'Lucifer of the Left'. His actions were, however, celebrated by the right-wing press.

> Thematic link: The Depression

The National Government

The cabinet of the National Government started with ten members, four each from Labour and the Conservatives, and two from the Liberal Party. It carried out emergency measures to deal with the government deficit, including slashing government expenditure and a 10% cut in unemployment benefit (which led to the Invergordon Mutiny over salary cuts in September 1931). A prime concern was the falling value of the pound and maintaining **the gold standard**. The government failed on this but the consequences of devaluation were not as dire as feared.

> Thematic link: Economic developments

Keynesian economics

The interwar governments largely stuck to classical economic ideas and policies. Unemployment was a huge challenge, especially when the Depression took hold. The economist John Maynard Keynes devised a new approach to government finances. **Keynesian economics** called for the following measures:

- Public works schemes should be initiated to reduce unemployment, improve the country's infrastructure and pump more money into the economy.
- The extra money should come from extra government borrowing, something that all parties tried to minimise. Keynes argued that this extra money would be subject to a 'multiplier effect': it would stimulate further economic growth.
- These projects would kick-start the economy and could be used to avoid the dips of the traditional trade cycle. Furthermore, the economic growth they would create would generate extra taxes for the government, reduce government expenditure on unemployment benefit and, therefore, pay for itself.
- Overall, Keynes called for much greater control by the government. A key aim was full employment, so that there was no wasteful spare capacity in the economy. Where the free market failed to provide employment and growth the government should step in.

These ideas were used to some degree by the National Government in the 1930s to address unemployment, but were not fully adopted in the interwar years. These ideas did have some success in the USA with Roosevelt's 'New Deal' and also with major public-work schemes in Mussolini's Italy and Hitler's Germany.

There was a good working relationship between MacDonald and Baldwin (who was well suited to the role of deputy prime minister) and the National Government was not dissolved following the financial crisis. A way forward including tariffs was agreed and a general election was held in October 1931. The National Government won a majority,

Key terms

The gold standard: The value of gold. When a government links the value of their currency to the gold standard, it is saying that it will exchange money for a specified amount of gold. The value of gold is set at a fixed price and the government agrees to buy and sell gold at this price, so it must have sufficient gold reserves to back the amount of money in circulation at any given time.

Keynesian economics: The philosophy developed by economist John Maynard Keynes, who encouraged government intervention in order to manage demand, create economic growth and redistribute wealth within society.

but it was now essentially a Conservative government. Many blamed the Labour Party for the latest financial crisis and for unemployment, though much of this was beyond their control.

The tariffs policy (10% on imported goods) brought in extra income for the government, removing the need for tax rises and helped British producers in the home market. Meanwhile, the lower value of the pound helped British exporters. Local authorities took advantage of the low interest rates (2%) and borrowed money to build houses, creating work and demand in the economy. It can be argued that the recovery that took place was not due to government action but rather to the economy naturally readjusting.

The National Government evidently retained electoral support, since it won a clear majority in the 1935 election. MacDonald, however, lost his seat and was suffering with poor health. He was replaced as prime minister by Baldwin, who was himself replaced by Neville Chamberlain in 1937. Standards of living rose somewhat, but unemployment remained a problem.

The abdication crisis and the emergence of radical political movements

The abdication

Edward VIII became King in January 1936 at the age of 41. He was unmarried and a popular but controversial character. He was good-looking and a renowned womaniser, with little regard for the conventions of court and his position in the royal family. Both his father and the politicians of the 1920s and 1930s had been concerned about his becoming king. The fact that he had served in the army and frequently visited the front lines during the First World War made him popular, as did his genuine concern over the impact of poverty on the British people.

Edward was having an affair with a married American woman, Wallis Simpson. She had been divorced once already and was granted a divorce from her second husband in October 1936. The issue was kept out of the press, but once it became clear that Edward intended to marry Wallis, Prime Minister Baldwin decided that he had to act.

Baldwin told Edward that the marriage would be highly unpopular with the people and his government. The Archbishop of Canterbury Dr Lang opposed the marriage on the grounds that Edward, as the head of the Church of England, should not marry a divorcee. Some of the press, including *The Times*, attacked the idea of the marriage and popular opinion seemed to be against it.

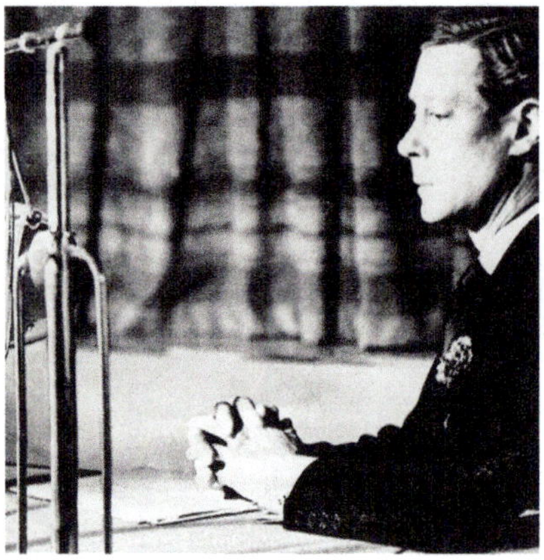

There was some support for the marriage from Churchill and Mosley as well as the *Daily Mail*. Edward offered the compromise of the wedding taking place, but his new wife remaining a private citizen and not queen. This idea was rejected by Baldwin and the cabinet. Edward abdicated and was succeeded by his brother, who became George VI. Edward did marry Mrs Simpson and the couple spent the majority of the rest of their lives in exile from Britain. Baldwin was seen as having handled the issue effectively and his reputation was restored. This did not last, however, as he and others would see their reputations shattered by the policy of appeasement and Britain's lack of adequate defences when war broke out in 1939.

The abdication crisis highlighted the deeply conservative moral attitudes of the establishment and political elites. While there was a degree of support in the popular press for the King and his right to choose his own wife, Baldwin and others saw this as a matter on which they were willing to resign. There was greater acceptance of divorce and remarriage within Britain and, therefore, the elites could be seen as being old-fashioned in their attitudes. The fact that as king Edward would be head of the Church of England was significant, as it meant that the head of the Church was not fully in line with the Church's teaching at that time.

ACTIVITY 3.10

1. Research the careers of Stanley Baldwin and Ramsay MacDonald.
2. Assess the view of C.L. Mowat that in the 1920s and 1930s Britain was led by 'pygmies and second class brains'. Is this a reasonable conclusion when Baldwin is compared with Lloyd George? Use the views of contemporaries and academics to help you.
3. Then hold a class debate: Did MacDonald betray the Labour party?

ACTIVITY 3.11

Using the film *The King's Speech* as stimulus material, consider why there was an abdication crisis and the nature of Baldwin's role in preventing a full constitutional crisis.

Figure 3.7: King Edward VIII preparing to broadcast his abdication speech, 11 December 1936

The abdication did have an impact on the position of the monarchy, but it is hard to judge what would have happened if it had not taken place. It is important to note that the private lives of the current royal family are still the focus of great press interest and royal marriages still of constitutional significance (Charles and Camilla, for example). The clash between public duty and private choice made Edward's decision a significant one – and his unique position as King led to the pressure to make a decision that otherwise would not seem to fully fit with societal belief at the time.

Radical movements: the British Union of Fascists (BUF)

The first Fascist movement in Britain was the British Fascisti, set up in 1923 by Rotha Lintorn-Orman. This movement was highly anti-communist but not massively distinct from the right wing of the Conservative Party. Its membership peaked at about 3000 in 1926, but then fell to around 300 by 1932.

In 1931 Sir Oswald Mosley left the Labour Party when it rejected his economic plans and formed the 'New Party'. A year later he formed the British Union of Fascists (BUF) following a visit to Rome, where he was inspired by the apparent achievements of Mussolini and his Fascist Party in Italy and wanted to emulate them in Britain. He believed he could get rid of unemployment and poverty through public work schemes, tariffs and government control. Mosley's personality cult ensured his domination of the party and clearly echoed Hitler's and Mussolini's.

The party had its own version of the Nazi brown shirts (the BUF's were black) and was known as the Defence Force. They marched and paraded in jackboots, gave fascist salutes and often used violence, especially against communist opponents. This was demonstrated in the 'Battle of Cable Street' in 1936, when a BUF march ended in violent clashes with anti-fascist demonstrators; and on other occasions too the Defence Force attacked crowds that opposed them. The Public Order Act of 1936 was specifically targeted at the BUF giving the police powers to ban their marches.

The party was highly anti-communist and also anti-Semitic – like the Nazis in Germany. It had a peak membership of 50 000 in 1934 and also received backing from the press most, notably the *Daily Mail* and its owner Lord Rothermere. The *Daily Mail* ran pro-BUF headlines and stories including 'Hurrah for the Blackshirts'[3] and claimed that the future of Britain depended on the BUF and 'the same directness of purpose and energy of method as Hitler and Mussolini'.[4] The party, however, remained a paramilitary organisation and did not contest the 1935 general election, so it is hard to judge the level of support it enjoyed. By the end of 1936 membership had fallen to 5000, suggesting the BUF was of little significance.

There is some suggestion that Mosley and the BUF had the support of King Edward VIII. The historian Pugh has gone as far as to suggest that, during the abdication crisis, Edward might have decided to keep his throne, dismiss Baldwin and appoint Mosley as prime minister. This does not appear to be fully convincing, as the BUF had no democratic mandate and Edward's priority was his marriage rather than political influence.

The BUF's popularity was certainly affected by increasingly anti-Nazi feeling in Britain and during the war it was banned and Mosley arrested.

Radical movements: the communists

The Bolshevik Revolution in Russia in 1917 inspired communist movements across the world and Britain was no exception. The fear of communism was always much greater than the actual size and influence of the communist movement. Two Communist MPs were elected in 1922 (Battersea North and Motherwell), but they made little impact. The membership of the Communist Party peaked at around 17 000 in 1926, when the General Strike took place and there was some Communist influence in some of the trade unions.

ACTIVITY 3.12

Research the career of Oswald Mosley:

- his time in the Conservative Party and crossing the floor
- his rise in the Labour Party and conversion to Keynesian economics
- the creation of the New Party and the BUF
- the influence of Mussolini and Hitler on his ideas
- the degrees to which he was pro-violence and anti-Semitic.

ACTIVITY 3.13

1. Research the BUF and the Communist Party in Britain. Look at their involvement in events in the 1920s and 1930s and investigate the level of support they enjoyed.
2. Evaluate the appeal of these radical political groups, but also their relative failure in Britain compared with their success in other European countries such as Germany and Italy.

During the Depression in the 1930s when the Communists might have hoped for more influence, since their claims that capitalism would fail appeared justified, their support actually fell. There were about 5000 members, no MPs and the actions of the movement were restricted to soup kitchens, hunger marches and confronting the fascist movement. The Communist Party of Great Britain were portrayed by some Conservatives and some of press as being a threat, but they were never strong enough to bear this out.

Economic changes

Increased state involvement during wartime

Traditionally, British economics adopted a laissez-faire approach: the economy was dominated by private enterprise. Increased state intervention was generally unwelcome, but during the First World War there was a substantial change in attitudes to state intervention in the economy.

The need to supply the army with men and materials was so pressing that civilians would experience shortages and this could lead to inflation. The free market would not be relied on to manage the economy, so a system of controls came into place. There had been a movement towards state control before the war, as the government had intervened in industrial disputes, and the state sector was still small, but growing rapidly: it doubled in the years 1900 to 1914.

New Liberalism could be argued to have changed attitudes towards state intervention, but there may simply have been a reaction to the socio-economic conditions in Britain before the First World War, rather than a shift in attitudes towards the state's relationship with the economy.

> **Thematic link: The reasons the coalition was formed**

Munitions

The Shell Scandal in 1915 highlighted problems and inefficiencies in the War Office and how these had hampered production. The War Office had, for example, been using over 2500 different companies. The new Ministry of Munitions, run by David Lloyd George, had a series of new powers set out in the Munitions of War Act of July 1915:

- Labour: further loss of engineers to the armed forces was blocked and trade unions had to accepted some semi-skilled and unskilled workers working in jobs previously reserved for skilled workers.
- Profits: munitions factories profits were limited to prewar level plus one-fifth.
- Workplaces: the state built 250 new shell factories, which it controlled.
- Supply: the ministry controlled the buying and supplying of goods to munitions factories and its new shell factories.
- Capital: the ministry had £2000 million to fund its expansion of production.

The Ministry of Munitions was an undoubted success. The level of control meant that prices were kept down; the ministry was, in effect, controlling 20 000 munitions factories and the supply chain, so the system was highly centralised and efficient. The methods created and standards set in the munitions industry spread into the rest of the economy, which started to adopt:

- standards of health and safety and employee welfare provision
- new technology (such as electricity) and mass production techniques
- research and development into producing more advanced weapons.

The Ministry of Munitions was certainly revolutionary during the war, but it was clearly a war industry meeting a specific need. Interestingly, the action around munitions spread beyond simply the industry itself, with several pubs in munition-producing areas being nationalised – giving the government greater control on opening times and the strength of drinks. Its impact after the war was limited.

Railways

The railways were essential to the movement of troops and supplies, and were therefore very quickly brought under government control. The 130 railway companies were guaranteed the maintenance of prewar profit levels. The move to state control, however, highlighted prewar inefficiencies and a great deal of duplication in the existing system. Although wartime experience did not lead to nationalisation, it did result in structural change after the war. By 1921 there were only four railway companies and an act of Parliament restricted the industry to this number.

Shipping

Britain was the world leader in shipbuilding at the outbreak of war, producing almost 60% of the world tonnage of ships launched in 1909–13. There was therefore no immediate need for government intervention. In 1916 the Ministry of Shipping was set up and in 1917 there was a crisis as almost 4 million tons of British shipping was sunk by German U-boats in the spring, a threat countered by the convoy system. The majority of merchant shipping was under military control. War losses sparked a construction boom, but in the longer term Britain would never recover its prewar dominance.

Mining

Coal mining was essential to war production and was put under government control. The need for control was highlighted by a strike in 1915 that threatened production levels. At this point the government introduced price controls and limited export licences. The level of control was increased further in 1917 with the appointment of a Coal Controller. His brief was to ensure the required coal supply and he succeeded, although the mines remained in private hands – in effect, there was nationalisation. There were, however, problems:

- Industrial relations remained poor.
- The industry did not modernise or introduce technical innovations.
- The legacy of the war would prove to be over-capacity and high wages.

Rationing

Britain had been highly dependent on cheap imports in the years leading up to the war, so when supplies were disrupted there were shortages, which started in late 1916. The Ministry of Food was set up in December 1916, but resisted the idea of food rationing. Lord Rhondda took over the ministry in June 1917. He introduced a subsidy to reduce bread prices and some voluntary rationing schemes were introduced. Full-blown national rationing began in 1918, affecting: sugar (until November 1920), meat (until November 1919), butter (lasted into 1920), jam and margarine.

Agriculture

The government was aware of the reliance on imported goods and moved to increase food production:

- The Cultivation Production Act (1917) meant that farmers could be forced to change land use from pasture (animal keeping) to arable (crop growing), though this was rarely used.
- The Corn Production Act (1917) guaranteed a minimum price for grain and introduced a minimum wage for agricultural labourers.

Key terms

Autarky: Economic self-sufficiency and independence.

Extra labour was made available through the Women's Land Army, soldiers and even prisoners of war. There were tensions; the farm lobby was very powerful in the Conservative Party, so the government aimed to persuade rather than force change, which was therefore slower than it might have been. The war also saw the introduction of daylight saving. This adjustment of the clocks was designed to help agricultural production.

Problems of the staple industries and mines

British staple industries faced a number of problems during the years 1918–1935.

- World trade had grown by at least 25% per decade between 1830 and 1914, but it only grew 8.5% in 1920s and fell by 35% between 1929 and 1933. Staple industries in Britain generally exported about 40% of their output (80% in cotton). Staple industries, therefore, were really badly hit by the international downturn from 1929 to 1935 (see Tables 3.3 and 3.4).
- British staple industries were also hit by other countries finding alternative sources (or increasing their own production) of staple goods, while British exports were not available. This meant that key export markets were lost and foreign competition increased.
- British staple industries had not modernised at the same rate as those in other countries. Techniques and machinery used in Britain were now outdated and required more manpower than did industry in other countries, notably the USA. A key example is in the mining industry where a great deal of British coal continued to be cut by hand.
- Because Britain was on the gold standard until 1931, the value of the pound, and therefore the price of British exports, was kept artificially high, and imports artificially low.
- Other countries were increasingly protecting their own industries with tariffs while, until 1931, Britain remained staunchly free trade. There was also a move towards achieving **autarky** by certain countries, notably Italy in the 1920s and Germany in the 1930s. Russia also largely withdrew from international trade after the Revolution of 1917, cutting out another market.

Industry	1929	1932	1936	1938
Coal	18.2	41.2	25.0	22.0
Cotton	14.5	31.1	15.1	27.7
Shipbuilding	23.2	59.5	30.6	21.4
Iron and steel	19.9	48.5	29.5	24.8
Average for all Industries	9.9	22.9	12.5	13.3

Table 3.3: Unemployment (%) in staple industries compared with national average[5]

Decade	Cotton	Other textiles	Iron and steel	Coal
1910–9	25	15	12	10
1920–9	24	12	12	8
1930–9	14	10	12	9

Table 3.4: The main components of British exports (% of total value)[6]

3 The Great War and its impact, 1914–39

⇄ **Cross-reference:** The General Strike, government finances and the gold standard

Figure 3.8: The negative cycle in the staple industries

(Lack of modernisation → Uncompetitive against foreign competititon → Falling profits → Lack of investment → Lack of modernisation)

British mines remained poorly equipped, and were far less mechanised than those in other countries. The refusal of the government to nationalise the mines meant that there was no major influx of investment. Industrial relations were also very poor, which culminated in the General Strike in 1926. The return to the gold standard in 1925 made exports uncompetitive and new countries, including Poland and Spain, started to mine their own coal. New fuels, such as oil and gas, were also a threat.

Year	Output (tons)	Exports (tons)
1913	287	98
1929	258	77
1933	208	57

Table 3.5: Coal production and exports[7]

Shipbuilding

Between 1920 and 1929 Britain produced 45% of the world's shipping tonnage – it had been 59% in 1909–13. The percentage of the world fleet registered in Britain in 1930 was 30%, compared with 41% in 1914. There were various reasons for this decline:

- The boom in production at the end of the war led to overcapacity to carry freight in the 1920s, causing the shipping rates to fall.
- Naval orders fell after the war.
- British designs were outdated compared with those being made in other countries such as the USA.
- British producers struggled against foreign shipbuilders that could undercut them on price.

Year	Ships built (tons)
1913	1 950 000
1920	240 000 (boom created by loss of shipping in First World War)
1925	800 000
1930	680 000
1939	1 000 000 (increase in demand due to rearmament)

Table 3.6: Shipbuilding in British yards[8]

Iron and steel

The British iron and steel industries were already falling behind competitors before 1914. The war reinvigorated demand, but from 1920 demand fell sharply. Further export markets were lost during the war, a free-trade policy allowed cheap imports to be dumped on the British market (a story being repeated in 2015 and 2016) and the Depression from 1929 to 1933 saw a further drop in demand, especially from the shipbuilding industry.

The move to rearmament in the late 1930s altered the fortunes of the declining staple industries as there was suddenly a much greater demand for steel and shipbuilding in particular (both of these stimulated demand for coal).

The General Strike, government finances and the gold standard

Strained industrial relations before the General Strike

In 1919 and 1920 there was a series of strikes that included riots and demonstrations among the Clydeside engineers and shipbuilders. The red flag was raised in Glasgow's George Square and the government had to use troops to restore order. There was also a major strike in the mining industry. The strikes were apparently politically motivated, with evident support for socialist ideas (shown by the flying of the red flag in Glasgow and demands for nationalisation in the mining industry) and there was fear of the spread of 'Bolshevism'. The striking workers could also be seen as being motivated by the need and desire for better pay and conditions. The short postwar boom gave trade unions the confidence to make demands on this front and the experiences of nationalisation during the war suggested that it might improve the lot of miners.

In 1921 almost 86 million working days were lost to strike action and the 'triple alliance' of railwaymen, miners and transport workers threatened to carry out common action. From this point on a general strike appeared a real possibility.

Even during the first Labour government industrial relations were poor. In February 1924, a dockers' strike ended in victory for the dockers, but this was not due to support from the Labour government: MacDonald would have been willing to use troops to unload ships if the strike had continued. Then in March 1924 MacDonald announced a state of emergency during a London tram and bus strike.

A number of factors contributed to the 1926 General Strike:

- The mining industry, which played a central role, had failed to modernise; conditions were poor and pay varied from mine to mine. Miners wanted the government to nationalise the mines and bring about much-needed modernisation but successive governments refused to do so.
- The coal industry and other staple industries were in decline and struggling against foreign competition in their export markets. Coal in particular was in difficulties, as

ACTIVITY 3.14

Examine the data and detail in this section.

1. How far did the following industries decline in the years between 1918 and 1939?
   - shipbuilding
   - coal
   - iron and steel.
2. Explain in your own words why the decline took place.
3. Explain the inter-relationship between the different staple industries.

France and Italy were receiving free coal from Germany and domestically they had to compete against the new fuels of gas, oil and electricity.
- Unemployment in the areas dominated by staple industries became entrenched as the export markets permanently declined. This '**structural unemployment**' kept wages low in staple industries.
- The introduction of the gold standard in April 1925 made British exports even less competitive.
- In June 1925 coal exports fell still further and owners announced cuts in wages, an end to national pay rates and increases in hours. A crisis was avoided by a nine-month subsidy from Baldwin's government and the setting up of a Royal Commission under Herbert Samuel.
- The Trades Union Congress (TUC) backed the miners, fearing that wages would be cut through all industries. This meant that a general strike was on the cards (though the TUC hoped it would not be needed).
- The Samuel Commission (published in March 1926) suggested that mine owners needed to modernise and that government subsidy should end. In the long term pay should not be cut (but short-term cuts might be needed) and hours should not be increased. The TUC accepted the findings, but mine owners and miners rejected them and the government did not step in. Mine owners announced a pay reduction from 30 April 1926, the miners a strike from 1 May.
- Mine owners locked out the miners on 30 April. Lord Birkenhead (the Lord Chancellor 1919–22 and then Secretary of State for India 1924–1928) famously said, 'It would be possible to say without exaggeration that the miners' leaders were the stupidest men in England if we had not on frequent occasion to meet the owners.'[9]
- The TUC and the cabinet entered negotiations. Some miners' leaders left early, and then Baldwin withdrew from negotiations when he heard that printers at the *Daily Mail* had refused to print an article attacking the trade unions. Baldwin saw this as a sign that the General Strike had started, so he went to bed, despite the TUC seeking further talks.

The strike, according to the TUC, was not designed to bring down the government and it only lasted from 4 to 9 May 1926 (except for the miners, who stayed on strike for the rest of the year before having to back down). There were outbreaks of violence and clashes as the strikers' jobs were taken by middle-class volunteers, some of whom fulfilled childhood ambitions of driving trains, and so on.

Consequences of the strike
The TUC made huge losses, and union membership fell. Baldwin designed the Trade Disputes Act (1927) to restrict union power and prevent another general strike. The act banned sympathetic strikes, allowed the seizure of union funds and reversed the 'contracting out' system of the political levy of the 1913 Trade Disputes Act. The act was seen as unnecessary and vindictive.

Thematic link: Trade unions

Government finances
The First World War placed a massive strain on government finances. The national debt in 1914 was £625 million. By the end of the war it was £7980 million. It continued to rise until 1939. Throughout the interwar years national debt was always more than 100% of gross domestic product. Government spending rose from one-eighth of national income before the war to more than half in 1919. The war also shifted the emphasis of taxation. Previously a large proportion of tax revenue (almost half) came from indirect taxation (tax on goods such as tobacco and alcohol), but during the war more tax was raised on incomes. Excess profits duty, raised from industries that benefited from the war effort, taxed any net profits that exceeded prewar levels.

Key terms
Structural unemployment: Unemployment caused by long-term faults in the economy.

ACTIVITY 3.15
1. Why did the General Strike happen?
2. Who should accept the most responsibility?

ACTIVITY 3.16
1. Research the events of the General Strike and the media coverage of it. Write two articles: one from a pro-striker's viewpoint and one against.
2. Examine Baldwin's role: how well did he handle the build-up to the strike and the strike itself?

Key terms

Retrenchment: Cutting back of government spending.

The postwar boom briefly eased problems with government finances. However, the level of government expenditure rose dramatically in 1921 as the economy slumped and unemployment reached 2 million. The government had extended the National Insurance Act and now could not afford the extra costs. The slump also led to a fall in government income, since falling profits and incomes yielded less tax. A policy of **retrenchment** was pursued led by Sir Eric Geddes, Chairman of the Committee on National Expenditure. What became known as the 'Geddes Axe' was responsible for £64 million of cuts that affected army, navy, education, health services and the building of council houses. These policies were arguably effective but they were massively unpopular.

Thematic link: Social policies

The different governments brought in a range of welfare reforms and there were attempts to find solutions to the housing problems. However, governments did try to keep spending low and economic orthodoxy was maintained. The key issue that successive governments failed to address and that drained their finances was unemployment (see Figure 3.9). Prewar unemployment levels had reached 8%, but the interwar period was a very different story.

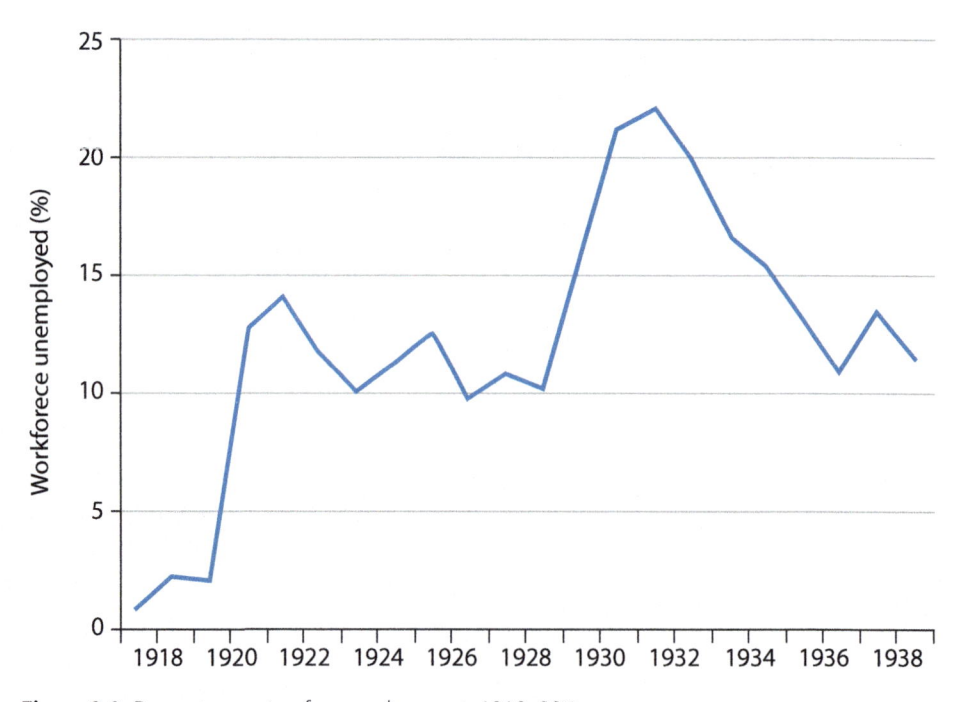

Figure 3.9: Percentage rate of unemployment, 1918–39[10]

ACTIVITY 3.17

Using the information in this chapter and your own research assess:

1. the financial records of the different interwar governments
2. the causes of problems in government finances
3. whether more effective policies could have been introduced.

The gold standard

Winston Churchill, the Chancellor of the Exchequer, decided in April 1925 to return Britain to the gold standard in order to help the economy return to its prewar strength (it was believed that the gold standard would control inflation and fix exchange rates, giving clarity and stability to British export industries). This has been judged by many (including, subsequently, Churchill himself) to have been a mistake, compounded by opting for the prewar value of $4.86 (Keynes argued that this was 10% too high). The gold standard had not been the cause of Britain's prosperity and the return to it at an inflated price caused problems. The overvaluing of the pound meant that British exports became more expensive and uncompetitive, hitting employment and wage rates in the staple industries that were reliant on export markets. It can be seen as one of the causes of the General Strike and to have damaged British economic performance from 1925 through to 1931.

To maintain the gold standard Britain had to keep interest rates high (to encourage foreign investment in British banks). If foreign money was withdrawn, British gold reserves would be depleted. To keep these international investors happy, the British government had to avoid long-term budget deficits and therefore imposed restrictions on government actions to deal with the Depression. The high interest rates also made borrowing expensive and discouraged companies and individuals from borrowing to invest in commerce or industry.

When the National Government abandoned the gold standard in August 1931, the value of the pound fell from $4.86 to $3.20. Inflation was feared but did not happen, exporters were helped and many politicians whose economic policies had been made overly complicated and ineffective by the gold standard wondered why the action had not been taken earlier (particularly those from the second Labour government).

Thematic link: The National Government

The Depression

When the Wall Street Crash of 1929 brought down the US economy, the USA withdrew the loans it had been making to Europe, leading to a worldwide depression in trade. The effects in Britain were beyond the control of the government. Unemployment rose dramatically and so did the cost of unemployment benefits. MacDonald's Labour government, following Keynes, introduced a small degree of funding for public works (£42 million), but then split over the need for cuts to spending and unemployment benefits in particular. MacDonald and Snowden agreed to join the Conservative-led National Government in 1931.

Cross references: The working classes; *The Road To Wigan Pier*; **Regional divisions**

As well as leaving the gold standard, the National Government carried out cuts in spending (£70 million, including a 10% cut in unemployment benefit) and cut interest rates from 12% to 6% in 1931 and then 2% in 1932, encouraging borrowing and spending by individuals, businesses and councils.

Economic policies from 1931

Various government measures contributed to a gradual recovery. In 1931 tariffs were introduced to protect domestic production. The Unemployment Act (1934) altered the administration of benefits, although it did nothing to solve unemployment. In 1935 the Special Areas Act made £2 million available to relieve structural unemployment: 44 000 workers were encouraged to move, and 30 000 men were retrained.

Generally, improvements in the economy were due to an upturn in the economic cycle rather than central government action. Local government played a strong role, however, with a boom in house-building.

Economic realignment

In this period there was a shift away from the traditional base of the British economy in the staple industries and towards new industries and the service sector. This realignment of the economy also led to a shift in the regional basis of employment.

New industries included car production, chemicals, electrical engineering and supply, plastics, rubber and synthetic fibre. These new industries used oil and electricity, not coal and steam, so they did not need to be located in the traditional industrial heartlands. They therefore largely developed in the South, the Midlands, and in particular in the South-East near the biggest market: London.

The new industries differed from the old staple industries not only geographically, but also in a number of other ways. They focused more on the domestic market rather than export, so they needed transport links to major markets in Britain rather than to ports for export. Technologically and organisationally the new industries embraced the latest ideas, research and methods, which made them radically different from the old staple industries. Staff training was also much better in the new industries.

The car industry

The development of the car industry was significant in Britain in the years 1914–39. The use of motor vehicles by the armed forces during the war helped build a skills base in terms of production, servicing and repairing of vehicles. Wartime developments fed into a thriving postwar industry. In 1923 the industry employed 120 000 people and this more than doubled to 250 000 by 1938. Mass-production techniques, pioneered by Henry Ford in the USA using production lines, were adopted. British manufacturers such as William Morris and Herbert Austin started to produce small cars that were affordable for the masses, including the Austin 7 and Morris Cowley. Major US firms such as Vauxhall (in Luton) and Ford (in Dagenham) set up large factories in Britain to produce for the British market.

The firms generally all produced for the home market (88% of all cars produced were sold in Britain) that was protected by a 33% tariff from 1915 and was buoyant enough to support the industry. Some high-end manufacturers such as Rolls-Royce did export. This new industry did not suffer the effects of the Depression in the same way as the old staple industries.

With high unemployment, the decline of the traditional industries, a General Strike and the Depression, it is easy to see the interwar economic picture of Britain as a grim one. It was, undoubtedly, a very difficult time for millions of Britons, but on average wages increased in real terms by about 33% between 1913 and 1938.

There were some aspects of change in terms of state intervention and certainly plenty of discussion of possible alternative approaches, such as Keynesian economics, but the realignment to a more state-controlled economy would not truly come to Britain until the Second World War. There was, however, certainly a realignment in British industry, as new industries developed away from the traditional base. Consumer goods – many of which were mass-produced – and retail started to be a significant part of the economy, fuelled by the increasing affluence of those in steady employment.

ACTIVITY 3.18

Research the growth of other new industries:
- electrical supply
- electrical engineering and electrical consumer goods
- chemical industry
- synthetic fabrics
- aircraft manufacture.

Look at how many people they employed, the markets they targeted, where they were based and the adoption of new technology and techniques.

Figure 3.10: 1927 Austin 7 Chummy

ACTIVITY 3.19

Study Table 3.7, which shows occupational groups as a percentage of the employed population.[11]

1. Describe what changes to the economy the table shows.
2. Using this table and the rest of the section evaluate the extent to which the British economy changed in the interwar years.

Occupational groups	1911	1921	1931
1) employers and business owners	6.7%	6.8%	6.7%
2) non-manual workers	18.7%	21.2%	23%
a) managers	3.4%	3.6%	3.7%
b) higher professionals	1%	1%	1.1%
c) lower professionals	3.1%	3.5%	3.5%
d) supervisors and inspectors	1.3%	1.4%	1.5%
e) clerical workers	4.5%	6.5%	6.7%
f) sales employees	5.4%	5.1%	6.5%
3) manual workers	74.6%	72%	70.3%

Table 3.7: Occupational groups as a percentage of the employed population

Social developments

Changes in the role of women during and after the war

The First World War can be seen as a turning point in the role of women in Britain: they gained political rights at the end of the war; their role in employment was transformed during the war; they gained great social freedom; and the advance of labour-saving devices and falling family sizes changed their role within the family.

The groundwork for much as this was set out before the war with the suffrage movement; female participation in the trade union movement (there were 437 000 female members by 1914) and improvements in female education (The Girls' Day School Trust established 33 girls' schools between 1872 and 1900, and universities created women's colleges).

Work during the war

Women were drafted into factories to replace the men who went off to war and to help the war effort. There were 500 000 women working in ammunition factories in July 1917 and 18 000 working in the Women's Land Army in 1918. Women entered new areas of work, such as the civil service and the professions. In 1917 there were almost 500 000 women working in local government and 60 000 in banking.

In numerous areas women showed that they were more than capable of fulfilling the roles previously carried out by men, where either physical and/or mental capability had previously been seen as barriers. Women were working in the steel industry, as plumbers and electricians and as doctors.

The suffragettes called off their campaign when war broke out and the suffrage movement set about supporting the war effort. Women's efforts during in the war were arguably the key factor in earning them the vote (though many women under 30 contributed), and the role of prewar movements should not be ignored. In addition, the Conservatives may have hoped that emancipating women would to some degree mitigate the impact of enfranchising working-class men.

Postwar developments

Timeline: women's emancipation

1918	The Representation of the People Act gave women aged 30 and over the vote in national elections.
1919	The Sex Disqualification Removal Act allowed women to stand as candidates for Parliamentary seats. The first elected were Countess Markievicz (a Sinn Feiner who therefore did not take her seat) and Nancy Astor (US-born wife of the owner of the *Observer* newspaper Viscount Waldorf Astor).
By 1923	There were 4000 female magistrates, mayors, councillors or guardians.
1928	Women gained the vote at the age of 21, the same age as men.
1929	Margaret Bondfield became the first female cabinet minister.

Movements such as Labour Women's sections of Cooperative Guilds offered opportunities for listening to speakers and discussing political issue. They also organised support for movements such as the Peace Ballot. Other organisations emerged to widen women's experiences and opportunities: The Women's Institute and Women's League of Health and Beauty.

Legal developments

The legal rights of women were improved in three important areas.

- The Matrimonial Causes Act (1923) meant that wives did not need to prove cruelty, desertion or another 'cause' as well as adultery as grounds for divorce. Grounds for divorce were further extended in 1927.
- The Guardian of Infants Act (1924) gave joint guardianship of children to both parents, rather than just the father. Custody that was in dispute would be settled by the courts.
- The New English Law of Property (1926) gave single women the right to hold and dispose of their property on the same terms as men.
- The Law Reform Act (1935) equalised the rules regarding property for married women, giving them the same control of their property as single women.

Work after the war

Wartime agreements had 'diluted' some jobs to make them accessible to women. The Restoration of Pre-War Practices Act (1919) ended the agreements, and some women lost their wartime positions. Middle-class women's organisations protested, but many women accepted the need to free up jobs for the returning men.

In the interwar years, middle-class married women rarely worked, but many working-class families with two incomes managed a good standard of living and could buy luxury goods. Britain had the same proportion of women employed as the USA in 1939 and far more than any other European country. Women remained largely in low-skilled jobs and were paid on average half as much as men. They were much less likely to be unionised than men.

Fashion and social change

Women's appearance changed dramatically after the First World War. They adopted shorter haircuts such as the 'bob', 'shingle' and 'Eton crop'.

The lighter fabrics used for clothing (often the new artificial ones, such as rayon and nylon) and shorter skirts were all designed to give a more 'boyish' figure. In the 1930s styles moved towards a more glamorous and groomed look. Changes throughout the

---

ACTIVITY 3.20

1. Did their 'war work' give some women the vote in 1918? Find different academic interpretations to support your arguments.
2. How far had women's lives in the postwar period really changed? Create a table identifying and contrasting elements of change and elements of continuity.
3. Research whether women's roles changed more depending on their class.

period, including the wide acceptance of cosmetics, were symbols of greater freedom and independence.

Social conventions relaxed over dating and women smoking in public. Sex and birth control remained fairly taboo subjects but there is evidence that the number of women who engaged in pre-marital sex was steadily increasing through the period. Some books and magazine articles promoted sexual enjoyment for both partners, but British society remained rather prudish.

The pilot Amy Johnson, who flew solo to Australia in 1930, was one of a number of remarkable women who showed that there were no limits to what women could do.

The working classes

The conditions of the working classes varied over time (unemployment fluctuated over time as did costs of living) and between regions (areas dominated by staple industries saw a long period of decline).

> **Thematic link: Staple industries and mines**

Because prices fell between 1920 and 1938, and fell more than wages, those in work saw an increase in their 'real wages'. Many of the working classes, however, struggled to stay in regular employment especially during the Depression.

Improving living standards

Overall, there was a wider variety of fresh food available (consumption rose by 88% for fruit, 64% for vegetables and 46% for eggs) and new branded pre-packaged goods became available (Kellogg's, Heinz and Bisto, for example). The working classes

Voices from the past

George Orwell: The Road to Wigan Pier

George Orwell's political writings, including *The Road to Wigan Pier*, *1984* and *Animal Farm*, continue to have strong resonance today. He was commissioned by Victor Gollancz (British publisher and humanitarian) to visit areas of mass unemployment in Lancashire and Yorkshire and describe what he found. The result was *The Road to Wigan Pier*. Orwell lived among the poor and unemployed, experiencing what the slums were like, the poor diet of the working classes, conditions in the mines and the unemployed searching for useable coal on the slag heaps.

When people live on the dole for years at a time they grow used to it, and drawing the dole, though it remains unpleasant, ceases to be shameful. In the back-streets of Wigan and Barnsley I saw every kind of privation, but I probably saw much less conscious misery than I should have seen ten years ago. The people have at any rate grasped that unemployment is a thing they cannot help. It is not only Alf Smith who is out of work now; Bert Jones is out of work as well, and both of them have been 'out' for years. It makes a great deal of difference when things are the same for everybody.

So you have whole populations settling down, as it were to a lifetime on the PAC (Public Assistance Committee). And what I think is admirable, perhaps even hopeful, is that they have managed to do it without going spiritually to pieces. A working man does not disintegrate under the strain of poverty as a middle-class person does. Take, for instance, the fact that the working classes think nothing of getting married on the dole.[12]

Discussion points:

1. How does Orwell suggest the experience of unemployment has changed?
2. What things give Orwell hope for the future?
3. Look at further extracts of *The Road to Wigan Pier* to get a full picture of:
   - living conditions
   - diet and health
   - work in the mines
   - life of the unemployed.

were strongly drawn to the new cheap foods, including sweets, sugar, white bread, processed and tinned foods and savoury snacks such as crisps.

As food became cheaper, it required a smaller percentage of the working-class family's budget (in 1914 it was 60%, in 1938, 35%). This meant that the working classes had money to spend on household goods (radios being a prime example), newspapers and leisure (working hours were falling and paid holidays were more common) and entertainment (the cinema was cheap and popular). Spending also increased on alcohol, tobacco and gambling (the football pools became a massive industry).

The working classes had gained access to a number of luxuries in clothing (cheap mass-produced suits and dresses were particularly popular with the young), food (cheap chocolate, fish and chips, and so on) and leisure (films and football pools). This did not, however, mean that poverty became a thing of the past. When times were hard Orwell and others found that members of working classes often went without necessities, rather than missing out on these new luxuries. Sweets and chips were cheaper than more nutritious foods.

Poverty remained a real issue for a significant part of the population. There were numerous investigations into poverty in the 1930s, including one by Seebohm Rowntree in York in 1936.

> **Thematic link: Standards of living**

Rowntree found that 7% of the population were in 'primary poverty' and 18% of the population overall were in poverty (the standards set were higher than those used in 1899). The 1936 report found that poverty and 'primary poverty' disproportionately affected young children. Just over half of working-class children were born into poverty and this had a significant impact on their health and life chances.

Other groups still badly hit by poverty were the elderly – despite the introduction of the pension (this was exacerbated by household means testing, which meant that many old people could not live with their families) – the sick, widows and the unemployed. Rowntree did, however, also find poverty among full-time workers, notably those in the building trades, agricultural labourers and transport workers. Even in better-paid industries workers would find themselves in poverty due to seasonal layoffs, short-time working and limited availability of shifts. The pawn shop in working areas often did a roaring trade, with family valuables being pawned between paydays to keep the family fed.

Regional divisions

There were two very distinct areas of Britain in the 1930s in terms of economic conditions: the South and the Midlands were, on the whole prosperous, unlike the North and West (Wales, north of England, Scotland, Northern Ireland). In 1934, for example, Jarrow (the North-East) had an unemployment rate of 68%, in Merthyr Tydfil (South Wales) it was 62%, and in St Albans (the South-East) it was 3.9%. Unemployment was a particular problem in the staple industries (see Table 3.8).

> **ACTIVITY 3.21**
>
> Create a spider diagram or chart on life for the working classes. Show both improvements and remaining problems.

3 The Great War and its impact, 1914–39

Industry	1929	1932	1936	1938
Coal	18.2%	41.2%	25%	22%
Cotton	14.5%	31.1%	15.1%	27.7%
Shipbuilding	23.2%	59.5%	30.6%	21.4%
Iron and steel	19.9%	48.5%	29.5%	24.8%
National average	9.9%	22.9%	12.5%	13.3%

Table 3.8: Unemployment in the staple trades compared with the national average.[13]

Unemployment in the staple industries was structural. The industries had become inefficient and overstaffed, profits had fallen and there was a poor level of investment. Where a staple industry dominated an area, unemployment was devastating (see Figure 3.11). The hardship in Jarrow was typical of this problem.

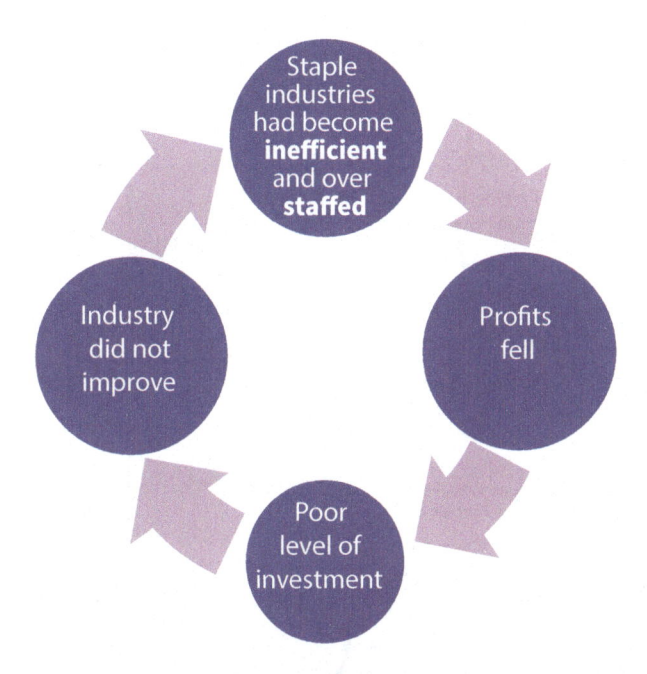

Figure 3.11: The vicious cycle of unemployment in the staple industries

The Jarrow March (1936)

After the closure of Palmer's shipyard, the last major employer in Jarrow, unemployment reached over 70%. A group of 200 men decided to march to London (300 miles away) to highlight their plight and demand the building of a new steel works. The local MP, Ellen Wilkinson, supported the marchers and wrote of the despair in the town with poverty, poor housing, lack of food, disease and high infant mortality rates. Support given by the Unemployed Assistance Board proved to be inadequate. The march gathered national coverage and support. The 200 men carried an oak box containing a petition signed by 11 000 people in Jarrow and further petitions gathered along the route. The men marched for 25, days starting at 8.45 each morning.

The marchers received considerable sympathy, and Ellen Wilkinson presented their petition to Parliament. No plan was put in place to help Jarrow, but a shipbreaking yard did open in 1938 and a steelworks in 1939.

As regional differences became more marked (unemployment was very high in some areas and relatively low elsewhere), some people moved to seek work. However, the changes were not very great (see Table 3.9), and government did little beyond the 1935 Special Areas Act to stimulate these movements.

The new industries, such as chemical, motor cars and other light industries took hold in the South-East and the Midlands. Populations in London and Coventry doubled, in Oxford grew by a third and Slough and Luton also saw notable growth. Morris Motors in Cowley in Oxfordshire recruited almost half its workforce from depressed areas in the 1930s, as the local supply of labour was exhausted.

Only some areas suffered from structural unemployment, but regional and seasonal factors affected employment in many places. In industrial towns such as Middlesbrough unemployment rose considerably in the winter, as the building trade needed fewer men and working hours were shorter. Seaside towns such as Blackpool had high levels of seasonal employment in the leisure, retail and hospitality sectors during the summer. In industries such as car production employment tended to be lower in the winter, so even in the 'good' times in the 1920s Britain suffered with seasonal winter unemployment.

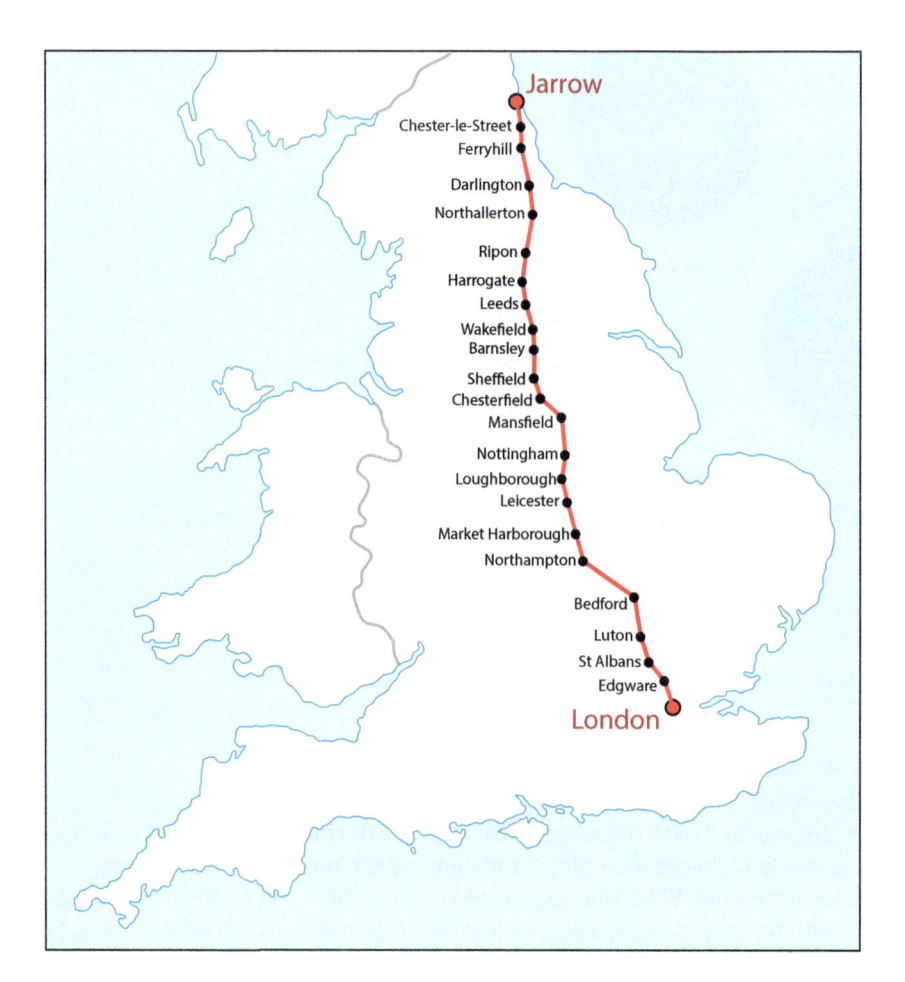

Figure 3.12: The route of the Jarrow March

3 The Great War and its impact, 1914–39

Area	1911–21 change in numbers	1911–21 percentage change	1931–9 change in numbers	1931–9 percentage change
South-East	488 000	4.2%	1 893 000	7.3%
East Midlands	296 000	7.4%	98 000	5.4%
West Midlands	108 000	5.1%	146 000	7.6%
East	32 000	1.8%	258 000	10.6%
North	677 000	5.6%	162 000	1%
South-West	−23 000	−1.2%	63 000	2.3%
Wales	237 000	9.8%	−128 000	−4.9%
England and Wales	1 817 000	5%	1 492 000	3.7%
Scotland	122 000	2.6%	164 000	3.4%

Table 3.9: Regional population changes.[14] (Numbers have been rounded. All changes shown are increases, except where shown as negative.)

ACTIVITY 3.22

Study the table of population changes:

1. Where is there the most significant growth in population?
2. What is happening in the areas where the staple industries were based?
3. What is happening in the areas where the new industries were based?

Figure 3.13: The Jarrow March of unemployed miners and shipbuilders from north-east England set out on 5 October

Cross-reference: Staples, new industries and foreign competition (Chapter 2)

Changing attitudes in the 1920s and the 'hungry thirties'

Judging how far social attitudes had changed or stayed the same across the interwar period is a difficult thing to do. A historian can look at key indicators in terms of contemporary literature, art and culture and also look at data showing changing attitudes to marriage, divorce and the conceiving of children. This section considers these different aspects, but, as always when making complex historical judgements, the more information you have, the better.

Literature

Stark realism and hatred of war played a key role in interwar literature. Siegfried Sassoon and Wilfred Owen, in their wartime writing on the brutality of war, developed a modern style with direct speech and colloquialisms. There was a series of anti-war books at the end of the 1920s, including *Death of a Hero* by Richard Aldington and Siegfried Sassoon's *Memoirs of a Foxhunting Man* and *Memoirs of an Infantry Officer*.

Writing of the 1920s and 1930s tended to be highly critical of the prewar institutions and ways of doing things. There was some popular comic writing in the 1920s, including P.G. Wodehouse's series of books about Bertie Wooster, a clueless aristocrat, and his brilliantly capable butler Jeeves.

Some interwar literature pushed the boundaries with its content. James Joyce's *Ulysses*, for example, featured unusual language, introspection and sexual content that led to it being initially banned in Britain. The writing of D.H. Lawrence proved to be particularly controversial: *The Rainbow* had strong sexual content, while his *Lady Chatterley's Lover*, published abroad in 1928, was banned in Britain until 1960.

In the 1930s writing with socialist messages included the works of J. B. Priestley (such as *English Journey of 1934*) and George Orwell's *The Road to Wigan Pier* (1937). Political writing flourished with the rise of fascism and the growing international tension and conflict, including the Spanish Civil War.

The 'Bloomsbury set', a group of mainly Cambridge-educated intellectuals, followed the ideas of the philosopher G.E. Moore, including 'art for art's sake'. They held left-wing liberal views, attacked militarism and supported female suffrage. The group included the economist J. Maynard Keynes, the writers Virginia Woolf, Leonard Woolf and E.M. Forster and the painters and art critics Roger Fry, Duncan Grant, Clive Bell and Vanessa Bell. The Bloomsbury set was criticised at the time for being too dominant in British art and culture. They were seen as being elitist and, by some, as morally dangerous, as they stood against the normal conventions of morality and monogamy.

Overall, literature in the 1930s had a more serious and political tone than in the 1920s, in line with the economic problems in Britain and growing international tensions.

> **Taking it further**
>
> Research the 'Bloomsbury set' – the different members, their work and beliefs.

Science

The advent of electricity and the internal combustion engine did much to change British society. Homes were changed by the development of labour-saving devices, and people now could enjoy independent travel. Science and technology did not become central to British culture or education, but Britain was a pioneer in developing radio and television.

Social trends

Arguably, the greatest changes in society during the interwar years affected women. Tables 3.10 and 3.11 illustrate some of the significant social trends that made women's lives very different from those of their mothers and grandmothers.

Year	Average number of divorces per year
1921–5	2848
1926–30	4052
1931–5	4784
1936–40	7535

Table 3.10: Average number of divorces per year in England and Wales[15]

Year	Average annual number of legitimate births per 1000 married women aged 15–44	Average annual number of illegitimate births per 1000 unmarried women aged 15–44
1911–15	190.7	7.9
1921–5	156.7	6.7
1931–5	115.2	5.5

Table 3.11: Fertility trends in England and Wales[16]

ACTIVITY 3.23

Using the details and data in this section as well as further research of your own, answer the following:

1. In what ways did British literature, art and culture change in the interwar years?
2. Was British culture in the 'hungry thirties' different from that in the 1920s?
3. Had society's attitudes altered on issues of:
   - marriage
   - divorce
   - family size?

The growth of the media

The press

In the 1930s newspapers played an enormous part in British society. In 1939, 69% of the population over 16 years old read a daily national paper. The percentage for the number reading a national Sunday paper was a startling 82%, not far under 100% of the literate adult population.

Tabloids	
News of the World	Circulation about 4 million, focused on sensational stories, often sexual ones
Daily Express	Circulation about 2.5 million, similar focus to the News of the World
Daily Herald	Circulation about 2 million, supported the Labour Party
Daily Mirror	Circulation of about 1.5 million
Daily Mail	Circulation of 1.5 million and notable for supporting the BUF in the 1930s and its role in sparking the General Strike in 1926
Broadsheet	
The Times	The mouthpiece of the establishment
Daily Telegraph	Strongly Conservative
Manchester Guardian	Supported Liberalism

Table 3.12: Key newspapers of the interwar period

ACTIVITY 3.24

Working in groups, divide the newspapers listed in Table 3.12 among groups in your class. Research the newspapers at this time and then present what you find to the class. Look in particular at changes in layout, changes in the style of headlines and the use of photographs and cartoons.

Magazines

In the interwar years there was a marked growth in women's magazines. These magazines had recipes, fashion tips and clothes patterns, tips on household management, romance and marriage. The problem pages were a particular hit, most notably in the biggest seller *Woman*, which sold 3 million copies in 1939. The women featured in its advertisements and articles were focused on their home (with a happy and well-fed husband and children), fashion and cosmetics. Whether the media helped shape women's role in society, or simply reflected it, is hard to judge.

There had been magazines aimed at children since before the First World War. There was a major innovation in the late 1930s when the coloured comics *The Dandy* and *The Beano* were launched.

Radio

A radio became a fixture in homes of all classes in Britain during the interwar years and listening to the wireless was a key leisure-time activity. The number of homes with licences grew from 36 000 in 1922 to 2 000 000 in 1926, then 34 000 000 in 1939.

There were commercial broadcasters, but the airwaves were dominated by the BBC. In the 1920s broadcasts consisted mainly of classical music and plays, but in the 1930s the focus moved to the mass market with light music, comedy, news and sports commentary. Coverage of test match cricket was highly popular, as were cup finals at Wembley and coverage of tennis at Wimbledon. Popular programmes at lunchtime and the evenings could attract audiences of up to 10 million.

The radio played a role in keeping the nation together and breaking big news such as the abdication and the outbreak of war. It was not much used for political control, as in, for example, Nazi Germany, but politicians such as Baldwin saw its significance and he made use of it during the General Strike.

Cinema

In the 1920s the cinema grew enormously and silent films offered images of romance, creating stars such as Greta Garbo, Rudolph Valentino, John Gilbert and Mary Pickford. There were also slapstick comedies from actors such as Buster Keaton. In the late 1920s, the 'talkies' (talking pictures) arrived, with Al Jolson in *The Jazz Singer*, for example. Cinemas holding up to 3000 people were built in town centres and entry was cheap enough for the working classes to go several times a week.

Social policies

Legislation and reforms in housing

Timeline: Housing policy

1918	Tudor Walter Report
1919	The Housing and Town Planning Act (Addison Act)
1922/23	Subsidy introduced to promote house-building
1924	The Wheatley Housing Act
1930	The Greenwood Housing Act
1935	The Housing Act
1938	The Housing Act
1938	Green Belt Act

Thematic link: The effects of changes in society and social policy

Homes fit for heroes

After the war Lloyd George promised to make Britain 'a fit country for heroes to live in', showing that there was a belief that housing in Britain was not up to standard. It also demonstrated the belief that it was intolerable for the men who had fought bravely in the terrible conditions of the First Word War to return to live in poor, squalid conditions. Christopher Addison was charged with improving housing to meet Lloyd George's promise. He estimated that 400 000 houses in Britain were unfit for human habitation and up to 800 000 were needed to replace the slums and make up for the shortfall in house-building.

The 1919 Housing and Town Planning Act appointed 11 regional commissioners whose job was to encouraged local authorities to build new houses with the support of central government money. The government would pay any difference between cost and rental income. Planning laws changed to make it easier for local authorities to demolish slums and buy land. The policy had an immediate impact, with 100 000 houses built with subsidies by July 1921 and this rose to 170 000 by the end of the government's term in office. The shifts in policy meant that housing needs would from then on be seen as a government responsibility.

However, there were some difficulties: many local authorities were reluctant to act; bricklayers were in short supply; builders often opted for more profitable work than working on council houses; and houses were built at a cost of £910, but a few years later falling costs for both materials and labour brought the price down to £385. Local authorities were now paying significantly less to build houses, and had to fend off criticism suggesting that they had wasted a great deal of money on house-building in the years straight after the war.[17]

The Addison Act followed the Tudor Walters Report, which had set high standards (including recommendations about low-density developments). This resulted in some of the best council houses of the 20th century. The houses had separate rooms for cooking, eating, living and sleeping – a vast improvement for those used to slum housing.

During 1922 and 1923, Neville Chamberlain introduced legislation to encourage authorities to build more houses. Central government would pay a subsidy of £6 a year for 20 years for each new house built. Then in 1924, the Housing Act, introduced by Labour minister John Wheatley, raised the subsidy from £6 to £9 per house and the payments would continue for 40 years, not 20. The act specified that the houses were to be for rent, not for sale, which benefited the working, rather than the middle, class. By the end of this scheme in 1933, 500 000 houses had been built.

Local Government Act (1929)

This act overhauled the organisation of local government. Councils received a grant from central government to cover the costs of their expanded roles – a fairer system since the responsibility of looking after the poor was no longer based on the ability to raise money locally. Poor Law unions and their boards of guardians were abolished. Rates were overhauled: significant cuts were introduced for railways and industrial buildings, and rates were removed from agricultural land and farm buildings.

Thematic link: Prosperity and poverty

The second Labour government
The Greenwood Housing Act of 1930 renewed subsidy for council house-building and organised the speeding up of slum clearance. The act was suspended between 1931 and 1934 due to the financial crisis, but it was reinstated by the National Government. Many jobs were created and more slums were cleared between 1931 and 1939 than in any previous period. Local authorities built over 700 000 houses and therefore managed to rehouse four-fifths of slum dwellers.

The Housing Act of 1935
The act set standards of overcrowding – two people per room including all living rooms and bedrooms – according to which only 4% of 9 million houses were overcrowded. It was estimated that 12% of the population lived in overcrowded conditions. The problem was especially acute in London, where, in 1933, half a million people, including almost half the families in Islington, Finsbury and Shoreditch, were living in houses of three or more families. Slum housing was also a major issue in Liverpool, in particular the ward of St Anne's, where 42% of families lived in houses of four or more families.[18]

By 1939, Britain had seen remarkable improvements in its housing stock:

- More than a million council houses had been built to provide accommodation to those needing rehoming following slum clearance.
- Three million homes had been built by the private sector.
- Two-thirds of homes in Britain were wired for electricity, giving access to electric lighting and electrically operated domestic appliances such as radios, irons and vacuum cleaners.
- In 90% of homes the main form of heating was open fires.
- Some 60% had supplementary electric or gas heaters.
- About a third of families earning under £300 a year had a piped hot water supply, two-thirds heated their water over an open fire or on the stove.
- Two-thirds of homes had a gas cooker.
- Some of the middle classes had 'Aga' or electric cookers.

The quality and level of housing certainly went up between 1914 and 1939 (though the population did so too). Governments invested more than £200 million – a huge sum – in building houses and clearing slums. The number of people per house fell from about 5.5 to about 3.5 (in part due to people having smaller families). The problem of overcrowding did not disappear, however, nor did the slums. In major cities there were still slums and areas of overcrowding (see Table 3.13), back-to-back houses remained and so did houses without lavatories.

City	Number of people living in overcrowded houses
London	500 000
Glasgow	200 000
Birmingham	68 000
Manchester	49 000
Sheffield	41 000
Leeds	38 000

Table 3.13: Overcrowding (more than two people per room in a house) in 1932[19]

Renting and owning
The building of council houses was the focus of government action on housing. These were constructed to a good standard by local authorities, based on the provisions of the various housing acts.

> **ACTIVITY 3.25**
>
> Using this section and other resources available, conduct further research into changes and legislation in housing. Assess the relative success of the policies introduced.

Private renting remained the basis of housing for most people in Britain. Around two-thirds of all households rented their homes from a private landlord. The rental market covered all aspects of the housing market, from grand villas in the suburbs to a single room in a slum house. The majority of poor housing was owned by private landlords and was often poorly maintained. Rents in the overcrowded slums could often be surprisingly high as people seeking work needed to be close to the key centres of employment. They varied enormously: working-class families might pay anything between 5% and 40% of their weekly income in rent.

The 1933 and 1938 Housing Acts removed rent controls on valuable houses, but maintained them on cheaper housing. Rents were decontrolled on a change of tenancy, which led to unfair evictions and wide variations of rent on identical houses. There was a growing backlash against private landlords as the contrast between the quality of repairs in council-owned and privately rented properties became stark.

Home ownership was growing. Over 2.5 million houses were built for private sale between the wars. A semi-detached house in the suburbs with a good size garden and garage could be bought for £450 (double the average annual salary of a professional). Mortgages in the 1930s were affordable, with low interest rates of around 4–5% (the base rate after 1932 was 2%). Deposits could be as low as £25. The housing market thrived and the urban centres sprawled, which started to raise concerns about the amount of rural land being lost and the impact of traffic.

In 1938, Labour won control of London County Council and Herbert Morrison, its chairman, pioneered a scheme to secure the protection of 25 000 acres of 'green belt' around London that resulted in the Green Belt Act (1938).

Education

The Fisher Education Act (1918)

Herbert Fisher, the president of the Board of Education, introduced his Education Act in 1918 aiming to improve the education of the working classes. Fisher, who was vice chancellor of the University of Sheffield between 1913 and 1917, believed that there was intellect among the working classes that was being wasted as they were not receiving sufficient education. The war had brought the classes together, as men from the upper and middle classes commanded and worked side by side with working-class men. This led many to reach the same conclusion as Fisher – that the working classes lacked education rather than intellect. Britain was also struggling to compete with other countries, especially the USA, in terms of having the educated workforce required for the postwar industries.

To improve the education of the working classes it was made compulsory for all children to attend school up to the age of 14. Extra free places were brought in for 'bright' children at secondary schools to ensure that working-class children were educated beyond **elementary standard**. The numbers of poor children staying in school beyond 14 was very small and few local authorities took advantage of the facility to provide 'continuation schools' for people up to the age of 16, as the idea was not backed with funds.

The reforms established national pay rates for teachers, and provided for the building and maintenance of nursery schools for under-fives, although this aspect of the act was neglected and very few of these were built. Spending on education was one of the casualties of government cuts when the postwar boom faded and the 'Geddes Axe' fell in 1922. State funding was cut for working-class students to attend either education beyond 14, or university.

Key terms

Elementary standard: The level of education someone would have expected to have reached by the end of primary school.

> **Thematic link: Government finances**

Labour government (1924)

The first Labour Government revived state scholarships to the universities, undoing the Geddes economies of 1922 and also increased the number of free places available to working-class students in grammar schools. Significantly, a review of education was set up under Sir Henry Hadow. The Hadow Report was presented in 1926 and was, arguably, a key moment in British education – or would have been if its ideas, which received widespread support, had been backed up with money in the interwar period. The report suggested that:

- There should be a break between primary education and secondary education at the age of 11.
- The existing secondary schools should be renamed 'grammar schools' and provide a highly academic education to the most-able pupils.
- New schools, called 'modern schools', should be created for the students who did not attend the grammar schools. These schools would be attended by the majority of children, with a leaving age of 15. Education in these schools would be less academic and more practical.

Amid the ongoing economic problems in Britain, education was not seen as a priority. There was no further significant government legislation and funding was highly limited. By 1939 very few of the working classes were receiving what might be considered 'advanced' secondary, let alone higher, education. This can be seen as a significant area of failure of the interwar politicians, as it was clear that the comparative decline of British industry was partly due to Britain's lower level of scientific and technical education compared with both Germany and the USA.

Welfare

Welfare is financial support given to those in need, for example the unemployed, the elderly, the sick and the bereaved. Welfare was a key issue at the end of the war as it left a significant number of war widows and war wounded. There were also large number of demobilised troops looking for work and leaving these war heroes without work or government support would have been politically damaging.

Unemployment benefit

Unemployment became a problem for the Lloyd George coalition government (1916–22) following demobilisation in 1918 and the ending of production in the munitions factories. An 'Out of Work Donation' (OWD) was introduced to ensure these groups were supported. It was paid to the unemployed without the requirement for a contribution to have been paid. The size of the unemployed person's family determined the amount of the payment, which was continued until the person found work. This was the first instance of a non-contribution-based unemployment benefit. OWD was discontinued in 1920.

In 1920, the Unemployment Insurance Act provided unemployment insurance for the majority of the workforce. It covered almost everyone who earned less than £250 a year – about 12 million people. The benefit could be claimed for 15 weeks at a rate of 15 shillings a week for men and 12 shillings for women. This was an increase in benefit levels, though a larger contribution was required. Agricultural labourers, domestic servants and the self-employed were excluded.

There was a fear that because long-term unemployment was concentrated in certain areas, this could lead to unrest or even revolution. This led to the introduction in 1921 of 'uncovenanted benefit' (benefit that did not require contributions) or 'dole'. This

---

ACTIVITY 3.26

Hold a class debate: 'This class believes that the interwar governments failed to improve educational provision for the British working classes.'

was paid for two periods of 16 weeks, with a gap in between, to those seeking work. The second set of 16 weeks was not based on contributions but on a means test. This was seen as a 'gift' from the government and set an important new principle that the government would take a long-term role in helping maintain those who, through no fault of their own, could not find work.

In the same year extra payments were made to those unemployed with dependants. The whole programme was expected to be largely self-supporting, but as unemployment rose in 1921 it became clear that unemployment benefit would become a drain on government finances.

The first Labour government (1924) ensured that unemployment benefit increased and made payment continuous by removing the 16-week block pattern.

In 1927 the Conservative government ended the distinction between covenanted (contribution based) and uncovenanted (non-contribution based) benefit. Unemployment benefit was now paid for an unlimited period for those genuinely seeking work. Extra benefit over and above the level of covenanted benefit was known as 'transitional benefit'. The workers' contribution from their wages was now higher than before and the weekly level of benefit was lower. These changes were significant: it was now accepted across the political spectrum in the British Parliament that it was the state's responsibility to look after the unemployed in the long term. This suggests that understanding of the reasons for unemployment had shifted since the period before the war.

The Labour Government (1929–31) ended the Poor Law, which was becoming too big a burden on local rates in certain areas. Up to 1.5 million people were reliant on workhouses and Poor Law infirmaries. The Poor Law system was replaced by Public Assistance Committees (PACs), run by local authorities, but funded by central government grants – a revolutionary move, since the Poor Law had existed since Tudor times and been the mainstay of welfare in Britain for hundreds of years. However, the same buildings were still being used and, to a degree, the same stigma remained with what people continued to call the workhouses.

Thematic link: The Depression

In one of its first emergency actions, the National Government (1931–35) cut unemployment benefit by 10%, one of several substantial cuts to government spending. The depression caused by the world economic crisis had led to a large deficit in government finances, and the Labour government had fallen, following a split over the cutting of unemployment benefit. In 1931 the level of contributions was £44 million but expenditure was £120 million in 'transitional' and other forms of unemployment benefit, as unemployment hit 2.5 million: the drain on finances was unsustainable.

The Unemployment Act of 1934 introduced a new system in relation to the payment of non-contribution-based unemployment benefit. PACs were replaced by the Unemployed Assistance Board (UAB) which had branches all over the country. There was a great deal of anger at the change as the level of assistance in some cases was lower than the rate paid by the old local PACs. The biggest protests were in the South Wales mining areas and the government returned the payments to the old levels. The 10% cut was reversed and was payable from the age of 14.

There is evidence to suggest the new system was generous: in some areas, particularly in the North, the payment was higher than some wages paid, particularly those in the 'sweated industries'. There was also heavy criticism as the entire household was means-tested, so that a man (as it usually was) might lose benefit if his children were working (and he therefore become financially dependent on them). The pensions of any elderly persons living with their families would be seen as part of the household income. Any savings were also included in the assessment, which penalised those who had been thrifty.[20]

Unemployment dropped in the mid-1930s, and in 1936 agricultural workers were brought into unemployment insurance for the first time.

Interwar governments overall made reasonable provision for the unemployed. Provision made by Lloyd George's government at the start of the 1920s was witness to a shift in government attitudes. It had become clear that some fundamentals of the economy had changed and the level of structural unemployment (about 1 million) would not shift throughout the interwar years. All the parties accepted that unemployment was often not the fault of the unemployed worker, but rather to do with the economic cycle, or the decline in staple industries. The very unpopular means tests and the frequent changes in the system also created confusion and discontent.

Pensions

The Lloyd George coalition government doubled the pension in 1919 to 10 shillings a week (it had been 5 shillings in 1908). It was, however, still not paid until the age of 70 despite growing calls for the qualifying age to be reduced. Pensions were subsequently further increased by the first Labour government (1924).

The next major piece of legislation was the Widows, Orphans and Old Age Contributory Pensions Act (1925), the work of Neville Chamberlain, a dynamic member of the Conservative front bench. Under this compulsory scheme, both the employer and the employee paid into the pension, supplemented by a contribution from the state. A contributing worker was entitled to a pension of 10 shillings a week (£1 for a married couple, 10 shillings for a widow, with extra payments made for dependent children) from the age of 65 to 70, which was not means-tested.

This contribution-based scheme, which only lasted for five years until the start of the non-contributory state pension, was thought to be complicated as it required gathering information on the level of contribution made – often involving lots of short-term employments with numerous employers – and then complicated calculations about the totals contributed. Critics on the left also saw this as more akin to forced savings rather than genuine government support, as the poor were largely receiving their own contributions back at a later date rather than being genuinely supported by the state. The Conservative government was cutting income tax at the same time, so, arguably, if they had not done so the whole scheme could have been funded through general taxation. The level of payments was also still far from generous.

Health insurance

> Cross-reference: Standards of living (Chapter 2)

Supporting the health and medical treatment of the British population was, arguably, the biggest failure of the interwar governments. There were some – but few – changes during the interwar years to the provisions of the 1911 National Insurance Act that had introduced health insurance for workers:

- 1919: Payment raised from 10 shillings to 15 shillings a week.
- 1926: The state reduced its contribution to the health insurance pot.
- 1926: A Royal Commission recommended that insurance be extended to cover the worker's wife and children, and that there were too many variations in the quality of provision by different companies administering the scheme and this needed to be addressed. Neither of these recommendations was met and insurance companies

ACTIVITY 3.27

Which government did the most to improve the lives of the unemployed?

Which government did the least good (or the most damage) to the lives of the unemployed?

ACTIVITY 3.28

1. Produce a diagram highlighting successes and failings in social policy in the interwar years. Include all the different areas of social policy.
2. Rank the areas of social policy in order of success for the interwar years.
3. Carry out research looking at material, such as the reports from Seebohm Rowntree and Lord Beveridge, to help you make a judgement on how far the provision of social policy had improved the lives of the British people.
4. Contrast the sections on social policy in this chapter with the corresponding sections in Chapters 1 and 2. Do your findings alter your view on the interwar governments?

continued to profit while little progress was made to improve the health of the nation.

The scheme, therefore, still only covered the worker, it did not pay for hospital treatment (which was expensive) and the number of hospitals remained dangerously low because the Ministry of Health did nothing to force local authorities to build them where they were required.

> Thematic link: The National Health Service

Ireland and Anglo-Irish relations

The British decision to declare war on Germany had a tremendous impact on Irish politics. Redmond reiterated the Irish Party's loyalty to the government. With Home Rule close, he was determined to reassure both the British and the unionists that nationalists presented no threat. However, his speech of 20 September, which made it clear that the Irish Volunteers would fight for Britain, led to division in the nationalist camp. Although 160 000 Volunteers supported Redmond, renaming themselves the National Volunteers, a group of 10 000, led by Eoin MacNeill, were opposed. They declared that 'Ireland cannot … take part in foreign quarrels otherwise than through the free action of a … Government of her own.'[21] However, Irish soldiers made significant contributions to the war effort. Around 100 000 Irishmen served in the British army. This included the Ulster Volunteer Force (UVF), who Carson had strongly encouraged to enlist.

Figure 3.14: A memorial to soldiers of the 36th Ulster Division in a Loyalist area of Northern Ireland, commemorating those who died in the Battle of the Somme

The Easter Rising

As the war progressed, moderate nationalists became frustrated. With stalemate in the trenches, Home Rule seemed a distant possibility. In addition, there was anger at the UVF's incorporation within the British army, while the National Volunteers were a separate entity. Carson's promotion to Asquith's coalition cabinet in 1915 did not help. Much anger was directed at Redmond, whose alliance with the Liberals appeared to have achieved little for the nationalist cause. As the IPP became increasingly unpopular, the IRB grew in influence, fostering ties with the Irish Volunteers.

Despite the growth of the IRB, few would have predicted an Irish rebellion during the war. Around 150 000 Irishmen were in active service by 1916 – the war had also brought prosperity, with growing demand for foodstuffs benefiting the Irish economy. In addition, Redmond managed to stop the British extending conscription to Ireland. The fact that a rebellion did occur was largely a result of the pressure applied by Patrick Pearse and James Connolly, supported by Tom Clarke and Sean MacDermott, who had persuaded the IRB's Military Council to support a rising by spring 1916.

For Pearse, the timing of the rebellion, even at such a critical stage in the First World War, was unimportant. He viewed himself as a romantic revolutionary, believing that to sacrifice himself in the nationalist cause was more important than a successful rebellion. Pearse argued that such a 'blood sacrifice' would stimulate nationalist feeling among his fellow Irishmen. Connolly was a socialist, who led the Irish Citizen Army, the group formed to defend Dublin's transport workers during a 1913 strike. He was convinced that only an independent Ireland could provide economic justice. Connolly claimed that the Irish masses, frustrated at the slow progress towards Home Rule and personally affected by losses on the Western Front, would support a rebellion during the war, ensuring success.

Thematic link: The growth of unionism and nationalism

Despite opposition from MacNeill, Pearse and Connolly gained support for their plans. They pointed to Roger Casement, an Irish Volunteer who had travelled to Germany in 1914, who would potentially provide support from Irish prisoners of war and the German government. In fact, support from POWs was limited. Furthermore, the navy intercepted a delivery of 20 000 rifles and ten machine guns in 1916. This did not discourage Pearse, and on Easter Monday, 24 April 1916, the Rising began.

Despite the rebels' unpopularity, the British reaction to the Rising changed public perceptions. First, martial law was declared. Coupled with the arrest of many Sinn Fein members, most of whom had no involvement in the Rising, this made many Irish people sympathise with the rebellion. The brutality of the 15 executions ensured that the rebels were viewed as martyrs. This was especially the case with Connolly, who was carried to his execution on a stretcher and shot sitting in a chair.

As anti-British sentiment grew, Asquith visited Dublin in May 1916. Recognising the limitations of a heavy-handed approach, he ensured that the remaining death sentences were commuted to life imprisonment. He also appointed Lloyd George to lead Home Rule negotiations with unionists and nationalists. Although Redmond was willing to compromise, accepting that all six Ulster counties should be temporarily excluded from Home Rule, Carson rejected Lloyd George's plans. This was a major setback. It also marked the decline of the Irish Party as a political force. During 1917, candidates supported by the militant Sinn Fein won three by-elections. Two of the victors, Joe MacGuinness and Eamon de Valera, had been involved in the Rising.

Voices from the past

Patrick Pearse

Bloodshed is a cleansing and a sanctifying thing, and the nation which regards it as the final horror has lost its manhood. There are many things more horrible than bloodshed; and slavery is one of them.[22]

Discussion point:

Explain why Pearse pressed ahead with the Rising, despite the limited chances of victory. Use the quote to help you.

3 The Great War and its impact, 1914–39

Statistics
- 1300 Irish Volunteers and 300 members of the Citizens Army (a workers' militia) were involved.
- 200 rebels and 250 Irish civilians were killed and 2000 wounded.
- 116 British soldiers and policemen were killed; and 300 to 400 wounded.
- Approximately 3000 people were arrested; 160 were imprisoned, and 1800 were interned (without trial).
- 90 rebels were sentenced to death; 15 were eventually executed.

Key events
1. The rebels entered central Dublin, without any violence, and took control of the General Post Office, which became their headquarters. Pearse proclaimed an Irish Republic.
2. By the next day, the British had brought in reinforcements. They shelled the GPO, causing the rebels to escape to other parts of the city.
3. Over the next five days, the British hunted down the rebels. Pearse surrendered on April 29th.

The Easter Rising 1916

Why did the Rising fail?
- The Rising did not attract public support. Few participated aside from the 1600 that belonged to the Volunteers or the Citizens Army.
- The Rising was condemned by Redmond and the Catholic Church. Many felt the rebels were betraying those Irishmen who had died on the Western Front, and others were angered that most of the casualties were Irish.
- MacNeill banned provincial units of the Volunteers from supporting the Rising.
- The seizure of German weapons and the capture of Casement on his arrival in Ireland meant that the rebels lacked foreign support.
- The British were quick to regroup, and easily outnumbered the rebels.

Figure 3.15: Details of the Easter Rising

The rise of Sinn Fein

The advance of Sinn Fein was the consequence of British actions after 1916. Anger at further imprisonments and the continuation of martial law led to militant nationalist feeling, and men in internment camps became increasingly radicalised as they were confined together. Support for Sinn Fein grew when, in early 1918, Lloyd George attempted to extend conscription to Ireland. This infuriated nationalists. John Dillon, leader of the Irish Party, told Lloyd George that 'all Ireland will rise against you'. Although an anti-conscription campaign forced the government to concede, the British responded by arresting 73 Sinn Fein leaders, claiming they were plotting with Germany. Public support for Sinn Fein continued to grow: in December 1918, they won 73 seats in the general election.

The 1918 election was a crucial turning point. The Sinn Fein MPs refused to take up their seats in the Westminster Parliament. Instead, they met in Dublin on 21 January 1919, as the Dail Eireann (Irish Parliament.) The Dail declared independence, demanding British withdrawal. De Valera was chosen as president of the Irish Republic. This was followed by two parallel developments:

- The Irish Volunteers, renamed the **Irish Republican** Army (IRA), murdered two police officers at Soloheadbeg in January 1919. This led to the Anglo-Irish War, fought between the IRA and British troops.
- Lloyd George moved to implement Home Rule through the Government of Ireland Act (1920).

Key terms

Irish Republican: An Irish nationalist who believes in full independence from the British Empire.

The Anglo-Irish War

After the first meeting of the Dail, the IRA announced that Ireland and Britain were at war. Despite limited Sinn Fein support, the IRA began a campaign against members of the Royal Irish Constabulary (RIC), the Irish police force. Between January and June 1920, sixteen RIC barracks were destroyed. In 1920 alone, 176 policemen were killed. While Lloyd George outlawed Sinn Fein and the IRA, he was anxious not to commit large numbers of troops to tackling a group he saw as a tiny 'murder gang'. However, as it became clear that the RIC was struggling, the government recruited a group of hardened former soldiers, known as the Black and Tans. They were joined by the Auxiliaries, a semi-military organisation of former army officers.

The second half of 1920 was marked by an escalation of violence. Martial law was reintroduced, as the IRA began to target civilians accused of sheltering policemen or soldiers. Using guerrilla tactics, the IRA's Flying Columns killed 18 Auxiliary soldiers at Kilmichael in November 1920. This was followed on 21 November by Bloody Sunday, on which 11 British civilians, believed to be intelligence officers, were shot in their homes. British soldiers took revenge that afternoon, firing into the crowd at Croke Park sports ground, killing 12 civilians and wounding at least 60 others. Auxiliary soldiers also burned the centre of Cork in December 1920 in response to an IRA ambush.

The Government of Ireland Act and the Anglo-Irish Treaty

While politics was changing in Ireland, the impact of the First World War was being felt at Westminster too. In response to the priorities of the Treaty of Versailles, the Liberal-Conservative coalition of 1918–22 united around the issue of self-determination. As they loosened their ties with the Ulster Unionists, the Conservatives largely abandoned their opposition to Home Rule. This gave Lloyd George the opportunity to resurrect the policy, in the hope of bringing peace to Ireland. In December 1919, a committee led by former unionist leader Walter Long made recommendations to the government; these became enshrined in the Government of Ireland Bill of February 1920.

> Thematic link: The National Government

Terms of the Government of Ireland Act
- The country would be divided into a six-county Northern Ireland and a 26-county Southern Ireland.
- Both new states would have a Parliament of two chambers, elected by proportional representation, and a government, accountable to their Parliament.
- While both Parliaments would have significant power over Irish affairs, the Westminster government would retain control over foreign and defence policy, as well as having ultimate supremacy.

The bill became law in December 1920. It had eventually won the support of the Ulster Unionists, who recognised that the Northern Irish Parliament would provide greater security in the light of IRA violence. The unionists won 40 of the 52 seats when Northern Irish elections were held in May 1921. Their leader, Sir James Craig, became prime minister.

Events in the South
Given the events of the Anglo-Irish War, the elections in the South were of little importance. Sinn Fein, unopposed in every constituency they fought, won 124 of the 128 seats. The bigger issue was how to bring an end to the ongoing violence between the IRA and British troops. The British public began to put pressure on the government to end the war. Trades unions, the Labour Party and influential newspapers expressed their concern at army atrocities. The US government was also opposed to

continued bloodshed, as was the British-based Peace with Ireland Council. The IRA also recognised the need for a truce – in the first half of 1921, 752 IRA soldiers and Irish civilians were killed. The fact that Northern Ireland now existed also removed a potential obstacle to negotiations. In June, King George V called for conciliation at the opening of the Northern Irish Parliament. The way was clear for a truce, which came into effect on 11 July.

The Anglo-Irish Treaty

The truce was followed by a summer of negotiations between the two sides, in the hope of arriving at a formal peace settlement. Lloyd George was adamant that Ireland should become a **dominion**, giving it the same status as Canada. This would give Ireland full control over domestic policy (an improvement on Home Rule), but Ireland would remain a member of the British Empire, with the monarch as head of state. In addition, partition would remain. Contrastingly, De Valera was determined that Ireland should become a fully independent country.

Despite these differences, Sinn Fein agreed to formal talks in London in October 1921. De Valera was absent from the autumn conference – he sent Arthur Griffith and Michael Collins as chief negotiators in his place. This made effective negotiation difficult, since de Valera insisted that all decisions had to be vetted by his cabinet in Dublin. It also weakened Collins, as de Valera used the opportunity to distance himself from the deals that were struck, in an attempt to turn Irish opinion against his rival.

The British delegation, which included experienced politicians such as Winston Churchill and Austen Chamberlain, held firm on the issue of Irish allegiance to the Crown and Ireland's status within the empire. They eventually persuaded the Irish to accept a 'free partnership with the other States associated within the British Commonwealth'. Collins was convinced that this would mean Ireland itself stayed outside the **Commonwealth**, but this was never the British intention. Tension grew within the negotiating team, especially as they failed to resolve the Ulster issue; the suggestion of an all-Ireland Parliament was rejected.

In December, the Dublin cabinet instructed their negotiators to reject the proposed oath of allegiance to the British monarch, ensure that Ireland remained outside the Commonwealth, and not to sign any treaty without the Dail's agreement. Despite de Valera's orders, the Irish delegation signed the treaty on 6 December. As the IRA's leading commander, Collins knew that a renewed war would be very difficult to win. He had also been swayed by Lloyd George's promise to set up a Boundary Commission to reconsider the borders of Northern Ireland.

British relief at the treaty was mirrored by renewed conflict in Ireland. De Valera was firmly opposed – although the new Irish Free State had full dominion status and could make its own laws, 'Dev' was not prepared to accept the oath of allegiance to the British Crown. Nevertheless, the Irish cabinet accepted the treaty by four votes to three and the Dail agreed to it by 64 votes to 57. De Valera also lost the subsequent vote of confidence in his presidency; he was succeeded by Arthur Griffith. A new provisional government was formed under the leadership of Michael Collins.

The British Army began to withdraw from Ireland, and the June 1922 election resulted in a large majority for Collins' pro-treaty faction, winning around 78% of the popular vote. Rather than ushering in a period of peace, this inflamed tensions – de Valera's anti-treaty group began a campaign of violence in both South and North, resulting in a brief, but bloody, civil war.

Key terms

Dominion: A country within the British Empire whose government was responsible for its own domestic affairs.

Commonwealth: A group of countries within the British Empire which had a greater degree of independence than other colonies.

ACTIVITY 3.29

Draw a diagram to show how successful Irish nationalists were between 1914 and 1921, and how this changed over time. As a minimum, make sure you include the outbreak of the First World War, the Easter Rising, the growth of Sinn Fein, the Anglo-Irish War and the Anglo-Irish Treaty.

Timeline: The Irish Civil War

1922	
April	A group of IRA members, the Irregulars, take control of the Four Courts, where Dublin's main courts are based
22 June	Unionist politician Sir Henry Wilson assassinated by two IRA members.
Summer	The Provisional Government reclaims the Four Courts; the Irregulars are pushed to the west of Ireland
August	Collins assassinated in a guerrilla attack
Nov–Dec	Execution of leading anti-Treaty figures, including Erskine Childers and Rory O'Connor
1923	
March	Several republican prisoners killed without trial in Kerry
April	Liam Lynch, the Irregulars' leader, killed, leading to the surrender of anti-Treaty forces

Voices from the past

Michael Collins (1890–1922)

From a letter written after signing the Anglo-Irish treaty

When you have sweated, toiled, had mad dreams … you find yourself in London's streets, cold and dank. Think – what have I got for Ireland? Something which she has wanted these past seven hundred years. Will anyone be satisfied at the bargain? … I tell you this; early this morning I signed my death warrant.[23]

Discussion points:

1. In no more than 50 words, explain the phrase 'this morning I signed my death warrant'.
2. Were Irish republicans right to blame Collins for the final treaty? Explain your answer carefully, presenting both sides of the argument.

Divided Ireland before the Second World War

The Irish Free State

While the Provisional Government had won the Civil War, its leadership was gone, Griffith having died suddenly ten days before Collins' assassination. As the new state came into being on 6 December, W.T. Cosgrave took over as Irish president, and began the process of restoring stability to Ireland. His first priority was dealing with the 12 000 republican prisoners who remained after the civil war. Overcrowding and brutality were common and 200 prisoners went on hunger strike. Although most prisoners had been released by 1924, the government maintained a tough approach to law and order, passing the Public Safety (Emergency Powers) Act in 1926. This allowed for internment in states of emergency. This act was tightened the following year after the assassination of Kevin O'Higgins, the minister for justice.

This period also saw the return to power of de Valera, who left Sinn Fein in 1926 in order to found a new party, Fianna Fail. The party aimed 'to secure the political independence of a united Ireland as a republic'.[24] Within a year, de Valera had been re-elected to the Dail, and by 1932, Fianna Fail was in power, with de Valera as prime minister. During the 1930s, de Valera led the efforts to make the Free State into an independent republic. This had already begun with the Statute of Westminster (1931), which recognised that dominions were not subordinate to Britain. De Valera's successful campaign to remove the oath of allegiance continued the process.

In 1936, the External Relations Act abolished the monarch's role in internal Irish affairs. De Valera's lasting legacy was the 1937 constitution, which strengthened the Irish government through the creation of a president as head of state. It also hinted at the ultimate desire to reunite the country – Article 2 referred to the national territory as 'the whole island of Ireland'. The constitution also reinforced another notable aspect of de Valera's Ireland – its socially conservative attitudes, reinforced by the power of the Church. Article 44 related to the 'special position' of the Catholic Church in the Irish state; Article 41 claimed, 'The State recognises that by her life within the home, woman gives to the State a support without which the common good cannot be achieved.'

Further evidence of the traditional nature of the new Irish state included the creation of the Committee on Evil Literature, which banned novels including Joseph Heller's *Catch 22*; and the attendance of 20% of the population at the Eucharistic Congress of 1932, promoting devotion to the Blessed Sacrament.

Northern Ireland

Although partition offered a solution to the 'Ulster problem', Northern Ireland faced conflict and division from its inception. Protestants made up 66% of the new state, but two of its counties, Fermanagh and Tyrone, both had a Catholic majority. After the 1920 election, Nationalist candidates opposed to partition refused to take their seats in the Northern Irish Parliament. In 1925, although they agreed to take their seats in Parliament this time, they refused to act as an official opposition to the unionist government. The Anglo-Irish War saw the rise of inter-communal violence in the North, with Catholics evacuated from Lisburn in August 1920, after attacks on their offices and homes.

Unemployment, which hit 40% in June 1921, increased the tensions and up to 9000 Catholics were sacked from their jobs to make way for Protestants. In the years 1920–1922 alone, 453 people were murdered in Belfast. The creation of the Royal Ulster Constabulary (RUC) was an attempt by James Craig to contain the situation. In reality, the anti-Catholic views of some RUC officers led many Catholics to support the IRA. Repressive legislation was introduced – the Special Powers Act of 1922 allowed the RUC significant powers of arrest and detention without trial.

ACTIVITY 3.30

Using the information in this section, and your own research, write short biographies of Michael Collins and Eamon de Valera.

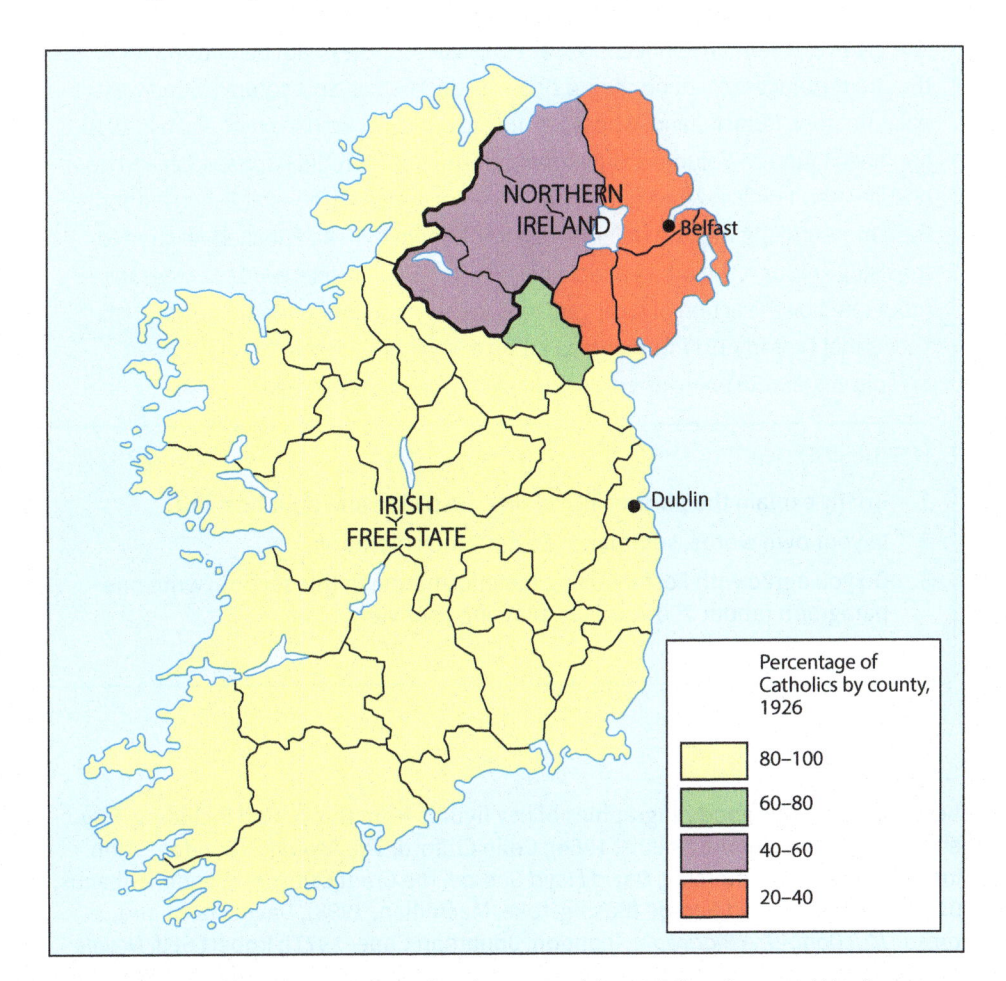

Figure 3.16: The Catholic population of each county of the Irish Free State and Northern Ireland five years after partition

In employment and local government, discrimination persisted. Only one-sixth of the RUC was Catholic. It was hard for Catholics to reach higher positions within the civil service. In 1921, the Northern Irish Parliament disbanded 21 nationalist local councils, replacing them with government-appointed commissioners. Electoral boundaries were redrawn to favour unionists, and proportional representation was abolished, confirming unionist dominance in the political arena. It was no surprise when, in 1924, nationalists won control of only two of 80 local councils. In response, Joseph Devlin and Cahir Healy created the Nationalist League in the North in 1928, in an attempt to unite a range of nationalist groups. It enjoyed a brief period of success, with 10 nationalist MPs being elected by the end of the decade, but it disbanded in 1934 after being opposed by both Sinn Fein and the Catholic Church. As a result, the unionists continued to dominate Northern Irish politics. The unionist Craig continued as prime minister until his death in 1940.

By the time war broke out in 1939, the religious and political divisions, both within Northern Ireland and between the two Irish states, were greater than ever.

Speak like a historian

R.F. Foster, Modern Ireland 1600–1972

The fifteen grisly executions in early May created as many martyrs. The case in law, given the German connection, was conclusive for the death penalty; but in the circumstances of Ireland during 1916, the decision against commutation was inflammatory. Rural Ireland, whose attitude towards separatist nationalism in 1915 had been found by Volunteer organizers a mixture of 'incredulity, suspicion and dour hostility' soon rediscovered traditional modes of resistance to established authority. Even more striking was the shift in 'respectable' opinion. The appalled reaction to the rising amongst the urban middle classes immediately afterwards … was rapidly moderated by the action of local garrisons; a survey of County Meath newspapers shows that by early 1917 Cumann na mBan and other extreme nationalist organisations were being given a new kind of respectful coverage.[25]

Discussion points:

1. Briefly explain the phrase 'incredulity, suspicion and dour hostility'.
2. In your own words, summarise Foster's interpretation.
3. Do you agree with Foster? Using the information in this section, write one paragraph (about 200 words) explaining your view.

Further reading

There are numerous good biographies of key figures from this period including: Roy Jenkins, *Asquith* (London, Collins, 1964); Colin Clifford, *The Asquiths* (London, John Murray, 2003); Roy Hattersley, *David Lloyd George, the Great Outsider* (London, Abacus, 2012); Ian Packer, *Lloyd George* (Basingstoke, Macmillan, 1998); David Marquand, *Ramsay MacDonald: A Biography* (London, Jonathan Cape, 1977); Robert Self, *Neville Chamberlain: A Biography* (Aldershot, Ashgate, 2006) and Tim Pat Coogan, *De Valera: Long Fellow, Long Shadow* (London, Arrow, 1995).

A key debate looks at the decline of the Liberal Party. Key texts include Paul Adelman, *The Decline of the Liberal Party, 1910–31* (Harlow, Longman, 1981). and the seminal

George Dangerfield, *The Strange Death of Liberal England, 1910–1914* (available online). *British Social Trends since 1900*, edited by A.H. Halsey (Basingstoke, Macmillan, 1988) is an excellent source of statistics about developments in the British economy and society from 1900 onwards. Charles Townshend, *Easter 1916: The Irish Rebellion* (London, Penguin, 2005) is a good summary of the motives, actions and impact of the nationalist rebels during the First World War.

> **Practice essay questions**
>
> 1. 'Britain lacked effective political leadership in the years 1918 to 1939.' Assess the validity of this view.
> 2. To what extent did economic policy of British governments change in the years 1918–1939?
> 3. 'The changing role of women was the most significant social development in Britain in the years 1914–1939.' Assess the validity of this view.
> 4. Using your understanding of the historical context, assess how convincing these three extracts are in relation to the impact of Eamon de Valera on Irish politics between 1921 and 1939.

Extract A

Diarmaid Ferriter, *Judging Dev,* Royal Irish Academy, 2007, pp. 366–7.

Prosperous modern Ireland often asks why prosperity did not come sooner and analyses the 1930s … from that perspective, as opposed to looking at the real and lasting achievements of an exceptionally talented state-builder … De Valera was careful about many things … this was particularly the case after the divisions of the Civil War era, when he adopted a clever and defiant but also a careful strategy to maximise independent Ireland's sovereignty and invest that sovereignty with dignity. It could not be achieved without compromise and difficulties, and sometimes mistakes. But by and large it worked, and it invoked … a strong sense of nationhood, while at the same time producing an exceptionally stable democracy … De Valera may have miscalculated in 1921 by believing … that his alternative strategy to the Treaty could have yielded greater independence, but he learnt from his mistakes in a way that benefited the country. The legislative record of Fianna Fail in the 1930s … is impressive … in the areas of housing, health and welfare provision.[26]

Extract B

T. Ryle Dwyer, *Eamon De Valera,* Paperview, 2006, p. 356.

[De Valera's] ultimate political legacy to the Irish people was a mixed bag, with positive and negative aspects. No subsequent political action can condone his mistakes or erase his share of the guilt for the events leading to the Civil War, but history is replete with examples of leaders who surmounted disastrous mistakes to enrich the lives of their people. Since nothing succeeds quite like success, his past errors and miscalculations took on a different aspect as a result of his achievements in the 1930s … when he made an invaluable contribution towards the preservation of democracy. Some Irish people genuinely feared that de Valera would try to set up a dictatorship when he came to power in 1932 … [but] de Valera had promised to adhere to democratic principles and he upheld his promise. In the process, he managed to take the gun out of twenty-six county politics, an achievement which was probably his greatest contribution to the modern Irish state.[27]

Extract C

Tim Pat Coogan *De Valera: Long Fellow, Long Shadow,* Arrow, 1993, pp. 696–7, and 700.

[De Valera's] behaviour after the Treaty was signed was irresponsible and caused lasting damage to his colleagues and to Ireland. The wading-through-blood speeches … were fiery, but cold-blooded, on all fours with his deliberate decision to utilise extremist support – the IRA – for his purpose … De Valera did not do or say anything that can be pointed to as enriching Irish culture or bringing Ireland into the mainstream of Western thought … The form of the Irish Church … was essential to de Valera, Man of Power … it provided him with an electorate indoctrinated by (the need to have) 'respect for those who rule over us' … Yet even though he held it for too long, de Valera played a decisive, and not dishonourable, part in holding the bridge for democracy … among de Valera's other … legacies were his Constitution … and his political party, Fianna Fail.[28]

Chapter summary

By the end of this chapter you should have gained a broad overview of the way in which British politics, economy and society developed in the years 1914–39:

- the impact of war on British parties and politics: the development of coalition government; the reasons for the decline of the Liberals; and impact on the development of Conservative and Labour parties
- the causes and consequences of electoral reform: successes and failures of the Conservative and Labour governments; the National Government and the challenges it faced, including the abdication crisis and emergence of radical political movements, including the BUF and communism
- the cause and consequence of economic developments including: increased state role in wartime; problems of the staple industries and mines; the General Strike; government finances and the gold standard; the Depression; economic realignment
- the significance of social developments such as: the changes in the role of women during and after the war; the condition of the working classes; regional divisions; changing attitudes in the 1920s and 'the hungry thirties'; the growth of the media
- the degree of success of social policies: legislation and reforms in housing; education and welfare
- the impact of the First World War and the Easter Rising on Irish nationalism, and the growing differences between the new Irish Free State and Northern Ireland.

Endnotes

1. M. Bentley, *Politics Without Democracy, 1815–1914*. London, Fontana, 1984, pp. 367–8.
2. *Workers Weekly*, 25 July 1924.
3. *Daily Mail*, 15 January 1934.
4. Ibid.
5. J. Stevenson, *British Society 1914–45*. London, Penguin, 1984, p. 270.
6. B. R. Mitchell and Phyllis Deane, *Abstract of British Historical Statistics*. Cambridge University Press, 1962.
7. D. Taylor, *Mastering Economic and Social History*. Macmillan Education, 1988, p. 543.
8. Ibid, p. 544.
9. Statement of 1925, as quoted in C.L. Mowat, *Britain between the Wars*. London, Methuen & Co., 1955, p. 300.
10. A. H. Halsey (ed.), *British Social Trends since 1900*, revised 2nd edition. Basingstoke, Macmillan, 1988, p. 174.
11. Ibid, p. 164.
12. G. Orwell, *The Road to Wigan Pier*. London, Penguin, 2001, p. 80.
13. Stevenson, *British Society 1914–45*, p. 270.
14. Halsey, *British Social Trends since 1900*, p. 112.
15. Ibid, p. 80.
16. Ibid, p. 43.
17. R. Pearce, *Britain: Domestic Politics 1918–39*. London, Hodder & Stoughton, 1992, p. 21.
18. Halsey, *British Social Trends Since 1900*, chapter 10.
19. Stevenson, *British Society 1914–45*, p. 227.
20. N. Lowe, *Modern British History*, 4th edition. Basingstoke, Palgrave Macmillan, 2009, p. 384.
21. From the manifesto of the Irish Volunteers, 24 September 1914, quoted in S.L. Gwynn, *The Last Years of John Redmond*. London, Edward Arnold, 1919.
22. P. Pearse, quoted in J. Valente, *The Myth of Manliness in Irish National Culture, 1880–1922*. Illinois, University of Illinois Press, 2010, p.103.
23. Quoted in J.A. Ranelagh, *A Short History of Ireland*. Cambridge, Cambridge University Press, 1999, p. 232.
24. Quoted in A. O'Day and J. Stevenson, *Irish Historical Documents since 1800*. Dublin, Gill & Macmillan, 1992, p. 188.
25. R.F. Foster, *Modern Ireland 1600–1972*. London, Penguin, 1988, p. 485.
26. D. Ferriter, *Judging Dev*. Dublin, Royal Irish Academy, 2007, pp. 366–7.
27. T. Ryle Dwyer, *Eamon De Valera*. Dublin, Gill and Macmillan Limited, 1998,, p. 356.
28. T.P. Coogan, *De Valera: Long Fellow, Long Shadow*. London, Arrow, 1993, pp. 696–7 and 700.

4 Transformation and change, 1939–64

In this chapter we will investigate the political, social and economic impact of the Second World War. In particular, we will look into:

- the impact of the Second World War on British politics: Churchill as wartime leader; domestic developments under Churchill; the Labour landslide of 1945; Labour ideology and policies

- developments in the political parties: Conservative dominance from 1951 and political consensus; division within the Labour Party; Conservatism and the Establishment; Labour victory in 1964

- economic developments and policies: mobilisation of resources in wartime; the postwar boom; balance of payments issues and 'stop-go' policies; changes to British industry and trade; new technology

- social changes and divisions: austerity and the impact of war; the growth of affluence; consumerism and changes for women and young people; immigration and racial tensions

- developments in social policy: the Beveridge Report; the Butler Act; the growth of the welfare state and the NHS; the development of education

- the condition of Ireland and Anglo-Irish relations: continuing North-South friction; the civil rights campaign.

The impact of the Second World War on British politics

Churchill as wartime leader

Timeline: The Second World War

1939	
3 September	Britain declares war on Germany
1940	
April	German invasion of Norway and Denmark
10 May	Chamberlain resigns; replaced by Churchill
May–June	Germans overrun Belgium, the Netherlands and northern France
27 May – 4 June	British troops evacuated from Dunkirk
22 June	Surrender of France
August	Battle of Britain begins
September	Hitler switches tactics, bombing London and other major cities
November	Aircraft from British carrier *Illustrious* sink half the Italian fleet
1941	
April	British soldiers withdraw from Greece to Crete; British troops driven out of Libya
June	British withdrawal from Crete
1942	
February	Fall of Singapore
March	Japanese occupation of Burma
July	First Battle of El-Alamein: Montgomery's Eighth Army drives Rommel out of Tobruk
Oct–Nov	Rommel's armies withdraw from Egypt
1943	
January	Tripoli captured by the Allies
8 September	Italy surrenders, entering the war on the Allied side
1944	
6 June	D-Day: Allied troops re-enter France
25 August	Paris liberated
December	German advance pushed back at the Battle of the Bulge
1945	
April	Japanese withdrawal from Burma
8 May	VE Day
5 July	General election: Attlee becomes prime minister
15 August	VJ Day

Hitler's refusal to withdraw his troops from Poland in September 1939 led to Chamberlain's declaration of war. However, the initial months of the conflict saw little action, becoming known as the 'Phoney War'. The British imposed a blockade and won a number of minor naval battles, but it was not until April 1940 that the war escalated, with the German invasion of Norway.

The Germans wanted to safeguard Narvik, the main outlet for Swedish iron ore used by the German arms industry. They landed at Oslo and other towns, taking the British by surprise. During a Commons debate on the issue, Chamberlain was attacked by fellow Conservative MPs, including Leo Amery, who proclaimed: 'Depart, I say, and let us have done with you. In the name of God, go.'[1] Although the government won the subsequent vote, its majority (normally 240) was 81. Chamberlain resigned; the King accepted his recommendation to summon Churchill as the new prime minister.

Churchill's difficulties

Churchill did not face an easy task. The war itself was going badly for the Allies – the Nazi invasion of the Netherlands, Belgium and France on 10 May demonstrated the strength of Nazi blitzkrieg tactics. The evacuation of 338 000 British troops from Dunkirk, in the face of attacks by the Luftwaffe, was portrayed as a triumph by the press and the government. The 'Dunkirk Spirit', encouraged by the prime minister, undoubtedly boosted British morale, but the reality on the ground was grim. The German capture of Paris and the French surrender led to a situation where northern France was under Nazi control, while the south of the country, under Marshal Pétain, collaborated with the Germans. Britain, whose troops had fully withdrawn from France by June, was now alone in the fight against Nazi Germany.

However, Churchill's difficulties were also political. He was not popular with his Conservative colleagues, many of whom distrusted him. His attacks on Chamberlain as an appeaser, and his support for Edward VIII during the abdication crisis, made many of his own MPs suspicious. Chamberlain's ally Rab Butler claimed the Conservatives had 'weakly surrendered to a half-breed American'. His reputation as a serial 'floor-crosser' (he had moved from the Conservatives to the Liberals and then back to the Conservatives during a long career) did not help. It was notable that, on Churchill's first appearance in the Commons as prime minister, he was cheered by Labour and Liberal MPs, whereas his own side largely cheered for Chamberlain. However, even many Labour MPs were dubious about Churchill. They remembered his enthusiasm for engaging the army during the General Strike.

Opposition to Churchill persisted during the war. In May 1941 and July 1942, Erskine-Hill, chairman of the 1922 Committee, met Lord Woolton to discuss the possibility of replacing Churchill. In August 1942, Woolton reported that the Party 'thinks that Winston has had his day'.

Churchill's advantages

Nevertheless, Churchill had several advantages. His consistent support for rearmament and opposing Hitler gave the impression of a strong war leader who would stand up effectively for British interests. A.J.P. Taylor claimed, 'it was as if all his life had been an unconscious preparation for this hour'.[2] He also chose his war cabinet and full cabinet carefully, making use of Labour and Liberal talents. The war cabinet included Chamberlain, Halifax, Labour leader Attlee and another Labour member, Arthur Greenwood. In the cabinet, Labour's Ernest Bevin was an effective minister of labour, and Conservative Lord Beaverbrook played a key role as minister of aircraft production. Other notable contributions were made by Labour's Herbert Morrison (Home Secretary) and Hugh Dalton (President of the Board of Trade), as well as Liberal leader Archibald Sinclair, who became Secretary of State for Air. The passing of the Emergency Powers Act in 1940 – which would give the government almost total power over property and British citizens – was an early indication of the strength of the Churchill administration.

> **Thematic link:** Mobilisation of resources in wartime

Churchill's leadership style

Historians have tended to emphasise Churchill's energy and enthusiasm for getting involved in all aspects of military strategy. This had its advantages, ensuring that generals were always in full control of their briefs as a result of Churchill's 'ceaseless prodding' for information and updates. Nevertheless, his style made him unpopular among civil servants, who tended to see him as a 'meddler', as well as some of his cabinet colleagues, who resented his long interventions during meetings. However, Alan Brooke, the Chief of the General Staff, was usually effective at dissuading Churchill from some of his more outlandish suggestions. To his credit, Churchill was content to delegate key decisions on the Home Front to his colleagues, especially Attlee and Bevin. He allowed himself to be overruled on a number of domestic issues, including the conscription of women in 1941 and the introduction of clothes rationing, both of which he personally opposed.

Churchill's greatest strengths were his will to win and his ability to boost the morale of the British people. His inspiring oratory, both on the radio and in the House of Commons, made a significant difference to the public's self-belief and contributed towards the success of the Home Front's efforts to keep troops well supplied.

Arguments in praise of Churchill's military leadership

In addition to his ability to inspire the armed forces and the public, there are several reasons why Churchill has been viewed as an effective wartime leader:

- During the Battle of Britain, the RAF resisted German attempts to target aerodromes and communication systems. On 8 August 1940, 31 German planes were shot down, compared with 20 British ones. Hitler called off his planned invasion of Britain on 15 September, after a day on which 60 German planes were lost. Churchill's leadership contributed, as did the skill of British pilots, aircraft production (496 were produced in July alone) and the work of 51 radar stations, which warned of German attacks.
- The war at sea was largely successful. The sinking of half the Italian fleet at Taranto, as well as the *Bismarck* in 1941, was an achievement. The navy provided escorts for convoys carrying supplies for the USSR.
- The battle of El-Alamein was an important turning point. Rommel's forces captured Tobruk in June 1942 but were driven back by Montgomery's Eighth Army. In October Rommel was chased out of Egypt, and by January 1943, Tripoli had been captured. British reinforcements made a difference: there were 230 000 British men to 80 000 Germans. The battles secured Egypt and the Suez Canal and stopped the Axis powers in Ukraine and the Middle East combining.
- D-Day was enormously successful. Some 326 000 men had safely landed by end of the first week. Over 3 million troops were eventually landed, leading to the liberation of Paris and, later, Brussels and Antwerp, enabling Allied troops ultimately to liberate Germany by May 1945.
- 'Carpet bombing' had an impact after July 1944. German synthetic oil production fell, leading to fuel shortages. The destruction of the Krupps armaments factory also had a significant effect – forcing the Germans to divert aircraft from the Eastern front which relieved pressure on the Soviets.

> **Voices from the past**
>
> ### Winston Churchill (1874–1965)[3]
>
> We have before us many, many long months of struggle and of suffering. You ask, what is our policy? I can say: It is to wage war, by sea, land and air, with all our might and with all the strength that God can give us; to wage war against a monstrous tyranny, never surpassed in the dark, lamentable catalogue of human crime. (13 May 1940)
>
> We shall go on to the end, we shall fight in France, we shall fight on the seas and oceans, we shall fight with growing confidence and growing strength in the air, we shall defend our Island, whatever the cost may be, we shall fight on the beaches, we shall fight on the landing grounds, we shall fight in the fields and in the streets, we shall fight in the hills; we shall never surrender. (4 June 1940)
>
> Never in the field of human conflict was so much owed by so many to so few. (20 August 1940)
>
> ### Discussion points:
>
> 1. Using evidence from these three speeches, explain how Churchill's oratory was effective in improving British morale.
> 2. To what extent was Churchill's oratory the most important factor in Britain's victory? Explain your answer, using evidence from this section and your own research.

Figure 4.1: A Supermarine Spitfire, armed with a 250 lb GP bomb under each wing

Arguments against Churchill's military leadership
However, there are a number of arguments to suggest that Churchill's military leadership had significant weaknesses:

- It can be argued that success in the Battle of Britain was more the result of Hitler's mistakes. Later in the battle, the British were struggling: 103 RAF airmen were killed between 24 August and 6 September. However, Hitler's decision to divert his aircraft to bomb British cities during the Blitz gave the British time to regroup.
- Churchill's decision to intervene in Greece was heavily criticised. The evacuation of 60 000 troops to Crete – itself not properly fortified and captured by a German parachute attack – was seen as a mistake. 36 000 British troops were killed. This was partly because Churchill failed to realise the importance of air support in naval operations.
- He was criticised during the war in the Mediterranean. The British were driven out of Libya by Rommel after troops and planes were diverted to Greece. Malta faced sustained German and Italian bombing and was almost starved into surrender. The loss of the *Ark Royal* aircraft carrier was a further embarrassment.
- Churchill underestimated Japan. Britain's early campaign in the Far East was disastrous. Japan took Hong Kong and captured all the airfields in northern Malaya. British ships *Repulse* and the *Prince of Wales* were sunk. Churchill also thought Singapore was unassailable (it was known as 'Fortress Singapore'.) In fact, the Japanese were able to cut off its water supply and force it to surrender.
- The 'carpet' bombing of German cities was criticised for its ineffectiveness and on moral grounds. 158 000 Allied airmen were killed during these bombing raids. Meanwhile, the killing of 50 000 German civilians on one night in February 1945 led to condemnation from some Labour MPs and, particularly, from the Church.

4 Transformation and change, 1939–64

Speak like a historian

David Reynolds and Robert Blake

David Reynolds is Professor of International History at Cambridge University. His area of expertise ranges across 20th-century international history, with a particular focus on the two world wars.

Recognition of Churchill's remarkable role in 1940 must be balanced by an acknowledgement that he was not always right in his decisions … however, a sober examination of Churchill's performance as war leader in 1940 does not belittle his greatness … it makes him more human.[4]

Robert Blake combined a distinguished career as a historian with an involvement in Conservative politics, both as a local councillor and as a member of the House of Lords. His *Conservative Party from Peel to Major* is a highly regarded and accessible history of the party.

His old fashioned … views on … the empire, and Britain's role in the world had been liabilities in the 1930s. So too had been his obvious fascination by war and the problems of war. Now in a desperate struggle for national survival, they became … virtues, along with his courage, tenacity, and a command over language unsurpassed by any previous Prime Minister.[5]

Discussion points:

1. Give three pieces of evidence to suggest that Churchill was 'not always right in his decisions'.
2. Do you agree with Reynolds that Churchill can still be regarded as a great leader, despite his failings?
3. Write a one-paragraph conclusion to the question, 'Which of these two interpretations do you find more convincing?'

Domestic developments under Churchill

As in the First World War, the experience of 'total war' led to significant developments in social policy and welfare under Churchill's coalition government. Two notable examples are the publication of the Beveridge Report in 1942 and the passing of the 'Butler' Education Act in 1944.

Cross-references: The Beveridge Report; The Butler Act

The Beveridge Report, which identified the five 'great evils' of want, squalor, disease, ignorance and idleness was debated by the Commons in February 1943. Within the cabinet, there were differences of opinion about how to react to the recommendations. Labour wanted to implement Beveridge's proposals immediately; Churchill, though largely supportive in principle, was adamant it was vital to win the war first.

Although Churchill's view largely prevailed, one of the report's suggestions was introduced before the end of the war – the introduction of child allowances of five shillings a week for each child after the first. A Labour resolution that the government should immediately implement the recommendations of the report was defeated in the Commons by 335 votes to 119. Nevertheless, Attlee worked hard behind the scenes to ensure that the rest of the report was not forgotten. Churchill's appointment of Lord Woolton as minister of reconstruction, and the introduction of three White Papers on health, employment, and social insurance in 1944, suggested that Attlee's efforts were not in vain.

The 1944 Education Act was an attempt to tackle the 'ignorance' identified as one of Beveridge's five great evils. Rab Butler, the Conservative President of the Board of Education, was determined to ensure that all children were given access to free secondary education. Alongside the Beveridge Report, the Butler Act laid the foundations for the work of the Attlee government and its successors in building the welfare state.

The Labour landslide of 1945

The defeat of Nazi Germany on 8 May marked a personal triumph for Churchill, whose reputation as a world statesman was secure. His position at home was more vulnerable. He had wanted the coalition to continue in office until Japan was defeated, but Attlee disagreed, triggering the first general election for ten years. Polling day was 5 July, but the votes were not counted until 26 July in order to allow members of the armed forces to vote. Parliamentary candidates, such as Labour's Jim Callaghan, who were serving overseas were provided with special transport home. Although the media expected a Conservative victory, Labour won by a landslide. Gaining 48% of the popular vote against 39.6% for the Conservatives, their majority was 146 seats; 250 of the 393 Labour victors were new Members of Parliament.

Reasons for Labour's victory

Although the scale of Labour's victory was a surprise, it can be explained with reference to several factors:

- Socialist ideas were popular among intellectuals. The 'climate of opinion' had swung to the left since the 1930s, evidenced by the prominence of the radical publisher Victor Gollancz, and the activities of the Left Book Club. Books such as Eleanor Rathbone's *A Case for Family Allowances* were widely read.
- Left-wing policies of state intervention, high spending and high taxation, as well as state control of railways and gas, had been necessary in order to win the war. Labour MP Michael Foot claimed: 'It was the nearest thing I have seen in my lifetime to the operation of a democratic socialist state.' The idea that government could, and should, pursue these policies seemed less radical than before the war. Full employment, free school milk and free school meals during the war demonstrated the benefits of this approach.
- Churchill therefore misjudged the national mood when he claimed during the campaign that Labour would bring 'the kind of features that were associated with the Gestapo'. Churchill also underestimated Attlee, whom he described variously as 'a sheep in sheep's clothing' and 'a modest little man with plenty to be modest about'.[6]
- Many middle-class families, shocked at the poverty of the evacuees they had welcomed into their homes, became convinced of the need for greater state intervention. There was also a feeling that the working people of Britain had 'earned' the right to better conditions, thanks to their war work, and a sense of outrage that similar expectations had not been met after 1918. Labour's clear proposals to implement the Beveridge Report were therefore popular. The

Conservatives showed less enthusiasm for the report and their policy proposals appeared vague in comparison.
- Churchill was popular (a fact his party recognised, naming their manifesto *Mr Churchill's Declaration of Policy to the Electors*) but the Conservative Party was not. Conservatives were held responsible both for the Depression and for the outbreak of war. Harold Macmillan claimed: 'It was not Churchill who lost the 1945 election; it was the ghost of Neville Chamberlain.'[7]

As a result of its participation in the wartime coalition, the Labour party was seen as competent and experienced. Other than Churchill, Attlee was the only politician to have been a member of the war cabinet throughout 1940–45. Arthur Greenwood had successfully set up committees of researchers and planners as minister with responsibility for reconstruction.

Labour ideology and policies

Labour's 1945 manifesto stated that 'the Labour Party is a Socialist Party, and proud of it'. Labour's socialist ideology was evident primarily in its proposals to nationalise key industries. The left-wing Aneurin Bevan, who as minister of health would introduce the NHS, ensured that the implementation of socialist principles remained firmly on the government's agenda. However, the new cabinet also contained a number of more pragmatic figures, including the Chancellor, Hugh Dalton; the Foreign Secretary, Ernest Bevin; and the Leader of the House of Commons, Herbert Morrison. The government's support for a mixed economy, as well as its implementation of the ideas of Beveridge and Keynes (both Liberals) suggested a more moderate, social democratic ideology.

Attlee faced significant challenges in managing his cabinet. Not only did the leading figures clash over ideology, but personal rivalries could also lead to hostility, especially in the case of Bevan and Bevin. Nevertheless, Attlee was able to control this group of strong and independent-minded personalities effectively. According to Peter Hennessy, he was good at 'using silence as a weapon, cutting off wafflers, absolutely brutal with the inadequate and the incompetent, far more effective than any Prime Minister since'.[9]

> **Thematic links: The Beveridge Report; the General Strike**

The implementation of the Beveridge Report was the key priority for the new government. However, it also introduced other important legislation.

The New Towns Act (1946) gave the government power to decide where new towns were built and to set up development corporations for the projects. The aim was to provide healthy environments which met the needs of their people. As a result of the act, 14 new towns were created, including Stevenage, Hemel Hempstead and East Kilbride.

The Trade Disputes Act (1946) reintroduced the political levy. Individuals now had to 'contract out' if they did not want to contribute to the Labour Party. The law repealed Baldwin's Trade Disputes Act of 1927, and returned the trade unions to the position which they held before the General Strike.

Nationalisation

Labour's other key priority was to **nationalise** key industries. The 1944 Labour Party conference had resolved that this would be the main solution in order to restore trade that had been disrupted during the war, revive declining industries, improve exports and restore prosperity. Left-wingers argued that nationalisation would lead to fairer treatment of workers, improved working conditions and full employment. Profits

---

Voices from the past

Sir Robert Bruce Lockhart (1887–1970)
Diary entry of 26 July 1945

The magnitude of Labour's victory was largely determined by the faulty election tactics of the Tories who turned what the vast majority of the public, and especially of the large class of new young voters, regarded as a most serious affair affecting their future lives into a kind of dog-fight of the last century in which abuse and slanging of the enemy takes the place of a constructive programme.[8]

Discussion points:
1. What does Lockhart mean by 'a kind of dog-fight of the last century'? Use evidence from Chapters 1 and 2 to help you.
2. Do you agree that Labour's victory was 'largely determined' by Conservative weaknesses?

Key terms

Nationalisation: The policy of bringing private companies into public ownership, under the ultimate control of the government.

would now go to the Treasury, rather than to private owners – these would be used to fund the growth of the welfare state. Clause IV of the party's constitution included a commitment to state control of 'the means of production, distribution and exchange'. Under the leadership of Morrison, Attlee's government began to put this into practice, with 2.3 million workers moving from privately to publicly owned industries.

> Thematic links: The growth of the welfare state; the constitutional crisis

ACTIVITY 4.1

Create a concept web to explain the term 'nationalisation'.

Timeline: Nationalisation of British industries

Date	Industry nationalised	Details
1946	Bank of England	Day-to-day management of the Bank would be carried out by its staff, but the Chancellor now had greater control over key monetary policy decisions, especially the setting of interest rates.
1946	Air transport	Reorganised into three companies: British Overseas, British European and British South American Airways
1947	Mining	1500 collieries and 400 smaller mines were brought under the control of the National Coal Board. Conservatives opposed this, but miners were generally supportive.
1948	Public transport	Controlled by British Transport Commission, divided into six boards.
1948	Electricity	The government took over around 500 generating companies and set up 14 area electricity boards to ensure consistent prices and voltage.
1949	Gas	Parliament agreed to this despite 800 Conservative amendments to the bill.
1950	Iron and steel	The Conservatives were opposed, as these industries were flourishing. After the Lords blocked the plans, the Parliament Act (1949) was introduced. This meant the Lords could now delay a bill for one year.

Nationalisation was part of a wider government emphasis on planning. The importance of planning was reinforced by the formation of the Economic Planning Council, set up in July 1947 under Sir Edwin Plowden, as well as the creation of the Import Programmes Committee and Production Committee.

> Cross-references: Mobilisation of resources in wartime; Changes to British industry and trade; Austerity and the impact of war

4 Transformation and change, 1939-64

Taking it further

Assessing the Labour Government

The 1945–51 Labour government has divided opinion like few others in history. Kenneth Morgan claims it 'was amongst the most effective of any British government since the passage of the 1832 Reform Act' and that 1948–50 was 'amongst the most thriving periods economically that the country as a whole had experienced since the late Victorian era'.[10] He points to the fact that Labour's policies were largely maintained at least until 1970. Boosted by its landslide victory, its innovative policies and focus on planning improved the economy. Inflation was brought under control and full employment achieved, and the balance of payments was healthy, buoyed by the increase in car exports to the United States.

Conversely, right-wing historians such as Corelli Barnett argue that Labour squandered resources on the welfare state, rather than using them to modernise industry. According to Barnett, the post-war economy was not strong enough to fund welfare on the scale implemented by Labour, affecting Britain's longer-term economic prospects and its ability to compete with Japan, the USA and West Germany. Once the profits of industry had been maximised, then the money could have been used to fund the NHS and social security. Barnett claims that 'the illusions and dreams of 1945 would fade one by one – the imperial and Commonwealth role, the world-power role, British industrial genius, and at the last, New Jerusalem itself, a dream turned to a dank reality of a segregated, subliterate, unskilled, unhealthy and institutionalised proletariat hanging on the nipple of state maternalism'.[11]

Martin Pugh argues against Barnett, suggesting that many factors caused Britain's economic decline and the government inherited a difficult economic situation after the war. He points to West Germany and France, where social security spending was similar to that of Attlee's government. Although spending was high, all three Labour Chancellors carefully spent within their means.

Nick Tiratsoo agrees, claiming that industry *was* modernised – new factories were given top priority in the government's building programme and working parties of experts, employers and workers were set up to improve performance. The British Institute of Management was established to improve standards, and many industrialists and workers visited the USA to investigate cutting-edge techniques.

Socialist historians such as John Saville have criticised the government from the left. They claim that Hugh Dalton and Stafford Cripps were not expert planners and were reluctant to take advice from those who were. Long-term targets for investment and production were rarely set; the approach was piecemeal. Workers rarely featured on the boards of nationalised industries, which tended to be highly bureaucratic; only 20% of industry was actually nationalised.

1. Copy and complete this table.
2. Write a paragraph to explain which interpretation is most convincing and why.

Historian	Summary of their interpretation	Evidence for this position	Evidence against this position
Morgan			
Barnett			
Pugh			

Developments in the political parties

Conservative dominance from 1951 and political consensus

After three years of **austerity**, Labour's electoral fortunes suffered. The 1950 election saw their majority cut to five. Although Labour won 46.1% of the vote, the Conservative share increased to 43.5%. Such a small majority was unsustainable, and Attlee called a second election in 1951. This time, the Conservatives were victorious. With a majority of 17, the Conservatives began a period of dominance that would last for 13 years.

> **Key terms**
>
> **Austerity:** A policy which involves government cuts; during times of austerity, the public are encouraged to live within their means.

Election	Winning party	Overall majority	Winning prime minister
1945	Labour	146	Attlee
1950	Labour	5	Attlee
1951	Conservative	17	Churchill
1955	Conservative	58	Eden
1959	Conservative	100	Macmillan
1964	Labour	4	Wilson

Table 4.1: Election results, 1945–64

Reasons for the Conservative victory in 1951

Churchill's victory was the result both of Labour weaknesses and a much more effective campaign than in 1945.

- The Labour government had become unpopular. Continued rationing and housing shortages, combined with an extended period of austerity, meant that the public were ready for a change.
- In contrast, the Conservatives had a wider appeal than in 1945. The party promised 300 000 new houses a year. Churchill's promises of 'more red meat' and to 'set people free' from socialist rules captured the national mood. In the midst of the Korean War, Churchill's credentials as a world statesman were in his favour.
- After 1945, Woolton had revitalised the Conservative Party. He successfully appealed to party members and business for £1 million for campaigning. He also began to encourage the selection of candidates from a wider range of social backgrounds. Woolton's membership drive was remarkably effective: by 1952, the membership had swelled to 2.8 million, including many younger members.
- The Liberal Party stood in only 109 constituencies. In the other seats, Liberal voters tended to vote Conservative, rather than Labour.
- The Conservatives had shown in opposition that they accepted most of the more-popular policies of the Attlee government, such as Keynesian economics and positive relations with the unions. Reginald Maudling prepared an Industrial Charter in 1947, which announced the party's commitment to a **mixed economy** and a **corporatist** approach to industry.

The Churchill government and the postwar consensus

Churchill's second period in power has often been viewed as a period of inertia and limited innovation. It is certainly true that Churchill himself, now 75, was tired and in poor health – much of the day-to-day running of the government was left to Eden. However, there was certainly some change: ID cards were abolished in 1952 and rationing finally ended in 1954. Churchill's cabinet also looked different from that of Attlee, thanks to the creation of ministerial 'overlords' who oversaw the running of

> **Key terms**
>
> **Mixed economy:** An economy in which some industries are nationalised and others are privately owned.
>
> **Corporatism:** A system of government in which both employers and trade unions take part in the decision-making process.

several departments each. These included Woolton (home affairs), and Lord Leathers, who oversaw transport, fuel and power.

Nevertheless, it soon became clear that the Conservatives would pursue similar economic policies to those of Attlee. Many of the leading members of Churchill's cabinet, including Butler (his Chancellor), Harold Macmillan at housing and Walter Monckton at labour were 'one nation Tories' who genuinely believed in a mixed economy. Historians have therefore labelled the period from 1945 to 1970 as the **postwar consensus**. Successive governments, Labour and Conservative, pursued Keynesian policies, extended the welfare state, aimed for full employment and accepted the mixed economy. They also had a corporatist approach to trade unions and business.

Churchill's government played its part in establishing this consensus. Iron and steel were denationalised, but the other nationalised industries remained. Meanwhile, the unions were given a prominent role. By 1958, employees had parity of representation on 850 committees.

> **Key terms**
>
> **Postwar consensus:** The period between 1945 and 1970, during which both Labour and Conservative parties pursued similar economic and industrial policies.

Taking it further

Historians have examined the consensus in depth. Michael Fraser questions whether the consensus existed at all, arguing: 'To say that the situation ... amounted to a consensus is a myth of more recent origin ... The real position was like that of two trains, starting off from parallel platforms ... and running for a time on broadly parallel lines but always heading for very different destinations.'[12]

Interestingly, two critics of consensus – Marxist historian Ralph Miliband and right-winger Nigel Lawson – nevertheless argue that consensus was a reality. Miliband writes 'one of the most important aspects of the political life of advanced capitalism is precisely that the disagreements between those political leaders who have generally been able to gain high office have very seldom been of the fundamental kind these leaders and other people so often suggest. What is really striking.... is not their many differences, but the extent of their agreement on truly fundamental issues.'[13]

Lawson claims that 'the Attlee government set the political agenda for the next quarter of a century. The two key principles which informed its actions ... big government and the drive towards quality, remained effectively unchallenged for more than a generation, the very heart of the postwar consensus.'[14]

A further perspective is offered by David Marquand, who claims that, not only did consensus exist, but that it had its origins not in 1945, but as far back as 1928.[15]

1. Work in groups of three. Divide Fraser's, Lawson's and Miliband's interpretations between you. For your interpretation, give it a mark out of 10 for how convincing you find it; explain your number using detailed evidence from this chapter.
2. Research David Marquand's perspective:
   - What evidence does he use to support his claim?
   - Do you agree with his interpretation? Use evidence from Chapters 3 and 4 to support your answer.

Eden's government

Churchill retired in April 1955, and was succeeded by Anthony Eden. The new prime minister called a general election for May, which saw an increase in the Conservative majority to 58; they won 345 seats, compared with Labour's 277. Labour had been riven by internal disputes, especially on defence and, in an era of consensus, struggled to argue that the Conservatives had wrecked their achievements of 1945–51. Aside from their proposals to abolish prescription charges and for the 11+ exam, Labour offered little in the way of creative thinking. Meanwhile, rising prosperity and living standards helped Eden, who was seen as a respected world statesman who would stand firm against the Soviet threat. The Conservatives made good use of television and radio, taking advantage of the fact that there were three times as many home television sets than there had been in 1951.

> **Cross-reference:** Division within the Labour Party

Timeline: Leaders of the Conservative Party

1937–40	Neville Chamberlain
1940–55	Winston Churchill
1955–57	Anthony Eden
1957–63	Harold Macmillan
1963–65	Alec Douglas-Home

> **Thematic links:** The postwar boom; the growth of affluence

It was clear that Eden would continue with a consensual approach to the economy. According to Hennessy, he was 'positively evangelical about industrial partnership as the banisher of class divisions between capital and labour.'[16] However, his government was dominated by one of the most significant foreign policy failures of the century, which centred on Egypt's Suez Canal. While Egyptian leader, Colonel Nasser, nationalised the Suez Canal, whose share owners were mainly British and French, Eden decided that firm action was needed. Britain, France and Israel secretly agreed the Protocol of Sèvres, under which Israel would attack the Egyptian army near the canal – this would then lead to military intervention by Britain and France in order to 'protect' the canal. In October 1956, Israel invaded the Sinai Peninsula and its troops moved towards the canal zone. Although the British and French bombed the area and landed paratroopers, a UN ceasefire came into force in November after US pressure. Britain and France reluctantly agreed to withdraw.

The crisis was a humiliation both for Britain and for Eden personally. Nasser's standing in the Middle East grew; meanwhile, Britain appeared weak on the international stage. It was clear that, as soon as the USA withdrew support, Britain was unable to conduct an effective foreign policy. Eden resigned, citing ill health – Suez was a major contributing factor.

Macmillan's government: 1957–63

Harold Macmillan was chosen as Eden's successor and made a positive start. He restored Conservative morale after Suez, was popular with both his cabinet and the public and immediately made good use of television to boost his appeal. He also appointed an impressive array of younger talent to his cabinet, including Julian Amery, Iain Macleod and Reginald Maudling. Like Eden, Macmillan was committed to the principles of consensus. He had been a successful housing minister, working hard to fulfil the pledge to build 300 000 new houses a year. His time as an MP in the deprived North-East during the Depression had an enormous impact. According to Attlee, Macmillan was 'a real left-wing radical in his social, human and economic thinking'.[17]

Macmillan claimed, 'I can never forget the impoverishment and demoralisation which all this brought with it. I am determined … never to allow this shadow to fall again upon our country.'[18]

It was no surprise when, in 1959, as living standards were rising, Macmillan won an easy election victory. With 365 seats to Labour's 258, the Conservatives now had a majority of 100. The 1959 budget had boosted the economy (see Figure 4.4) and even beer duty had been cut – a popular move! Labour was again hampered by internal divisions. The electorate were not convinced by Gaitskell's pledge to increase benefits while keeping income tax at existing levels. Meanwhile, the Conservatives exploited Macmillan's popularity: he spoke at 74 meetings during the campaign.

> Cross-reference: Division within the Labour Party

Macmillan's domestic policies

In addition to continuing with a consensual economic approach, Macmillan's government passed a number of significant pieces of legislation.

The Rent Act (1957) allowed landlords to charge higher rents to help improve their property. Labour claimed it was a 'landlords' charter', which would exploit vulnerable tenants. As a result of the act, 810 000 properties moved out of rent control. The act also allowed for rent increases in the remaining 4.3 million controlled properties.

The Life Peers Act (1957) introduced peers to the House of Lords who were appointed, rather than inheriting their title. By safeguarding the position of existing hereditary peers, the act did not go far enough for those seeking radical reform or the abolition of the Lords.

The Homicide Act (1957) reserved the death penalty for five special cases of murder. The aim was to gradually accustom the public to the idea of abolishing capital punishment by monitoring the effect of reducing the deterrent. This was a response to recent controversial hangings, including that of Ruth Ellis (the last woman to be executed in Britain).

Assessing the Macmillan government

> Thematic links: The postwar boom; the growth of affluence

Decolonisation, reforms to the Lords and criminal justice, and growing affluence have been viewed positively by most historians of the Macmillan government. However, several criticisms can also be made:

- Despite rising prosperity, the economy had stagnated by 1963. In January of that year, unemployment stood at 900 000. Conservative Chancellors had failed to find a solution to the issue of how to stimulate economic growth and a balance of payments surplus without causing spiralling inflation.
- **Stop-go policies** were reactive and short term. They failed to address deep-seated problems of industrial decline and the fact that British exports were hampered by its isolation from the European Economic Community (see Figure 4.4).
- It can be argued that, while living standards did increase during these years, there would have been even greater affluence without the negative impact of stop-go policies, which limited long-term prosperity.
- The positive relationship with the unions meant that the issue of union reform was not tackled, nor were necessary wage freezes introduced. Unions were excluded

Key terms

Decolonisation: The process by which countries within the British Empire gradually became independent, most remaining as part of the Commonwealth.

Stop-go policies: Short-term policies, which combine economic stimulation packages in times of economic downturn and measures to cut growth during periods of high inflation.

from the Monopolies and Restrictive Practices Act of 1956 and have been blamed for the limited productivity of these years. In 1957, 8.5 million working days were lost to strike action.

Macmillan's final years

By 1962, Macmillan appeared vulnerable. Economic problems were followed by the loss of the Orpington by-election, where a Conservative majority of almost 15 000 became a Liberal majority of 7855. Macmillan's response was a brutal cabinet reshuffle, soon nicknamed the 'Night of the Long Knives' – seven members of the cabinet, including Chancellor Selwyn Lloyd, were sacked. This did not have the desired effect, leading both to internal party divisions and to the growing impression of a government in crisis. The Profumo scandal weakened Macmillan further.

> **Cross-reference:** Economic developments and policies

The Profumo affair

John Profumo, Macmillan's Secretary of State for War, had been introduced to Christine Keeler, a showgirl and model, by Stephen Ward in 1961. Ward was an osteopath and artist who was friendly with many members of the Establishment, including Lord Astor, a Conservative peer. It was at Astor's home at Cliveden that Keeler and Profumo began their affair. In itself, Profumo's relationship may not have been the stuff of scandal, but the fact that Keeler was also in a relationship with a Russian naval attaché, Captain Ivanov, made Profumo's behaviour a huge security risk at the height of the Cold War. When rumours of his affair began to circulate in March 1963, Profumo told the Commons that there had been 'no impropriety' in his dealings with Keeler and that their relationship had ended in 1961.

As more detail emerged in the press, it became clear that Profumo had lied. He resigned from the cabinet and as an MP. The impact on Macmillan was significant. Macmillan found the whole affair distasteful and struggled to talk publicly about it. Harold Wilson used this to attack Macmillan for his weakness and complacency in the light of the Soviet threat. It was for this reason that the Profumo affair was a factor in Macmillan's decision to retire.

Macmillan's government was also damaged by the Rachman affair. Peter Rachman was a London landlord whose widespread exploitation of his tenants reflected badly on the government's decision to pass the Rent Act. Macmillan's resignation in 1963 led to a further crisis, with the appointment of Alec Douglas-Home itself a controversial issue.

> **Thematic link:** Conservatism and the Establishment

Division within the Labour Party

After the landslide victory of 1945, the 1950s were difficult years for the Labour Party, which was riven by internal division. To some extent, the battle lines had already been drawn during the Attlee government, when Bevan and Wilson resigned over the introduction of NHS charges. Bevan became the focus for Labour dissent, especially after his rival Hugh Gaitskell assumed the Labour leadership in 1955.

> **Thematic links:** The growth of the NHS; nationalisation

ACTIVITY 4.2

Use the information in this chapter, as well as your own research, to write a short biography of Harold Macmillan in no more than 300 words.

Timeline: Leaders of the Labour Party

1935–55	Clement Attlee
1955–63	Hugh Gaitskell
1963–76	Harold Wilson

The most divisive issue for Labour was defence. In the early 1950s, Bevan, supported by Wilson, Richard Crossman and Barbara Castle, opposed the official pro-nuclear, pro-American policy. By 1951, there were 32 MPs who could be identified as 'Bevanites'. The situation had worsened by 1952, when 57 Labour MPs risked dismissal after ignoring the party whip on defence issues. In 1954, Bevan defied Attlee's instructions to support proposals in the Commons for the manufacture of a hydrogen bomb.

Another controversial issue within the party was public ownership of industry. Gaitskell hoped to rewrite Clause IV of the party's constitution, which had committed it to wholesale nationalisation. He was supported in this by Labour right-winger Tony Crosland, who believed in a bigger welfare state, but funded by economic growth and built on efficiently managed industry within a mixed economy. This issue led to intense conflict at successive Labour conferences during Gaitskell's period as leader. While trade union leaders, such as Arthur Deakin of the Transport and General Workers' Union, Tom Williamson of the Municipal Workers and William Lawther of the Miners' Union, supported the leadership on defence, they were opposed to any abandonment of the commitment to nationalisation.

Speak like a historian

J.E. Cronin

Labour ceased to offer a compelling reformist vision or even a clear alternative to the Tories. Its middle-class supporters soon began to swing back and forth between Labour and the Conservatives depending on the fickle perceptions of the moment, and its working-class base to alternate between abstention and reluctant support.[19]

Discussion points:

1. In under 50 words, summarise Cronin's interpretation of Labour's problems.
2. Using the information in this chapter, and your own research, explain how convincing Cronin's explanation is, with reference to the years 1945–64.

Figure 4.2: Aneurin Bevan speaking against unilateral nuclear disarmament at the 1957 Labour Party Conference

It appeared in 1957 that the situation might improve: Bevan was appointed Shadow Foreign Secretary, and made a devastating speech promising that, if in power, he would not allow future Foreign Secretaries to go 'naked into the Conference Chamber' – a reference to the possibility of unilateral nuclear disarmament. Although this speech played a key role in the rapprochement between Bevan and Gaitskell, it outraged Bevan's former supporters on the left, who maintained their opposition to the leadership. Despite a passionate speech at the 1959 party conference, promising to 'fight, fight, and fight again to save the party that I love',[20] Gaitskell was defeated on the issue of Clause IV by an alliance of unions and left-wingers. A year later, he also lost the conference vote against unilateral disarmament.

Conservatism and the Establishment

> **Cross-reference:** Consumerism and changes for women and young people

Throughout its history, the Conservative Party had been closely linked to 'the Establishment'– those groups who had traditionally possessed significant influence in Britain, including politicians, senior civil servants, bishops of the Church of England, the aristocracy, leading financiers, and Oxford and Cambridge academics. Writing in 1955, British journalist Henry Fairlie defined the Establishment as 'not only ... the centres of official power – though they are certainly part of it – but rather the whole matrix of official and social relations within which power is exercised'.[21]

The links between Conservatism and the Establishment remained strong during the 1950s and early 1960s. An example is the ties between the public school system and the party. Eden, Macmillan and their successor, Home, were educated at the same school (Eton College), as were nine members of Macmillan's 1957 cabinet. The Conservatives also remained intimately connected to the aristocracy. For example, Macmillan was married to Lady Dorothy Cavendish, daughter of the Duke of Devonshire. However, by the 1960s, the relationship between Conservatism and the Establishment was a factor in the party's downfall. This was especially true after Macmillan's resignation in 1963.

The appointment of Lord Home

On Macmillan's resignation, the traditional method of choosing a Conservative leader was set in motion. Party grandees 'took soundings' from leading figures in order to find the most suitable candidate. From his hospital bed, Macmillan pushed for his Foreign Secretary, Lord Home, to succeed him. When the Lord Chancellor, Viscount Dilhorne, reported back on the soundings, he wrongly claimed that an overwhelming majority of the party also favoured Home. It is believed that, in fact, at least 9 of the 20 cabinet members favoured Rab Butler.

The old-fashioned method of selection, the misrepresentation of the party's views, and the decision to sideline Butler, angered many Conservatives. The choice of the first peer to become prime minister since Lord Salisbury, when there were 363 Conservative MPs from whom to choose, did not sit well with modern Britain. Home renounced his peerage, but the damage was done. Wilson, now Labour leader, exploited this to the full, claiming that Home's lack of Commons experience, plus his inability to empathise with the experiences of ordinary working people would make him a bad prime minister. This message resonated with the electorate, and after 363 days as prime minister, Home lost power (see the section 'Labour victory in 1964').

Establishment values

As the Establishment maintained its influence during this period, the attitudes and values associated with it remained strong. In particular, the culture of **deference** towards those in authority (whether national institutions, or individuals such as parents and teachers) continued. The idea that the Establishment knew what was right for the rest of society remained a powerful one. It was not only Conservatives who held this view: Labour politician Douglas Jay had written in 1937 that 'in the case of nutrition and health ... the gentleman in Whitehall really does know better what is good for people than the people know themselves'.[22]

Nevertheless, as the public reaction to Home's appointment demonstrates, these values were slowly being questioned. The development of youth culture (see 'Consumerism and changes for women and young people') had an impact on 'old-fashioned' notions of deference. The growth of consumerism helped to disperse power more widely in society, as well as being linked to the adoption of less traditional values

> **Key terms**
>
> **Deference:** Showing respect to, and accepting the wishes of, those in authority; respecting the established institutions of society.

4 Transformation and change, 1939–64

Voices from the past

Harold Wilson (1916–95)

Although proud of his Yorkshire background, Wilson was educated at Wirral Grammar School. He then spent several years in Oxford: as a research fellow at University College, he contributed to the preparation of the Beveridge Report in 1942. Elected an MP in 1945, Wilson became President of the Board of Trade in 1947 – the youngest cabinet member since Pitt the Younger. Along with Bevan, he later resigned from the cabinet over the issue of NHS charges. Wilson was never comfortable during his rival Gaitskell's period as leader, and challenged him unsuccessfully for the position in 1961. On Gaitskell's death, however, he was elected Labour leader; a year later, he was prime minister, ending 13 years of Conservative dominance. Wilson is one of only two postwar prime ministers to have held the post on two separate occasions (1964–70 and 1974–76).

from the USA. The growth of satire, particularly the television show *That Was the Week that Was*, which mocked Establishment figures, was another factor in the decline of traditional attitudes.

Eventually, even the Conservative Party accepted that attitudes to the Establishment were changing. Home's successor as leader was Edward Heath, who had attended a state grammar school. While the Establishment remained influential, it was no longer the dominant force it had been before the war.

Labour victory in 1964

Labour's narrow victory in the 1964 general election, with the largest swing since 1945, brought an end to a long period of Conservative dominance – 317 Labour MPs were elected, against 304 Conservatives and nine Liberals. There were several reasons for the first Labour victory for 14 years:

- The electoral disaster of 1959 had forced Labour to think carefully about its future. The question 'can Labour ever win?' began to circulate widely, leading some of Gaitskell's opponents to rein in their activities. In 1961, Gaitskell won a conference vote on unilateral disarmament and by the time of his death in January 1963 he was in a commanding position within the party.
- Labour's campaign slogan, 'New Britain' fitted the public mood that it was time for a change. Labour exuded a sense of hope and their rhetoric and policies matched the spirit of the 1960s. Wilson spoke of 'the white heat of the technological revolution'[23] and promised the modernisation of industry, effective economic planning, scientific development and improved welfare, in order to compete with the USA and Japan.

Cross-references: Conservatism and the Establishment; Social changes and divisions

- In contrast, Home struggled during the campaign. General dissatisfaction with the Macmillan government, as well as the circumstances of Home's appointment, put him in a difficult position. He was heckled at numerous public meetings, including a particularly difficult one in Birmingham Rag Market a week before polling day.
- The contrast between Wilson and Home as individuals was also striking. Wilson had taught economics at Oxford, whereas Home had recently made an ill-judged joke about using matchsticks to compensate for his lack of understanding of economic matters. Wilson performed better than Home on television; although Home held eight open-air meetings a day, television reached a much wider audience.

Hidden voices

Bill Deedes, Home's media minister

'[Home] is not a presidential candidate but a traditional parliamentary leader.'[24]

Discussion points:

1. Explain what Bill Deedes means by the description 'a traditional parliamentary leader'.
2. To what extent does Deedes' point explain Labour's victory in 1964?

ACTIVITY 4.3

Construct a graph, detailing the number of seats won by Labour and the Conservatives for every election between 1945 and 1964. Annotate your graph, summarising why the victorious party won on each occasion.

Economic developments and policies

Mobilisation of resources in wartime

> **Cross-reference:** Increased state involvement during wartime (Chapter 3)

Like the First World War, the Second World War involved 'total war' – the British economy would be fully geared towards winning the conflict. This would not be easy, given the parlous state of the economy. In 1914, Britain had 13.6% of the world's manufacturing capacity, but this figure had fallen to 9% by 1938. The 1930s had also seen various balance of payments crises, and the country's gold and international currency reserves were lower than at the outbreak of the First World War. It was entirely possible that the war would bankrupt Britain: careful mobilisation of resources would be needed. A key figure in this was Ernest Bevin.

Figure 4.3: British women working at a small-arms factory during the Second World War

The coalition government put in place a number of measures:

- Rationing was introduced. This covered a wide range of foodstuffs, including meat, cheese and butter. Fuel and clothing were also rationed.
- Both men and women could be conscripted into work that the government had classified as essential. The National Service No. 2 Act took all single women of 20 and 21 into war service; in 1942, the age was lowered to 19. Churchill argued that 'millions of new workers will be needed, and more than a million women must come boldly forward into our war industries – into the shell plants, the munition works, and into the aircraft factories'.
- The most famous group of conscripted workers were 'Bevin Boys'. These were men aged between 18 and 24, whose National Service numbers were entered in a fortnightly ballot: those whose final digit matched that week's randomly drawn number were sent to work in the coal mines. The deeply unpopular scheme ran from 1943 to 1948.

Voices from the past

Ernest Bevin (1881–1951)

Like his colleague Aneurin Bevan, Ernest Bevin progressed into Labour politics via trade union activism. After leaving school at 12, he became an official in the Dockers' Union and then a leading figure in the National Transport Workers' Federation. In 1922, he founded the Transport and General Workers' Union, serving as its General Secretary for the next 18 years. In this role, he consolidated the unions' links with the Labour Party, as well as standing firm against far-left infiltration of party and unions. As the wartime minister of labour, his direction of industry was crucial to the war effort. Appointed as Foreign Secretary by Attlee, Bevin was a loyal member of the Labour government, taking a firm line against the communist threat during the Berlin blockade and the Korean War. His rivalry with Bevan was legendary: on hearing a colleague describe Bevan as 'his own worst enemy', Bevin responded, 'Not while I'm alive he ain't!'[25]

- Order 1305 was passed, forbidding strikes. As a union man, Bevin was able to get away with this controversial measure!
- Tax on incomes over £1000 per year rose to 38%. Tax on unearned incomes over £1000 was set at 94%. Also, luxury items were subject to a tax equivalent to 100% of their full value.
- Millions of acres of spare land were to be used for crop production. By 1945, the amount of arable land under cultivation had increased by over 50%.

The British public played a vital role in supporting the government's efforts. Many bought war bonds – almost £8.5 billion was raised in this way, represent an average saving of £177 per person. Although women's conscription was a significant social change, people accepted the necessity. The Wartime Social Survey found that 97% of all women agreed that women should do war work. Encouraged by the government, civilians also saved and collected aluminium pans and iron railings for war materials. Rationing was respected (albeit grudgingly) by most; only a minority made use of the black market, which gave access to luxuries. The public accepted not only income tax rises, but also cuts in the production of consumer goods: the production figure for 1944 was 54% that for 1939. Some citizens took up second jobs – it was not unusual to see a vicar working as a postman, for example.

> **Thematic link: The impact of the Second World War on British politics**

In terms of military victory, the result of this cooperation between the people and the authorities was positive. For instance, 130 620 bomber planes were produced between 1940 and 1945. This compared favourably to the 17 498 made by Germany in the same period. However, despite the combined efforts of government and the public, the economy struggled to cope with the strain of war. British gold reserves had fallen to £3 million by 1941 and, by the end of the war, Britain's overseas debts were over £3 billion. The situation would have been even worse had it not been for Lend-Lease. This scheme, introduced in March 1941, involved the US government supplying its allies with food, fuel, arms and transport. Thanks to Lend-Lease, the British received $750 million worth of arms in 1941 alone.

Hidden voices

Mollie Panter-Downes (diarist)

It is the stiffest dose of totalitarian principles that a democracy has ever had to swallow in order to save the democratic ideal from totalitarian destruction.[26]

Discussion points:

1. What paradox does Panter-Downes identify? Explain her point in your own words.
2. Using the evidence from this section, do you agree with Panter-Downes?

> ### Speak like a historian
>
> #### Arthur Marwick
>
> Arthur Marwick was a leading British social historian, who wrote detailed accounts of the work of civilians and, especially, women during both world wars. Marwick was notable for his role as the first Professor of History at the Open University.
>
> Conscription played a very minor role in the changes in women's employment during the war. In practice, only single women of the age group 19–24 were called up, and they were given the choice of serving in the Women's Auxiliary Services, in civil defence, or in certain … forms of civilian employment. At the end of the war there were rather fewer than half a million women enrolled in the WRNS, the ATs and WAAF … in civilian trades, women's employment expanded most noticeably in light engineering and agriculture.[27]
>
> Discussion points:
> 1. In fewer than 50 words, summarise Marwick's interpretation.
> 2. Using the information in this section, as well as your own research, write two paragraphs, one supporting Marwick and the other opposing his view.

The postwar boom

> **Thematic link:** Social changes and divisions

After the hardships of the Depression, the sacrifices made during war, and a period of austerity under Attlee, the 1950s was a time of economic growth, during which consumption increased and the population became more affluent. In London in particular, industry expanded. A prominent example was Royal Dutch-Shell, a large international business with its headquarters in the capital. The British steel industry was also booming. The Steel Company of Wales, based in Port Talbot, had one of the world's most modern mill systems and employed 20 000 people. In the chemicals industry, ICI employed 6000 research workers and was noted for spending more on research and development than all Britain's universities put together! British-based P&O had become the world's largest shipping line, with 366 vessels in total.

Firms which began to apply contemporary market research and advertising techniques found that success followed. A prime example was Unilever, which produced goods ranging from frozen food to toothpaste. Unilever also invested heavily in training its managers, which had not previously been a priority in British industry.

The boom was borne out by the figures for economic growth, which averaged over 4% a year during Macmillan's premiership.

> **Cross-references:** Changes to British industry and trade; The growth of affluence

Firm	Main products
Ferranti	Electronics
AEI	Engines, light bulbs, fridges, washing machines
Rolls-Royce	Cars
Vickers	Shipbuilding, artillery manufacture, aircraft
Guest, Keen and Nettlefolds	Wheels, turbine blades

Table 4.2: Leading manufacturers

Hugh Fraser III	Charles Forte
Set up House of Fraser in 1948. Established Universal Investment Trusts. Added the John Barker group (1957) and Harrods (1959) to his investments.	Expanded a group of roadside cafés into an enormous catering and hotel business. Set up the Little Chef and Happy Eater chains. Established Britain's first motorway café.

Table 4.3: Enterprising businessmen

> Thematic link: Austerity and the impact of war

Balance of payments issues and 'stop-go' policies

The extent of Britain's reliance on US support was revealed when President Truman decided to end the Lend-Lease programme in 1945. The fragility of the economy meant that Britain's ability to produce and then export large quantities of goods was weakened. Economist and government adviser John Maynard Keynes was sent to Washington to negotiate an interest-free loan of $6 billion, but the USA was unwilling to accede to his demands. In 1946, Britain eventually received a loan of $3.75 billion, to be repaid at 2% interest. Those repayments would begin in 1951.

The loan was, in some ways, a poisoned chalice. It was almost entirely used up within a year. More worryingly, as part of the deal, Britain also had to make the pound sterling freely convertible (exchangeable) for dollars from July 1947. Almost immediately, countries with **sterling balance** took $1 billion from British reserves. As a result, the government was forced to suspend convertibility. Stafford Cripps also chose to **devalue** the pound, from $4.02 to $2.80, in 1949 in an attempt to boost British dollar reserves.

This crisis set the scene for the next 15 years. Despite the growth of affluence and the development of new technology, the economy remained unstable and the government tended to react to crises rather than engaging in long-term planning. The next decade was marked by numerous balance of payments crises and subsequent stop-go policies in response. Between 1947 and 1950, the USA rearmed in response to the Soviet threat. This forced up raw material prices, making imports expensive. Although British exports were 17% higher than their 1939 level, the cost of imports led to a balance of payments deficit of £438 million. When Britain accepted £1.263 billion in **Marshall Aid**, the economic situation looked more promising – by 1950, exports were 75% above their 1938 level. However, the positive outlook was short-lived.

Key terms

Sterling balance: Pounds earned from buying British exports; under the terms of the US loan, these could now be sold to Britain in exchange for dollars.

Devaluation: The official lowering of the value of a country's currency, setting a new fixed rate with respect to a foreign country's currency.

Marshall Aid: Economic support given by the USA to European countries to help them recover after the Second World War. The aim was partly humanitarian, but the USA also hoped to strengthen its European trading partners, as well as reducing the link between poverty and the growth of communism.

Timeline: Chancellors of the Exchequer, 1945–64

Years	Chancellor	Prime minister
1945–47	Dalton	Attlee
1947–50	Cripps	Attlee
1950–51	Gaitskell	Attlee
1951–55	Butler	Churchill
1955–57	Macmillan	Eden
1957–58	Thorneycroft	Macmillan
1958–60	Heathcoat-Amory	Macmillan
1960–62	Selwyn Lloyd	Macmillan
1962–64	Maudling	Macmillan/Home

The changing balance of payments and stop-go policies: 1951–64

STOP! (1951–52)
Churchill inherited a balance of payments deficit of £700 million. As Chancellor, Butler responded by introducing credit restrictions, cutting food subsidies, and reducing imports by £600 million. Interest rates were increased from 2% to 4%. These policies, aided by Korean War, led to a balance of payments surplus of £300 million in 1952.

STOP! (1955–56)
In response, Butler and his successor, Macmillan, pursued policies to slow the economy. Purchase tax was increased, and the bank rate rose to 5.5%. Hire-purchase deposits were increased in an attempt to lower inflation and reduce imports. These policies were successful: the balance of payments was in surplus by 1956.

STOP! (1958–59)
Thorneycroft then proposed spending cuts of £163 million. Although Macmillan supported cuts, he felt those suggested by his Chancellor were too deep. While Thorneycroft compared Britain's liabilities (£4 billion) to its assets (£850 million), Macmillan remembered the human cost of economic contraction in the 1930s. In the face of opposition, Thorneycroft resigned. Nevertheless, some cuts were enacted by his replacement, Heathcoat-Amory.

STOP! (1960–63)
Selwyn Lloyd attempted to tackle this situation in 1960. Credit was restricted, interest rates rose, 10% was added to purchase tax, and import duties were increased. A pay pause was introduced: there were no wage increases for government employees for 12 months; 35 outstanding pay claims were not addressed. The National Economic Development Council and the National Incomes Commission were set up in 1961 and 1962 respectively, in an attempt to bring together the government, business, and the unions to discuss production targets, wages, and central planning. However, the unions' reluctance to engage with the NEDC, and their boycott of the NIC meant both institutions were of limited importance.

GO! (1953–54)
As the economy contracted, Churchill's government decided to cut the bank rate. Industry began to expand, investment increased, full employment was achieved, and there was a rise in exports. The boom continued into 1955 as income tax was cut by 6d. just before the election. During the boom, wages rose, increasing the demand for British-made goods. In response, prices went up, and inflation began to climb. Growing demand was also met by increasing imports, leading to a balance of payments deficit in 1955.

GO! (1957–58)
Macmillan's first Chancellor, Peter Thorneycroft originally pursued policies to stimulate the economy. Taxes were lowered and credit restrictions eased; at first, exports boomed. However, as consumer demand increased, so did imports, as well as prices. In response, some workers demanded higher wages; where demands were not met, strikes were often the outcome. This affected production and exports, leading to a balance of payments deficit.

GO! (1959)
One of the most controversial features of 'stop-go' policies was the creation of economic booms just before general elections. 1959 was a prime example: in time for polling day, Heathcoat-Amory cut taxes, relaxed credit controls, allowed wage increases, and lowered the bank rate from 7% to 4.5%. Macmillan won with a handsome majority, but the subsequent increase in imports led once more to a balance of payments deficit.

GO! (1963–64)
The final year of Conservative goverment saw a big increase in imports, leading to a balance of payments deficit of £748 million in 1964. This was also the result of high production costs, which made British exports expensive. In the light of growing competition, British products were often priced out of the market.

Figure 4.4: Stop-go policies, 1951–64

4 Transformation and change, 1939–64

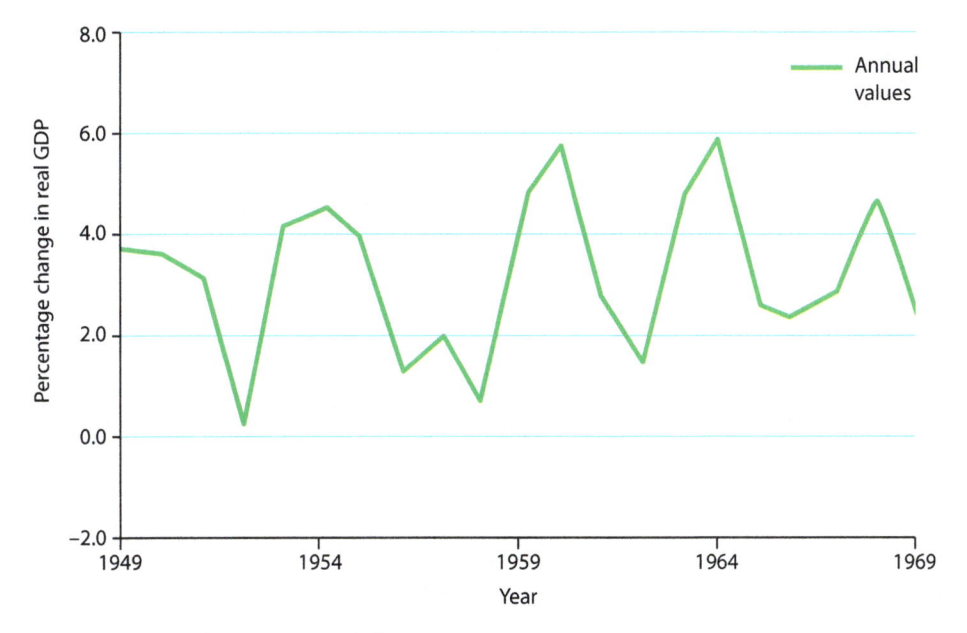

Figure 4.5: Annual UK GDP growth from 1948

ACTIVITY 4.4
What conclusions can you draw from the graph in Figure 4.5 about the economic policies of governments between 1949 and 1964?

Cross-reference: The Depression (Chapter 3)

Changes to British industry and trade

As trade and industry began to recover after the Second World War, there were notable changes in terms of technology and the administration of leading firms. Many of these changes built on the developments of the interwar years, including the growth of the chemicals and car industries and the improvement of management techniques (see 'Economic realignment'):

- US management techniques were increasingly studied and copied by British firms. '**Corporate raiding**' grew, as tycoons took over and reorganised poorly managed businesses.
- The power of good advertising was also recognised: a number of American advertising firms set up headquarters in London.
- There were changes to the mining industry: the introduction of large super-pits provided the opportunity to use modern, safer technology, but also led to the loss of 200 000 jobs.
- The aircraft and chemical industries expanded significantly.
- The system of **Resale Price Maintenance**, which had allowed manufacturers and suppliers to set the retail price of their goods, was abolished by Home's government. This lowered the cost of living, as well as increasing competition on the high street, leading to the growth of large supermarket chains.

Thematic link: Developments in technology

Transport
The immediate postwar period was also marked by significant changes to the transport industry. The opening of the 8-mile Preston bypass in December 1958

Voices from the past

Peter Thorneycroft
Dear Harold … was a great spender. He'd been brought up in areas of great unemployment and he thought that writing cheques was the best way of dealing with it. This wasn't my view or the view of the junior ministers.[28]

Robert Blake
Macmillan perhaps had too much fear of unemployment and too little of inflation.[29]

Discussion points:
1. To what extent do Thorneycroft and Blake support each other's views of Macmillan?
2. Using this section and also Chapter 3, explain why Macmillan had a 'fear' of unemployment.
3. How convincing do you find Blake's view? Explain your answer, using evidence from this section and also from the section 'Political developments'.

> **Key terms**
>
> **Corporate raiding:** The process of buying a large stake in a company, then using voting rights as a shareholder to force the company to make significant changes to management practices.
>
> **Resale Price Maintenance:** A system which obliged shops to sell goods at standard prices set by suppliers, preventing undercutting, but reducing competition.

marked the beginning of a programme of motorway construction that would see 300 miles built by 1964. The bypass was the first new major road in Britain for 20 years. It was the result of years of pressure, including a 1941 cabinet committee report criticising existing congested roads; Frederick Cook's 1942 memorandum, arguing that motorways would both help industry and improve road safety; and the 1949 Special Roads Act.

Of particular note were the 67 miles of the M1 opened in 1959, which included the country's first service stations – Newport Pagnell and Watford Gap. The programme reflected a widespread encouragement of road transport, led by transport minister Ernest Marples. The first parking meters were introduced, as were yellow lines and Britain's first major roundabouts.

As road transport developed, railways were drastically pruned. Dr Richard Beeching, the new head of British Rail, published his controversial *The Reshaping of Britain's Railways* in March 1963. He recommended the closure of one-third of the existing routes, 2361 stations and 5000 miles of track. While Beeching defended his proposals as rational and cost effective, his committee and its plans were much criticised. Opponents pointed to the fact that the committee featured several businessmen (Beeching himself was a former director of ICI), but no railway specialists. Others were convinced the report was a spiteful response to recent railway strikes. In any case, the impact of the 'Beeching Axe' was significant. Large amounts of trade were diverted from trains to lorries; this process was accelerated by the denationalisation of road haulage, meaning that 24 000 lorries were now privately owned.

The growth of the car industry

The most significant change was the growth of the car industry. The merger of the Austin Motor Company and Morris Motors to form the British Motor Company in 1952 was a particularly important event. Making effective use of newspaper and magazine adverts, the company enjoyed huge success with their Morris Minor, which became the first British car to sell over a million. Designed by Alec Issigonis, and costing just £350, it was cheaper than its rivals. Its success confounded the BMC's owner, Lord Nuffield, who had described it as 'that damned poached egg designed by that damned foreigner'.[30] Another popular development was the introduction of the Mini in 1959 – its small size and fuel economy made it an attractive proposition for British consumers.

Figure 4.6: The Morris Minor

> **Cross-references:** New technology; Consumerism and changes for women and young people

Growing competition

Despite these positive developments, the wider picture for British industry was worrying. While regular 'stops' and the cost of Britain's nuclear programme limited industrial investment and expansion, foreign industry flourished. Competition from India led to the decline of the British textile industry. However, the major threats came from West Germany, the USA and Japan. Buoyed by US investment, West Germany's share of world trade grew nearly four times as fast as Britain's. Meanwhile, Japan outperformed Britain in a variety of fields, including shipbuilding, camera and electronics technologies and motorcycle production. The growth of Honda, Kawasaki and, especially, Yamaha, with its popular Suzuki model, demonstrated Japan's increasing advantage. By the end of the 1950s, Japan was producing an average of 500 000 motorcycles a year, compared with the British average of 140 000.

The problem of growing competition was not helped by the reluctance of some British industrialists to embrace change. For instance, of the 300 000 British companies that existed, only 1% were listed on the stock market. It can also be argued that upper-class Conservatives, such as Macmillan, were suspicious of self-made entrepreneurs, viewing them as vulgar *arrivistes*.

Country	Change in GDP (%)	Change in exports (%)
France	5.0	8.1
Italy	5.1	11.7
Japan	9.5	15.4
UK	2.7	4.1
USA	3.7	5.1
West Germany	5.7	10.8

Table 4.4: Increases in GDP and exports in selected countries 1951–73

Key terms

Arriviste: A person who has recently attained wealth, status, or power, sometimes by dubious means and often unexpectedly.

Speak like a historian

Keith Middlemass

Keith Middlemass, an economic historian, suggests the following explanation for Britain's economic malaise:

The continued survival of a mass of small firms, reliant on sheltered domestic markets, which were unable or unwilling to reform their practices or their low productivity.[31]

Discussion points:

1. Pick out two key phrases which Middlemass uses to support his interpretation.
2. Is the reason identified by Middlemass the key factor in Britain's economic problems? Explain your answer, using all the information in this section.

New technology

The promotion of new technology was a priority of Stafford Cripps, President of the Board of Trade from 1945 to 1947. He commissioned the Council of Industrial Design to stage the 'Britain Can Make It' exhibition at the V&A Museum in September 1946. The exhibition celebrated British production of consumer goods, as well as showcasing advances in science and technology. Over 1.4 million people visited, including 43 000 trade visitors and 7000 trade buyers from 67 countries, leading to orders totalling more than £25 million. Despite the austerity of the Attlee years, the exhibition highlighted the encouraging progress that was being made in the technological field.

During the 1950s, British technology improved rapidly, notably in the production of industrial glass and in the chemicals industry. The start of the offshore gas industry was another sign that British technology was both effective and competitive. Furthermore, in 1956, the nuclear power station at Calder Hall was connected to the National Grid, becoming the first nuclear power station to provide energy commercially. Its Magnox gas-cooled reactor used cutting-edge technology. Ten similar power stations soon followed – British nuclear technology was flourishing.

ACTIVITY 4.5

1. Plot the information in Table 4.4 on a graph.
2. Working in groups of six, research one of the countries in the table, looking for reasons to explain their economic performance. Share your findings, and use them to annotate your graph.

Concorde

Another major development in British technology was the jet engine. The most exciting example of this was the Concorde project, which gained approval from Macmillan's cabinet in 1962. This involved British and French cooperation: British Aerospace and Aérospatiale worked together to design the airframe, while Rolls-Royce and the French firm Snecma developed the jet engines. Concorde's first flight on 2 March 1969 marked a watershed in air travel. Its maximum cruising speed of 1354 miles per hour, more than twice the speed of sound, allowed it to travel from London to New York in three hours.

Figure 4.7: Concorde

Social changes and divisions

Austerity and the impact of war

The bleak economic outlook in 1945 was felt across the country (see 'The changing balance of payments and stop-go policies'). Rationing continued well after VJ Day; the public were particularly upset that bread and potatoes, neither of which had been rationed during the war, were included in 1946 and 1947 respectively. The fact that food allowances tended to be lower than during the war did little to help matters. By the 1951 general election, meat, butter, sugar and tea were still rationed.

It was not only war that hit the economy. That most British of problems, the weather, had an enormous impact during the bitterly cold winter of 1946–47:

- In January 1947, the minimum recorded temperature in England was −21°C.
- February 1947 saw an average of 1.1 hours of sunshine per day; in many places, snow fell on 26 of the 28 days in the month.
- Ferry services between Dover and Ostend were suspended owing to pack ice.
- Frost destroyed 70 000 tons of potatoes.
- 300 major roads became impassable during the crisis.

Coal supplies were already low at the beginning of winter: stockpiles contained enough coal to last for just four weeks, compared with the prewar average of 10 to 12 weeks. Fearing a coal shortage, many people bought electric fires, putting a strain on electricity supplies. When snow hit, wagons became stuck and roads were closed, making it very difficult to transport coal. Stockpiles remained at the pit, becoming frozen and unusable. As the demand for coal and electricity rose significantly, fuel rationing became particularly severe.

At the height of the crisis, the government made it illegal to use electricity in the home between 9 a.m. and 12 p.m., and 2 p.m. and 4 p.m. Coal shortages also caused temporary factory closures, leaving 2 million people without work. Food rations were cut even further, and there was little light relief: television was temporarily suspended, radio broadcasts were decreased and newspapers reduced in size. Although the crisis had subsided by April 1947, its impact on public morale was significant; it was undoubtedly a factor in Labour's declining electoral fortunes in 1950 and 1951.

> **Thematic link:** Conservative dominance from 1951

During this period, the government kept tight control over profits, interest rates and rents. A culture of lavish spending and excessive money-making was discouraged. Building materials were rationed; priority was given to essential buildings, such as schools, factories and council houses. While this made economic sense, the low priority given to building cinemas and dance-halls was unpopular with the public.

4 Transformation and change, 1939–64

Voices from the past

Stafford Cripps (1889–1952)

Cripps detailed his priorities as follows: 'First are exports, second is capital investment in industry, and last are the needs, comforts and amenities of the family.' The public had to 'submerge all thoughts of personal gain and personal ambition'.[32]

Discussion points:

1. Explain why exports were Cripps' first priority.
2. To what extent were Cripps' policies effective? Use the information in this section, as well as sections 'The impact of the Second World War on British politics' and 'Economic developments' in this chapter to write approximately 300 words in answer to this question.

The Chancellor, Sir Stafford Cripps, also kept careful control over imports, focusing on buying supplies of raw materials for industries that exported most of their goods. This included the chemicals and aircraft industries, as well as shipbuilding and motorcycle manufacture. However, the drive for exports resulted in shortages of consumer goods for the British people. The situation became especially severe after the government's devaluation of the pound in August 1949. This led to spending cuts of £120 million. In the face of criticism from the left, Cripps claimed that only the economic growth provided by increasing exports could lead to a fairer, socialist society.

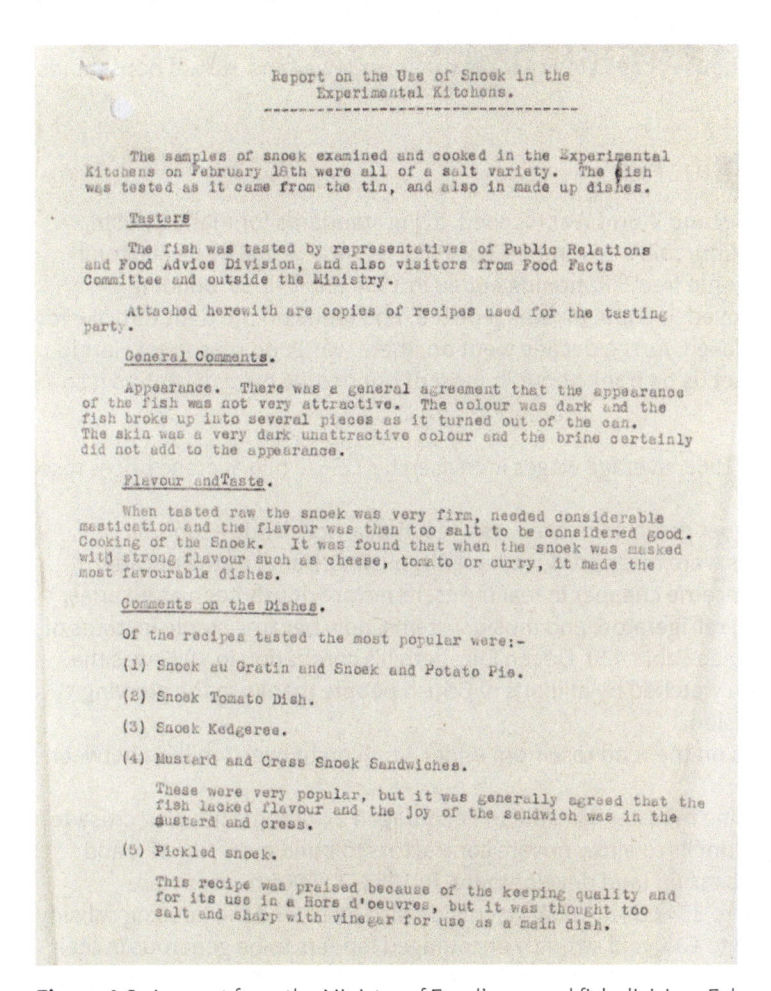

Figure 4.8: A report from the Ministry of Food's canned fish division, February 1948, on the benefits of snoek, a cheap South African import encouraged by Cripps. Snoek was to become a hated symbol of unpopular austerity policies, and much of the consignment was eventually used instead for cat food.

> **Cross-reference:** Balance of payments issues and 'stop-go' policies

Despite frustration at continued rationing and grumbling about Cripps' suggestions for frugal living (see Figure 4.8), the public played its part in cooperating with austerity. Trade unions largely accepted a policy of wage restraint between 1948 and 1950, even though the cost of living was rising as prices increased. There were exceptions, notably the dock strikes of 1948 and 1949 – during the second strike, the army was enlisted to transport food. Bevin angered left-wing MPs by reintroducing Order 1305, granting the government the power to arrest and imprison strikers.

Society during the era of austerity

Although the period from 1945 to 1951 was one of significant change in terms of politics and welfare politics, British society retained many prewar features. According to social historian David Kynaston, 'society remained riddled by petty snobbery and the infinite gradations of class'.[33] Kynaston argues that the town planning system, which focused on building concrete council flats, made it difficult for working people to achieve their ambition of having their own home and garden. He also points to the snobbery of liberal intellectuals, who criticised workers' leisure choices, especially their preference for football and holidays at Butlins. Middle-class Britons remained significantly better off than their working-class counterparts, earning on average 50% more. In addition, working-class housing remained poor: one-third of all dwellings had no fixed bath, 15% of houses consisted of three rooms or fewer and 18% of households shared a lavatory.

The growth of affluence

As the impact of the Second World War receded, living standards for many British people began to rise. Churchill's government of 1951–55 took seriously its electoral promise to 'set the people free'.[34] Rationing ended in 1954 and Cripps' building restrictions were removed. Income tax was reduced, and limits on the right to strike for higher wages were relaxed. As the decade went on, there was good reason for Harold Macmillan to claim, 'Let us be frank about it; most of our people have never had it so good.'[35]

- Between 1951 and 1963, average wages increased by 72%, while average prices rose by only 45%.
- The sales of consumer goods increased, as a result of a worldwide economic boom. These goods were mass produced, readily available and, as the decade progressed, they became cheaper in real terms. Items previously seen as luxuries, such as televisions, refrigerators and music systems, now became staple features of many households (see Table 4.5). Queen Elizabeth II's coronation in 1953 was the first major occasion watched by millions of British people thanks to the growing popularity of television.
- The number of cars on the road rose from under 3 million to over 7 million between 1951 and 1963.
- As Churchill's housing minister, Macmillan encouraged a 'national housing crusade', instructing local councils to allow private contractors to build more houses, and abolishing Labour's tax on land development. In 1953, 327 000 houses were constructed, rising to 354 000 in 1954. Macmillan also increased the housing subsidy from £22 per home to £35, and strongly encouraged lenders to be generous in their provision of mortgages.
- The support given to farmers by Attlee's government continued: between 1960 and 1961, £100 million in government grants was given to farmers. This resulted in increased production and greater efficiency and made an increasingly wide selection of food available to the British people.

- Working people were increasingly able to afford holidays, evident in the popularity of Billy Butlin's holiday camps during the 1950s. These provided affordable accommodation and on-site entertainment for around the cost of a week's pay. New Butlins camps were opened in Brighton in 1953 and Blackpool in 1955.
- As the economy grew, social mobility increased, particularly for young working-class men, who helped to fill the growing number of vacancies for professional administrators and other white-collar workers. This also helped to narrow divisions between the middle and working classes.

Appliance	1945	1965
Vacuum cleaner	32	81
Electric iron	65	94
Electric cooker	16	36
Telephone	21	35
Television	0.25	85
Refrigerator	2.1	46
Washing machine	3	58

Table 4.5: Percentage of British households owning consumer goods in 1945 and 1965

Problems during the era of affluence

> **Cross-references:** Changes to British industry and trade; The development of education

The governments of this period can, nevertheless, be criticised for short-term economic policies and the growing failure to compete with Japan and the USA. Historians have also pointed to the poor quality of many of the houses built during the 1950s, as well as the fact that other essential buildings, such as hospitals and technical schools, were not built in sufficient numbers during the age of affluence.

Consumerism and changes for women and young people

Consumerism

> **Thematic link:** Conservatism and the Establishment

The growth of affluence had a significant impact on British culture. As wages increased and unemployment fell, income gaps narrowed between the rich and the middle classes, as well as between middle and working-class people. As a result, consumerism became a feature of British life, cutting across social divisions. Whereas previously class divisions had been evident in fashion and clothing, the 1950s and early 1960s was notable for the popularity of 'classless' clothes, such as blue jeans and T-shirts. Meanwhile, many working-class families, able to afford their own homes and cars, increasingly resembled their middle-class counterparts (who had often lost their servants during the era of austerity).

The growth of shopping centres and supermarkets was another notable feature of the decade. The number of British supermarkets rose from 50 in 1950 to 572 by 1961. The majority of these belonged to new companies, such as Fine Fare, Premier and Victor

ACTIVITY 4.6

1. Construct a graph to represent the information in Table 4.5.
2. Does your graph prove that Britain had become an affluent nation by 1965? Explain your answer carefully.

Value, which had 330 stores between them. Supermarkets stocked produce previously rarely seen in Britain, including aubergines, spaghetti, pizza and garlic.

Advertising also grew significantly in the 1950s. The introduction of commercial television in 1955, as well as increased availability of colour magazines such as *National Geographic*, meant that luxury goods were advertised on a scale previously unknown in Britain. By 1960, industry had recognised that consumers were concerned not just with essential goods, but with comfort, status and 'lifestyle choices'. The next decade was marked by the growth of specialist retailers, most significantly in the fashion industry, who aimed to allow people to show an individual identity.

These developments were not without their critics. Many in the Establishment, including sections of the Conservative Party, saw consumerist values as a threat to British tradition and a potential destabilising factor in society. A different critical perspective was provided by Richard Hoggart in *The Uses of Literacy* (1957): he argued that the growth of advertising and consumerism was a threat to authentic British working-class culture.

> **Thematic link: Growing competition**

> **Cross-references: The growth of affluence; Changes to British industry and trade**

Voices from the past

Motion passed at the 1962 Conservative Party conference

This Conference, while appreciating that successive Conservative governments have caused the material standard of living to rise faster during the past eleven years than ever before in our history, calls upon Ministers to emphasise that this is but one side of a policy founded on the true Tory principles of duty and service.[36]

Discussion points:

1. Explain the phrase 'this is but one side of a policy founded on the true Tory principles of duty and service'.
2. Why do you think the Conservative Party conference agreed to this motion?

Women

The era of affluence also led to significant changes in the position of women in British society. In the century from 1851 to 1951, the percentage of women who worked outside the home remained at around 35%, despite the temporary increases during the two world wars. By 1960, the figure had risen to 42%. Office work and teaching both saw a dramatic increase in the number of female employees. This radically altered society's expectations of a woman's role: as late as 1942, William Beveridge had argued, 'The great majority of married women must be regarded as occupied on work which is vital but unpaid, without which their husbands could not do their paid work and without which the nation could not continue.'[37]

The situation changed particularly sharply for married women. It had been unusual for married women to work outside the home before the Second World War. By 1951, the proportion of working women who were married was 40%; by 1961, the figure was over 50%. There were a number of reasons for these developments:

- The Attlee government appealed for women to go out to work during the economic crisis of 1947. By the end of the year, 800 000 more women were in paid employment than in 1939.
- As the economy expanded, the clerical sector grew, increasing employment opportunities for women. The growth of the light engineering and electrical industries, which relied on the production line approach, encouraged unskilled women into the factories.
- The increasing availability of consumer goods encouraged women to go to work in order to boost their household income and take advantage of the products on sale.
- In parallel with this, many of those products were labour-saving devices, such as washing machines, which made it easier for women to combine paid employment with their domestic role.
- By the mid-1950s, the birth rate was much lower than in previous decades (partly a result of the growing availability and use of contraception). As a result, married

women spent only four years on average in pregnancy and caring for infants before returning to work. This compared with 15 years in the late 19th century.

Despite these developments, women did not achieve full equality with men, nor were expectations of their role transformed completely:

- It was still assumed that women would play the leading role in the home. This was reinforced by magazines such as *Woman's Own* and *Woman's Realm*, which around 80% of women read at least once a week. This assumption was also perpetuated by schools, where girls received lessons in cookery, household management, darning, sewing and, in some cases, how to iron a shirt properly.
- Although girls were increasingly encouraged to consider paid work, the focus was on those jobs which they could realistically combine with their domestic role. These included teaching, nursing and dentistry. Few women entered science or engineering.
- In 1950, only a small minority of women attended university; the figure was especially low among working-class women.
- Although equal pay was achieved for female teachers and civil servants in the years 1954 to 1955, this was not the case for other female employees, including the large number of factory workers. The Equal Pay Campaign Committee (which had fought for these improvements) was dissolved in 1955, with no prospect of further progress being achieved in the foreseeable future.

Nevertheless, the 1950s was undoubtedly a decade of significant progress for British women. The opportunity to go to work gave a growing number of women a sense of independence. This was particularly true given the nature of that work – far fewer women (around 23% of those employed) were in domestic service than in the early part of the century (when the figure was around 40% of working women).

Cross-references: The Beveridge Report; The Butler Act

Speak like a historian

Stephanie Spencer

Increased educational opportunity following the 1944 Education Act, together with an economic background of full employment, gave female school leavers a choice in their post-school employment. In popular memory, and in the women's magazines of the time, a woman's place appears securely centred on domesticity ... For girls their expectations of imminent full-time domesticity constrained their employment decisions.[38]

Discussion points:

1. What is Spencer's interpretation of the place of women in the 1950s?
2. Write one paragraph supporting Spencer's interpretation, using the information in this chapter.
3. Carry out your own research to help you write a paragraph opposing Spencer's interpretation.

Young people

The 1950s were also a time of significant development for young people. The growth of 'youth culture' and the rise of the 'teenager', partly the result of the 1944 education reforms, led to profound and lasting social change. In the 1950s, an increasing number of working-class children progressed from grammar school to university and by 1955, only one-third of men had the same social status by occupation as their fathers. As social mobility increased, class distinctions became less influential and youth culture emerged, crossing class boundaries.

> **Cross-references:** The postwar boom; The growth of affluence; The Butler Act

Increased affluence also contributed to the developing youth culture. Many teenagers in the 1950s were in paid work, so had significantly greater spending power compared with their predecessors. Affluent young people could now afford to carve out their own identity, freed from the economic pressures of the 1940s, where the priority had been simply avoiding poverty and hunger. Businesses increasingly focused their marketing and advertising on young people, helping to create a teenage identity that transcended class divisions and set them apart from the older generation.

By the end of the decade, there were numerous cafés and milk bars designed for teenagers. Young people could also be identified by their transport, especially fuelled scooters, and their music. Here, the influence of US culture was crucial: rock 'n' roll was enormously popular among British teenagers. American film stars such as James Dean and Marlon Brando became role models for young people in Britain.

The widening generation gap led to tensions between young people and their parents. Sections of the press began to condemn rock 'n' roll, linking it to riots and rising crime. For some of the older generation, the rise of youth culture was one of many examples of the 'permissiveness' of British society. They pointed also to the 1957 Wolfenden Report, which called for the decriminalisation of homosexuality and the acquittal from obscenity charges of the publishers of D.H. Lawrence's sexually explicit novel, *Lady Chatterley's Lover*, in 1960.

In 1951, a new trend emerged in the USA and Britain for Edwardian 'drape' jackets, tight drainpipe trousers, a bootlace tie and heavily greased hair with a quiff at the front. By 1952, this trend had been adopted by young men from East and North London, particularly Tottenham and Highbury. *The Daily Express* coined the term 'Teddy Boys' to describe these teenagers, who tended to be semi-skilled workers. The Teddy Boy was the first significant group identity adopted by large numbers of British teenagers: the fashion spread, across London, then to the south coast, before reaching the Midlands and the North by 1956. The public reaction to Teddy Boys reflected the fears of the older generation about youth culture – they were portrayed as violent gangs, responsible for rioting and disorder. To some extent, this was true: when the film *Blackboard Jungle* (accompanied by Bill Haley's 'Rock Around the Clock') was shown in Elephant and Castle in 1956, a group of Teddy Boys began to riot. This behaviour was copied across the country wherever the film was shown. It was also the case that Teddy Boys were instrumental in the 1958 Notting Hill riots (see 'Immigration and racial tensions'). However, the majority of Teddy Boys were just interested in belonging to a group and challenging the norms with regard to fashion and culture.

Changing youth culture was also reflected in the work of writers nicknamed the 'Angry Young Men'. The group, including Kingsley Amis, John Osborne and Alan Sillitoe, railed against consumer culture and growing materialism. They also argued that, despite economic changes, class divisions, snobbery, and the power of the Establishment remained poisonous influences on British society. Amis' *Lucky Jim* (1954) and

Osborne's *Look Back in Anger* (1956) were widely read and represented another challenge by the younger generation to traditional social values.

The changes of the 1950s in youth culture paved the way for the developments of the early 1960s. Pop music was key to expressing teenage identity, just as rock 'n' roll had done during the previous decade. The Beatles, in particular, were the focus of adulation from a generation of teenagers forging their identity in the age of mass culture. (So much so that 'Beatlemania' made it so difficult to perform effectively that the Beatles stopped giving live concerts after 1966.)

Changing fashions, including the introduction of the miniskirt in 1962, demonstrated that an identifiable youth culture (although it would perpetually change) was now an established part of British society.

Immigration and racial tensions

One of the notable features of the immediate postwar period was the growth in the number of immigrants from former British colonies. The British Nationality Act of 1948 enabled subjects of the empire to settle in Britain without a visa. The act was partly a response to labour shortages, particularly in the NHS. Many businesses also actively encouraged New Commonwealth immigration, advertising for recruits across former colonies. Between 1955 and 1962, around 472 000 people emigrated from Commonwealth countries to Britain. The annual figure grew steadily during the period: for example, 46 800 Commonwealth immigrants entered the country in 1956, compared with 136 400 in 1961. Over 60 000 immigrants arrived from India between 1947 – when it gained independence and the partition of the country caused immense upheaval – and 1955.

Meanwhile, the 492 arrivals from Jamaica on the *Empire Windrush* in 1948 marked the beginning of a period of West Indian immigration. By 1955, 18 000 Jamaicans had settled in Britain and between 1961 and 1962, 98 000 West Indians entered the country. They were motivated not only by the provisions of the Nationality Act, but also by high unemployment at home, and the perception of a higher standard of living in Britain, especially the quality of healthcare offered by the NHS.

While immigration from the New Commonwealth was significant, other groups also settled in Britain. During the 1950s, an average of 30 000 immigrants arrived each year. The figure for the 1960s was close to 60 000, with 223 000 people entering the UK in the years 1961–62 alone. Non-Commonwealth immigration was due to a number of causes. In the aftermath of the Second World War, Britain recruited displaced people as European volunteer workers to boost industries needed for economic recovery. Many of these workers came from Poland: by 1951, there were 162 339 Polish-born people in England, compared with 44 642 in 1931.

A further group of Eastern European immigrants arrived in 1956 and 1957, following the Soviet crushing of the Hungarian uprising in 1956. Around 21 000 Hungarians settled in Britain during this time. The postwar period also saw a sharp rise in Irish immigration; this was primarily the result of difficult economic conditions in the early years of the Republic.

Postwar immigrants settled in a variety of areas. Some Pakistani communities formed communities in Lancashire and West Yorkshire, working in particular in the textile industries of Manchester and Bradford. Many had done similar jobs at home, so had the necessary skills. Others settled in the West Midlands, especially Birmingham, working in car plants and engineering works. Most West Indian migrants settled in London, particularly Notting Hill and Brixton. London was also the destination for many migrants from India, especially those from Punjab – many found work in manufacturing and textiles. Irish migrants tended to settle in major cities, particularly London, Glasgow, Liverpool and Manchester.

ACTIVITY 4.7

1. Construct a timeline, detailing the key dates concerning immigration.
2. Drawing on the sections 'Economic development' and 'Social changes and divisions' in this chapter, can you make any links between the economic situation in the 1950s and 1960s and the public and political reaction to immigration?
3. Look back at your assessment in Activity 3.28 of successive governments on social policy. Has this chapter changed, or added to, that assessment? If so, how and why?

> **Cross-reference:** The condition of Ireland and Anglo-Irish relations

Reaction to immigration

The reaction from the British public was mixed. In some communities, immigrants were welcomed; many from the Indian subcontinent found that those who had served there during the war were among the most sympathetic. However, there were violent clashes in other communities, including Nottingham and Notting Hill in 1958. Although immigrants officially enjoyed full civil rights, in reality they could be less tolerantly received. Pubs often refused to serve them and some, particularly West Indian immigrants, faced discrimination in housing and employment. In London, in particular, the relationship between new arrivals and the police was a tense one.

To understand the British reaction to immigration, it is important to consider the wider social and economic context, especially in the large cities. Historian David Goodhart criticises postwar governments, claiming, 'As the incoming groups after 1948 became more different, less effort was made to integrate them ... the real failure ... was not to prepare those existing citizens for something as (significant) as large-scale immigration.'[39] In addition, during periods of economic downturn, immigrants would tend to be blamed for unemployment and poverty within working-class communities.

David Mason argues that 'the arrival of large numbers of migrants, particularly in inner city areas with the most acute housing problems, inevitably exacerbated already

Hidden voices

Smethwick, 1964

The 1964 election ended a period of Conservative dominance; the national swing from Conservative to Labour was 3.5%. However, in the West Midlands constituency of Smethwick, the swing was in the other direction. Labour's Shadow Home Secretary, Patrick Gordon Walker, lost the seat to his Conservative challenger, Peter Griffiths, on a 7.2% swing. Gordon Walker had won 20 670 votes in 1959; his total in 1964 was 14 916. The reason for this peculiar result was immigration, which had been the key issue in Smethwick during the campaign. The local Conservatives' election slogan ('If you want a nigger for a neighbour, vote Labour') had provoked condemnation across the country. However, Griffiths had refused to disown the slogan, claiming, 'I would not condemn any man who said that ... I regard it as a manifestation of popular feeling.'

During the election campaign, Griffiths attacked Walker for his opposition to the Commonwealth Immigration Act, arguing 'how easy to support uncontrolled immigration when one lives in a garden suburb' – a reference to Walker's decision to live in Hampstead, far from industrial Smethwick. In contrast, Griffiths emphasised the fact that he was a local councillor who understood the concerns of the people of the town. Despite the uncompromising racism of the campaign, it struck a chord with local voters, many of whom were affected by housing shortages and the perpetual fear of unemployment. The strength of feeling was clear as Walker left the count having lost his seat: some of Griffiths' supporters shouted, 'Where are your niggers now, Walker?'

When Griffiths took his seat in the Commons, Harold Wilson encouraged Douglas-Home to disown him, claiming, 'If Sir Alec does not take what I am sure is the right course, Smethwick Conservatives can have the satisfaction of having sent a member who, until another election returns him to oblivion, will serve his time as a parliamentary leper.'[40] Although the first part of Wilson's prediction came true (Griffiths losing his seat to Labour's Andrew Faulds in 1966), the second part did not: 25 of Griffiths' colleagues walked out of the Commons in protest at Wilson's insulting language.[41]

The polarised reaction to events in Smethwick reflected growing tensions, which would explode later when Enoch Powell's 1968 'Rivers of Blood' speech divided the nation.

Discussion points:

1. What conclusions can you draw from the Smethwick election about British attitudes to immigration?
2. Explain the phrase 'parliamentary leper'.
3. Explain Griffiths' reference to 'living in a garden suburb'.

serious shortages.'[42] Working-class concerns were evident in a 1958 letter sent by the Assistant General Secretary of the TUC to the Ministry of Labour, which suggested that the government should consider migration controls and expressed concern about Indian and Pakistani immigration in particular.

The political reaction was somewhat more sympathetic. Britain's fascist party, the National Front, had minimal influence and lacked electoral support. Although some Conservative MPs had serious fears about the issue, most kept them private, expressing them in the privacy of the newly formed Monday Club, a right-wing faction within the party. Conservatives were aware that at election time, Labour would portray them as heartless and bigoted. Nevertheless, as early as 1951, concerns were being expressed in cabinet. Churchill told his colleagues that 'Keep England White' was a good slogan.[43] More subtly, Duncan Sandys warned the cabinet that uncontrolled immigration would cause serious social problems in London and Birmingham.

In 1952, ministers discussed papers that could authorise the Home Secretary to 'arrange for officials of the departments concerned to examine the possibilities of preventing any further increase in the number of coloured people seeking employment in this country'. The papers also suggested that the Chancellor should 'arrange for concurrent examination of the possibility of restricting the number of coloured people obtaining admission to the Civil Service'.[44] Cabinet also discussed plans to deport immigrants who had been convicted of crimes or who were seen as a 'charge on public funds'. Divided between those who desired immigration controls and others who supported unlimited immigration, Cabinet decided not to take action on the papers. A similar decision was taken in September 1958: there were to be no immigration controls.

The Commonwealth Immigrants Act (1962)

As it happened, immigration fell slightly in 1958 and 1959, but rising numbers from 1960 led to growing unemployment among immigrants. Fearing the subsequent impact on the welfare bill, the Commonwealth Migrants Cabinet Committee recommended that controls be introduced. The proposal was accepted and became enshrined in the Commonwealth Immigrants Act (1962):

- Immigrants who could show they had a job to come to and those with close relatives already in Britain were allowed to enter.
- The law was initially intended to last for a five-year trial period.
- Labour criticised the act as racist – it placed no restrictions on immigrants from outside the Commonwealth, many of whom were white. Gaitskell referred to it as 'cruel and brutal anti-colour legislation'.[45]

Developments in social policy

The Beveridge Report

Thematic links: Domestic changes under Churchill; Liberal social reforms

The Beveridge Report was a major turning point in British social history. Beveridge's committee identified five significant problems, which it named 'giant evils'. The report also suggested a range of solutions (see Table 4.6).

Voices from the past

William Beveridge (1879–1963)

Educated at Charterhouse and Oxford, Beveridge is remembered as the architect of the welfare state. His experiences while working at Toynbee Hall in the East End of London (despite his father's disapproval) instilled in him the belief that state intervention was necessary in order to tackle poverty. As a civil servant, he worked for a time as Churchill's personal assistant, a role in which he helped to draft the 1911 National Insurance Act. He later became director of the London School of Economics and then Master of University College Oxford in 1937. While undertaking the latter role, he was asked to chair a committee of civil servants investigating the provision of social insurance. The resulting Beveridge Report (1942) was largely implemented by Attlee's Labour government of 1945–51, though its guiding principles were upheld throughout the years of consensus.

Figure 4.9: Sir William Beveridge in 1942

A/AS Level History for AQA: Challenge and Transformation: Britain, c1851–1964

'Giant evil' identified	Proposed solution
Want	Child allowances and insurance schemes
Squalor	Rapid house building programme
Idleness	Full employment as a key aim of government
Ignorance	Universal free secondary education
Disease	A National Health Service, free at the point of use and subsidised by taxes.

Table 4.6: The 'giant evils'

Reaction to the Beveridge Report

The response of the press and the public to Beveridge was largely enthusiastic. Within a year, 265 000 copies of the report sold, an unprecedented number for a government publication. According to a 1942 poll, 95% of people had heard of the report; again, this is unusually high!

However, the report was not universally popular. Some on the left of the Labour Party felt it was not radical enough; others saw it as an attempt to protect capitalism by giving it a slightly more human face. They felt the report did not go as far as the Labour conference's proposals for a comprehensive social security scheme, an NHS and family allowances. Beveridge's Liberal background made him the target of Labour suspicion – Hugh Dalton claimed that 'he is not "one of us" and has no first-hand knowledge of industrial conditions'.[46]

Some sceptical historians have picked up on these criticisms, claiming that the report's proposals did not go beyond rationalising pre-existing schemes, such as those introduced by Lloyd George. Its provisions were, therefore, far from generous or comprehensive. Others have claimed that it favoured men and discriminated against working women.

Thematic link: Social policies

Hidden voices

On the Beveridge Report

'The central proposals (of the Report) must surely be accepted as the basis of government action.' (*The Times*, December 1942)

'One of the most remarkable state documents ever drafted' (*The Economist*, December 1942)

Discussion points:

1. Neither *The Times* nor *The Economist* is a left-wing publication. Why do you think both were so enthusiastic about the Beveridge Report?
2. Write (a) one paragraph to agree with *The Economist's* verdict, and (b) one paragraph to disagree.

Voices from the past

The Beveridge Report, 1942

Organisation of social insurance should be treated as one part only of a comprehensive policy of social progress. Social insurance fully developed may provide income security; it is an attack upon Want. But Want is one only of five giants on the road of reconstruction and in some ways the easiest to attack. The others are Disease, Ignorance, Squalor and Idleness.[47]

Discussion points:

1. Explain the phrase 'a comprehensive policy of social progress'.
2. Using the information in this section, do you agree with the report that want (or poverty) was 'the easiest to attack'?

The Butler Act

> **Cross-reference:** Domestic developments under Churchill

Before 1939, only 20% of all children above the age of 14 had remained in education. The Butler Act raised the school leaving age to 15, and set up a Ministry of Education to 'direct and control' local authorities. Local Education Authorities (LEAs) were to provide secondary schools 'sufficient in number, character and equipment to afford all pupils such variety of instruction and training as may be desirable in view of their different ages, abilities and aptitudes'. The act also made both a daily act of Christian worship and religious education compulsory, but did provide a 'conscience clause' allowing certain pupils to be excluded from these if their parents' beliefs required it.

In response to the Butler Act, most LEAs introduced an exam for children in their final year of primary school. The '11+', as it became known, was used to determine which type of secondary school each child would attend:

- Those who passed the 11+ would go to a grammar school.
- Those who failed the exam would attend a secondary modern.
- In some areas, those identified as having a particular aptitude for practical work would be sent to a secondary technical school.

This approach, known as the tripartite system, was suggested in the Hadow Report of 1926. Many educationalists, pleased at the improved provision of free secondary education, were nevertheless disappointed with the tripartite system. They favoured the comprehensive system, in which all students, regardless of ability, would attend their local secondary school. They argued that the tripartite system limited equality of opportunity. On the other hand, the growth of grammar schools did make it possible for a greater number of high-achieving working-class children to attend university.

Speak like a historian

Michael Barber
On the 1944 Education Act

It seems to me ... that those responsible for education in the early 1940s ... did things well ... the policy process between 1941 and 1944 was on the whole, excellent. The ability of R.A. Butler to combine a ... vision of the future with the immediate political imperatives was also remarkable.[48]

Discussion points:

1. Write two bullet points (no longer than 20 words each) to summarise Barber's view in your own words.
2. How convincing do you find Barber's view?

Voices from the past

Richard Austen ('Rab') Butler (1902–82)

A political veteran by the time of his retirement in 1964, Butler was elected as Conservative MP for Saffron Walden in 1929. He was appointed Under-Secretary at the India Office in 1932 – the first in a series of important front-bench positions. He then moved to be Lord Halifax's deputy at the Foreign Office, in which role he was a firm supporter of appeasement. Despite this, he played a key role in Churchill's wartime government. As minister of education, his act of 1944 transformed education provision across the country. In Churchill's postwar government, Butler continued his Labour predecessors' Keynesian policies in his role as Chancellor. His later career was tinged with disappointment; though commonly expected to get the job, Butler was passed over twice for Conservative leader, on both Eden's and Macmillan's resignations. A party loyalist, he nevertheless served Home effectively as Foreign Secretary.

> Thematic link: The development of education

The growth of the welfare state

Having been denied the opportunity to implement most of the Beveridge report during the war, Attlee made it his priority once elected in 1945. The report was implemented via a series of acts.

> Thematic link: The impact of the Second World War on British politics

National insurance

The National Insurance Act (1946) extended the 1911 act to cover all adults. The national insurance scheme was compulsory – in return for a weekly contribution from workers, employers and the government, a range of benefits was available. These now included sickness and unemployment benefit, widows' and orphans' pensions, maternity allowances and death grants to help families with funeral expenses. Old age pensions were provided for women from the age of 60; men had to wait until they were 65. The individual pension paid was 26 shillings a week; a married couple would receive 42 shillings. Although the act made more generous provision than Beveridge had envisaged, it was criticised by some Labour MPs for not providing an adequate level of support for the most vulnerable in society.

The National Insurance Industrial Injuries Act (1946) made it compulsory for workers, employers and the government to make weekly contributions to a fund which would compensate injured workers and provided pensions for those who were disabled. The act built on previous Workmen's Compensation Acts – these had attempted to support those who were injured in the workplace, but it had been a lengthy and expensive process for a worker to prove an injury had been caused at work.

The National Assistance Act (1948) aimed to support those for whom the National Insurance Act did not provide an adequate 'safety net'. This included people who had joined the national insurance scheme for the first time, who were not entitled to full pension benefits for ten years. It also included many of the elderly, whose only income was the non-contributory pension – at ten shillings a week, this was very limited. The Assistance Act also aimed to support women whose husbands were in prison, unmarried mothers, the blind, the deaf and the disabled. National Assistance Boards were established to provide for all of these groups; individuals could apply to these boards for financial help. Support came in the form of cash benefits, but also included the provision of extra local services, such as old people's homes and accommodation for the disabled. All of this extra assistance was funded through central government taxation. This was a significant move away from a situation where local support would depend primarily on the willingness and financial health of local authorities.

Housing

Tackling the 'giant evil' of squalor was a particular challenge. There was already a serious housing shortage in 1939. During the 1930s, an average of 350 000 houses were built annually, but this had not been enough to address the problem fully. The onset of war made the existing problem much worse. The destruction of 700 000 homes as a result of German bombing meant that the housing crisis had to be a priority for the new government. Resources had, inevitably, been directed elsewhere during wartime – only 3000 new houses had been built in 1945. The return of around 5 million members of the armed forces increased the urgency of the situation. In March 1945, the wartime government announced that 750 000 new houses were needed immediately.

After Attlee's victory, Bevan was appointed to oversee Labour's house-building drive. Despite shortages of raw materials, significant progress was made: 140 000 houses were built in 1947 and over 284 000 in 1948. Between 1949 and 1951, the annual average was 200 000 new houses. Most of these were council houses. Although some of these dwellings were intended to be only temporary (such as the aluminium-framed 'pre-fabs'), Bevan insisted on a minimum standard. This included three bedrooms and an indoor bathroom and toilet. Bevan's other important contribution was to introduce rent controls in order to protect tenants from exploitative landlords.

> ### ACTIVITY 4.8
> What conclusions can you draw from the graph in Figure 4.10 about:
> - how successfully 'squalor was tackled' between 1945 and 1964?
> - the existence of the postwar consensus?

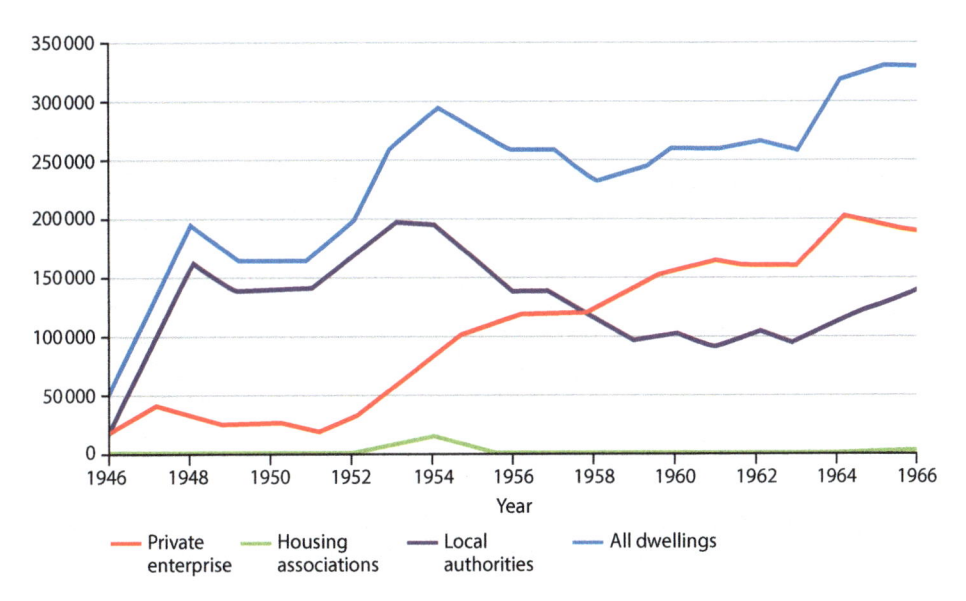

Figure 4.10: House-building: permanent dwellings completed, by tenure

The growth of the NHS

Despite Bevan's efforts, the housing shortage remained a problem. The postwar increase in marriages and the subsequent 'baby boom' were partly responsible. By 1951, there were still 750 000 houses fewer than households in Britain. In London and other major cities, 'squatters' occupied empty properties, demanding water and bedding. As a result of continued shortages, many families found themselves accommodated in temporary hostels.

The NHS Act (1946)
This was one of the most significant pieces of legislation of the 20th century. The key principles behind the new services were:

- Everyone would receive free medical care. This included treatment by GPs, specialists, opticians, midwives and dentists; hospital treatment; maternity and child welfare services; and access to medicines and drugs.
- The system would be funded through income tax and National Insurance contributions.
- Hospitals were nationalised. The aim was to provide all patients with an equal standard of care. England and Wales were divided into 14 areas, each under the control a regional hospital board. Scotland had five regional boards.
- Hospital boards were appointed by Bevan and were responsible for controlling general policy. The day-to-day running of hospitals would be by local management committees. There were 388 of these in England and Wales and 84 in Scotland.

> ### Voices from the past
>
> #### Aneurin (Nye) Bevan (1897–1960)
>
> A towering figure in the politics of the 20th century, Bevan became a miner at the age of 13 in his home town of Tredegar. He became active in the South Wales Miners' Federation, acting as chairman of his union lodge by the time he was just 19. In 1929, Bevan was elected as MP for Ebbw Vale. He spent the next 16 years criticising not only the national governments of Macdonald and Baldwin, but also the wartime ones of Chamberlain and Churchill. His role as Health Secretary in the Attlee government was a historic one – the introduction of the National Health Service transformed British society.
>
> Bevan also had responsibility for the crucial housing programme. After his resignation over prescription charges, Bevan became a dissenting figure within his own party, especially after Gaitskell's election as leader. However, it was the left he angered after 1957, criticising unilateral nuclear disarmament in his role as Shadow Foreign Secretary.

Reaction to the NHS

Bevan had good reason to be confident that his plans would be accepted. The British Medical Association had recognised the need for a system of universal healthcare as far back as 1918, and a report published in 1930 (*General Medical Services for the Nation*) had repeated the call for such a system. Successive wars from the Boer War onwards had revealed the poor health of many within the army, and the Second World War was no different.

> Cross-references: Chapter 2: Social change; Social policies

However, many Conservatives were opposed to the plans and proposed an amendment on the NHS bill's second reading in May 1946. Although this was defeated by 359 votes to 172, the party continued to oppose the bill on its third reading. While Conservative opposition was unsuccessful, the bill being given royal assent by the end of the year, it reflected the wider concerns of many doctors. Many GPs were opposed to being employees of the government, fearing that their professional independence would be jeopardised. They also felt that the positive relationships developed with their patients would be weakened. In a ballot of November 1946, 55% of BMA members voted not to cooperate with Bevan's proposals. In February 1948, as the act became a reality, 90% of the BMA threatened to boycott the NHS.

Defying his reputation as a combative politician, Bevan worked hard to compromise with the doctors. GPs would now receive fees based on the number of patients on their lists. There would no longer be full-time contracts which enabled doctors to give some of their time to private patients. This allayed the fears of most doctors, and as the NHS came into existence, over 90% cooperated.

The NHS in practice

The NHS soon became an accepted and important feature of British life. It often claimed to be the third biggest employer in the world, beaten only by Stalin's Red Army and the Indian state railways! It undoubtedly had a positive impact on the health of the population, especially the working classes. By the 1950s, there had been a significant reduction in deaths from tuberculosis, diphtheria and pneumonia.

However, it proved difficult to fund the new services: the NHS cost £400 million in its first year alone. By September 1948, the number of prescriptions had doubled and by 1951 the figure was 19 million a month. This contrasted to a monthly average of 7 million prescriptions under the previous system. In addition, 5 million pairs of glasses were given out in the first twelve months and the demand for false teeth was double that expected. Despite opposition from Bevan and Harold Wilson, both of whom resigned from the cabinet, the Labour Government reluctantly introduced proposals to allow prescription charges in January 1951. The Conservatives, while now fully supportive of the NHS, introduced the first charges, of one shilling, in 1952.

> Cross-reference: Conservative dominance from 1951 and political consensus

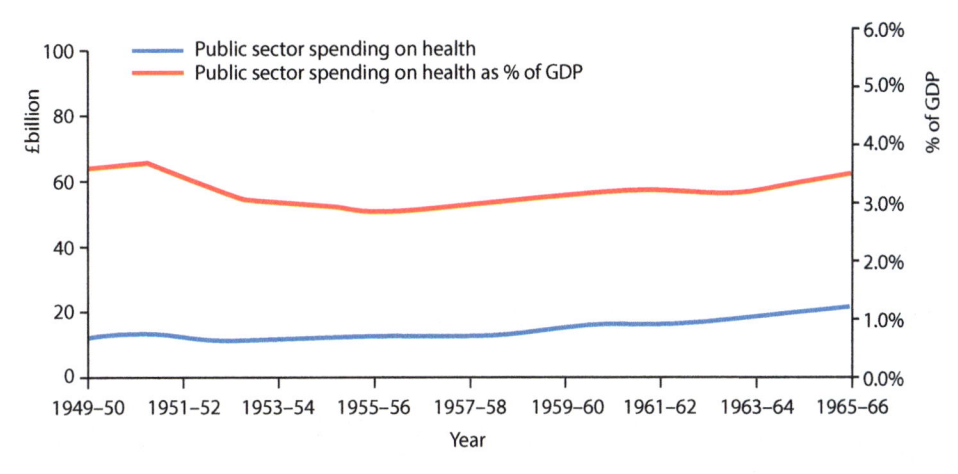

Figure 4.11: Public spending on health in the UK, in real terms and as a percentage of gross domestic product (2014/15 prices)

> ### Speak like a historian
>
> #### Alan Sked and Chris Cook
>
> In their book *Post-War Britain: A Political History*, Sked and Cook say that the NHS:
>
> … constituted an almost revolutionary social innovation since it improved the quality of life of most of the British people … it was soon to become the social institution of which the British would feel most proud.[49]
>
> #### Discussion points:
>
> 1. What do Sked and Cook mean by the phrase 'an almost revolutionary social innovation'?
> 2. Using the three graphs in Figures 4.12 to 4.14, as well as the rest of this section, write approximately 200 words in support of this interpretation and around 200 words against it.

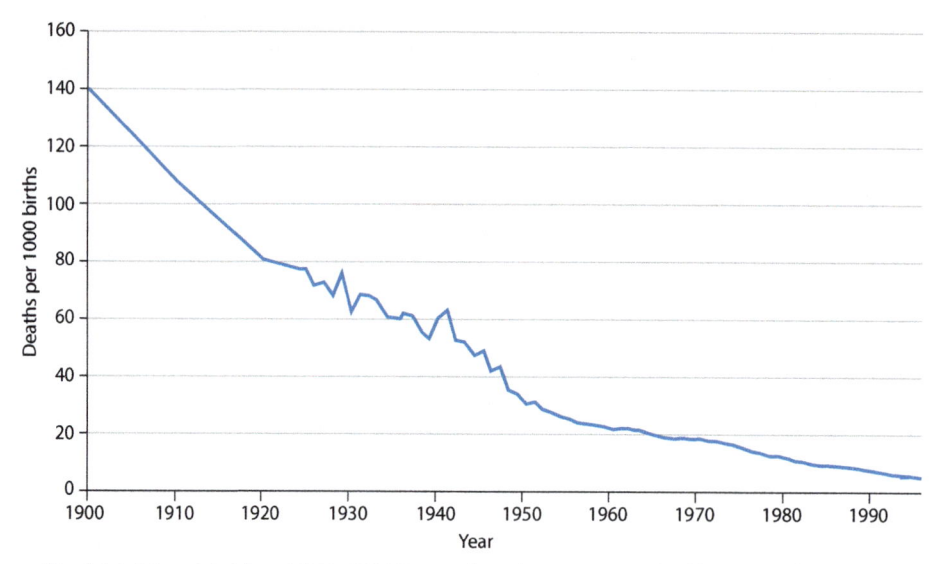

The data is interpolated from 1900 to 1924: it was collected every ten years in 1900, 1910 and 1920. From 1924 an annual record was taken.

Figure 4.12: Infant mortality per 1000 births, 1900–1990

The figures are estimated from 1996.

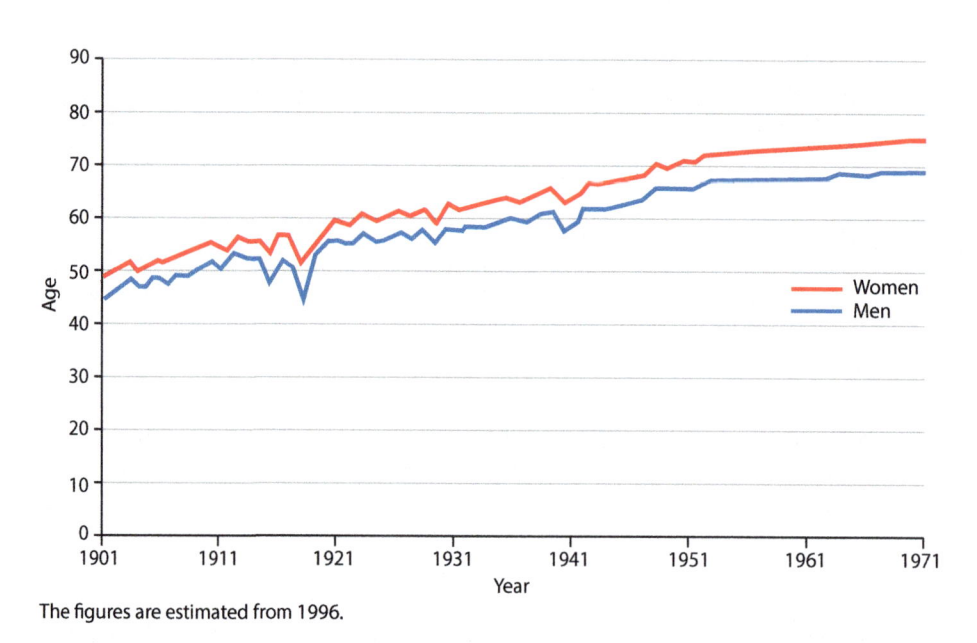

Figure 4.13: Life expectancy at birth, 1901–1971

The development of education

Education reforms to tackle the 'giant evil' of ignorance began even before the election of the Attlee government. The Butler Act had been introduced by the wartime coalition. It was the role of the Attlee government to ensure that the act was fully implemented. As well as implementing the tripartite system, the Attlee government ensured that pupils were provided with free school meals and milk and extended the medical services provided within schools. Education reforms went beyond schools: the Youth Employment Service was established, and the postwar period saw a significant expansion of university and technical education.

In line with the postwar consensus, the Conservative governments of the 1950s pursued similar education policies to those of the Labour government. David Eccles, appointed education minister by Churchill in 1954, implemented proposals for improving technical schools. The positive impact of education reforms was demonstrated by the fact that in 1955, twice as many children remained in full-time education to the age of 17 than in 1951. Reforms were continued during the Eden and Macmillan eras: colleges of advanced technology were established, as were university institutes of technology. The number of technical schools was also increased.

A significant development of 1963 was the government's adoption of a report produced by the Committee on Higher Education, chaired by the eminent economist, Lord Robbins. The committee was established in an attempt to address restricted access to higher education. Only 4% of 18-year-olds entered full-time university courses in 1963 – entry figures were even lower for working-class boys (3%) and working-class girls (1%). Despite the fact that a rising number of young people were obtaining the required entrance qualifications, many academics remained opposed to increasing numbers. However, there was growing economic competition from countries whose higher education systems were less restrictive, and this persuaded the government to tackle the issue.

The Robbins Report stated that university places 'should be available to all who were qualified for them by ability and attainment' and proposed granting university status to all colleges of advanced technology. Robbins also proposed that the number of full-time university students should rise to 217 000 by 1974, with 'further big expansion' by 1980, to ensure that all who were qualified and wanted to attend university were able to do so. The government's swift acceptance of the report led to the creation of a number of new universities, including York, East Anglia, Lancaster, Warwick and Kent. By 1969, the number of students in higher education (212 000) had already surpassed Robbins' target.

Thematic link: The Butler Act

Criticisms of the Conservative education policy

Both educationalists and Labour MPs had a range of concerns about the tripartite system. They felt the Attlee government should have adopted a more imaginative approach than either that provided by Butler or the 1926 Hadow proposals. There were objections to the principles behind the system: many felt it was wrong to make life-changing judgements about a child's ability at the tender age of 11. In addition, a large number of working-class children ended up at poorly funded and badly run secondary moderns, having failed the 11+.

Many critics questioned the need for selective secondary education, when it was possible to run a perfectly effective comprehensive system in primary schools. The objections were also practical: it soon became clear that the quality of education was inconsistent across England. A well-off authority such as Lancashire could subsidise technical schools too: 40% of school places were in these institutions or grammar schools. Contrastingly, 85% of secondary-age children in Surrey attended secondary modern schools. An intelligent student who would have enjoyed a grammar school education in Lancashire may just have missed out in Surrey.

A further criticism of 1950s education policy concerns the limited number of new nurseries, schools and colleges that were built. Although Eccles' work to improve technical schools was important, these schools were in a poor condition and his intervention was seen by many as too little, too late.

ACTIVITY 4.9

Produce a concept map to explain the term 'welfare state'. Use the information from the whole of this section to help you.

The condition of Ireland and Anglo-Irish relations

Continuing North-South friction

The North during the Second World War

Northern Ireland benefited economically from the war. Londonderry was a significant naval base and northern industry, geared to the production of war materials, prospered. An important role was played by Harland and Wolff's shipyard in Belfast, where workers made munitions, replacement ships and aircraft. New airfields were also built in order to ensure protection for Atlantic convoys. The resulting job creation meant that unemployment fell to 5%. As the economy boomed, temporary workers arrived from the South, though the government was quick to remind them that this was not a permanent arrangement. A more encouraging sign in terms of North-South cooperation was the Free State's loan of its fire engines when Belfast struggled to cope with German bombing raids.

> Thematic link: The Easter Rising

Unlike the rest of the UK, conscription was not extended to Northern Ireland. Although unionist politicians were supportive of conscription, the British government feared the impact it would have on nationalist groups. Nevertheless, 38 000 volunteers (including 7000 women) were recruited to the armed forces. The impact of war was felt in a variety of ways. Rationing was as much a feature of life as in the rest of the UK; 300 000 US troops were stationed in the province from 1942 and new military bases were built as a result.

Most alarming was the fact that, although Belfast was an important port, Northern Ireland was not well defended, lacking anti-aircraft technology and searchlights. Seven heavy guns were little defence against German bombing. 700 people were killed during a raid in April 1941, and a massive attack in May, involving 86 000 devices, destroyed many factories. Across the two raids, half of the homes in Belfast were damaged.

As in the First World War, nationalist activity remained prominent. Early in the war, the IRA began a campaign of violence in England, with seven towns bombed during 1939–40. The worst of these atrocities was in Coventry, where five people were killed. As a result, two IRA members were hanged in 1940, having been convicted under the Prevention of Violence (Special Provisions) Act of 1939. The Northern Irish government reintroduced internment. IRA prisoners responded by going on hunger strike. As a result, two died in 1940 and another in 1946.

The Irish Free State during the Second World War

In the Free State, de Valera's decision to remain neutral during the war was controversial, increasing tensions between North and South. The British no longer had control over Irish ports (which had been given to the control of the Irish government in 1938) and feared that Ireland would become a base for German spies. Churchill then exacerbated North/South tensions by mooting the idea of a united Ireland in return for Britain regaining the Irish ports. Given Churchill's praise for Northern Ireland's war efforts and his talk of an 'unbreakable bond' between the province and the rest of the UK, it was no surprise that unionists felt both confused and angry.

Despite every other Commonwealth country supporting Britain, de Valera remained steadfast. In reality though, the British did receive some help from their neighbours: 43 000 Irishmen enlisted in the British army and, especially after Dublin was bombed by the Germans in May 1941, de Valera gave the British covert support. This included providing weather reports and releasing RAF pilots grounded in Ireland – a gesture not extended to the Germans. Like his northern counterparts, de Valera introduced anti-IRA measures including the Offences against the State Act, which established military tribunals. He also reintroduced internment in 1940, despite a campaign by his opponents to label it unconstitutional.

North and South after the Second World War

The years immediately after the war saw further tension between North and South. De Valera's decision in 1948 to leave the Commonwealth and to introduce the Republic of Ireland Act formally ended the association between the Free State and the British monarch. Angered by the act and under pressure from unionists, the British responded with the 1949 Ireland Act. This declared that Northern Ireland remained part of the United Kingdom and would continue to do so unless the province's Parliament decided otherwise. For nationalists, it now seemed even more urgent to campaign for a united Ireland.

At the beginning of the 1950s, there were encouraging signs of cross-border cooperation. North and South cooperated on a drainage scheme enabling the building of a hydroelectric generating station on Lough Erne. In 1951, the South took over the management of the Great Northern Railway and in 1952, Foyle Fisheries was established by the Republic. Ministers and civil servants from both nations collaborated on these projects.

Nevertheless, it was impossible to ignore the growing differences between the two countries. The Republic remained heavily Catholic: at least 90% of the population were regular churchgoers, and education and welfare services were often in the hands of the Church. In contrast to the North, where the NHS was now in operation, healthcare in the Republic was heavily influenced by the Catholic authorities. Health minister

ACTIVITY 4.10

Create two parallel timelines for the years 1939–45, one for Northern Ireland and one for the Irish Free State. Add links between the two timelines where appropriate.

Hidden voices

Sheila Cloney and the Fethard Boycott

Sheila Cloney's story embodies both the tense relationship between North and South, and the enormous contrasts between the two nations. She and her husband Sean lived in Fethard-on-Sea, a village in the Republic of Ireland. As a Protestant, she had agreed with her Catholic husband that their two daughters would be exposed to both traditions. When the parish priest, Father Laurence Allen, told Sheila that her daughters were to go to the local Catholic school, she fled across the border with her children in April 1957. After arriving in Belfast, she was eventually smuggled to Scotland by associates of Ian Paisley.

Another Fethard priest, Father William Stafford, ordered local Catholics to boycott the two Protestant shops in the village; meanwhile, the Protestant school was forced to close when its Catholic teacher walked out. Catholic labourers stopped working for Protestant farmers, and shots were fired outside Protestant homes.

The boycott was condemned in Northern Ireland and briefly achieved worldwide attention. However, it was generally well supported by the local Catholic community, apart from some IRA members who remembered the Church's opposition to their activities during the civil war. The most vociferous supporter of the boycott was the Bishop of Galway, Michael Browne, who announced: 'there seems to be a concerted campaign to entice or kidnap Catholic children and deprive them of their faith. Non-Catholics, with one or two honourable exceptions, do not protest against the crime of conspiring to steal the children of a Catholic father, but they try to make political capital when a Catholic people make a peaceful and moderate protest.'

The boycott ended in September 1957, after condemnation from de Valera, who described it as 'ill-conceived, ill-considered and futile' and Sheila Cloney and her daughters returned home in December. Tensions did not disappear, however. The Protestant Church of Ireland blamed Cloney herself, using the opportunity to criticise her decision to enter a 'mixed marriage'. It was also noted that many Catholic customers never returned to the Protestant shops in Fethard.[50]

Discussion points:

1. What does the story of Sheila Cloney reveal about (a) the role of the Church in the Republic of Ireland, and (b) the relationship between North and South in 1957?
2. Why do you think the Church of Ireland condemned Sheila Cloney, rather than criticising the Catholic Church?

Noel Browne was forced to abandon a proposed scheme to give free medical relief to mothers and children under 16, in the face of Church claims that it would undermine family responsibility.

The impact of the welfare state

> **Thematic link: The growth of the NHS and the welfare state**

At a time when the Republic's economy was struggling with limited industry, rising unemployment and farmers facing tough foreign competition, the positive impact of the welfare state in the North heightened tensions. The New Housing Trust built 100 000 new houses in the North; they were even distributed fairly between Catholics and Protestants. Over 500 000 northern workers had insurance against unemployment or illness by 1952 and family allowance was paid for at least 220 000 children. Most significant of all, the NHS helped to reduce the death rate in Northern Ireland from the UK's highest in 1939 to its lowest by 1962.

Government funding for industrial development had a positive impact on the North: over 4700 new jobs were created in 1946 and 111 new factories had opened by the early 1960s. Education minister Samuel Hall-Thompson introduced scholarships for bright children from poor backgrounds, as well as free school meals, in 1947. One unexpected development of these improvements was the decision of some northern Catholics to shift the focus of their campaigning. The advantages of the British welfare state meant that a united Ireland appeared less attractive, so the focus changed to improving those aspects of northern life which remained unacceptable. The priority would now be tackling widespread discrimination and fighting for full civil rights.

Evidence of segregation and discrimination

There was a wide range of evidence which civil rights campaigners were able to use in order to show that discrimination was widespread:

- The education system was almost entirely segregated – mixed schools and colleges did exist, but were a rarity. Segregation also extended to sports teams, scout troops and youth clubs.
- There was widespread discrimination in employment: 90% of Harland and Wolff workers were Protestants, as were 94% of senior civil servants and at least 90% of RUC members. The B-Specials (the province's volunteer police force) contained even fewer Catholics than the RUC. Many jobs were allocated on the basis of recommendations from employers' families and friends; often, the **Orange Order** played a key role in recruitment too. Formal and fair interviews were uncommon. As a result, the proportion of Catholics who were unemployed was three times that of Protestants. In periods of economic crisis, such as 1958, this discrimination tended to become even more marked.
- Counties with a significant Catholic population, such as Londonderry, Tyrone, and Fermanagh, saw less investment in industry than in Protestant counties. Only 16 of the 111 new factories in the postwar period were built in those counties.
- The allocation of council housing also tended to favour Protestants.
- Property qualifications were imposed both for general and local elections. The vote was restricted to owners or tenants of dwellings; the majority of the 25 000 people now denied the vote were poorer Catholics. As a result, Catholics tended to be under-represented on local councils, even in areas with a large nationalist population. Loopholes that had been closed in the rest of the UK, allowing some businessmen and university graduates to have two votes, remained in Northern Ireland. Most of these voters were Protestant.
- The RUC and particularly the B-Specials could be aggressive in their dealings with the Catholic community, leading to growing resentment among nationalists.

Key terms

Orange Order: Officially called the Loyal Orange Institution, it was founded in 1795, during a period of intense conflict between Protestants and Catholics. Its members swore to uphold the Protestant faith and the Protestant king. Its name refers to William of the Dutch House of Orange, who defeated the Catholic James II at the Battle of the Boyne in 1690, cementing his position as King William III. Members are noted for their orange sashes and their annual marches on 12 July, the routes of which have been a source of conflict with the Catholic community. The Order is closely linked to Northern Ireland's unionist parties and remains a conservative organisation dedicated to maintaining the province's place within the UK.

- Orange Order marches were often deliberately re-routed through Catholic areas. The Flags and Emblems (Display) Act of 1954 was also provocative. This law made it illegal to interfere with the Union flag when it was in a public place. However, the police had the right to remove other flags from public or private property. This led to the removal of numerous Irish tricolours.

> **Thematic link: Divided Ireland before the Second World War**

Figure 4.14: Portadown members of the Orange Order gathering for their annual parade to Drumcree

In the light of this discrimination, sectarian tensions grew. This was evident in the actions of nationalist councils, who could be equally discriminatory in their allocation of resources. In nationalist Newry, for example, of 765 new council houses built, only 22 were given to Protestants.

Tension was also evident in the continued activity of the IRA. Although Sinn Fein gained only 155 000 votes in the 1955 election, the IRA believed this was enough of a mandate for a new campaign of violence. Between 1956 and 1962, the IRA's Operation Harvest, involving the 'flying squad' tactics honed by Michael Collins, was put into action. The operation failed to improve the civil rights of northern Catholics, partly because the IRA had been infiltrated by MI5 and partly because nationalist militancy made unionists even more determined not to make concessions.

By 1962 the IRA had adopted a new approach. Its emerging leaders, Cathal Goulding and Roy Johnstone, adopted radical socialist ideas in an attempt to unite the working class in support. This ultimately led to a split with more conservative IRA figures such as Joe Cahill and Sean MacStiofain.

Voices from the past

Terence O'Neill (1914–90)

A Unionist MP since 1946, O'Neill became prime minister of Northern Ireland in 1963. In this role, he encouraged economic modernisation as a way of attempting to heal cross-community divisions within the province. He was also keen to improve relations between Northern Ireland and the Republic of Ireland. O'Neill faced criticism from the emerging civil rights movement, who believed his gestures were rarely followed by concrete actions to tackle anti-Catholic discrimination. On the other hand, he was also condemned by more militant unionist politicians, such as Paisley and Brian Faulkner, who believed his approach to be too liberal. Mounting pressure from both sides, coupled with the beginnings of the 'Troubles' led O'Neill to resign in 1969.

ACTIVITY 4.11

Refer to table 4.7:

1. What percentage of the voters in North ward and Waterside ward were Catholics?
2. What percentage of the voters in South ward were Protestants?
3. What conclusions can you draw from this data? Present your answer in three key bullet points.

Council ward	Protestant voters	Catholic voters	Protestant councillors	Catholic councillors
North	3946	2530	8	0
South	1138	10 047	0	8
Waterside	3697	1852	4	0

Table 4.7: Voting for Londonderry Council, 1964

Unionist divisions and sectarian violence: 1963–64

Coinciding with the IRA split between the radicals Goulding and Johnstone and the conservatives Cahill and MacStiofain, Terence O'Neill emerged as the province's prime minister, and this offered some hope to Catholics. O'Neill aimed to limit Catholic support for a united Ireland by improving living standards in the North. He embarked on a gradual programme of reform, working towards Catholic civil rights. The creation of new towns at Antrim, Ballymena and Craigavon was another encouraging sign.

Although Harold Wilson gave his full backing, Prime Minister O'Neill faced strong criticism from Paisley, who formed the Ulster Protestant Action group with the stated aim of preserving preferential treatment for Protestant workers during times of recession. Paisley's condemnation demonstrated the difficulties that Catholics would face in their fight for civil rights. Despite his reforming instincts, O'Neill was increasingly frustrated by opposition from fellow unionists. Furthermore, Paisley's actions resulted in growing tension. A notable example was the RUC's removal of an Irish flag from Billy McMillen's office window in the Divis Street area of West Belfast in September 1964. McMillen was an Independent Republican election candidate and the RUC's decision was the result of threats of direction action by Paisley and his supporters. Several days of rioting ensued.

Speak like a historian

Sabine Wichert

O'Neill had tried to bring Northern Ireland into the twentieth century, but the political values of the province were nineteenth-century ones: the transformation of a liberal democracy into a full mass-democracy had happened slowly elsewhere, the impact of international politics on the radicals in the province, however, demanded an acceleration of the speed with which reforms were implemented, and this in turn could not keep pace with the mutually contradictory reformist and conservative expectations. Between these forces, O'Neill's policies foundered and Westminster had to be asked to intervene, ending fifty years of unionist rule. A final assessment of the reasons for O'Neill's failure cannot yet be made: but it looks as if bad luck and accident, as so often in history, were the main causes.[51]

Discussion points:

1. Summarise Wichert's interpretation in your own words (no more than 50).
2. Carry out some research on Terence O'Neill, and begin an answer to the question 'How convincing is Wichert's interpretation of O'Neill's career?'

4 Transformation and change, 1939–64

Voices from the past

John Hume (b. 1937)

An article by the Nationalist leader in the *Irish Times*, 1964

Weak opposition leads to corrupt government. Nationalists in opposition have been in no way constructive. They have … been loud in their demands for rights, but they have remained silent and inactive about their duties. In 40 years of opposition, they have not produced one constructive contribution on either the social or economic plane to the development of Northern Ireland … it is this lack of positive contribution and the apparent lack of interest in the general welfare of Northern Ireland that has led many Protestants to believe that the Northern Catholic is politically irresponsible and therefore unfit to rule.[52]

Discussion points:

1. What does Hume mean by the phrase 'they have remained silent and inactive about their duties?'
2. Are you surprised by Hume's argument? Explain your answer carefully.
3. Write a paragraph explaining how a nationalist opponent of Hume might argue against him.

The civil rights campaign

The effects of the economic boom were rarely felt by northern Catholics, many of whom were confined in the poorest areas of the province. Even by 1961, 20% of houses had no piped water supply and 23% had no flushing toilets. Many of these houses were inhabited by Catholics. In the nationalist areas of Dungannon, County Tyrone, there had been no new council houses in the years 1945–63. When a number of bungalows in the town were chosen for demolition in 1963, 17 Catholic families squatted in them as a protest. Attempts by the Unionist council to evict them failed. In the light of press criticism and public sympathy, councillors instead promised to speed up the local house-building programme.

Key in the protest was the new Homeless Citizens' League, founded by Patricia McCluskey. This was the beginning of a civil rights movement, inspired by the work of Martin Luther King in the USA, which would grow to be a significant force by the end of the decade. Inspired by the successful protest, McCluskey's husband, Conn, founded the Campaign for Social Justice (CSJ) on 17 January 1964. The CSJ, chaired by Patricia McCluskey, soon produced a dossier revealing the extent of housing discrimination in Dungannon. After over a hundred years of nationalist campaigning, it was clear that Irish Catholics would continue to make their voices heard.

Further reading

There are several good biographies of the leading figures during this period. Roy Jenkins' *Churchill* (London, Pan, 2002) is a comprehensive and entertaining account of this complex character. Francis Beckett's *Clem Attlee* (London, Haus, 2015) and Nick Tiratsoo's *The Attlee Years* (London, Continuum, 1991) give positive, but objective, summaries of Attlee's government, while D.R. Thorpe's biography of Harold Macmillan, *Supermac* (London, Pimlico, 2011) is a detailed and informative chronicle of the events of 1957 to 1963. Terence O'Neill's autobiography (London, Rupert Hart-Davis, 1972) gives an important moderate-unionist perspective on developments in Northern Ireland.

There are many very good general accounts which cover this period. Brian Harrison's *The Transformation of British Politics* (Oxford University Press, 1996) is a scholarly, but accessible, work covering the leading policies and political figures. Martin Pugh's *State and Society* (London, Bloomsbury, 2012) covers both political and social developments in detail. John Ramsden's *An Appetite For Power* (London, HarperCollins, 1998) is an invaluable source of information about Churchill, Eden and Macmillan. David and Gareth Butler's *Twentieth Century British Political Facts* (Basingstoke, Palgrave Macmillan, 2000) is a superb reference point for electoral statistics and details of party

Voices from the past

From the founding statement of the CSJ, January 1964

[The CSJ has been established] for the purpose of bringing the light of publicity to bear on the discrimination which exists in our community against the Catholic section of that community representing more than one-third of the total population.

Discussion points:

1. Using this statement, the information about the McCluskey family and your own research, summarise the aims and methods of the CSJ.
2. Using the information on Ireland from previous chapters, write two paragraphs exploring similarities and differences between the CSJ and earlier nationalist organisations.

politics. Peter Hennessy's *The Prime Minister* (London, Penguin, 2000) is a fascinating insight into the personalities of the various figures who occupied Downing Street during this period.

Two interesting perspectives from social historians are provided by Juliet Gardiner, whose *Wartime Britain: 1939–1945* (London, Headline Review, 2004) chronicles the experiences of ordinary British people, and Stephanie Spencer, author of *Gender, Work and Education in the 1950s* (Basingstoke, Palgrave Macmillan, 2005), who examines the often-conflicting pressures faced by British women.

> **Practice essay questions**
>
> 1. 'The years 1945 to 1964 were a period of consensus in economic and social policy.' Assess the validity of this view.
> 2. To what extent were the five 'great evils' identified by the Beveridge Report effectively tackled between 1942 and 1964?
> 3. 'The period 1939 to 1964 was a period of significant social and cultural change.' Assess the validity of this view.
> 4. Using your understanding of the historical context, assess how convincing these three extracts are in relation to the state of the British economy between 1945 and 1964.

Extract A

Rex Pope, *The British Economy since 1914: A Study in Decline?* Abingdon, Routledge, 2013, pp. 52, 88, 91.

[In the 1950s] Britain's … growth record was impressive by historical standards, trade was buoyant, there was full employment, and living standards remained the best in Europe …The … increased commitment of resources to education and welfare was beneficial to economic growth. So was the … pent-up demand for … consumer goods. [However, this was the period] when British decline became the accepted and unchallenged economic and political wisdom. The explanation lies in the comparative performance of the British and other economies and the painful realisation … that Britain was eventually overtaken … Criticisms of government drew attention to the supposed effects of 'stop-go' policies … in fact, the resulting economic fluctuations of the 1950s … were mild by the standards of what preceded them. There is a little more substance to the suggestion that the … potential of nationalised industries was subordinated to short-term political … objectives.[53]

Extract B

George Bernstein, *The Myth of Decline: The Rise of Britain Since 1945*, London, Pimlico, 2004.

For every piece of evidence of Britain's failure in the post-war period, there was counterbalancing evidence of economic success: relatively high inflation … and low growth rates for the economy as a whole compared with competitor nations were balanced by historically low unemployment, low poverty, and high growth rates compared with Britain's past … Britain came out of the war with serious economic problems … it is something of a miracle that the Labour government was able to combine economic recovery with achieving its many policy goals. By the 1950s, the people of Britain were seeing … unparalleled prosperity that allowed standards of living to shoot up. Throughout the decade, however, there was evidence that the economy was not altogether equipped to take on the demands that were put on it ... The expansive economy that assured full employment led to a balance of payments deficit ... while the tight economic policies that were necessary to defend sterling led to unemployment.[54]

Extract C

Alan Booth, *The British Economy in the Twentieth Century.* Basingstoke, Palgrave Macmillan, 2001, pp. 3 and 6.

Britain had emerged from the war effectively bankrupt, with an overstretched economy and massive popular expectations of economic and social improvement. For a decade and a half, economic progress appeared satisfactory, and the British began to come to terms with the idea of affluence, but in the later 1950s, British mass opinion suddenly awoke to the realisation that other countries were growing much faster and overtaking our living standards. Areas of strength were increasingly difficult to find. Britain's share of world trade now contracted alarmingly ... Governments came to believe that their hold on office depended on their ability to manage the economy effectively, or at least to persuade other people that the opposition was even less competent. The bear pit of party politics is scarcely the best backdrop to ... investigation of economic strengths and weaknesses.[55]

Chapter summary

By the end of this chapter you should have gained a broad overview of the way in which British politics, economy and society developed in the years 1939–64. You should also understand:

- the way in which the Second World War transformed attitudes towards the role and aims of government, making a landslide Labour victory possible
- the policies of successive governments between 1945 and 1964 and the debate about whether these amounted to a postwar consensus
- the fluctuating fortunes of the British economy, including: the economic problems caused by total war; the postwar boom; and the impact of stop-go policies on trade and industry
- postwar social changes, including: the rise of consumerism; the gradual change in the role of women in British society; the growth of 'teenager culture'; and the impact of growing Commonwealth immigration
- the impact of the Beveridge Report on the growth of education, the NHS and the welfare state, and the debate about the extent to which the 'Five Great Evils' were tackled
- the growing divide between the political and social landscape of Northern Ireland and the Republic of Ireland and the pressures in the North that led to the rise of the civil rights movement.

Endnotes

[1] Hansard, House of Commons Debate, 5th series, v.260, c.1150, 7 May 1940.
[2] N. Lowe, *Mastering Modern British History*. Basingstoke, Palgrave Macmillan, 2009, p. 544.
[3] D. Cannadine, *Blood, Toil, Tears and Sweat*. Boston, Houghton Mifflin, 1989, pp. 4, 149, 165.
[4] D. Reynolds, *Churchill, A Major New Assessment of His Life in Peace and War*, ed. R. Blake and W.R. Louis. Oxford, Oxford University Press, 1993, p. 241.
[5] R. Blake, *The Conservative Party from Peel to Major*. London, Arrow, 1998, p. 249.
[6] Lowe, *Mastering Modern British History*, pp. 475–6.
[7] Quoted in J. Turner, *Macmillan*. Abingdon, Routledge, 2014, p. 92.
[8] R. Bruce Lockhart, *The Diaries of Sir Robert Bruce Lockhart*, Vol. 2 1939–1965. London, Macmillan, 1973, p. 474.
[9] P. Hennessy, 'Never Again: Britain 1945–51', in Lowe, *Mastering Modern British History*, p. 476.
[10] K. Morgan, *Labour in Power*. Oxford, Oxford University Press, 1984, p. 402.
[11] C. Barnett, *The Audit of War*. London, Pan, 1996, p. 304.
[12] M. Fraser quoted in P. Hennessy and A. Seldon, *Ruling Performance: British Governments from Attlee to Thatcher*. Oxford, Blackwell, 1989, p. 310.
[13] R. Miliband, *The State in Capitalist Society*. Pontypool, Merlin Press, 2009, p. 69.
[14] N. Lawson quoted in P. Hennessy, *The Prime Minister: The Office and its Holders Since 1945*. London, Penguin, 2000, p. 151.
[15] D. Marquand, quoted in M. Pearce and G. Stewart, *British Political History 1867–1995*, London, Routledge, 1992, p. 516.
[16] Hennessy, *The Prime Minister*, p. 210.
[17] Quoted in J. Margach, *The Abuse of Power*. London, W.H. Allen, 1978, pp. 116–17.
[18] Quoted in P. Dorey, *British Conservatism and Trade Unionism*, Farnham, Ashgate, 2009, pp. 170–1.
[19] J.E. Cronin, *Labour and Society in Britain 1918–1979*. London, Batsford, 1984, p. 13.
[20] Quoted in F. Mount, *The New Few*. London, Simon & Schuster, 2012, p. 119.
[21] H. Fairlie, 'Political Commentary', in *The Spectator*, 23 September 1955.
[22] D. Jay, *The Socialist Case*. London, Faber & Faber, 1937, p. 317.
[23] Speech at the Labour Party Conference, Scarborough, 1 October 1963: http://nottspolitics.org/wp-content/uploads/2013/06/Labours-Plan-for-science.pdf.
[24] Quoted in Hennessy, *The Prime Minister*, p. 284.
[25] See, for example, Peter Wilby, 'Why Labour politicians hate each other and I loved reading Melanie Phillips', *New Statesman*, 3 October 2013.
[26] M. Panter-Downes, *London War Notes*. Farrar, Straus and Giroux, 1971, p. 433.
[27] A. Marwick, *Britain in the Century of Total War*. London, The Bodley Head, 1969, p. 291.
[28] P. Thorneycroft, quoted in Hennessy, *The Prime Minister*, p. 266.
[29] Blake, *The Conservative Party from Peel to Major*, p. 281.
[30] Quoted in A. Marr, *A History of Modern Britain*. London, Pan, 2009, p. 169.
[31] K. Middlemass, quoted in Marr, *A History of Modern Britain*, p. 179.
[32] Lowe, *Mastering Modern British History*, p. 580.
[33] D. Kynaston, *Austerity Britain 1945–1951*. London, Bloomsbury, 2007, p. 174.
[34] Blake, *The Conservative Party from Peel to Major*, p. 267.
[35] At a Bedford rally, 20 July 1957.
[36] Recorded in the Annual Conference, National Union of Conservative and Unionist Associations, Volume 81, October 1962, p. 8.
[37] W. Beveridge, quoted in M. Pugh, *The Making of Modern Britain*. Oxford, Blackwell, 2002, p. 266.
[38] S. Spencer, *Gender, Work and Education in the 1950s*, Basingstoke, Palgrave Macmillan, 2005, p. 3.
[39] D. Goodhart, *The British Dream*. London, Atlantic Books, 2013.
[40] *Hansard*, House of Commons, 5th series, vol. 701, col. 71.
[41] S. Jeffries, 'Britain's most racist election: the story of Smethwick, 50 years on', *The Guardian*, 15 October 2014.
[42] D. Mason, *Race and Ethnicity in Modern Britain*. Oxford, Oxford University Press, 2000, p. 26.
[43] In P. Buchanan, *Churchill, Hitler and the Unnecessary War*. New York, Crown, 2008, p. 405.
[44] P. Addison, *Churchill on the Home Front 1900–1955*. London, Faber & Faber, 2013, p. 416.

[45] In M. Pearce and G. Stuart, *British Political History 1867–2001*. Abingdon, Routledge, 2002, p. 483.

[46] Hugh Dalton, *The Second World War Diary*, ed. B. Pimlott. London, Cape, 1986, p. 564.

[47] Report on Social Insurance and Allied Services ('The Beveridge Report'), 1 December 1942, p. 6.

[48] M. Barber, *Making of the 1944 Education Act*. London, Cassell, 1994, pp. ix and x.

[49] A. Sked and C. Cook, *Post-War Britain: A Political History,* quoted in Lowe, *Mastering Modern British History*, p. 574.

[50] T. Fanning, 'One Woman, Two Children and a Town Torn in Two by Religion', *Belfast Telegraph*, 1 April 2010.

[51] In J. Elvert (ed.), *Northern Ireland, Past and Present.* Stuttgart, Franz Steiner Verlag, 1994, p. 199.

[52] J. Hume, *Irish Times*, 18 May 1964.

[53] R. Pope, *The British Economy since 1914: A Study in Decline?* Abingdon, Routledge, 2013, pp. 52, 88 and 91.

[54] G. Bernstein, *The Myth of Decline: The Rise of Britain Since 1945*. London, Pimlico, 2004.

[55] A. Booth, *The British Economy in the Twentieth Century*. Basingstoke, Palgrave Macmillan, 2001, pp. 3 and 6.

Glossary

Arriviste — A person who has recently attained wealth, status, or power, sometimes by dubious means and often unexpectedly.

Austerity — A policy which involves government cuts; during times of austerity, the public are encouraged to live within their means.

Autarky — Economic self-sufficiency and independence.

Balance of payments — The difference between revenue from exports and spending on imports – this can be a surplus (revenue greater than spending) or a deficit (spending greater than revenue).

Balance of trade — The value of exports minus the value of imports. The visible balance of trade is based on the value of physical goods being exported and imported. The overall balance of trade is also affected by 'invisible' imports and exports: services and non-physical goods, such as City financial services for foreign firms.

Boer War — The Second Boer War took place from 1899 to 1902. It was fought in South Africa between the British and a group of settlers of Dutch extraction known as the Boers. Britain won the war, but at terrible cost and with great difficulty. The war raised many questions about empire and Britain's position as a great power.

Borough — A town that sends an MP or MPs to Parliament, traditionally a town with a corporation and privileges granted by a royal charter.

Catholic emancipation — the process by which historic restrictions on Irish Catholics were lifted, giving them equal civil rights to non-Catholics. Emancipation was granted by the Roman Catholic Relief Act (1829).

Chartist movement — A working-class political movement that was active from 1836 to 1848, which petitioned for further political reform following the 1832 Reform Act. Their charter comprised six demands, including universal male suffrage, secret ballots and annual parliaments.

Children's Charter — A collection of measures of 1906–09 introduced as part of Liberal social reform to help children. It included free school meals, compulsory medical inspections in schools, separate courts for child offenders and a 'free place' system in secondary schools for bright working-class children.

Church of England — The founding church of the now-worldwide Anglican Church; the established church in England following the reformation in the 16th century. It is headed by the British monarch and combines Protestantism with some Catholic traditions.

Coalition — An alliance between different political parties which is temporary. Parties form a coalition when no party has a clear majority, or at a time of national emergency when party differences are put to one side.

Colourable employment — Giving people fictitious or nominal jobs as a cover for paying them to vote for a particular candidate.

Commonwealth — A group of countries within the British Empire which had a greater degree of independence than other colonies.

Conscription — The calling up of people for compulsory military service.

Conservative Party — The political party that emerged from the Tory Party in the 1830s under the leadership of Robert Peel.

Constituency — An area in which a group of voters live. In the 19th century in Britain there were two types of constituency: boroughs and counties.

Constitution — The set of rules that sets out how a country is governed, and defines the relationship between different political institutions and between government and the people. Some countries have a codified constitution (written in a single document) and others, such as Britain, have an uncodified constitution: an accumulation of laws, convention and precedent.

Corporate raiding — The process of buying a large stake in a company, then using voting rights as a shareholder to force the company to make significant changes to management practices.

Corporatism — A system of government in which both employers and trade unions take part in the decision-making process.

County — The main subdivision of the UK (such as Yorkshire and Lancashire). Traditionally counties sent MPs to Parliament to represent the rural community.

Coupon election — In the general election of 1918 there was a coalition between the Conservatives and the Liberals who chose, after the Maurice debate, to follow Lloyd George. The term 'coupon' was a reference to a letter every official coalition candidate had, signed by Bonar Law and Lloyd George, endorsing them and ensuring they were not opposed by another Conservative or Lloyd George Liberal. 88% of those with a 'coupon' were elected.

Decolonisation — The process by which countries within the British Empire gradually became independent, most remaining as part of the Commonwealth.

Deference — Showing respect to, and accepting the wishes of, those in authority; respecting the established institutions of society.

Democracy — 'The rule of the people', taken from the Greek *demos* (people) and *kratos* (rule). A democracy is a system whereby the people choose the government; this is normally done through the electing of representatives. A 'full' or 'true' democracy will have universal suffrage for adults.

Denomination — A sub-group of a major religion; for example, Anglican, Baptist and Roman Catholic are all different Christian denominations.

Devaluation — The official lowering of the value of a country's currency, setting a new fixed rate with respect to a foreign country's currency.

Disestablishment — The process of removing a church from its status as the official, 'established' state Church. In Irish terms, this meant ending the established status of the Anglican Church.

Dominion — A country within the British Empire whose government was responsible for its own domestic affairs.

Elementary standard — The level of education someone would have expected to have reached by the end of primary school.

Established church — In Britain, the Church of England is the established church. It hosts official ceremonies such as coronations, royal weddings and funerals, and so on.

Glossary

Establishment	The elite group which dominated British politics, key institutions such as the Church, armed forces and civil service and, to an extent, British society as a whole.
Eugenics	The idea that society could be improved through promoting selective breeding and even sterilisation of some members of society.
First Great Reform Act	Passed in 1832, this gave the vote to middle-class men for the first time, reformed the political system and got rid of many of the smaller constituencies, replacing them with ones that better reflected the new centres of population among other significant changes.
First past the post	A voting system whereby the country is divided into constituencies (areas) of roughly equal population. The votes at an election are counted for the constituency and the candidate with the most votes wins the seat. This system can lead to the number of seats a party wins not reflecting their share of the overall vote across the country.
Fixed tenure	The principle which ensured that tenants had a guaranteed right to remain on their land for a fixed period of time, without threat of eviction.
Franchise	The right to vote in political elections, also referred to as suffrage.
Free sale	The principle which allowed a tenant to sell their 'interest' in a piece of land to the next tenant.
Free trade	International commerce (trade) which is not subject to tariffs, quotas or other interference from government.
Gold standard	The value of gold. When a government links the value of their currency to the gold standard, it is saying that it will exchange money for a specified amount of gold. The value of gold is set at a fixed price and the government agrees to buy and sell gold at this price, so it must have sufficient gold reserves to back the amount of money in circulation at any given time.
Government	This group of politicians, called ministers, is led by the Prime Minister, and each has particular responsibilities. The two houses of Parliament and the civil service run the government of Britain under the leadership of the government. Senior members of the government, such as the Home Secretary and Foreign Minister, belong to the cabinet. Ministers are, in most cases, drawn from the two Houses of Parliament.
Hegemony	Dominance or power over others.
Hereditary peer	Someone who becomes a peer (holder of high social rank such as Duke, Earl, Baron or Marquis) when it is passed to them following the death of a relative who had been the holder of the peerage.
High farming	Farming that was considered to be excellent, often involving new techniques, technology and ideas that improved production.
Home Rule	A system by which Ireland would have its own Parliament, responsible for Irish domestic affairs, but would also remain under the ultimate control of the Westminster Parliament. Westminster would be responsible for foreign and defence policy, and Ireland would remain part of the British Empire.
House of Commons	The lower house of Parliament in Britain where laws are debated and voted on. The House of Commons is composed of elected MPs from Britain's constituencies. During the 19th century the House of Commons became more powerful than the House of Lords.
House of Lords	The upper house of Parliament in Britain, where laws are debated and voted upon. The House of Lords in the 19th century comprised hereditary peers along with bishops and archbishops from the Church of England.
Irish Republican	An Irish nationalist who believes in full independence from the British Empire.
Keynesian economics	The philosophy developed by economist John Maynard Keynes, who encouraged government intervention in order to manage demand, create economic growth, and redistribute wealth within society.
Laissez-faire	An economic system that is free from government intervention
Liberal Party	A political party many agree was formed in 1859 at the Willis's Rooms meeting. It was a coalition of Whigs, Radicals and Peelites who united together.
Lib-Lab MPs	These were Liberal MPs financially supported by trade unions. Alexander McDonald and Thomas Burt, both supported by the Miners' Federation of Great Britain, were the first two such MPs to be elected in 1874.
Mandate	The political authority to carry out a policy, or set of policies, based on legitimate political power. For example, a political party that wins a clear majority in the House of Commons is said to have a mandate from the electorate to carry out its manifesto.
Marshall Aid	Economic support given by the USA to European countries to help them recover from the Second World War. The aim was partly humanitarian, but the USA also hoped to strengthen its European trading partners, as well as reducing the link between poverty and the growth of communism.
Marxism	A political ideology devised by Karl Marx that sees human history as a struggle between the classes. It criticised free market capitalism and argued that workers were being exploited by those who owned businesses and that, in time, the workers would rise up in revolution.
Maurice debate	In May 1918 General Sir Frederick Maurice, the retired Director of Military Operations, accused Lloyd George of misleading the House of Commons about the numbers of British troops in France and his promises to hold troops back in Britain. Asquith called for a select committee to look into the allegations and was supported by 98 Liberal MPs. This incident led to the Liberals splitting into two completely separate parliamentary parties.
Minority government	A party that does not have over 50% of the seats in the House of Commons so has to rely on the support of other parties to pass legislation and is vulnerable to a vote of 'no confidence'.
Mixed economy	An economy in which some industries are nationalised and others are privately owned.
National efficiency	There was concern that Britain was declining compared to other world powers and that the reason for this was the poor health and education of the work force in Britain, making them increasingly inefficient compared to their German and American contemporaries.
Nationalisation	The policy of bringing private companies into public ownership, under the ultimate control of the government.

Nonconformist	A member of a Protestant church that dissents (disagrees with and differs) from the established Church of England.
Obstructionist tactics	Blocking the passage of a bill through the Commons by talking for so long in a debate that the bill runs out of parliamentary time.
Orange Order	Officially called the Loyal Orange Institution, it was founded in 1795, during a period of intense conflict between Protestants and Catholics. Its members swore to uphold the Protestant faith and the Protestant king. Its name refers to William of the Dutch House of Orange, who defeated the Catholic James II at the Battle of the Boyne in 1690, cementing his position as King William III. Members are noted for their orange sashes and their annual marches on 12 July, the routes of which have been a source of conflict with the Catholic community. The Order is closely linked to Northern Ireland's unionist parties and remains a conservative organisation dedicated to maintaining the province's place within the UK.
Paper duties	Taxes on paper and printing industries, notably on newspapers.
Parliament	The legislature (law-making body) of Britain comprising the upper house (the House of Lords) and the lower house (the House of Commons).
Peelites	Supporters of Robert Peel's repeal of the Corn Laws in 1846, which caused the Conservative Party to split.
Plural voting	A situation where some people had more than one vote. For example, if they lived in one constituency and had business premises in another, they would have a vote in each constituency. This system favoured the wealthy and meant that there was no level playing field in British democracy.
Postwar consensus	The period between 1945 and 1970, during which both Labour and Conservative Parties pursued similar economic and industrial policies.
Private member's bill	A bill put forward by a member of the House of Commons who is not a member of the government.
Proportional representation (PR)	A voting system whereby the number of seats a party receives is based on the share of the vote the party received. For example, if a party wins 25% of the vote then they gain 25% of the seats in Parliament.
Protectionism	The policy of a government that 'protects' its country's industry from foreign competition through tariffs, quotas and so on (the opposite of free trade).
Rates	Local taxes, usually calculated on the basis of the value of a person's property or dwelling.
Resale Price Maintenance	A system which obliged shops to sell goods at standard prices set by suppliers, preventing undercutting, but reducing competition.
Retrenchment	Cutting back of government spending.
Service industry	A business that does work for a customer, or provides goods, but is not involved in manufacturing.
Socialism	A political ideology which calls for the creation of a society in which property, wealth and work is shared out equitably and members of society work cooperatively. Socialists often disagree over how this society will be brought about.
Sterling balance	Pounds earned from buying British exports; under the terms of the US loan, these could now be sold to Britain in exchange for dollars.
Stop-go policies	Short-term policies, which combine economic stimulation packages in times of economic downturn and measures to cut growth during periods of high inflation.
Structural unemployment	Unemployment caused by long-term faults in the economy.
Suffrage	The right to vote in political elections, also referred to as franchise.
Syndicalism	A form of revolutionary socialism that aims to overthrow the capitalist system and replace it with a socialist system based on the trade union movement. Syndicalists looked to the trade unions as the workers' movement that had the power to bring down the employers and, through a general strike, the power to gain control over the economy and society.
Tariff	Taxes imposed on imported goods by a government to protect the country's own industries against foreign competition.
Tariff reform	A strengthening of the tariff system to boost protection.
Three Fs	This was the stated aim of the Land League: fair rents, fixity of tenure, and free sale.
Tory	A parliamentary party who supported the established church and political order. The term has continued to be used in reference to the Conservative Party and its supporters.
Tory paternalism	An element of Conservative ideology focused on the idea that the elites should look after the lower classes as a parent would look after their children. It was seen as the motivation for social reform and a counter to growing demands for further reform and, later, socialism.
Trade union	A union of skilled workers from particular crafts or skills (such as the Amalgamated Society of Carpenters). These organisations sought to improve the conditions of their members and focused on self-help and self-education.
Treating	Giving or offering food and, more often, drink in order to influence how people vote.
Underconsumption	J.A. Hobson argued that for the economy to perform well, the well-off needed to buy goods to feed the circulation of money through the economic cycle of shopkeeper–manufacturer–wages for the worker. If the well-off saved money instead, the economy would underperform.
Whigs	A political faction that became a political party. They supported the powers of Parliament and the rights of Nonconformists. In 1859 the Whigs combined with the Radicals and Peelites to form the Liberal Party.
Yield	In agriculture it is the amount of crops/produce that can be grown on a given piece of land, a higher yield means more produce. In investments the yield is the amount of profit made on an investment.

Bibliography

Chapter 1

Aldous, R. *The Lion and the Unicorn, Gladstone vs Disraeli*. New York, W.W. Norton, 2007.

Bagehot, W. *The English Constitution*. London, Chapman and Hall, 1867.

Benson, J. *The Working Class in Britain 1850–1939*. London, I.B. Tauris, 2003.

Boyce, D.G. *The Irish Question and British Politics 1868–1986*. London, Palgrave Macmillan, 1988.

Cannadine, D. *The Decline and Fall of the British Aristocracy*. London, Yale University Press, 1990.

Chadwick, E. *The Present and General Condition of Sanitary Science*. London, Meldrum, 1889. Available at https://en.wikisource.org/wiki/The_present_and_general_condition_of_sanitary_science.

Chadwick, E. *The Sanitary Condition of the Labouring Population (1842)*. Edinburgh University Press, 1965.

Easson, B. and McIntyre, J.E. *Early Victorian Society: The Two Nations*. Edinburgh, Blackie, 1979.

Evans, E. *The Complete A–Z 19th and 20th Century British History Handbook*. London, Hodder & Stoughton, 1998.

Gash, N. *Aristocracy and People, Britain 1815–1865*. London, Hodder & Stoughton, 1991.

Hobsbawm, E.J. and Wrigley, C. *Industry and Empire: From 1750 to the Present Day, Volume 3, The Penguin History of Britain*. London, Penguin, 1968.

Hobsbawm, E. *The Age of Capital, 1848–1875*. London, Weidenfeld & Nicolson, 1975.

Kinealy, C. *A New History of Ireland*. Stroud, The History Press, 2008.

Lowe, N. *Mastering Modern British History*. Basingstoke, Palgrave Macmillan, 2009.

Mathias, P. *The First Industrial Nation*. London, Methuen and Co, 1969.

O'Day, A. and Stevenson, J. (eds), *Irish Historical Documents since 1800*. Dublin, Gill & Macmillan, 1992.

Peasant Life in the West of England (1872), available at https://archive.org/stream/peasantlifeinwes00heatuoft/peasantlifeinwes00heatuoft_djvu.txt.

Smiles, S. *Self-Help*. London, John Murray, 1866.

Snow, J. *On the Mode of Communication of Cholera, 2nd edition*. London, John Churchill, 1855.

Taylor, D. *Mastering Economic and Social History*. London, Palgrave Macmillan, 1988.

Thompson, E.P. *The Making of the English Working Class*. London, Penguin, 2013.

Tonge, N. *Industrialisation and Society 1700–1914*. London, Thomas Nelson and Sons, 1993.

Winstanley, M. *Gladstone and the Liberal Party*. London, Routledge, 1990.

Chapter 2

Altholz, J.L., *Selected Documents in Irish History*, London, Routledge, 2000.

Boyce, D.G. and O'Day, A. *The Ulster Crisis*, Basingstoke, Palgrave Macmillan, 2006.

Chamberlain, J., *The Radical Programme* (1885). Available at https://archive.org/details/radicalprogramme00chamiala.

Cook, C. and J. Stevenson. *Handbook of Modern British History, 1714–1987*. Harlow, Longman, 1988.

Coogan, T.P. *De Valera: Long Fellow, Long Shadow*. London, Arrow Books, 1993.

Green, E.H.H, 'Neutering Mr Balfour's poodle', *Modern History Review*, 7.4, April 1996.

Harris, B. *The Origins of the British Welfare State: Society, State and Social Welfare in England and Wales, 1800–1945*. Basingstoke, Palgrave Macmillan, 2004.

Hattersley, R. *The Edwardians*. Stroud, Abacus, 2006.

http://labourlist.org/2014/04/keir-hardies-sunshine-of-socialism-speech-full-text/

Judd, D. *Radical Joe: A Life of Joseph Chamberlain*. London, Faber, 1993.

Kinealy, C. *A New History of Ireland*. Stroud, The History Press, 2008.

Lyons, F.S.L. *Charles Stewart Parnell*. Dublin, Gill & Macmillan, 2005.

Mathias, P. *The First Industrial Nation: An Economic History of Britain, 2nd edn*. London, Methuen and Co. Ltd, 1969.

O'Day, A. and Stevenson, J. (eds), *Irish Historical Documents since 1800*. Dublin, Gill & Macmillan, 1992.

O'Day, A. *Irish Home Rule 1867 to 1921*. Manchester University Press, 1998.

Parry, J., *The Rise and Fall of Liberal Government in Victorian Britain*. Yale University Press, 1993.

Peaple, D. and T. Lancaster. *British History for AS Level, 1867–1918*. Ormskirk, Causeway Press, 2000.

Perkin, H. *The Rise of Professional Society: England Since 1880*. London, Routledge, 1989.

Pugh, M. *The Making of Modern British Politics: 1867–1945*. Oxford, Wiley, 2002.

Read, D. *Edwardian England*. London, Harrap, 1972.

Saul, S.B. *The Myth of the Great Depression*. Basingstoke, Macmillan, 1969.

Sykes, A. *The Rise and Fall of British Liberalism, 1776–1988*. Harlow, Longman 1997.

Taylor, D. *Mastering Economic and Social History*. Macmillan Education, 1988.

Ward, R. *The Chamberlains*. Stroud, Fonthill, 2015.

Winstanley, M. *Gladstone and the Liberal Party*. London, Routledge, 1990.

A/AS Level History for AQA: Challenge and Transformation: Britain, c1851–1964

Chapter 3

Adelman, P. *The Decline of the Liberal Party, 1910–31*. Harlow, Longman, 1981.

Bentley, M. *Politics Without Democracy, 1815–1914*. London, Fontana, 1984.,

Clifford, C. *The Asquiths*. London, John Murray, 2003.

Coogan, T.P. *De Valera: Long Fellow, Long Shadow*. London, Arrow Books, 1993.

Dangerfield, G. *The Strange Death of Liberal England, 1910–1914* (available online).

Dwyer, T.R. *Eamon De Valera*. Dublin, Paperview, 2006.

Ferriter, D. *Judging Dev*. Dublin, Royal Irish Academy, 2007.

Foster, R.F. *Modern Ireland 1600–1972*. London, Penguin, 1988.

Gwynn, S.L. *The Last Years of John Redmond*. London, Edward Arnold, 1919.

Halsey, A.H. (ed.) *British Social Trends since 1900, revised 2nd edition*. Basingstoke, Macmillan, 1988.

Hattersley, R. *David Lloyd George, the Great Outsider*. London, Abacus, 2012.

Jenkins, R. *Asquith*. London, Collins, 1964.

Lowe, N. *Modern British History, 4th edition*. Basingstoke, Palgrave Macmillan, 2009.

Marquand, D. *Ramsay MacDonald: A Biography*. London, Jonathan Cape, 1977.

Mitchell, B.R. and Deane, P. *Abstract of British Historical Statistics*. Cambridge University Press, 1962.

Mowat, C.L. *Britain between the Wars*. London, Methuen & Co, 1955.

O'Day, A. and Stevenson, J. *Irish Historical Documents since 1800*. Dublin, Gill & Macmillan, 1992.

Orwell, G. *The Road to Wigan Pier*. London, Penguin, 2001.

Packer, I. *Lloyd George*. Basingstoke, Macmillan, 1998.

Pearce, R. *Britain: Domestic Politics 1918–39*. London, Hodder and Stoughton, 1992.

Ranelagh, J. *A Short History of Ireland*. Cambridge University Press, 1999.

Self, R. *Neville Chamberlain: A Biography*. Aldershot, Ashgate, 2006.

Stevenson, J. *British Society 1914–45*. London, Penguin, 1984.

Taylor, D. *Mastering Economic and Social History*. Palgrave MacMillan, 1988.

Townshend, C. *Easter 1916: The Irish Rebellion*. London, Penguin, 2005.

Valente, J. *The Myth of Manliness in Irish National Culture, 1880–1922*. Illinois, University of Illinois Press, 2010.

Chapter 4

Addison, P. *Churchill on the Home Front 1900–1955*. London, Faber & Faber, 2013.

Barber, M. *Making of the 1944 Education Act*. London, Cassell, 1994.

Barnett, C. *The Audit of War*. London, Pan, 1996.

Beckett, F. *Clem Attlee*. London, Haus, 2015.

Bernstein, G. *The Myth of Decline: The Rise of Britain Since 1945*. London, Pimlico, 2004.

Blake, R. *The Conservative Party from Peel to Major*. London, Arrow, 1998.

Booth, A. *The British Economy in the Twentieth Century*. Basingstoke, Palgrave Macmillan, 2001.

Bruce Lockhart, R. *The Diaries of Sir Robert Bruce Lockhart, Vol. 2 1939–1965*. London, Macmillan, 1973.

Buchanan, P. *Churchill, Hitler and the Unnecessary War*. New York, Crown, 2008.

Butler, D. and G. *Twentieth Century British Political Facts*. Basingstoke, Palgrave Macmillan, 2000.

Cannadine, D, *Blood, Toil, Tears and Sweat*. Boston, Houghton Mifflin, 1989.

Cronin, J.E. *Labour and Society in Britain 1918–1979*. London, Batsford, 1984.

Dalton, H. *The Second World War Diary*, ed.

B. Pimlott. London, Cape, 1986.

Dorey, P. *British Conservatism and Trade Unionism*. Farnham, Ashgate, 2009.

Elvert, J. (ed.), *Northern Ireland, Past and Present*. Stuttgart, Franz Steiner Verlag, 1994.

Fanning, T. 'One woman, two children and a town torn in two by religion', *Belfast Telegraph*, 1 April 2010.

Gardiner, J. *Wartime Britain: 1939–1945*. London, Headline Review, 2004.

Goodhart, D. *The British Dream*. London, Atlantic Books, 2013.

Harrison, B. *The Transformation of British Politics*. Oxford, Oxford University Press, 1996.

Hennessy, P. and Seldon, A. *Ruling Performance: British Governments from Attlee to Thatcher*. Oxford, Blackwell, 1989.

Hennessy, P. *The Prime Minister: The Office and its Holders*. London, Penguin, 2000.

Jeffries, S. 'Britain's most racist election: the story of Smethwick, 50 years on', *The Guardian*, 15 October 2014.

Jenkins, R. *Churchill*. London, Pan, 2002.

Kynaston, D. *Austerity Britain 1945–1951*. London, Bloomsbury, 2007.

Lowe, N. *Mastering Modern British History*. Basingstoke, Palgrave Macmillan, 2009.

Margach, J. *The Abuse of Power*. London, W.H. Allen, 1978.

Marr, A. *A History of Modern Britain*. London, Pan, 2009.

Marwick, A. *Britain in the Century of Total War*. London, The Bodley Head, 1969,

Mason, D. *Race and Ethnicity in Modern Britain*. Oxford, Oxford University Press, 2000.

Miliband, Ralph. *The State in Capitalist Society*. Pontypool, Merlin Press, 2009.

Morgan, K. *Labour in Power*. Oxford, Oxford University Press, 1984.

Mount, F. *The New Few*, London, Simon & Schuster, 2012.

O'Neill, T. *The Autobiography of Terence O'Neill, Prime Minister of Northern Ireland 1963–1969*. London, Rupert Hart-Davis Ltd, 1972.

Panter-Downes, M. *London War Notes*. Farrar, Straus and Giroux, 1971.

Pearce, M. and Stuart, G. *British Political History 1867–2001*. Abingdon, Routledge, 2002.

Phillips, M. 'Why Labour politicians hate each other and I loved reading', *New Statesman*, 3 October 2013.

Pope, R. *The British Economy since 1914: A Study in Decline?* Abingdon, Routledge, 2013.

Pugh, M. *State and Society*. London, Bloomsbury, 2012.

Pugh, M. *The Making of Modern Britain*. Oxford, Blackwell, 2002.

Ramsden, J. *An Appetite For Power*. London, HarperCollins, 1998.

Report on Social Insurance and Allied Services ('The Beveridge Report'). 1 December 1942.

Reynolds, D. *Churchill, A Major New Assessment of His Life in Peace and War*, ed. Robert Blake and William Roger Louis. Oxford, 1993.

Spencer, S. *Gender, Work and Education in the 1950s*. Basingstoke, Palgrave Macmillan, 2005.

Thorpe, D.R. *Supermac*. London, Pimlico, 2011.

Tiratsoo, N. *The Attlee Years*. London, Continuum, 1991.

Turner, J, *Macmillan*. Abingdon, Routledge, 2014.

Wilby, P. 'Why Labour politicians hate each other and I loved reading Melanie Phillips', *New Statesman*, 3 October 2013.

Acknowledgements

A/AS Level History for AQA: Challenge and Transformation: Britain, c1851–1964

The authors and publishers acknowledge the following sources of copyright material and are grateful for the permissions granted. While every effort has been made, it has not always been possible to identify the sources of all the material used, or to trace all copyright holders. If any omissions are brought to our notice, we will be happy to include the appropriate acknowledgements on reprinting.

The publisher would like to thank the following for permission to reproduce their photographs (numbers refer to figureure numbers, unless otherwise stated):

Front Cover: Keystone Features / Getty Images, **page 1**: World History Archive / Alamy Stock Photo, **figure 1.3**: INTERFOTO / Alamy Stock Photo, **figure 1.5**: Private Collection / Bridgeman Images, **figure 1.6**: Georgios Kollidas / Alamy Stock Photo, **figure 1.7**: INTERFOTO / Alamy Stock Photo, **figure 1.8**: Classic Image / Alamy Stock Photo, **figure 1.10**: Pictorial Press Ltd / Alamy Stock Photo, **figure 1.12**: North Wind Picture Archives / Alamy Stock Photo, **figure 1.15**: The Print Collector / Alamy Stock Photo, **figure 1.17**: Illustrated London News / Getty Images, **page 52**: Heritage Image Partnership Ltd / Alamy Stock Photo, **figure 2.2**: GL Archive / Alamy Stock Photo, **figure 2.3**: World History Archive / Alamy Stock Photo, **figure 2.5**: Heritage Image Partnership Ltd / Alamy Stock Photo, **figure 2.6**: Private Collection / Bridgeman Images, **figure 2.9** World History Archive / Alamy Stock Photo, **figure 2.10**: Hulton Archive / Getty Images, **page 105**: Classic Image / Alamy Stock Photo, **figure 3.1**, IanDagnall Computing / Alamy Stock Photo, **figure 3.2**: Culture Club / Getty Images, **figure 3.3** INTERFOTO / Alamy Stock Photo, **figure 3.5**: Mary Evans Picture Library / Alamy Stock Photo, **figure 3.7**: Pictorial Press Ltd / Alamy Stock Photo, **figure 3.10**: Motoring Picture Library / Alamy Stock Photo, **figure 3.13**: World History Archive / Alamy Stock Photo, **figure 3.14**: Elizabeth Leyden / Alamy Stock Photo, **page 158**: Keystone Pictures USA / Alamy Stock Photo, **figure 4.1**: War Archive / Alamy Stock Photo, **figure 4.2**: Joseph McKeown / Getty Images, **figure 4.3**: Everett Collection Historical / Alamy Stock Photo, **figure 4.6**: Heritage Image Partnership Ltd / Alamy Stock Photo, **figure 4.7**: Antony Nettle / Alamy Stock Photo, **figure 4.9**: Pictorial Press Ltd / Alamy Stock Photo, **figure 4.14**: Portadown, Northern Ireland, United kingdom, UK, Britain.

The publisher would like to thank the following for permission to reproduce extracts from their texts:

Chapter 4: Reproduced with permission of Curtis Brown, London on behalf of The Estate of Winston S. Churchill © The Estate of Winston S. Churchill

Index

abdication crisis 120–1
Act of Union, 1800 43
affluence, postwar 186–7
agricultural workers 31
agriculture 20–1, 28, 43–4, 72–3, 123–4
alcohol, control of 42
American Civil War 22, 23
Anglo-Irish relations 43–9, 94–102, 147–54, 202–7
Anglo-Irish Treaty 151
aristocracy 7–9, 28–9, 32
army reforms 42
Artisans' Dwelling Act (1875) 42
Asquith, Herbert H. 107
Attlee, Clement 164–5, 168
austerity, postwar 184–6

Bagehot, Walter 7
balance of payments 179–80
Baldwin, Stanley 116–18
Balfour, Arthur 97
Bedchamber Crisis 4
'Beeching Axe' 182
Bevan, Aneurin (Nye) 173, 197
Beveridge, William 193
Beveridge Report 163–4, 193–4
Bevin, Ernest 176–7
Birmingham 88
'Bloomsbury set' 138
Boer War 65, 89
British Union of Fascists 121
Butler, Richard Austen (Rab) 195
Butler Education Act 164, 195
Butt, Isaac 47

Caird, James 20
Campbell case 117
car industry 74, 130, 182
Cardwell, Edward 42
Chamberlain, Joseph 56–7
Chancellors of the Exchequer, postwar 180
child labour 34–5, 43
Children's Charter 93
cholera 41
Church of Ireland 44
Churchill, Winston 160–4, 168–9
cinema 140
civil service 42
coal mining 23, 73–5, 123, 125
coalition governments
    First World War 107–10
    interwar 115–16
    Second World War 176–7
Collins, Michael 151–2
Commons, House of 6
Commonwealth immigration 191–3
Communist Party 121–2
Concorde 184
conscription 109
Conservatism 14–16, 174–5
Conservative Party 9–11, 112
    governments 1886-1905 53–5, 87, 88–9, 97
    interwar governments 116–18
    governments 1951-64 168–75
Conspiracy and Protection of Property Act (1875) 38
consumerism 187–8
cooperatives 37
Corn Laws 8, 20
Corrupt Practices Act (1883) 18–19
cotton industry 23
councils, local 87–8, 141
Criminal Law Amendment Act (1871) 38
Cripps, Stafford 185

Dangerfield, George 110
Davitt, Michael 47
de Valera, Eamon 151–2, 202–3
Depression, Great (from 1873) 27–8, 69–71
Depression, interwar 129
Derby, Earl of 9–10
Disestablishment of the Church of Ireland 44
Disraeli, Benjamin 10, 11, 14–15, 18
drunkenness 42

Eden, Anthony 169–70
education 39–40, 143–4, 200–1
Education Act (1870) 40
Education Act (1880) 40
Education Act (1902) 89
Education Act (1918) 143
Education Act (1944) 164, 195
Edward VIII 120–1
electoral reform 2, 12, 17–20, 113–15, 147–9
electrical industry 75
emigration 32
Establishment, the 14, 174–5
exports, invisible 75

Fabian Society 59–60

Factory Acts 43
Fascists, British Union of 121
fashion 132–3
Fenians 44–5
Fianna Fail 152
First World War 106–13, 122–4
Fisher Education Act (1918) 143
food adulteration 42
Forster's Education Act 40
franchise 16–20, 113–15
free trade 12–13, 24, 76–7
friendly societies 36–7

Gaitskell, Hugh 173
General Strike 126–9
gentry, landed 28–9
Germany, economic competition from 26, 70–4, 182–3
Gladstone, William 6, 10–13, 17–19, 44–8, 55–8, 94–7
gold standard 128–9
Gorst, John 15
Government of Ireland Act 150
Great Depression 27–8, 69–71
Great Exhibition (1851) 21
Great Famine 43
Great War 106–13, 122–4
Green, T.H. 64

Hadow Report 144
Hardie, Keir 60
health insurance 146–8
high farming methods 20–1
Hobson, J.A. 64
Home, Lord 174–5
Home Rule, Irish 47–8, 55–6
    Bills 94–7, 99–102
Hornby v Close case 38
House of Commons 6
House of Lords 5–6, 66–7
housing 34, 140–3, 196–7
'Hyde Park Railings Affair' 18

immigration 191–3
Independent Labour Party 60
industry 21–2, 71–5, 181–3
interwar years 113–22, 124–47
invisible exports 75
IRA (Irish Republican Army) 149–50, 202, 205–7
Ireland 43–9, 94–102, 147–54, 202–7
Irish Free State 152–3, 202–3

219

Irish National Land League 47
Irish National League (INL) 47–8
Irish nationalism 46, 98
Irish Parliamentary Party (IPP) 47–8
Irish Potato Famine 43
Irish Republican Army (IRA) 149–50, 202, 205–7
iron and steel industry 23–4, 73–5, 126

Jarrow March 135–7

Keynsian economics 119–20

Labour Party 60–2, 67–9, 112–13, 172–3
interwar governments 117, 118–19, 142, 144
1945-1951 government 164–7
1964 government 175
laissez-faire 12–13
Land Acts, Irish 45–6, 47–8, 97
Land War, Irish 46–7
landed gentry 28–9
leisure 85, 134
Liberal Party 9–11, 55–7, 108–11
government 1892-1895 87–8
governments 1906-1914 89–94, 99–102
Liberalism 12–14, 62–5
Licensing Act (1872) 42
literature, interwar 138
living standards 85–7, 133–4
Lloyd George, David 65, 92–3, 107–10, 115–16, 149, 151–2
local government 87–8, 141
Lockhart, Sir Robert Bruce 165
Lords, House of 5–6

MacDonald, Ramsay 117, 118–19
Macmillan, Harold 170–4
magazines 140
Malthus, Thomas 36
Marx, Karl 58–9
media 139–40
Melbourne, Earl of 4
merchant shipping 21, 22–3, 43, 123
middle classes 8, 29–30, 33
migration 32
mining industry 23, 73–5, 123, 125
monarch, role of 3–5
Mosley, Sir Oswald 121
motor car industry 74, 130, 182
motorways 182
Mundella's Education Act 40
munitions 122–3

National Assistance Act (1948) 196
national debt 127

National Government 119–20
National Health Service (NHS) 197–9
National Insurance Act (1911) 91, 92–3
National Insurance Act (1946) 196
nationalisation 165–6
nationalism, Irish 46, 98
New Liberalism 62–5
new model unions 37–8
New Unions 38–9
newspapers 139
Nonconformists 13
Northern Ireland 153–4, 202, 204–7

One Nation Conservatism 14–15
O'Neill, Terence 205–6
Orange Order 204–5

Paisley, Ian 206
Palmerston, Viscount 9
Parliament 3–7
Parliament Act (1911) 66–7
Parnell, Charles Stewart 47–8, 95
Pearse, Patrick 148
Peel, Sir Robert 8–11
Peelites 9
pensions 93, 94, 146
People's Budget (1909) 65–6, 89–90
Phoenix Park murders 48
Plimsoll, Samuel 43
Poor Law 35–6
postwar boom 178–9
poverty 33–6, 86, 134
Primrose League 15–16, 81
Profumo affair 172
prosperity 32–3
protectionism 76–7
public health 41–2

racial tensions 191–3
radio 140
railways 22, 123, 182
rationing 123, 184
Redistribution Act (1885) 19–20
Reform Act (1832) 2, 17
Reform Act (1867) 12, 17–18
Reform Act (1884) 17, 19–20
retail industry 84–5
Robbins Report 201
Royal Commission on the Poor Laws 89
Russell, Lord John 9–10

Salisbury, Lord 53, 55
Samuel, Herbert 64
science and technology 138, 183–4

Second World War 159–64, 176–7
secondary education 201
Secret Ballot Act (1872) 18–19
self-help 36–7
servants 30
service industries 84–5
Sheffield Outrages 38
shipbuilding 22, 73, 125–6
shipping 21, 22–3, 43, 123
Sinn Fein 149–50
slums 34
Smethwick election result (1964) 192
Smiles, Samuel 36
Smith, Adam 24
Social Democratic Federation 59
social reform legislation 41–3, 87–94
socialism 58–60
Solemn League and Covenant 99–100
standards of living 85–7, 133–4
staple industries 73–5, 124–6, 134–5
steel industry 23–4, 73–5, 126
'stop-go' policies 179–80
suburbs 30
Suez crisis (1956) 170
suffrage, women's 80–2, 113–14
supermarkets 187–8
syndicalism 79–80

Taff Vale judgement 62, 78
tariff reform 76–7
taxation 89–90
technology 138, 183–4
Teddy Boys 190
Tory party 10
towns, expansion of 82–4
trade and industry 21–2, 181–3
Trade Disputes Act (1906) 67–8, 79
trade unions 13–14, 37–9, 61–2, 77–9
Trades Union Congress (TUC) 38
transport industry 181–2

Ulster Custom 45
Ulster Unionists 98, 99, 150
unemployment 135–7
unemployment benefit 144–6
United States, economic competition from 26, 70–4, 182–3
university expansion 201
upper classes 28–9, 33
urbanisation 82–4

Valera, Eamon de 151–2, 202–3
Victoria, Queen 3–5
Villa Toryism 19

Index

wages 33–4
welfare state 196–7
Whigs 9
Wilson, Harold 174–5
women
 changing role of 131–3, 139, 188–9
 voting rights of 80–2, 113–14
workhouses 35–6
working classes 30–1, 33–6, 54–5, 87, 133–4, 143–4
World War I 106–13, 122–4
World War II 159–64, 176–7

youth culture 190–1